My Uncle Zhou Enlai

By Zhou Erliu

Published by
ACA Publishing Ltd
University House
11-13 Lower Grosvenor Place
London SW1W 0EX, UK
Tel: +44 (0)20 7834 7676
Fax: +44 (0)20 7973 0076
E-mail: info@alaincharlesasia.com
Web:www.alaincharlesasia.com
Beijing Office
Tel: +86 (0)10 8472 1250
Fax: +86 (0)10 5885 0639

Author: Zhou Erliu
Translator: Hui Cooper
Editor: Jantine Broek
Cover art: Daniel Li
Proofreading: Dwight Lou, Wynn Moodie

Published by ACA Publishing Ltd
This English edition is published by arrangement
with Yilin Press, Ltd

© 2015, by Zhou Erliu
ALL RIGHTS RESERVED. NO PART OF THIS
PUBLICATION MAY BE REPRODUCED IN MATERIAL FORM,
BY ANY MEANS, WHETHER GRAPHIC,
ELECTRONIC, MECHANICAL OR OTHER, INCLUDING
PHOTOCOPYING OR INFORMATION STORAGE, IN WHOLE OR IN PART, AND
MAY NOT BE USED TO PREPARE
OTHER PUBLICATIONS WITHOUT WRITTEN
PERMISSION FROM THE PUBLISHER.

The greatest care has been taken to ensure accuracy but the
publisher can accept no responsibility for errors or omissions, or
for any liability occasioned by relying on its content.

ISBN 978-1-910760-27-7

Printed and bound by CPI Group (UK) Ltd, Croydon CR0 4YY

A catalogue record for *My Uncle Zhou Enlai* is available from the
National Bibliographic Service of the British Library.

Contents

Preface XI

Part One   The Zhou Clan 3

    1.   The Origin of the Zhou Clan 3

    2.   Five Generations in Succession 8

        2.1   The Five-Generation Zhou Clan Starting from Mr Qiaoshui ... 8

        2.2   The Affection Between Family Members 10

    3.   From Zhou Dunyi to Our Clansman Lu Xun 12

    4.   The Family Tradition and Motto 18

    5.   Zhou Yuantang and His *Verses in Haichao Study* 21

        5.1   "I Ought to Be a Remarkable Man" 21

        5.2   The Poem of *Liu Hou* 26

    6.   Qi Ba's Uncle Zhou Henai 28

    7.   Shaoxing *Shiye*, a Profession Handed Down through Generations 34

    8.   "Driven to Revolt" 36

    The Family's Cultural Relics and Qi Ba and Qi Ma's Letters (Part One) 38

    1.   The Tombs of the Ancestors 39

    2.   Relics From When Qi Ba Studied in Europe 42

    3.   Qi Ba's Letters from London, England (1921) 44

    4.   The Postcard Qi Ba Sent from Paris, France (1922) 49

Part Two   **Aibao, Qi Ba and Qi Ma** 53

            The Riddle of My Birth 53

                1. The Secret Shelter: 'Sir Zhou's Mansion' in Hongkou, Shanghai 56

                2. The Days I Spent with Qi Yeye 60

                3. "An Orphan on an Isle" 62

                4. My Ordeal in the City of Gaoyou 64

                5. Finding Qi Ba in Shanghai 66

                6. Three Visits to Sir Zhou's Mansion 67

                7. A Bayonet Digging into My Back 74

                8. On the March to the Southwest with the PLA Second Field Army 76

                9. The Two Speeches by Liu Bocheng and Deng Xiaoping ... 78

                10. I Become Acting Director of the Grain Bureau 84

                11. I Am Admitted to Nankai University and My Relation to Qi Ba Is Exposed 86

                12. The Interesting Interpretation of My Name, 'Zhou Erliu' 89

            The Family's Cultural Relics and Qi Ba and Qi Ma's Letters (Part Two) 92

Part Three   **The Years of National Construction** 101

                1. Conversations About Social Issues 104

                     1.1 The Family Origins and Political Convictions 104

                     1.2 The National Minority Autonomy System 108

                     1.3 Heart-to-Heart Communication during a Cultural Exchange 117

                2. Qi Ba's Reflections during the Early Post-Liberation Period 119

                     2.1 Opposing Excessive Actions in the Land Reform Movement 119

	2.2	Vigilance for the Ultra-Left 'Valorous Elements' 121
	2.3	Safeguard the Interests of the Newborn Middle-Class Peasants 122
	2.4	Respect Market Regularity, Comply with the Change in Supply and Demand 123
	2.5	Let the People's Hands Lead the Market 125
3.	Around the Time of 'Great Leap Forward' 127
	3.1	Playing Ping-Pong with Qi Ba 127
	3.2	"I Speak as My Conscience Dictates" 129
	3.3	To Be More 'Leftist' or More 'Rightist'? 130
	3.4	How to Approach the Struggle within the Party and Prevent Being Privileged 132
	3.5	Can Sulphuric Acid Billow in a Plant? 137
	3.6	An Innovative Experiment Comes to a Premature End 139
	3.7	Qi Ba Returning to His Alma Mater, Nankai University 142
	3.8	In Doubt, but No One Dares to Speak the Truth 147
	3.9	I Visit the 'Chinese Miracles' 148
	3.10	The Taiwan Issue 154
4.	"I Raise My Hat to Salute Intellectuals" 159
	4.1	Chen Laozong Solves My 'Ideological Problem' 159
	4.2	"Today, I Raise My Hat to Salute You!" 163
	4.3	The *Shiwu Guan* Opera Becomes a Model 165
	4.4	Recording History Truthfully 168
	4.5	Qi Ba's Interesting Remarks on Basic Training for English Students 170
	4.6	The Soulmate of Translators and Interpreters 172
	4.7	A Search Spanning Half a Century 178

The Family's Cultural Relics and Qi Ba and Qi Ma's Letters (Part Three) 183

1. Qi Ma's Letter from Beijing (1956) 183

| | | 2. | Four Precious Presents .... 187 |
| | | 3. | The Lost Cultural Relics .... 197 |

Part Four The Years of the Cultural Revolution 205

  1. My Confusing and Bitter Experience................................207
     - 1.1 The Work Groups and the Two-Line Struggle 207
     - 1.2 The First Time I Write to Qi Ba about Political Issues 209
     - 1.3 My Visit to a Foreign Country with Wu Han Is Suspended... 213
  2. Qi Ba and the Other Leaders 216
     - 2.1 Chen Yi 216
     - 2.2 He Long.. 218
     - 2.3 Peng Dehuai 219
     - 2.4 Lin Biao... 220
     - 2.5 Li Fuchun.. 221
     - 2.6 Zhang Xiruo... 222
  3. US President Richard Nixon Visits China...........................224
     - 3.1 The Foreign Ministry and the Ministry of Public Security's Joint Circular... 224
     - 3.2 Qi Ba Is Unaware that He Is Seriously Ill 226
     - 3.3 Qi Ba's Chopsticks and President Nixon's Wine Glass 229
     - 3.4 The Week that Changed the World 231
     - 3.5 The Five Principles of Peaceful Coexistence and the Shanghai Communiqué... 233
     - 3.6 The Story of the Maotai Liquor.. 234
  4. Qi Ba and the Gang of Four..236
     - 4.1 Criticise Lin, Criticise Confucius and Criticise the Duke of Zhou 236
     - 4.2 The Photo that Stunned Viewers 239

	4.3	Zhang Chunqiao's Unreasonable Behaviour	243
	4.4	The Truth about the Creation of the Ballet *Red Detachment of Women*	244
	4.5	*The White-Haired Girl* Becomes *The Red-Haired Girl*	246

5. The Last Days 248

    5.1 My Last Reunion with Qi Ba 248
    5.2 Qi Ma's Special Words to Me 249
    5.3 The Deeply Touching National Day Reception of 1974 255
    5.4 "This Cultural Revolution Has Cut Off 10 Years of My Life" 257

6. Qi Ba Passes Away 258

    6.1 The Funeral that Shook the World 258
    6.2 The Gang of Four Falls from Power 265
    6.3 The Odd Behaviour of Cao Yi-ou, Kang Sheng's Widow 266

Part Five Everlasting Memories 273

1. Zhou Enlai in the Minds of the Founders of the PRC 275

    1.1 General Yang Chengwu 276
    1.2 Huang Zhen 280
    1.3 Geng Biao 284
    1.4 Wang Bingnan 288
    1.5 Wu Xueqian 291

2. Qi Ba and His Chinese and Foreign Friends 294

    2.1 Xu Beihong and Lao She 294
    2.2 Guo Moruo 296
    2.3 Mei Lanfang 300
    2.4 Jin Shan 303
    2.5 Israel Epstein 305
    2.6 Anna Louise Strong 306

		2.7	Ma Haide	308
		2.8	Rewi Alley	309
		2.9	Edward Heath	311
		2.10	Felix Greene	312
		2.11	Dai Ailian	313
	3.	The Painters Who Cherished the Premier's Memory		316
		3.1	Wu Biduan	316
		3.2	Shang Chengzuo	319
		3.3	Huang Zhou	320
		3.4	Wu Zuoren	322
		3.5	Mu Lingfei	323

Part Six Corrections, Additions and Clarifications of the Historical Facts 329

1. The Recipient of Zhou Enlai's Letter in 1921 Was His Second Uncle, Zhou Yikang 330

2. Zhou Enlai Did Not Go Directly to France to Study and Work 330

3. The Young Zhou Enlai Did Indeed Visit Shaoxing 330

4. Zhou Enshou's Reasons For Dropping out of the Revolutionary Ranks 332

5. Cheng Yizhen Gave Cover to Zhou Enlai and Deng Yingchao 336

6. Zhou Enzhu As Deputy Manager of the Shanghai Xiangsheng Car Company 339

7. Ma Shijie's True Experiences in His Old Age 342

8. The Strict Pursuit of a Policy to Avoid Nepotism 347

9. Treating Relatives Equally 352

10. 'Dislike, But Don't Avoid the Old Fogy' Zhou Yiliang 356

11. Shen Junru and Zhou Enlai Were Not Acquainted with Each Other during the Anti-Japanese War..359

12. How Dick Wilson Invented His Story 360

13. The True Story about Mrs Li Zhifan and Edgar Snow 363

14. The Utterly Absurd Book, *A Heavy Load on Dad*....................366

Part Seven Acting on the Teachings of the Deceased Qi Ba 373

Qi Ba and Qi Ma's Words Will Forever Warm Our Hearts..373

1. "You Are an Honest Child'"... 373
2. "Answer Them Based on Facts".. 375
3. The First Lesson I Learnt during My Foreign Exchange Practice.. 377
4. Rare Open Praise from Qi Ba.. 380
5. Qi Ba Calls Me a "Little Jack-of-All-Trades" 382

1. The Publication of the English Edition of *Speeches & Writings by Deng Xiaoping*..384

   1.1 A Party Committee Meets with Diverging Opinions....... 385
   1.2 I Am Mildly Rebuffed at My First Meeting with the Publisher... 386
   1.3 Who Can Resolve This Difficult Problem?........................ 387
   1.4 Maxwell's Wish... 398

2. The Three Generations of India's Prime Ministers and the Five Principles of Peaceful Coexistence 390

3. The Often-Told Tale of Joseph Needham and Lu Guizhen..397

   3.1 How Did Joseph Needham 'Discover' China?................... 397
   3.2 Lu Guizhen Gains Support from Zhou Enlai..................... 399
   3.3 I'll Always Remember Them with Deep Affection............. 402

4. Dr Runcie, the Archbishop of Canterbury, Visits China for

    the First Time...404

 5. My Joint Research with Professor Fei Xiaotong.................407

   5.1 Mr Fei Invites Me to Work on the Seventh Five-Year Plan Research Project.. 408

   5.2 Hu Yaobang Writes "Boldly in Support" on My Report 411

   5.3 Professor Fei Carries On with the Development Studies Throughout His Later Years 412

   5.4 Mr Fei, Huan Xiang and I Discuss the Wenzhou Model 414

   5.5 "We Do Well When We Work on Things in Tandem" 416

 6. Former British Prime Minister James Callaghan Visits Huaian 418

   6.1 Fei Xiaotong Meets Mr Callaghan by Chance....................... 418

   6.2 Setting out to Huaian in Advance to Make Arrangements.. 420

   6.3 Hu Yaobang Gives Callaghan a Courteous Reception.......... 422

   6.4 "China's Main Architect" 423

   6.5 Callaghan's Practical Deeds for the Chinese People 427

Concluding Remarks.. **429**

Additional Comments:

  The Work Engaged in by the Author in Recent Years for Passing on and Carrying Forward the Spirit of Zhou Enlai....................431

Preface

Zhou Yikang (my grandfather) and Zhou Yineng (Zhou Enlai's father) were cousins, belonging to the second household and the seventh household, respectively. Although my grandfather was a second son, he was adopted by the first household to carry on the family line, as they had no male child of their own; hence, he literally became head of the whole extended Zhou family. Once, my uncle Zhou Enlai (hereafter referred to as *Qi Ba*, literally meaning 'seventh father') seriously told me that I was the first grandson of the first household, which I'd previously had no idea about. My grandfather and the father of Qi Ba's father were not only male cousins with the same surname and grandfather, but they also had an unusual relationship, moving to Huaian from Shaoxing at the same time and living together after the move, with no distinction between each other. My grandfather was a *juren* (a successful candidate in the imperial examination at provincial level) towards the end of the Qing dynasty, and once worked as chief clerk in the provincial governor's court. He then became an official, taking up the position of prefect of the Zhili prefecture. During the time of the Republic of China, he was an adviser as well as secretary to the military governor of Jiangsu province. Besides having a stable income for himself, he found Qi Ba's father a job to work with him, and he also financed Qi Ba to study overseas. During the years of revolution, my family moved around and lived in Beijing, Tianjin, Nanjing and Shanghai, and several times when his life was in danger, Qi Ba took refuge with my family. In those days, Qi Ba's father was a permanent resident with my family and became a secret liaison contact for his son. My father was the youngest of his male generation, 10 years junior to Qi Ba. Under Qi Ba's influence, he also worked for the revolution at one point.

When my family lived in 44 Yong-an-li, North Sichuan Road, Shanghai, my mother died soon after giving birth to me. At the time, Qi Ba and my aunt Deng Yingchao (referred to hereafter as *Qi Ma*, literally meaning 'seventh mother') took refuge with my family. So when I was an infant, I was lucky to have the care and love of both of them, which have been with me ever since. From 1939 to 1942, my father, my stepmother and my other family members all went to Chongqing or northern Jiangsu. Only I was left behind to attend school in Shanghai, so Qi Ba humorously called me "an orphan on an isle". In 1946, he found me through an independent democrat, and he and Qi Ma then began supporting me directly. From 1946 to 1949, the expenses they provided were my only income. From 1954 to 1964, I needed to look after my grandmother and mother-in-law and often spent more than I actually had, so they would cover some of my extra expenses. Every month for a period of time, they gave my daughter Rmb30 for living expenses. Throughout my life, they have taken the greatest possible care of me; their teaching and ideological education have formed my own code of conduct. Either by chance or by arrangement, it happened quite often that after he, as premier, had visited some foreign countries, I would then accompany a Chinese cultural delegation visiting the same countries. At home, I would accompany foreign guests to places he had just inspected; hence he joked with me, saying that I had copied him and followed in his footsteps. At one point during my career, I concurrently held the positions of deputy director of the International Liaison Department of the Central Committee, director of the Committee for Cultural Relations with Foreign Countries under the Ministry of Culture, vice president of Beijing University and director of the Institute of Social Science, as well as that of head of the Centre for Sociological Research and Development Studies of China. I was the cultural counsellor at the Chinese Embassy in the UK for five years, and for many years I have been engaged in foreign affairs. Therefore, on various occasions I have met with the leaders of the UK, Ethiopia, India, Nepal, the US, Uganda and Yemen. While communicating with these noted political figures, I always followed the teachings of Qi Ba, being discreet in words and deeds. I have done some practical work for the development of friendship between China and foreign countries, with which I have achieved some good results. Meanwhile, while communicating with these foreign dignitaries, as well as with various noted domestic figures, I heard of their high praise of Qi Ba in person. My aim in writing this book is to preserve authentic material relating to

Preface

him, his ideology, as well as his actions during his lifetime. There are a few noted features in this book:

1) Some material has never been published before. I regard it as my duty to reveal these precious historical items to the public in my remaining years.

2) Many sections in this book are taken from discussions between Qi Ba and myself.

3) The Chinese and foreign personalities mentioned in the book are those who Qi Ba either knew very well or with whom he had an important association.

4) The contents of this book may enhance the comprehensive understanding of Premier Zhou Enlai both domestically and internationally, giving impetus to further research about him.

Zhou Erliu in front of the bust of Zhou Enlai at the Zhou family residence in Huaian.

Part One

Part One

The Zhou Clan

From 1946, when I met Qi Ba at his residence in Shanghai, until 1966, before the Cultural Revolution started, he often talked to me about our family and its origins. On several occasions, he spent nearly half a day or even a whole night talking about it. He was very busy, so why did he pay so much attention to this topic? The centenarian hall of the Zhou clan in Shaoxing that we are part of has many different branches, which throughout history have become established in a number of different places. In Qi Ba's time, members of the family clan were scattered everywhere, working in all sorts of jobs, and their political choices were varied. Did he have any affection or principles toward our old Zhou family? Or was there any family tradition or motto that had been handed down from our ancestors? His great-great-grandfather wrote many poems that were printed in a booklet by the family's descendants. All his life he loved this booklet dearly, and even kept it with him during the Cultural Revolution, the 10 years of hardship; but why did he treasure this booklet so much? What spiritual comfort did the poems give him, or what indication was there of the cultural traditions of our family? He told me in person that after his retirement he would write a novel called *Households of an Extended Family*, which would be based on the evolution of the extended family: Chinese society in microcosm. What is the relationship of his unfinished but long-cherished novel to his own family? The answer may be found in the long and uninterrupted cultural genealogy of our family.

1. The Origin of the Zhou Clan

In 1955, Qi Ba received my father at his residence in the West Flower Hall

The young Zhou Enlai.

in Zhongnanhai, Beijing. I was a student at Nankai University in Tianjin and was invited to attend the meeting; therefore, I had the chance to listen to their conversations. Of all the subjects they discussed, the topic of the Zhou clan impressed me the most. But before I give a detailed account of this, I would like to select a few written records by my forefather Zhou Wenhao for reference:

Originally, Zhou was the name of a reigning dynasty in the city of Zhouyuan in Qishan, now Qishan county, in Shaanxi province. When Duke Dan Fu, the 13th grandson of Houji (the son of Emperor Ku), led his people to settle in the city, he used its name as the title of their dynasty. After Emperor Ping (770BC-720BC) moved the capital to Luoyang, he granted his youngest son the manor estate of Rufen, where 19 generations lived until the estate was seized by the Qin state. After they settled in the city of Runan, they adopted the name Zhou as their surname, rather than the original surname of Ji. In the reign of Emperor Wu Di of the Jin dynasty, minister Jun of the Zhou family married Luoxiu, a girl from the Li family. They had three sons: Yi, Song and Mo, who all became famous officials, making the Zhou family prominent. During the Tang dynasty, Chongchang was a prefecture chief whose descendants migrated to Yingdao county, now Daozhou prefecture in Hunan province, after seven generations. Then, after several sucessive generations, Zhou Dunyi was born. He lived at the foot of Lianhua Peak on Mount Lu, where he built a hut he named 'Lianxi study'. His sons and grandsons multiplied and moved to the cities of Yangzhou and Yizhou. During the Southern Song dynasty, they migrated to the south of Mount Kefeng in eastern Zhejiang province and lived by Lake Luoshi, where the locals had built a temple to commemorate Emperor Hui of the Zhou dynasty. To avoid wars breaking out, ancestor Zhou Qing moved to the city and lived in Jingshui Lane in Kuaiji county. Then, in the year of Xinyou (1381) of Emperor Hongwu of the Ming dynasty, they moved to Yongchang Lane.

— Copied from the original manuscript by Zhou Wenhao in September 1824.

Zhou is the most common surname in China; much of the research done about its origins is rich in detail, but presents many different views. The above quotation was taken from *Textual Research on the Origin of the Zhou Clan*, a record of my family origins. From the text we can see that it is a copy of a previous record kept by our ancestor, Zhou Wenhao. In 1943, my great uncle Zhou Songyao recopied it: it has been preserved until the present day.

Qi Ba said to my father that because of the amount of time that had passed, as well as the many changes, it was very hard to check the records of our ancestors for correctness. For example, the records lacked a detailed description of Zhou Mao, our earliest ancestor to migrate. Even Zhou Songyao, the transcriber himself, only half believed what he was copying. So Qi Ba said: "Neither you nor I are experts in this respect, so we have to leave it to the researchers. But these records do have some degree of moral impact on future generations, as when we were young we felt that we were the legitimate descendants of the Yan and Yellow Emperors, and when we met with adversity, we had the feeling that we were the offspring of members of the nobility who had just met with misfortune, so we should never reconcile ourselves to falling behind." When he said this, he and my father smiled, looking into each other's eyes. "We Chinese, no matter what our surname is, are fond of claiming kinship to a famous ancestor, which is a feudal cultural tradition. From a positive point of view, it can enhance the strong sentiment that we are all Chinese, which makes it much easier for family members to establish a strong belief that everyone has a duty to their country." My father nodded his head in agreement.

Afterwards, I would meet many foreign friends at work, and some of them were the authors of monographs of Zhou Enlai. They apparently had an interest in his family background; out of curiosity, they asked me: "Is Zhou Enlai a direct descendant of Huangdi [the Yellow Emperor]?" My reply had always been based on the principles of conversations between him and my father. In recent years, members of the Zhou family clan around the world and related experts actively took part in research into the origin of the Zhou clan, and, after a comprehensive study incorporating all sources, the initial conclusion was that Zhou Enlai might have been the 127th grandson of Huangdi.

The chart of the Zhou clan generations in succession. For the full translation, see Appendix 1.

2. Five Generations in Succession

In 1939, during the period of cooperation between the nationalists and the communists, Qi Ba returned to Shaoxing, where he acquired some important data about the five-generation Zhou clan, starting from Mr Qiaoshui. He took the information to Chongqing and handed it to my father to make into a chart. After 1949, Qi Ba's younger brother, Zhou Enshou, made some slight modifications.

2.1. The Five-Generation Zhou Clan Starting from Mr Qiaoshui

Mr Qiaoshui lived during the period when Emperor Jiaqing was on the throne (1796-1820). He had five sons: Junhou (who was childless), Junang, Junlian, Junlong and Junpang. The five brothers were very close and never divided up the family property. Junang had his second son adopted by Junhou, who then provided much assistance to Junlong, enabling him to start to work as a private adviser. Afterwards, Junang and Junlong went to Huaian with the minister responsible for water transportation of grain to the capital. The two families lived in an old-fashioned courtyard house at 7 Fuma Lane in the northwest corner of the city of Huaian, sharing the courtyard and living like one family. Although the five brothers lived far apart in Shaoxing and Huaian, the affection among them never faded, but became stronger as time went by.

Portrait of Zhou Enlai's great-grandfather, Mr Qiaoshui.

Junang had three sons – Yiyu, Yikang and Yiliang – while Junlong had four sons: Yigeng, Yineng, Yikui and Yigan. Qi Ba was the eldest son of Yineng, but was adopted by his uncle Yigan, who had no sons. Yigeng had no sons either and adopted Yineng's younger son, Enshou. So, for the consideration of the family clan, he had two of his sons adopted, which showed how strong their filial bond was. As for myself, I am the eldest grandson of Yiyu, the adoptive father of my father. From my childhood, by family convention, I called Qi Ba's birth father Yineng *Qi Yeye* (or *Yaya* in the Shoaxing dialect, literally 'seventh grandfather'), who would follow his son around and who had not had the luck to see any of his own grandchildren but me when he lived with us in the cities of Shanghai, Zhenjiang and Yangzhou.

The fourth generation had large numbers of members who lived at scattered locations around the country, so it is difficult to arrange them by seniority. Therefore, we followed the seniority of our grandparents and called Premier Zhou Enlai *Qi Shu* or *Qi Bo* ('seventh uncle') and his wife Deng Yingchao *Qi Ma* ('seventh mother'). But as for myself, from when I first learnt to speak, I followed my grandmother and Qi Ba's father, as well as Qi Ba and Qi Ma themselves, in calling him *Qi Ba*, and I never addressed him differently. Qi Ba and Qi Ma called me by my infant name *Aibao* ('love treasure'), and only after I began working did Qi Ma gradually change it to *Erliu*. For some reason, only the first, the second and the eighth households continued the tradition to have *Er* in their names, so there are Zhou Erliu (me), Zhou Erqi, Zhou Erjun, Zhou Erhui and Zhou Ercui.

2.2. The Affection between Family Members

Overall, a strong sense of identity is one of the most distinctive features among members of the Zhou clan, which has been passed on from generation to generation. One reason for maintaining such a tradition is that the Zhou clan has a long history of culture, not merely of blood ties. For example, all the households of the extended family have acknowledged that Zhou Dunyi from the Northern Song dynasty was our earliest ancestor, and generally they also attach great importance to the education of the younger generation. A second reason is that the various households were often on the move and lived in many diverse locations. Our branch of the clan moved to Shaoxing in Zhejiang province during the early Ming dynasty, and afterwards migrated to Huaian, Yangzhou and Shanghai. But no matter where they were, all branches of the clan agreed that Zhou Mao was the first of our ancestors to migrate. The family trees

The family tree of the Zhou family, showing five generations and starting from Zhou Yuantang

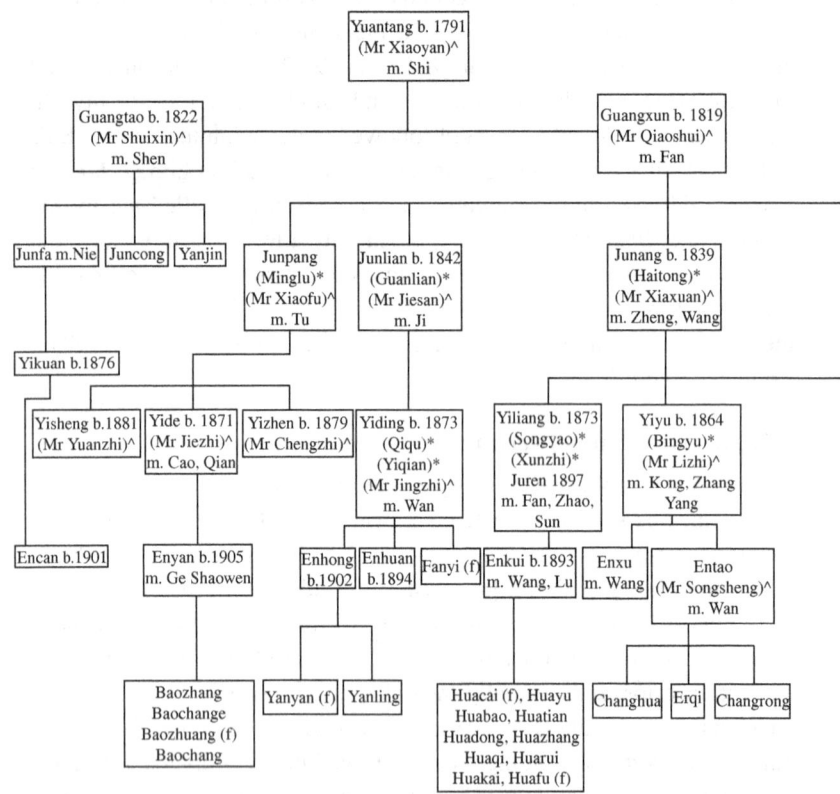

Portrait of Zhou Enlai's great-uncle, Zhou Junang, and great-aunt.

Portrait of Zhou Enlai's great-grandfather, Mr Qiaoshui, and great-grandmother.

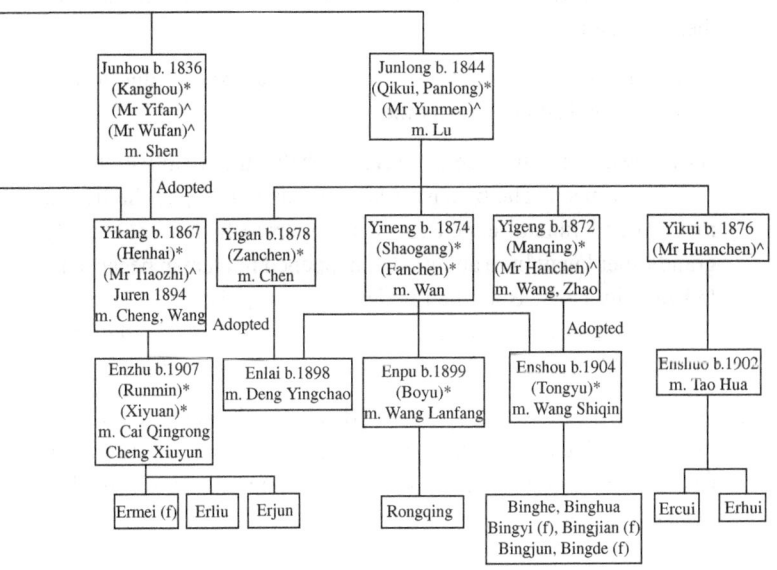

Juren is a degree for the imperial exam for the civil service.

* Style name (courtesy name)

^ Name used to show respect to elderly men.

of both Zhou Enlai and the writer Lu Xun have identical records relating to this. Nowadays the descendants of the clan are even more scattered, both at home and overseas, but the affection between blood relations that can be traced to the same origin will never end, and indeed it is not an easy thing to do so. The characteristics of the clan's closeness, from my generation dating back to the generation of my great-great grandfather, can be summed up as follows:

1) When family fortunes decline and households move elsewhere – as happened with my great-grandfather's generation, when four out of five brothers moved to Huaian from Shaoxing, and two of them lived in the same courtyard house – the family members continue to have a close relationship.

2) A large number of clan members lived a long way from each other, but they regarded Shaoxing as their place of origin and the land of their ancestors.

3) Family members transfer wisdom and impart knowledge to and also guide and support each other.

4) As always, family members relieve and help other family members in times of need. The better-off households would pay the living, medical and funeral expenses for the worse-off households. My grandfather knew little about what happened in Huaian because he left the city early. But when he learnt from Qi Ba that his young nephew Zhou Enshuo did not know what to do after his father died of illness, he immediately paid for the funeral and adopted the boy.

5) Be doubly related and interdependent. The brother of Qi Ba's mother married my grandfather's sister, and the younger generation have never forgotten this special relationship and have stayed in contact ever since.

3. From Zhou Dunyi to Our Clansman Lu Xun

After the liberation of China (1949), Qi Ba resided and worked in the West Flower Hall in the Zhongnanhai compound, which had been the mansion of the prince regent towards the end of the Qing dynasty. In the

Portrait of Zhou Dunyi.

courtyard, there is a pavilion called *buranting* (literally 'unsoiled pavilion'). Friends who knew something about my family history once asked me if the pavilion had anything to do with Zhou Enlai, or if the pavilion was named by him. This is an interesting question, and we can find the answer in the famous sentence: "It [the lotus] grows out of the mud but remains unsoiled." This also gives us some ideas about the thoughts of its author, Zhou Dunyi.

Zhou Dunyi (1017-1073) was originally named Zhou Dunshi, but he changed his name to avoid having a similar character as the one in Emperor Yingzong's personal name. His father died when he was 15, and from 24 on he worked as a magistrate in places such as Qianzhou, Hongzhou, Chengzhou and Hezhou. Wherever he took his position, he did not fear the remoteness or the dangers of the journey. He gave his court judgments in an honest and fair way and he understood and sympathized with the people. He helped the distressed and offered succour to those in peril, bringing benefits to the common people. He spent most of his salary to help the people, so that he rarely had any savings during his lifetime. He was just like his favourite flower, the elegant and dignified lotus, which 'grows out of the mud but remains unsoiled, cleansed by the pure water but not seductive.' He was one of the forefathers of neo-Confucianism and a key figure in the development of Confucianism, who carried on traditions of the past while ushering in the future, and who had a far-reaching influence on the history of thought in China. In fact, he was a typical example of the Chinese traditional cultural practice of absorbing every school's strong points and establishing his own.

Qi Ba was his 33rd grandson. As a descendant, and even more as an outstanding representative of the Zhou family himself, when he was young he was hugely proud of his ancestor, regarding him as a role model. His ancestor's ideological doctrine, which comprised moral integrity as well as a certain attitude to the conduct of an official while in office, had an immeasurable influence on him. In September 1946, when I was 15 years old, I was asked to go to meet him in his mansion in Shanghai. Before we ended our conversation there, he asked me if I had studied *On the Love of the Lotus (Ai Lian Shuo)*, a work of prose by Zhou Dunyi. "I learnt about it when I was in primary school," I told him. He was very pleased and said: "It was our ancestor who wrote this famous prose work. As his descendant, living in this complex city of Shanghai, I hope you will be like the lotus which grows out of the mud but remains unsoiled, waiting to greet the arrival of victory." In 1954, I was a student at Nankai University in Tianjin. During the winter holiday Qi Ba sent people to ask me to go to Beijing. I stayed in the West Flower Hall. As the premier, he was occupied with a myriad of state affairs, attending all sorts of major events and important activities. Even after returning to his residence, he usually carried on working deep into the night, sometimes until the crack of dawn. One night, our conversation lasted almost for the whole night, which was a rare occasion in my life thus far. He did not have time to give full expression to his views, so he let me stay in a room in the eastern wing and then urged me to stay there for the whole holiday. Such an opportunity was exceptional for my generation. During the following nights, he would make use of every spare second to talk to me. Occasionally, he talked about Zhou Dunyi, but the contents were much wider and deeper – maybe because I was a university student and I could comprehend them. "Our ancestor Zhou Dunyi used the yin-yang doctrine to explain the 'universe-in-itself', and he enriched and developed the basic subject of philosophy, which is not an ordinary contribution [to Chinese culture]. He highlighted the delicate beauty of human nature and attached importance to the conscience and intelligence of human beings, and then carried out a theoretical exploration of human nature. After gaining a thorough understanding of all sorts of theories invented by his forefathers, he formed his own original ideas. His work *Explanation of the Diagram of the Supreme Polarity* has been gradually accepted by people around the world. Therefore, he is not only a great master of Confucian teaching and the forefather of neo-Confucianism, but also a representative figure of traditional Chinese culture with international repercussions." Today, Zhou Dunyi is listed as a UNESCO Eminent Personality, which has proved the exceptional insight and judgement of Qi Ba.

Regarding the prose of *On the Love of the Lotus*, he repeatedly said to me:

"In the Northern Song dynasty, Zhou Dunyi had seen the trend of a feudal society that had passed its zenith and was on the wane. He used vivid artistic language to express his noble and unsullied aspirations through the lotus flower. His well-turned epigrammatic phrase, 'grows out of the mud but remains unsoiled', applies theory to reality and hits home. He predicted the unavoidable fall of a prosperous feudal society and then put forward a way of self-restraint and self-cultivation, so the well-known saying has become the symbol of an ideal moral quality." Many years later, when I discussed this with Nan Huaijin, the great master of Chinese cultural studies, he spoke highly of Zhou Dunyi, while holding in great esteem the original views of Qi Ba. It is a pity that I was young and ignorant at the time, feeling there was no free movement inside the compound and requesting several times that he should let me return to university as soon as possible. Time never flows backwards. Nowadays, when I think of it, I feel lost, blaming myself for not fully appreciating the chance to listen to his teachings. The 'unsoiled pavilion' had been named before Qi Ba moved in, but the coincidence is amusing, leading to endless afterthoughts from us.

Lu Xun (1881-1936) – a pseudonym for Zhou Shuren – was from Fupengqiao in Shaoxing, the 32nd grandson of Zhou Dunyi. He was born to a declining scholar-official family and became a great writer, thinker and revolutionary by integrating his rich personal experiences with the fate of the nation. The spirit of Lu Xun is called the spirit of the Chinese nation, which influenced many Chinese people then and afterwards.

Around the time when the May Fourth Movement took place, Lu Xun worked for the magazine *New Youth* and became a leading figure in the new cultural movement. This happened at the time when Qi Ba was studying at Nankai University and was one of the student leaders. He once invited

Portrait of Lu Xun.

Lu Xun to give a speech in the city of Tianjin. He could not make it, but he asked his younger brother Zhou Zuoren to go instead. Though the two had never met before, they had a mutual understanding and trust. Qi Ba spoke highly of the efforts leftist writers had put into the campaign to resist Japanese aggression and save the country. His admiration and respect for Lu Xun were well known. During several commemorative activities after the death of Lu Xun, Qi Ba gave some important speeches, and also wrote some articles that were published in the newspapers.

When I attended school in Shanghai, he emphasised during our conversations that Lu Xun was also an extraordinary man from the Zhou clan, and he asked me to use the ancient sage as an example for steeling my will, growing up and becoming a useful person. I knew that he had the greatest esteem for Lu Xun. I still remember once discussing Lu Xun in the presence of him and Qi Ma. I was studying at Nankai University, and one night Wang Zhangli and I went to see a film in an open field. One part of the documentary film showed the back of a woman who looked like Qi Ma; she turned round and we saw that she was Xu Guangping, Lu Xun's wife. Afterwards, when we were in the West Flower Hall, we told Qi Ba and Qi Ma about it, which drew laughter from them. Qi Ma said: "Your Qi Ba once told Xu Guangping: 'We are the same family and you are senior to me.' And Xu Guangping went to find the family tree to confirm it." Then Qi Ba asked me: "There are many well-known sayings and epigrams in Lu Xun's works. Which one is your favourite?" "I feel the same as the majority of people," I replied without thinking, "and my favourite saying is: 'Fierce-browed, I coolly defy one thousand pointing fingers; head bowed, like a willing ox, I serve the children.'" He said that he also liked that one and he had written a forward for it, and explained further: "Lu Xun used the refined language of a poet, expressing the heroic common aspirations of the Chinese nation a few words while issuing summons of the time and giving people a sense of mission – a skill out of the ordinary for a great writer. But things are not that simple; 'one thousand' indicates numerous people, and here it means the reactionaries. From the development of history, they are outwardly strong, but inwardly weak, and eventually they will meet their doom; however, it is possible to run wild for a while, and there is no lack of shameful followers. When the balance of force between the enemy and our own is unfavourable to us, the enemy will oppress people without mercy; hence, the revolutionaries and the people must first have the spirit of Lu Xun to coolly defy, to die rather than submit; secondly, we must, like Lu Xun, be possessed of ideals, have confidence in the future and carry on fighting tenaciously." With regard to 'the children', he said: "What Lu Xun is saying is that we should be like an ox, willing to serve the children, or 'people'; in today's language, it means that you should serve the people willingly and wholeheartedly." Now, the image of Qi Ba in his old age, wearing a badge inscribed with the words 'Serve the People', flashes across my mind. Because he had overworked himself over a long period of time, he looked a bit weary, but his eyes still showed extreme determination. In fact, the poem shows not only Qi Ba and Lu Xun's similar aspirations, but is a realistic portrayal of both men. From the inscription commemorating the second anniversary of Lu Xun's death on 19 October 1938 to the speech given at the memorial service for Lu Xun on 26 October 1946, Qi Ba passionately praised the noble character of Lu Xun and his persistent fighting eight times, both in speeches and written inscriptions. During his speech in October 1938, he said: "Based on our blood line, Lu Xun and I may be members of the same clan, because we are both from the Zhou family of Shaoxing in Zhejiang province. But I do not want to call him 'the nobleman from my family', only to commemorate him with an ancient poem: 'Only the toughest grass can withstand strong winds; the true and faithful can easily be spotted in times of trouble.'" Qi Ba praised Lu Xun as being the toughest grass and belonging to the true and faithful; but actually, in my opinion, their age, circumstances, character and career are all different, so Qi Ba's words of praise apply to both of them.

In 1982, I made an effort to go to the Lu Xun Memorial Hall in Shaoxing and pay Mr Jin, the curator of the hall, a visit. He told me that of the family trees of both Zhou Enlai and Lu Xun only fragments remained, so it is hard to confirm their blood relations. Luckily, with the efforts of academics who based their research on records supplied by the descendants of Zhou Dunyi, it has been checked, and it transpires that Lu Xun and Zhou Enlai are the 32nd and 33rd grandsons of Zhou Dunyi, respectively. At this late hour, I would like to emphasize that in the long history of the Chinese people, multiplying in an endless succession, of which our ancestry is an example, this old family can still produce great men like Zhou Shuren (Lu Xun) and Zhou Enlai, whose hearts are linked and who have a spiritual affinity. It is an inevitability rather than an accidental historical coincidence. Let's hope the rebirth of the old family is the epitome of Chinese society in the present age, from which we can predict the gradual rejuvenation of the whole nation.

4. The Family Tradition and Motto

Qi Ba told me that, from his own experience, the formation of the character and accomplishments of people in modern times mainly relied on three aspects: family education, school education, and social education. He said that he was born into a large, declining, feudal family; however, the long and deep cultural history of the family could not be ignored, and has indeed been passed on from generation to generation, nourishing the descendants, and has had immense influence on himself. This family tradition of almost one thousand years has the following distinguished principles, which can be traced to the same origin:

1) Be honest and upright, preserving a good name and integrity, and treating sincerity as the most important thing. Our forefather Zhou Dunyi was an official all his life; he had a reputation of being honest and upright. His adage, "The lotus grows out of mud but remains unsoiled," is known in every household in China. As a descendant, throughout his life, Qi Ba believed in "treating honesty and sincerity as being the most important attributes", as initiated by his ancestor. During his 26 years as premier of the most populous country in the world, from the beginning to the end, he was honest, self-restrained, and maintained personal integrity during chaotic times. These qualities of his are universally recognized and historical facts, often heard and well remembered by not only the Chinese people but people around the world, arousing widespread admiration. When I visited the Zhou Enlai Memorial Hall, I left the following message, to express the same feeling of mine: "Hovering in the universe,

your loyal heart is as bright as the sun and the moon; the love left by Zhou Enlai has spread all over the world."

2) Rejuvenate China and be ready to offer our services wherever they are needed. The Zhou clan is large with a long history, originating from an ancient Chinese civilization. Before our ancestors adopted the name of the reigning dynasty as their family name, their surname was Ji, and people generally regarded them as the direct descendants of the Yellow Emperor (the ancestor of the Chinese nation). Therefore, Zhou family members have a strong sense of historical purpose. This family clan originated in the northwest of China, and from Shaanxi and Henan it spread to other parts of the country. The branch that Qi Ba belongs to migrated to Hunan, Jiangxi and Zhejiang provinces, and their descendants, because they worked as private advisers to the local government, moved from place to place. They went to Jiangsu, Henan, Hunan, Hubei, and Hebei provinces, and following that moved to the larger cities, such as Tianjin, Beijing, and Shanghai. After Qi Ba started school, revolution, and work, he left footprints in every corner of the country. When he was a teenager, he boldly spoke his mind: "Study for the rise of China." In the northeast, he left the following inscription in the notebooks of his classmates: "Work together with one heart; a brilliant prospect can be expected any day." In 1917, before he went to Japan to study, he wrote down for his classmates: "Be ready to realise your aspirations anywhere in the country." In 1939, during the war of resistance against Japan, he visited his old home in Shaoxing and wrote an inscription for Mr Cao Tianfeng, quoting the powerful and rousing verses of Mr Shen Fu to express his own feeling and pledging to campaign to resist the Japanese aggression: "Don't ask if it is a victory or a defeat, because it is a trifling thing; after all, China belongs to the Yan and Yellow Emperors."

3) Study for the purpose of application, seeking truth and being pragmatic. When he was young, Qi Ba once wrote a couplet: "Reading books that have no words or sentences; working with

those who have heroic spirit." He loved this couplet very much and pursued its spirit accordingly as a way to get on in the world, to conduct or to run a country. After he grew up to be a professional revolutionary and in his old age, when he was the country's premier, he initiated the principle of 'live and learn' and earnestly practised what he advocated. Not only did he learn from books and from practice, but also from the common people whenever he had the chance. He even took the opportunity to learn from visiting foreign guests. During his lifetime, he often quoted a popular saying: "Act as one's conscience dictates." Because many of our family members worked as private advisers, they (including himself) paid attention not only to knowledge from the books that were necessary for examinations, but also to experiences in management summed up by their forefathers.

4) Strict family education to raise the greatest talents. The branch to which Qi Ba belonged was not a prominent family of officials nor a wealthy business family, but a big family whose members traditionally became private advisers. The usual and expected model for family development was the following: study the classics of Confucianism; take examinations; pass the examination at a provincial level; become a private adviser; become an official. Among his father's generation, there were three *juren* with whom he had been in touch, and they had all followed this pattern. The vocations of the other family members were varied, but the number undertaking teaching or clerical work was not small; the elders who had succeeded in their careers often regarded raising talented family members as their task. Outstanding youngsters would find favour in their eyes and be given guidance and financial help. Qi Ba was such an example, and in the course of his learning and growth he constantly received aid and help from his uncles.

5) Never cease writing. Poems were handed down from

generation to generation. Zhou Yuantang, Qi Ba's great-great grandfather, was an example. He failed his examinations but turned himself into a poet, well known to the local people, and his beautiful verses have been handed down through generations. After him, all three *juren* of the family (recently some academics have found, during their research, that there should be four, but Qi Ba only mentioned three in our conversations), had their poems passed on, such as *Ode to the Soul* and *Self-Admonishment*. These poems revealed, between the lines, the sentiments of being upright and self-disciplined as well as the poets' views of life. This is the influence formed in the history and culture of a large family clan. In my view, those of our ancestors who left these poems behind and whose poems have had huge influence on Qi Ba are Zhou Dunyi, Zhou Yuantang and Zhou Henai.

5. Zhou Yuantang and His *Verses in Haichao Study*

5.1. " I Ought to Be a Remarkable Man "

Zhou Yuantang was Qi Ba's great-great grandfather and his influence on him is still unknown to the world. He was born in 1791 and died in 1851. Although he wrote a lot during his lifetime, because of the wars only the manuscript of *Verses in Haichao Study* has been preserved. He wrote these verses before he was 22 years old and they were copied by his grandson Zhou Angjun (my great-grandfather). His great-grandsons, Zhou Henai (my grandfather), Zhou Bingyu, and Zhou Songyao, printed them and then passed them on to future generations. Qi Ba kept the 135 poems under his pillow, and they accompanied him during the 10-year catastrophe of the Cultural Revolution and until his death. The cultural traditions of the Zhou clan come down in a continuous line, and when Qi Ba was at primary school in Shenyang, his compositions stood out from those of his fellows. His *Thoughts on the Second Anniversary of the Dongguan Model School* was marked as excellent and was on show at the Fengtian (now Shenyang) provincial cultural exhibition. It was also included in the booklet on records of the national Chinese language and literature

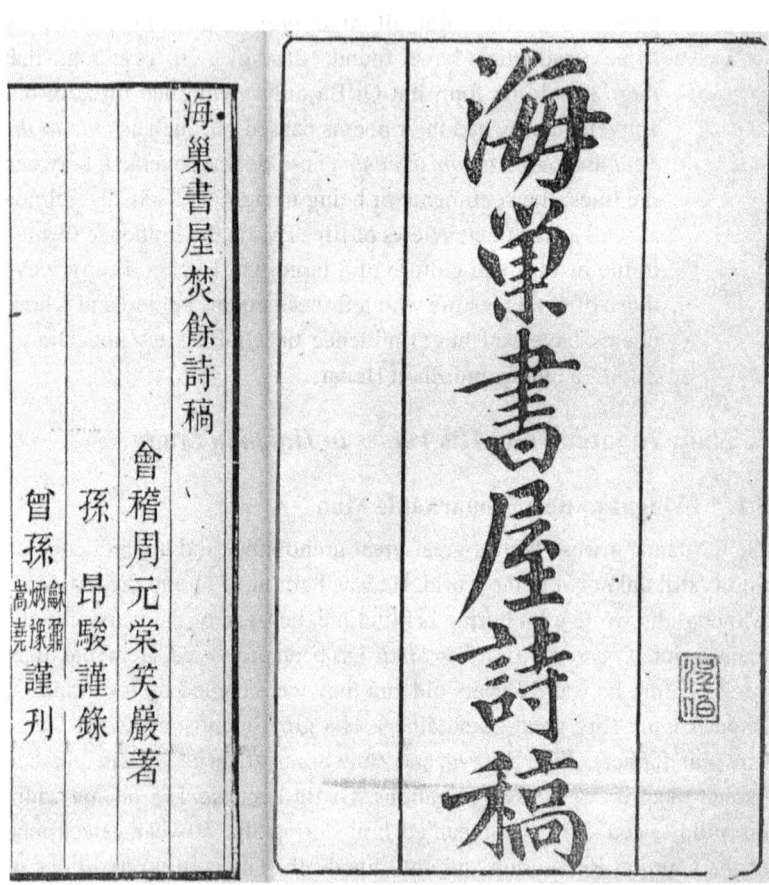

The book cover of the *Verses of Haichao Study*. "The surviving verses of Zhou Yuantang (Xiaoyan) of Kuaiji after his study caught fire. Recorded by Angjun (grandson of Zhou Yuantang). Printed by Henai, Bingyu and Songyao (great grandsons of Zhou Yuantang)."

for the exhibition of Fengtian cultural products. During his school days in Nankai, he studied very hard while remaining concerned about social conditions, and he expressed his feelings in his articles. Along with his classmates, who shared common ideals, he produced the *School Spirit and Career Dedication* newspapers. He had his own column, *Feifei's Random Notes* ('Feifei' was Qi Ba's pen name at the time), in which he published his poems and reviews.

A Random Verse on a Spring Day (2/2) (1914)

Cherry blossoms redden the paths,
Willow leaves green the edge of the ponds.
In the twittering of swallows,
To another year my yearning marches.

Student Zhou Enlai at Nankai School.

In this poem, the scenes of his school's surroundings aroused his strong feelings for his hometown, Shaoxing. Although he was born and brought up in Huaian and later went to school in Liaoning and Tianjin, and visited many other places in both the north and south of the country, his feelings for the hometown of his ancestors never faded. He knew the scenery and customs of Shaoxing very well. Besides having an encyclopaedic knowledge of the city, his love for Shaoxing had much to do with his great-great-grandfather Zhou Yuantang's poems, as well as with his thoughts after reading them. Zhou Yuantang was a man of sentiments; he wrote his poems masterfully — flowers blooming and fading, rice fields, and the tilling of fields are all included in his poems.

Spring is Gone

Melancholy, the sights and sounds of spring briskly reappear,
The crying cuckoos amuse themselves in the setting sun.
The Supreme Being blames not the spring breeze,
He lets the sunlight go anywhere it shoots.

He was also optimistic and broadminded, bemoaned neither autumn nor winter, and declared without reservations that "I am healthier in autumn". He was content living in honest poverty and he was able to see the true meaning of life in his learning and reflection.

Random Thoughts in an Autumn Night (3/3)

I am healthier in autumn, so
My verses are longer as I have more to say.
A twisting stream runs past my little window,
Broken bamboo slips send forth wafts of sweet fragrance.
Brush in hand, I write down some good verses,
Taking a rest, I drink wine to my heart's content.
The qin* curtains and the meditation beds,
Graciously I call them couch of learning.

(* musical instrument)

Although he had experienced the decline of his family, he himself chose to live in poverty, keeping his personal integrity intact all his life. When we read this beautiful line of verse, "I ought to be a remarkable man", it still makes us, the descendants, feel as though we have seen him in person.

That's Me (2/2)

Human feelings of sympathy are as thin as paper, and the way of the world is insipid as water. How to conduct myself is not within my own power to decide, but I ought to be a remarkable man. When I do things I shall never fall into evil ways, and when I speak I shall never slander. I say what I truly feel and I do what satisfies my essential being. I plough the fields of ink-slab where there is no border to designate. The pen is my weapon, so there is no need to have bows and arrows. I'd like to be a gifted scholar and leave all small tricks behind. Frustratingly, I have gained no scholarly honour and official rank — it is merely that I had no chance to obtain it. In this life, I may drift from place to place; yet I can teach what I know to students. I only hope I can finish my education and prove myself a man of ability, which will delight my parents and relatives as well as the heavens.

Scripts of *Liu Hou*.

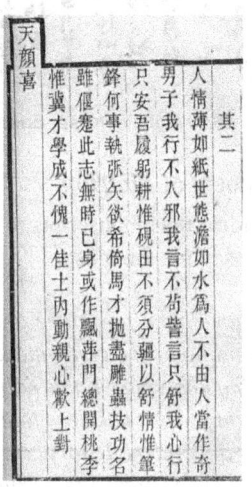

Scripts of *That's Me 2/2*.

When I read these verses, I remember the famous poem Qi Ba wrote before he travelled to Japan to study in September 1917. What a coincidence that the heroic spirit of the young Qi Ba, who was willing to sacrifice everything to save China, is the same spirit that his great-great-grandfather had!

> O, heroic! Eastward flows the Yangtze river,
> The poem I sang filled me with enthusiasm.
> Determined, I head eastward.
> My country is on the edge of a precipice;
> To save it, I study various subjects extensively.
> O, profound! Follow the example of the monk,
> Facing the wall in mediation for 10 years,
> Great attainments will be achieved.
> Aspiration unfulfilled? I am a hero still.

Zhou Enlai's verse, *Eastward Flows the Yangtze River*.

5.2. The Poem of *Liu Hou**

When I studied the manuscripts of Zhou Yuantang, the following poem *Liu Hou* impressed me the most:

> Heroes have been few since ancient times, and those few are either too unbending or too restrained. It is not unusual to draw one's sword to help, but knowing what is noble and displaying one's ability is more vital. Zifang was a peerless talent; the way he was presented with the book** is a wonderful story. He was humiliated and ordered to fetch and put the shoe back on for Huang Shigong, who was impressed with his fortitude and humility at the bridge. Armed with knowledge of the

art of war, he talked stratagems with various tricks up his the sleeve. Having double pupils in his eyes, he beat his opponents with ease. He managed state affairs with feminine looks, and after winning merit, he retired from office. How shabbily the rulers of the Han dynasty treated their heroes.

* Liu Hou, Marquis of Wencheng of Liu, is Zhang Liang (courtesy name 'Zifang'), who helped Liu Bang to establish the Han dynasty in 206 BC.
** The book was *The Art of War* by Taigong.

Zhang Liang, who was good-looking, was a man of learning and talent. He assisted Liu Bang in establishing the Han dynasty. But after this accomplishment, he retired from political life, spending the remainder of his life in seclusion, which might have been the best choice for an intellectual in a feudal society. In the poem it is said that since ancient times, historical figures who can be truly called heroes are few. Often they were either too strong-willed or too self-restrained. A true hero should be one who is adept with both the pen and sword, who can also temper force with mercy and who is always of superior attainments, cultivation and talents. In this 100-word poem, the 20-year-old Zhou Yuantang summarised the extraordinary abilities and wisdom as well as the life achievements of Zhang Liang, whom he aspired to be like. He described and commented on Zhang Liang's features, learning and character, which showed his talent as well as his literary foundation as a young poet. However, what amazed me most is that, by chance, he became an unusual predictor. Qi Ba's outstanding yet hard life, which was full of ups and downs, tested and verified his prediction, and at the same time it also tested and verified the powerful spirit of traditional Chinese culture. Coming from a big declining feudal family, he finally turned himself into a great statesman acknowledged the world over. All this was related to the inherited family culture; hence, it is not at all surprising that he kept this collection of poems with him all his life. We can imagine that he repeatedly studied them, as well as drew inspiration and comfort from them. Qi Ba had visited the Liu Hou temple; standing there pondering, he was reluctant to leave when he finished the tour. And coincidentally, he wrote a poem at Nankai School which alluded to Zhang Liang.

A Random Verse on a Spring Day (1/2) (1914)

In the fields outside the town that stretch as far as the eye can see,
Smothering fumes are whirling.
Deer are chased on the Central Plain*
Another Bolang(sha)** is at heel.

> *   meaning to try to seize control of the country.
> ** reference to Zhang Liang's attempted assassination of Emperor Qin Shi Huang in a place called Bolangsha in 218 BC.

6. Qi Ba's Uncle Zhou Henai

Among the family members, the one who had the most influence on Qi Ba was his uncle Zhou Henai (my grandfather). His courtesy name was 'Tiaozi' and, according to local custom, the family clan respectfully called him 'the revered Mr Tiaozi'. He was originally called Yiding, but he later changed it to Yikang and finally to his formal name, Henai. He was born in Huaian on 5 January 1868, the second son of Junang. He was engaged to Gao, but she died young, so next he married Wang (who suffered from a congenital mental disease), and then married Cheng. He had a reason to change his name and give himself a courtesy name: he was an adopted son of his uncle Jinhou, who was childless, so after the adoption his name was changed. Afterwards, one of his cousins changed his name,

Portrait of Zhou Henai, the second uncle of Zhou Enlai and grandfather of Zhou Erliu. He became the head of the extended Zhou family after he was adopted by his uncle. He was the first *juren* of the modern-day Zhou family.

but unfortunately one of the characters in his cousin's new name was the same one as in his name. To avoid confusion, he changed his name again, choosing 'Henai' as his formal name. Because his adopted father was the eldest of his generation, he took the place of first son of the first household. Thinking that he should have breadth of vision, and that bearing that came with being head of the extended family, he gave himself a name (Tiaozi) that was meant to mediate relations among family members.

He was diligent in his studies. When he was young, he received an academic degree as a student of the imperial college (the highest educational administration in feudal China) and the title of candidate for dean. He believed that as head of the extended family, he should care for everybody else. Several times he declined, out of modesty, the chance to take the imperial examination, insisting that other elder family members take it before him, and only took it himself in 1894. He was successful and became the 107th *juren* of his province. He was sincere and kind, though not very good at flattering others; nor did he like to be an official. Therefore, he often took the role of assistant instead. He was once the chief clerk at the court of Governor Chen Kuilong in Jiangsu province, and followed the governor to Kaifeng in Henan province and later to Wuhan in Hubei province. In 1909, he was the prefect of Dingzhou prefecture, Hebei province. His official cap showed that he was once a salt commissioner. He was unemployed after the 1911 revolution, but then became engaged in trade. In 1917, he went to Nanjing and became an adviser as well as secretary to the military governor, Li Chun. He died in Shanghai in 1921. Because he both left home and died early, later generations knew little of him.

Portrait of Zhou Henai.

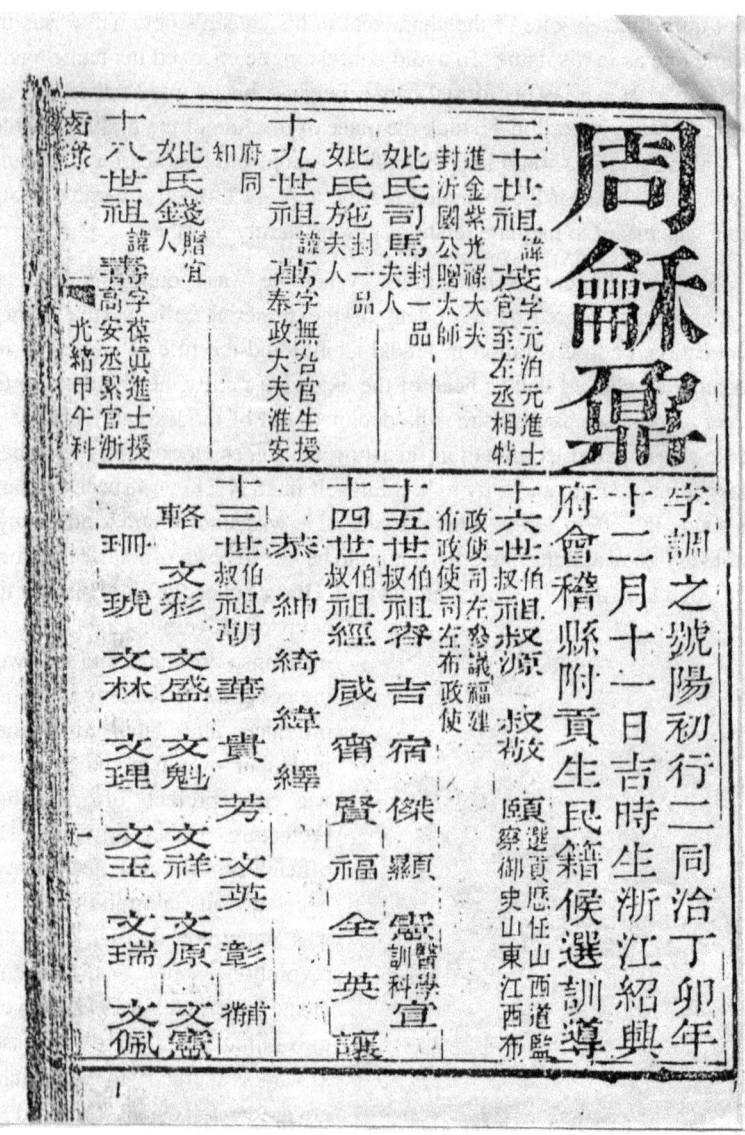

The archive copy showing Zhou Henai being announced as a successful candidate for the imperial examination at the provincial level. For the full translation, see Appendix 2.

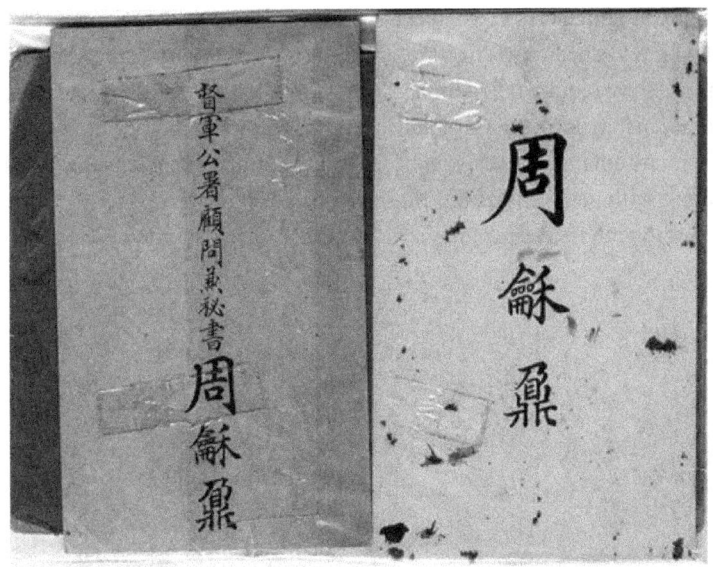

Zhou Henai's name card. "Zhou Henai. Adviser and secretary to the military governor's office."

He liked literature and the arts very much. Qi Ba once told me that he was versed in the south Kunqu opera, being well known in our hometown. Smiling, Qi Ba said: "It seems that literature and the arts are the tradition and the hobby of our family." Full of pride, he then said to me: "Your grandfather was an expert in Kunqu opera!" He left behind about 100 poems, some of which influenced Qi Ba; hence, they should not be ignored in any research on the influence that the family had on Qi Ba.

Self-Admonishment

Don't take having or not having affection for fame for granted,
Gaining honour or being down on one's luck is decided by nature.
There is no coincidence, but you must come to terms with your fortune,
Fame does not require being high up, but to reasonably handle affairs.

This poem was the work of Mr Tiaozi. Qi Ba liked it very much when he was a young man. As I remember it, he took the matter so seriously that he asked me to check it word for word, especially the following sentence: "Fame does not require being high up, but to reasonably handle affairs". He knew that his uncle was an official for many years, but did not follow the common customs. He never sought fame and fortune and was reasonable in dealing with daily affairs. Qi Ba talked to me about these poems many times, urging me to learn from our ancestor and strictly abide by them.

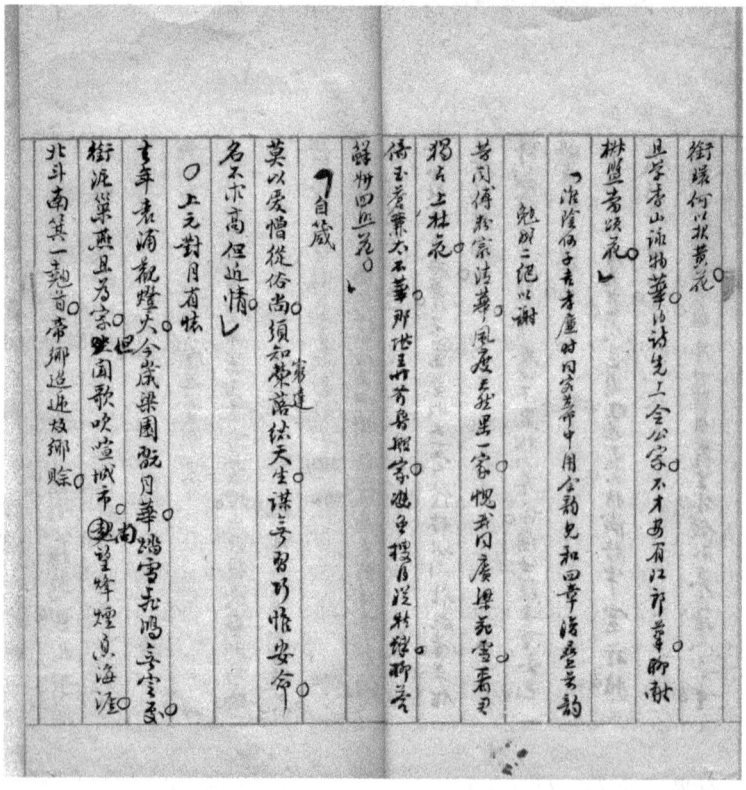

The manuscript of Mr Tiaozi's (Zhou Henai's) poem. For the full translation, see above.

Mr Tiaozi was broadminded and of a kindly disposition. He helped the distressed and those in peril. He fully embodied the regal manner of a head of a first household, and the other family members had the greatest esteem for him. When Qi Ba was a student in Tianjin and went to Beijing to perform in stage plays, he often went to the residences of his uncle, who would help him financially. Probably because my grandfather saw in his nephew a boy of outstanding ability, believing that he would win our family glory by realising his ambition, he went all out to help him without showing the slightest reluctance, including risking his own life to give Qi Ba shelter. Once, Qi Ma told me that in those years Qi Ba took part in student activities, organising demonstrations and rehearsing progressive plays. Such activities were risky, so many family members opposed his involvement; but my grandparents supported him, even though they were worried for his safety. Qi Ba played a female part in the play *One Yuan Coin*. The organisers invited the parents and guardians to watch, and my grandparents went. My grandmother often laughed when she said to me: "Enlai dressed as a girl to act in a modern play, and he looked nice." And whenever these events were recalled, Qi Ba would show his profound gratitude to my grandparents.

During his time in Japan, in 1918, he wrote down one event in his diary which had something to do with my grandfather.

16 January, Wednesday

The day before yesterday I received a letter from my teacher, Mr Gao. He said that after he read my letter he knew that I did not have enough money, and he is thinking about looking for a part-time teaching job so that he can give me some help. He blamed me for not telling him the truth about my situation. After I read his letter, I was both moved and surprised. When I wrote my letter, I was afraid that he would be worried about me, so I told him only part of my situation. I did not tell him that my financial situation was very difficult, but only said that sometimes I did not have enough money to spend. I never expected that my teacher would have such a plan to help me. It is rumoured that he wants to ask my Gan Ba to tell my uncle about this. He can't do that! I have already troubled so many friends, how can I trouble my family at home? Worse still, he himself is not in an easy situation; he is already overdrawn at the bank. If he does send me money, I would be very uneasy in my mind. Besides, I am not a person who is unable to bear any hardships. If the situation at home is like this, how can I be in the mood to enjoy ease and comfort?

The 'Gan Ba' in the letter is Zhou Yineng, his birth father; because he was adopted by his uncle he called his birth father and birth mother *Gan Ba* ('nominally adoptive father') and *Gan Ma* ('nominally adoptive mother'). He was hard up in Japan, but he was independent and eager to outdo others, so he was reluctant to ask for help. After my grandfather found out about his situation, he sent him money.

The teacher, 'Mr Gao', was Gao Yiwu, Qi Ba's kind and respectable teacher in Shenyang. He liked and admired his student very much. He was not only the teacher who taught the young Qi Ba, but also the teacher who introduced him to the revolutionary path. He gave Qi Ba the courtesy name 'Xiangyu' ('soaring over the world') when he graduated from the Dongguan Model Primary School in Shenyang. Later, when he moved to Beijing to work, they stayed in touch.

7. Shaoxing *Shiye*, a Profession Handed Down through Generations

Mr Tiaozi got on in life as a *juren*, but, living in the late Qing dynasty and the beginning of the Republic of China, when China was experiencing great change, the last generation of *shiye* (private advisers) experienced many spells of both good and bad fortune. In his poem, he wrote:

> We poor scholars have no land but ink-stones,
> In a good year we have wine to drink and clothes to keep us warm.
> When drunk, I got the idea of being a hero, and
> I went hunting at night on the Tianshan mountain.
> No sign of the beacon fires, but
> We've lost islands to the enemy.
> Hearing the music drifting in the air above our land,
> I, in vain, worry for my country.
> You high-ranking officials do need to pay
> A debt of gratitude for the high life you are enjoying.

For people like him, who lived on their learning, the minimum salary was not enough to make ends meet. Whether he was poor or not, he always held the ideal of repaying the country with supreme loyalty and to do something to one's credit. The political situation at the time was bad: wars raged all over the country; the national crisis had not ended; a large number of high officials still sought pleasure rather than think of serving their country. He was indignant, saying: "We *shiye*, who are in such a minor position, worry for our country, but those people are unpatriotic and ungrateful." *Shiye* became a traditional profession in Shaoxing, starting in the middle to late Ming dynasty and flourishing in the Qing dynasty, declining and terminating in the late Qing dynasty and during the early years of the Republic. They had been active in feudal ruling organizations for about 300 years. Generally, according to the division of duties, there were secretaries for official documents and correspondence, for jurisprudence and for tax collection. Qi Ba once humorously said that the Shaoxing *shiye* people saw in the operas were always drunken men of letters with a red nose, often masterminding a scheme for some officials who were avoiding doing a good deed. However, he said that the development of the profession of private adviser as well as the imperial examination system had respective historical reasons, and were also the historical factors which influenced the development of the modern system of civil servants in the West. Later, I personally exchanged ideas about this with many politicians and sociologists in Western Europe, and they all thought that the modern civil service systems in their countries could not have come into existence without the influence of the Chinese imperial examination system.

Qi Ba's father's generation produced three *juren*, which were grand events for the Zhou clan. Beside Zhou Henai, there were Zhou Songyao and Zhou Jiachen, who was a distant uncle, all three of them becoming secretaries of government officials.

After the 1911 revolution, the feudal system was replaced by republicanism. Many private advisers became government secretaries at all levels, and this special group, which developed under specific historical conditions, gradually stepped down from the stage of history. The same applied to the three *juren* of the Zhou family. According to Qi Ba, my grandfather Zhou Henai had concurrently been adviser and secretary to the military governor of Jiangsu province. His uncle Zhou Songyao had been secretary to Yuan Shikai, who considered student leaders and communists to be guilty of heterodoxy and unworthy descendants. However, with the developing situation, he slowly changed his attitude, particularly in his old age. In short, with the gigantic social change that the Republicans brought, the Shaoxing *shiye* model became redundant, and the younger members of the family had to try to find another way to earn a living. Going to a modern school or going to study abroad was not an easy thing to do, so the later generations felt that their future was bleak. Being at a loss as to what to do, they became dispirited, which was one of the major factors for the decline of the Zhou family clan. But those private advisers were intellectuals, who not only had poems and articles to pass on but who were also equipped with professional knowledge about assisting the administration. Among them, some were outstanding; therefore, defaming the whole group does not correspond to the real situation.

8. "Driven to Revolt"

At the end of the Qing dynasty, China was poor and weak; foreign aggressors came one after another, society was characterised by turbulence, and the masses lived in dire poverty. Many formerly large families found themselves in a crisis. Our family clan lived on being scholars; they had inkstones, but no land, so this background led to the downturn of the family. Especially after the end of the Qing dynasty, China had sunk into long-term infighting among warlords, and national calamity followed on the heels of impoverished families; hence, our family clan steadily deteriorated. When Qi Ba was a teenager, our family clan had been in decline for some time. Not only was his birth father absent from home all year round, but his birth mother and adoptive mother died one after the other, so he had to depend on pawnshops to live. Luckily, several uncles gave him support. With such a family background, and with his indomitable will and his noble ambition, he walked along the twisting, varied and colourful path of pursuing his studies. He once told me that he was driven to revolt and joined the revolution. I think he meant that the fall of the family and the ongoing social tumult were too much to bear, or, as he said: "In short, caused by national calamity and the family's poverty."

The Zhou Clan

The fall of a feudal family can have all sorts of consequences. From a negative point of view, they can be of every description, with a marked imprint on society. During one conversation between myself and Qi Ba, he gave a detailed account of the negative elements affecting our family clan. His appraisal was quite objective, and amongst all of the family's social relations, he pointed out 14 unhealthy relationships. I can still remember them, and they are: the secretary of a warlord chief; feudal bureaucrats; unhealthy private advisers; historical counterrevolutionaries; a dandy; a dissipated and impoverished family; those who died from taking drugs; those who launched an all-out attack against communism overseas; gambling addicts; those who committed economic wrongdoings, forfeiting their integrity and separating from the revolutionary ranks; reactionary members of the army; traitors; and vagrants.

Among the relatives in Huaian, there was an uncle who had a strong feudal ideology and a hot temper. He felt repulsion for Qi Ba's anti-feudal ideology and once cursed him, calling him a rebel who had moved away from the Confucian doctrine. He would sometimes intimidate Qi Ba or inform the townsmen of this "unworthy descendant". This reminds me of Qi Ba's proposal for a novel based on our family after his retirement. Our family has a tradition of writing poems, but writing a novel that would be based on the household's evolution within the family clan was pioneering. It's a pity that he couldn't fulfill his wish. He took the view that he should be a thorough materialist, namely, seeking truth from facts and setting an example. He had determined the true nature of his family background as a large, declining feudal family — not a revolutionary family, as someone once postulated.

My Uncle Zhou Enlai

The Family's Cultural Relics and Qi Ba and Qi Ma's Letters (Part One)

In the early 1940s, there was an unusual period of time during which my relatives left Shanghai one after another, leaving me, a 12-year-old boy, behind to attend school. My school was the Nanyang Model Middle School and I was one of the few boarders.

When my family members moved away from our home in 5 Shunde Lane, Route Tenant de la Tour (now Xiangyang Road South), after a discussion with the landlord, they stored the books and items left by our ancestors in a storeroom for me to look after. When I organised or aired them, I found that, besides the books, there were letters between Qi Ba and my grandfather and my father, manuscripts of my grandfather's poems, the family album, and some souvenirs sent by Qi Ba from France. Regarding them as priceless artifacts and as valuable as my life, I kept them safe with me in all conditions in the following decades. Even shortly before the liberation, with the enemy's bayonets pointed at my back, some of them were firmly placed next to the skin of my chest, never leaving me for a moment. I have tried to keep my promise that as my life is preserved, so shall these items be. It has been over 70 years, and I feel that I can comfort the spirits of the deceased. To me, every item has a touching past and is a piece of vivid history. In this book, I will present the illustrations and the stories behind them. The letters of Qi Ba and Qi Ma, which are included in this book, have never been published or analysed; they show the authentic family history. Hence, this correspondence is exceptionally significant to a study of Zhou Enlai.

These letters cover the period between 1920 and the early stages of the Cultural Revolution, and are extremely rich in content. They were either written when he studied in France, or written and sent home secretly when he was in an area controlled by the Kuomintang (KMT or nationalists). They either display the course of the early development of his ideology, or they show his care and love for his nephews and the arrangements for their schooling. They either embody the affection among family members that should respect the aged and love the young, or mirror the changes of society in different periods of history. These letters chronologically record the past events of three generations over half a century, centering around Qi Ba. The space and time span of these letters is large, which was rare in the past. They are not only my companions, but also examples, giving me infinite strength, and I believe that this precious historical evidence should be shown to the public. The interpretation of each letter is based on the background, the characters, the content and their implications. The full text of photocopies of the letters will be attached for the sake of reference.

In 2008, to mark the 110th anniversary of Qi Ba's birth, some extracts from his correspondence were on show in the Memorial Hall in Shanghai, which is the site of the first national congress of the CPC. Tens of thousands of visitors went to the exhibition. Besides commending the contents of the letters, many visitors gasped with admiration at Qi Ba's calligraphy of neat, regular and semi-cursive script.

1. The Tombs of the Ancestors

Qi Ba attached great importance to these historical relics, and if it were not for his efforts to maintain his rescue operation, the calamity of the Cultural Revolution would have brought even greater damage to the Chinese people. He was in contact with my grandparents as well as myself, and he lived with them occasionally, so he was familiar with the relics that had commemorative value to the family. In the decades from 1946 onwards, from time to time he would ask me about the whereabouts of each of them. If one of them had gone missing, he would be disappointed and very unhappy.

The tombstone of Mr Jingshang.

Regarding the ancestral graves, he vigorously maintained that the tombs should be flattened and the land be used to plant grain. In Shaoxing, after the remains of our ancestors were buried deep and the tombstones were removed, I went out of my way to try and buy back the tombstone of the revered Mr Jingshang, as well as those of his son and his grandson. These tombstones were inscribed with an elegiac address. But the local officials told me that they had been taken by the locals and used as building materials. I was very disappointed and regretful. However, after making every possible effort, I finally found Mr Jingshang's tombstone, which is now stored in the ancestral residence in Shaoxing.

In March 1939, Qi Ba visited the grave of his paternal great-great-grandfather, Mr Jingshang (formal name Zhou Wenhao). Jingshang lived in poverty, so he wished for his eldest son, Yuantang, to pass the imperial examination at provincial level after his success at county level. But Yuantang failed, so like his father he, too, became a private tutor. Yuantang's son Qiaoshui also became a private tutor after his success at the imperial examination at county level. Yuantang's grandson, Zhou Angjun, also passed the imperial examination at county level, but because his grandfather and father died one after the other, he lost the opportunity to carry on with his studies. By

A rubbing made from the tablet inscription for Mr Jingshang.

The tombstone of Mr Qiaoshui, the great-grandfather of Zhou Enlai.

The Zhou Clan

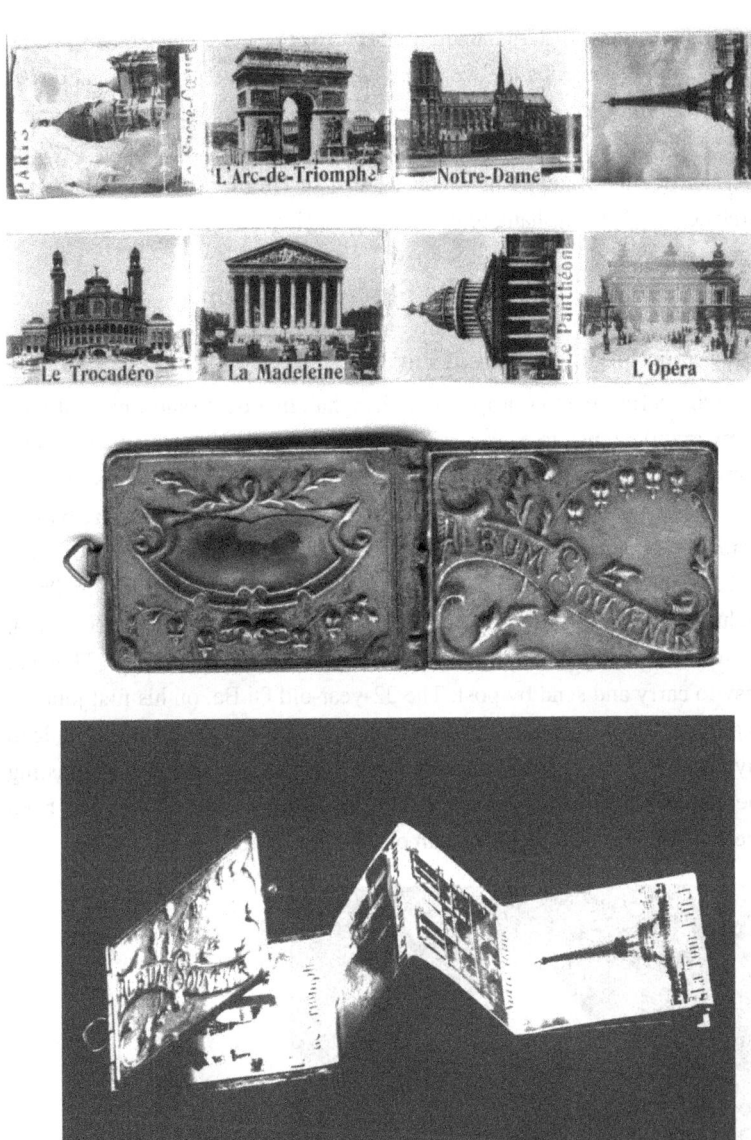

The scenic folding cards of Paris, sent by Zhou Enlai from France in the 1920s.

arrangement of his maternal uncle, he began a career as a magistrate's private adviser, and this occupation would be taken on by successive generations of the Zhou family. My grandfather, Zhou Henai, finally succeeded in becoming a *juren,* the first of the successive generations. It was an unquestionably grand occasion for the Zhou clan, which we can see from the inscription on the tombstone of Mr Jingshang (erected by Zhou Henai in 1921).

2. Relics From When Qi Ba Studied in Europe

2.1. Scenic Folding Cards of Paris

In 1920, Qi Ba went to Europe from Shanghai. In order to show his gratitude to my grandparents, in each port where the ship docked he would buy them some little presents with distinctive features depicting local history and culture. These two elegant metal scenic folding cards from Paris are typical examples of them. They are exquisite and unique, 4 centimetres long and 2.5 centimetres wide, each containing eight classic pictures of Paris, including the Eiffel tower, Notre Dame, the Arc de Triomphe and L'Opéra. As souvenirs, they have some cultural and historical significance. They are easy to carry and send by post. The 22-year-old Qi Ba, on his first journey to a major Western country, hand-picked these gifts to show his gratitude to my family. To me, they are not ordinary gifts from overseas, but everlasting mementos worth passing on to future generations. One of them has been presented to the National Museum of Chinese History by my father.

The mini peep show sent by Zhou Enlai from France in the 1920s.

2.2. Mini Personal Peep Show

When Qi Ba sent us the scenic folding cards, he also sent us a personal miniature peep show made of ivory. It is the same size as the scenic cards. The size of the lens is the same as a miniature pearl, but through it, you can clearly view the pictures of Paris inside. It is a typical and exquisite artifact. The peep show and the scenic folding cards verify that Qi Ba had an excellent ability to appreciate works of art.

The drawing pin box Zhou Enlai sent from Germany in 1922.

2.3. The German Drawing Pin Box

Because living in Germany was cheaper in early March of 1922, Qi Ba moved to 54 Kaiserallee, Wilmersdorf, Berlin. By then he had become a communist and actively engaged in local activities. In October of that same year, he and Zhang Shenfu convinced Zhu De to join the CPC. The 24-year-old Qi Ba asked somebody to bring a box of German drawing pins for his 14-year-old cousin, Zhou Enzhu (my father), at home. When I started primary school, in year one, my grandmother handed me the box to keep. My father told me that it was an essentially commemorative present, but with a sense of humour. Its imprint originally meant 'a lucky fellow'. The instruction said that the pins were made of high-quality celluloid, which was strong, convenient for travelling, and would not break after being used. Qi Ba showed consideration for the safety of his family at home, using the drawing pins to tell his young cousin that in Europe he had formed his political convictions, which he would pursue all his life.

3. Qi Ba's Letters from London, England (1921)

After the May Fourth Movement in 1919, Qi Ba strongly felt that the student movement needed to sum up their experiences and draw lessons from them. When he was with the Awakening Society, he gained a theoretical level of understanding of the ideas of all sects, short of on-the-spot examination. During his time in Japan, he discovered that "Japan's today will never be China's tomorrow", meaning that China's development and transformation should not follow the path of Japan's. In view of the above reasons, he felt that it was necessary for him to go to some of the European countries, such as Great Britain, to do some investigating. He seized the opportunity of a work-study programma and went to France, waiting to go to the UK. By the end of December 1920, after he "spent about 10 days in Paris, observing the spectacular views of the Capital of Flowers", he was scheduled to go to England, but the departure was delayed due to illness, and he did not arrive in London until 5 January 1921. After he finished registering with Edinburgh University, he wrote to the relatives of his father's generation. The addressee was his second uncle Zhou Yikang (not Zhou Yiding, his fifth uncle, which was wrongly circulated for 30 years). He also wanted the letter to be read by Zhou Yiliang, his sixth uncle. After some effort from me, the above misinformation was completely cleared up around 2008. This letter was written in cursive script, showing Qi Ba's characteristic style. His handwriting is elegant and intelligent, and there is strength as well as grace. The lengthy letter runs to nearly 1,000 words and flows smoothly, showing fully that his thinking is thorough and detailed. In his bearing, he stands head and shoulders above all others. It is the longest letter to his uncles that I have ever seen. Up to now, the full content has not been included in any published collection of Zhou Enlai's correspondence, and I hope this letter will draw the attention of both readers and researchers.

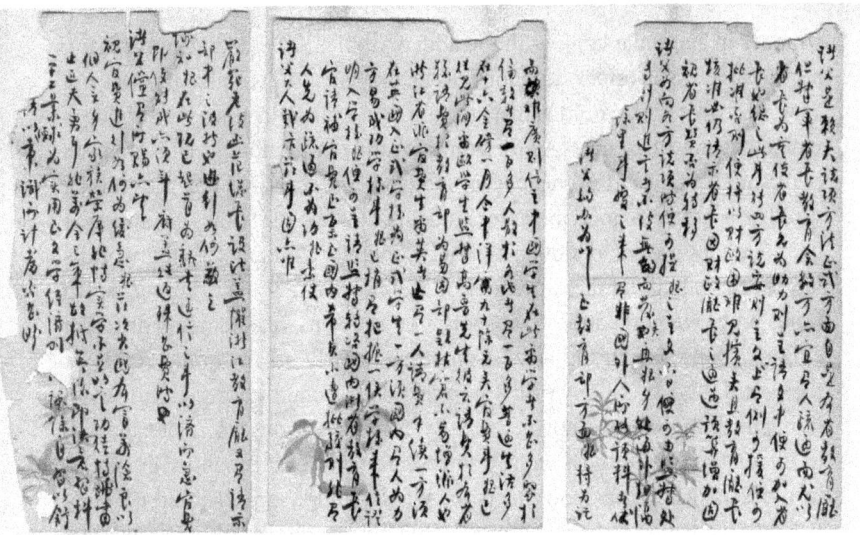

The letter sent by Zhou Enlai from London in 1921.

On 18 October 1920, Qi Ba left Tianjin for Shanghai, where he would board a ship to France. He stopped at Nanjing and stayed with his uncle Zhou Yikang for a while. He got some money from him and then travelled to Shanghai. At that time, Zhou Yikang was adviser as well as secretary to Li Chun, the military governor of Jiangsu province. Qi Ba did not know his uncle Zhou Yiliang very well at the time. It was said that he was the secretary general of Governor Li Chun, but at the time, when he was mentioned in the letter, he was at home with nothing to do, not knowing whether he should join Wang Shizhen or not. We have not been able to substantiate the facts. Wang Shizhen styled himself Pinqing; he was a veteran of the Beiyang warlords and had once been premier and, concurrently, chief of staff. He also served as the governor of Jiangsu, Anhui and Jiangxi provinces from December 1920 to January 1921. He was an old acquaintance of Zhou Yiliang. In his letter, Qi Ba asked Zhou Yiliang to seek Wang Shizhen's help with applying for a state grant. Zhou Yiliang failed, and as a result Qi Ba left the UK and went to Germany and France instead. Zhou Yikang sent him some money, but unfortunately, he died in 1921.

Qi Ba stated in his letter that when he first arrived in the UK, he was a stranger in a strange land; with the added problem of the language barrier, he was at a loss. Besides, London was an expensive city, so his life was not easy. He wrote: "I would rather go to a quiet place than stay in London, which has unsettled me." As for going to study at Edinburgh University in Scotland, he said: "It is cheaper in Scotland, and the air is cleaner and the weather is better; a good place for students." What will attract the attention of the reader are his comments about London: "London was the world's largest capital city at the time, four or five times larger than Beijing, seven times bigger in population. Transportation is extensive, and many different ethnic groups live in the city. It possesses nearly all the grand sights of the world, and it is the world's political and economic centre. However, living in London does not necessarily mean that you can understand it; to understand it we must engage in research and experiment with single-hearted devotion. London reflects the whole world, so we should not only listen to the lectures in the classroom, but also undertake research into this social phenomenon."

Europe is the hometown of Marxism, and London is a mirror of the world: a typical developed capitalist city. As a young student, Qi Ba decided to make an on-the-spot examination, then compare the historical development between Russia and Great Britain. And such a comparison could help him to answer the question of which path China must take. Afterwards, based on his examination, he made a timely and resolute political choice, whose significance would speak for itself.

He attached great importance to social practice. Being aware that London was the reflection of the world, all phenomena in the city should be studied and tested. In his early years, he was able to pursue this principle of combining 'study and experiment', so that in later years he became a popular and great statesman, to which his early travelling as well as the development of his ideology had given adequate indications.

In one letter, he wrote: "...earnestly hope that my uncles can do this for me." ('This' here means to secure a state grant for him to study in Europe.) He repeatedly requested his uncles to mediate with their contacts, and from this we can see that he was more or less aware of the harmful effect the long-standing abuse of power in old China had on society, and that he

The Zhou Clan

Zhou Erliu and Wang Zhangli outside 17 rue Godefroy, Paris. In 1974, when Deng Xiaoping was in Paris, he failed to revisit 17 rue Godefroy, the former residence of Zhou Enlai near the Place d'Italie. After Zhou Enlai's death in 1976, the French proposed to install a plaque at the address. In 1978, when the Chinese premier Hua Guofeng visited France, he, along with the French President Giscard d'Estaing and the mayor of Paris, Jacques Chirac, attended the ceremony to unveil the plaque. In 1982, Zhou Erliu and Wang Zhangli paid a special visit to the former residence of Zhou Enlai. The room is quite small and can only accommodate a single bed, a square table and two wooden chairs, which embodies Zhou Enlai's attitude: concerning himself with the world despite living in a small room.

appreciated the difficulty of governing such a society. His sharp insight still makes us think today and realize why he hated these bad habits of society so much and why he spent his whole life trying to get rid of them. After he became premier, he painstakingly sought to practise what he preached by governing the country in an honest and transparent way and relentlessly playing an exemplary role. He mentioned to his uncles that "virtue is the foundation for an individual, and family honour or disgrace can only rely on real learning", suggesting the idea of seeking common ground while, by then, differences had already formed between them. So, in front of the two aged feudal scholars, it was better for him to talk more about how to honour his ancestors than to stress that the purpose of his studying overseas was the rise of China.

"Merely to organise strikes is courage without discipline, and it is not a completely safe tactic." This sentence particularly catches the eye of the reader. From founding the Awakening Society to throwing himself into the May Fourth Movement, followed by being arrested and expelled from school; these experiences had made this young student leader more mature. He thought repeatedly and deeply about the limitations of the student movement, and these thoughts impelled him to make a correct political choice among numerous '-isms' and trends of thought as quickly as possible. It is especially worth pointing out that he had returned from Japan, and had formed his view that Imperial Japan would become a powerful enemy of China, but would never be an example for China to follow. He examined the origins of several progressive ideologies. He could never stop where he was, because of the obstacles. The key thing to remember is that he missed no chance to establish his own political, beliefs after a thorough study and comparison of all available ideas, and, after the decision, kept this faith all his life. He said: "My '-ism' has been decided, and I will not change it." In short, this letter is valuable and rare; it is not only a record of his political life and the evolution of his thoughts in his early political life, but also betokens the political beliefs that he was about to form. It represents a crucial turning point in his life: namely, a young school-leaver, who possessed advanced ideology and took part in the mass movement, had gradually turned into a professional revolutionary. He was both wise and courageous, and he remained faithful and unyielding to his beliefs. He was loved by his countrymen. He was a universally acknowledged statesman and a great historical figure. He has made outstanding contributions to the founding of the CPC and the construction of the new China.

4. The postcard sent by Qi Ba from Paris, France (1922)

This postcard was sent to Shanghai from Paris on 12 September 1922. The cartoon-like picture on the card is a sister playing with her brother. It has a greeting in French, but Qi Ba added an English one. On the other side of the card were the receiver (my father) and the sender (Qi Ba himself), with the Chinese New Year's greeting, the date, and the location (Paris). Because my grandfather died of illness in 1921, my grandmother and my 13-year-old father were in deep sorrow and even in a state of panic. According to Qi Ba, he purposefully selected this card and some other small gifts, sending them to Shanghai to comfort his aunt and cousin while remembering his deceased uncle, as well as to express his gratitude to him.

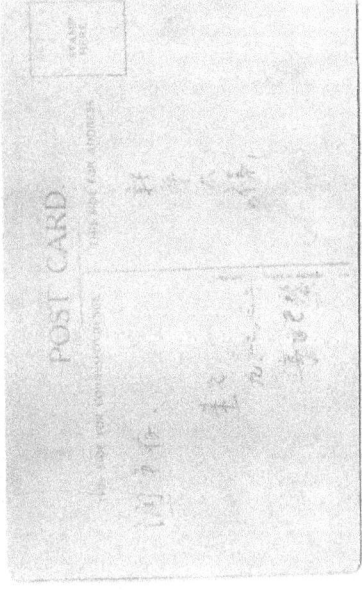

The postcard sent to Zhou Enzhu in Shanghai by Zhou Enlai from Paris, France in 1922. "Happy New Year to brother Run from Brother Lai, Paris, 9 December 1922."

Part Two

Aibao, Qi Ba and Qi Ma

The Riddle of My Birth

My birth mother, Cai Qingrong, was from an office worker's family in Anhui province. She was born in 1908, but the date of her death is unknown. From around 1927 to 1929 she studied at Datong University in Shanghai, where she came to know Zhou Enzhu and married him. She gave birth to a boy whose infant name was Aibao, but whose official name was Zhou Erliu.

However, Qi Ma and my stepmother, Ma Shunyi, told me that I was not born in 1929, but in late 1930 or early 1931. My stepmother's explanation was that my father lied to her about being a widower with a son, because he was worried that she would not want to marry him after the death of his first wife. In 1931, when Qi Ma stayed with my family, she saw me struggle to crawl on the floor, not looking at all like a two-year-old child. I also asked my father about this, but he angrily responded: "I'm your father. It is not appropriate for you to ask me

Zhou Erliu's birth mother, Cai Qingrong.

May 1931, Zhou Erliu at home in 44 Yong-an-li, North Sichuan Road, Shanghai. At the time, Zhou Enlai, Deng Yingchao and Zhou Enlai's birth father, Zhou Yineng, were taking cover at the address.

such a question." From the photos and letters left behind by my birth mother, I could see that she was a beautiful and gentle woman. She had an English name, Helen, and could play the piano and write good English. My stepmother told me that my maternal grandfather was a clergyman. Regrettably, I have not been able to seek out my mother's relatives, because none of them have paid me a visit in the last few decades; nor do I have their names or addresses.

When Qi Ba was less than six months old, he was adopted by his uncle, Zhou Yigan, who was seriously ill and died soon after the adoption. Before Qi Ba was ten years old, both his birth mother and adoptive mother died, one after the other. His birth father was not at home for most of the year, so he was looked after by his other uncles and spent his childhood and youth, which were permeated with hardships, in Huaian, Liaoning and Tianjin.

I was born in Shanghai, and my birth mother died soon after giving birth to me. My father was constantly ill and consequently weak, but mainly he was absent from home nearly all year round. Our separation was about more than us living together; for some time, we did not even know if he was still alive. My stepmother was cold and ignorant. When I was 14 or 15 years old, she even drove me out of the house. After leaving my grandmother, on whom I depended for survival, I was homeless, wandering the streets of Shanghai, sometimes in rags but always hungry. Luckily, Qi Ba found me then and began helping me with my life and studies. This surprisingly similar early-life experience that we shared made him profoundly understanding and sympathetic towards my situation, showing special loving care for me whom he would sometimes address as "orphan on an isle", "orphan with wholehearted devotion", or "orphan who is not an orphan". In the following decades, he would teach me and guide me constantly. He was universally recognised as the world's busiest man; meanwhile, I was the only junior relative of his that he spent time training and educating. The spiritual strength he bestowed upon me pointed my life in the right direction, and became an unlimited resource for me. He himself turned into a teacher and an example for me to follow for how to conduct myself in society. Hence, although my growing up was full of hardships and marred by the fickleness of human relationships, it was also filled with endless gentle and touching moments.

1. The Secret Shelter: 'Sir Zhou's Mansion' in Hongkou, Shanghai

From 1927 to 1931, because of the failure of the Great Revolution (the first revolutionary civil war in China, which lasted from 1924 to 1927), ostentatious and bustling Shanghai suffered from the carnage of war. At the time, Qi Ba was working with the party's Central Committee in Shanghai as one of its major leaders, who took responsibility for the daily work. Because their life, as well as their work, was highly secretive, they had to strictly follow the rules of the underground, keeping their address a secret and moving from place to place, as any slight carelessness could result in being exposed and, consequently, cause both irretrievable damage to the party and the loss of human lives. Under such circumstances, my family living at 44 Yong-an-li, North Sichuan Road (now the Sichuan North Road), which was not known to anybody, became an immediate shelter for Qi Ba at critical moments. The regular residents, earlier or later on, included my grandparents, Qi Ba's birth father, Qi Ba and Qi Ma, my grandmother's younger brother, my parents, and me. Occasionally, Qi Ma's mother, Ms Yang Zhende, would also come to stay.

Located in a quiet corner of the Hongkou area nearby Changchun Street, the house was a grey, three-story stone structure with both Western and Chinese features. The lane connected to Duolun (Darroch) Road, which would become the 'street of famous figures', so named because some prominent cultural figures, such as Lu Xun, Guo Moruo and Uchiyama, lived on that street at some point. Besides paying us nightly visits, at times Qi Ba came by during the day. When my parents got married, he and Qi Ma came for the wedding. The master of the wedding ceremony was Mr Shen Junru, the dean of the Shanghai law school, who stayed in touch with Qi Ba and Qi Ma from then on. My grandmother's younger brother, Cheng Shaoqin, also attended the wedding ceremony. Although they were childhood playmates, Qi Ba failed to recognise him, because they had not seen each other for many years. At the time, Qi Ba was 'most wanted' by the nationalist government, and he felt unsettled in the presence of a 'stranger'. My grandmother then had to introduce her brother to Qi Ba; smiling, she said: "This is your little uncle, who was your childhood playmate." They then began to talk in an easy manner, and have continued to write to each other since then.

Aibao, Qi Ba and Qi Ma

From 1927 to 1931, Zhou Enlai's birth father was a permanent tenant at 44 Yong-an-li, North Sichuan Road, Shanghai, and was a liaison between his son and my family. In 1931, before and after the Wu Hao incident, Zhou Enlai and Deng Yingchao stayed at the address many times before leaving Shanghai for the central base in Jiangxi.

Regarding this period of time, everyone in my family remembers the day in May 1931 when, without any notice from Qi Ba's birth father, who was the liaison person between him and us, my father was woken up at midnight by someone calling out to him, quietly but rapidly: "Runmin, open the door." He hurriedly opened the door and saw Qi Ba, dressed like a businessman in a long gown and a top hat, while Qi Ma was dressed like a lady from a wealthy family. He let them in immediately. After they settled down, they began to tell my family what had happened. Because Gu Shunzhang, the man who was responsible for security within the party, had shamelessly defected, they had had to destroy all documents and urge all the leaders of the Central Committee, as well as the staff, to move away immediately. The two of them needed to take cover in our house before deciding what to do next. At this dangerous time, my whole family had to act normally, not showing any sign that something was wrong. They went out less, instead playing Beijing opera on the gramophone to entertain the senior family members or playing with me, the newborn baby. Sometimes Qi Ba would put on an apron and cook our meals.

After I had grown up, Qi Ba and Qi Ma talked to me several times, telling me that after they unluckily lost their own baby, I was the first baby of the Zhou family they had known. They loved me very much and would often play with me. According to them, they would often burst into laughter when they saw me clumsily crawl on the floor, and they would throw me in the air and then catch me in their arms. When they did this, I did not cry, but was laughing and giggling as if I was welcoming them to live with us. Qi Ba once said to me about this period of time: "We were bound by a common cause and went through thick and thin together. There were tensions within, but relaxation externally; we lived in a joyous atmosphere." "We were dealing with your grandmother, who only knew a few Chinese characters," Qi Ma cut in, "and your young father and mother, who were lacking life experience, and you, a baby who could not walk but had learnt how to crawl. So we had to remain calm, or it would cause unnecessary panic and affect the overall situation."

Zhou Erliu and Wang Zhangli outside 44 Yong-an-li, Sichuan North Road, Shanghai.

The ceremony for unveiling the plaque at Sir Zhou's Mansion in Sichuan North Road, Shanghai. The backdrop reads: "Opening ceremony for the former site of comrade Zhou Enlai's early revolutionary activities in Shanghai."

As everyone knows, 'Sir Zhou's Mansion' on rue Massenet (Sinan Road) was in fact the office of the CPC in Shanghai. The building has been listed as 'revolutionary memorial hall' and has become one of the main revolutionary sites in Shanghai. However, my family's former residence in Sichuan North Road was very similar to Sir Zhou's Mansion. The people living there were Zhou Enlai's relatives, whom he trusted, and it was where he would take shelter whenever he was in imminent danger. But few people knew about it, and as a result such a valuable historical site has almost been forgotten. To make future generations fully aware of the cultural and historical significance of this site, I began to travel between Beijing and Shanghai after the downfall of the Gang of Four in 1976, exchanging views with the people concerned. I won their approval and support, but due to a change of personnel or some other reasons, the decision to make the house a revolutionary site was repeatedly delayed. In 2008, when we celebrated the 110th anniversary of the birth of Zhou Enlai, feeling that time waits for no man, I appealed to various organisations and finally won the support of the memorial hall of the first National Congress of the CPC, as well as the support of many related comrades from the Hongkou district. Veteran underground member Mr Zhu Huatong supplied evidence, and the problem was finally solved satisfactorily: at last, the building on 44 Yong-an-li, Sichuan North Road, Shanghai, Zhou Enlai's most important and most secret shelter in his early revolutionary activities, was named a historical and cultural site under state protection. The ceremony was held on 5 March 2009, and I was very happy with the result, believing that by visiting the site people will increase their knowledge and understanding of Zhou Enlai's revolutionary life.

2. The Days I Spent with Qi Yeye

My grandfather died long before I was born, but Qi Yeye stayed with my family for quite a while, so there was a deep affection between us, which has stayed with me all my life. He was Qi Ba's birth father, the seventh son of his generation.

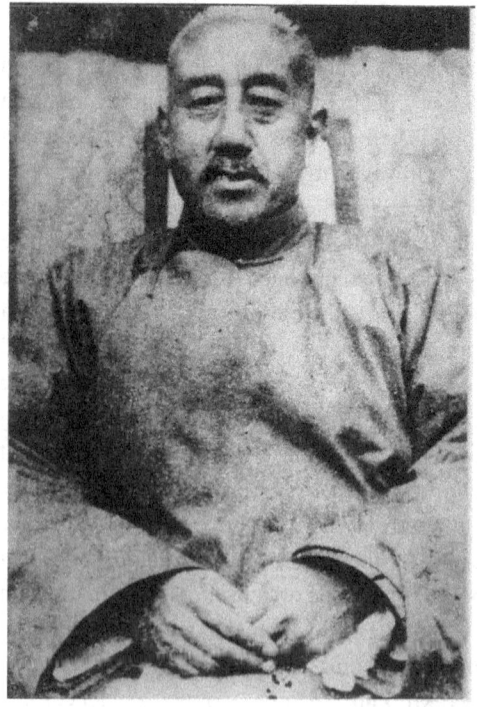

Zhou Enlai's birth father and Zhou Erliu's Qi Yeye, Zhou Yineng.

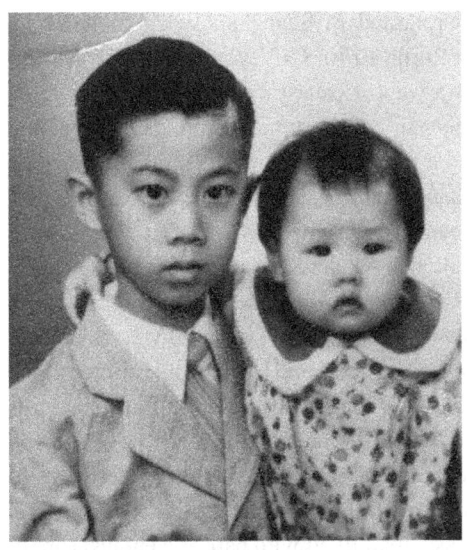

Zhou Erliu with his sister, Zhou Ermei, in 1939.

In 1932, I followed my grandmother and lived in Zhenjiang and Yangzhou for a while. Qi Yeye then joined us. Once, when we were in Zhenjiang, a neighbour's house caught fire; flames raged and smoke drifted in all directions. In spite of his old age, Qi Yeye helped to move items. When I was young, I was mischievous and ignorant. I often went to the river and climbed Mount Jin, and sometimes I would jump over the railing and stand on the edge of the cliff. My grandmother would be terrified, but my dear Qi Yeye would ignore the danger and also jump over the railing, carrying me back to the road. My grandmother would then recover from the shock, feeling a sense of relief.

Around 1934, Qi Yeye and my grandmother's brother came to live with us in Yangzhou. In earlier years, my grandfather had found them both jobs to work with him, and they were very grateful. This time, they came to help my grandmother make preparations for a Buddhist-style memorial service for my grandfather. I can still remember the scene: several old-style square tables for eight people were piled on top of each other, covered with cloth, and the tin candle holders that were as tall as me were taken out. Incense was lit and a thin layer of smoke slowly rose inside the hall, sending out a strong smell of sandalwood. Several Buddhist monks in monastic habit walked around the hall, chanting from scripts. The whole family paid devout respects to my deceased grandfather, and the grand religious ceremony left a deep impression on me. After the indoor ceremony, we also went to the tomb, where I was shown how to pour spirits on the ground and how to go down on my knee to show my respect.

In about 1938, my family returned to Shanghai, living in Huayuan Lane in rue Père Robert (now Ruijin Erlu). Qi Yeye came to live with us again, often taking me out for a walk. I clearly remember that he wore a long gown and cotton shoes, his hair cut short: the picture of a sincere and kind-hearted old man. He lived a frugal life and would sometimes share a steamed bun with me. More than once he picked up anti-Japanese leaflets from the ground, which had been left by somebody, and asked me to push them through the neighbours' kitchen windows, then urged me to run away fast. During this operation he would keep watch for me. When the foreign police of the French Concession were on patrol he would wave his hand, warning me; but when the Chinese police came by he would try to talk to them, which shows that he was quite experienced at this. Our house was in the French Concession, and when the Japanese bombers came to drop bombs on the Chinese city, he would take me to the second floor to stand on the balcony and watch. Filled with indignation, tears would cover his face as he cursed loudly. He was a man filled with patriotic enthusiasm. In 1938, Qi Ba arranged for his father to meet him in Wuhan. Afterwards, both of them went to the southwest region and through Guiyang, until Qi Yeye arrived in Chongqing, where he lived until his death.

Qi Ba also wrote to my father, urging him to go Chongqing as well. In January 1939, he left Shanghai and went to Hong Kong. From Hong Kong, he travelled to Vietnam, and then to Chongqing. After his departure, my grandmother, stepmother, brother and sister all left Shanghai. They went to stay with my stepmother's father, leaving me behind in Shanghai alone to attend school, beginning the period of hardship that would result in Qi Ba calling me "an orphan on an isle".

3. "An Orphan on an Isle"

I was 12 years old in the early 1940s, and a boarder at Shanghai Nanyang Model Middle School. During this period of time, when I returned home to organise things, I found the family's cultural artefacts and the correspondences between Qi Ba and my father and grandfather. I have kept them safe with me ever since.

The school rented a three-story building outside the campus for the boarders. There was no teacher to look after us, only a doorman. I was one of the few boarders. Whenever it was the weekend or a holiday, the other roommates would go home, leaving me behind on my own. At Chinese New Year, there were just two people in the whole building: the doorman and me. The days were very hard, because there was nothing to do. The doorman would sometimes lock the door and go out drinking. Several times I was locked outside at night, and I would either wait nearby for his return or just wander about on the streets in the freezing temperatures.

One night during term, the neighbour's house caught fire. The doorman and the other students all left the building, except me, who was fast asleep. They missed me in the chaos. I was only woken up after the fire was put out and they came back. I told them that I had no idea there had been a fire, and they said that I was a lucky boy to still be alive.

I slept in the lower berth with nothing but a pillow and a quilt, but some better-off roommates had their clothing targeted by thieves. One night, the thieves took away a leather jacket and some other expensive clothes, using some hooks to get them past me. In the morning, a pile of human faeces was found in the courtyard. Adults told us it was the bandits' habit, indicating that their actions had been a success and also warning the victims that they should not report to the police. Parents and neighbours talked about the matter, saying that it had been done by a ferocious gang of criminals who, if discovered, would cruelly kill any witnesses. They all said that I was lucky to have fallen asleep, or the consequences would have been severe.

Later, the Japanese occupied Shanghai. Several of our school's patriotic teachers went missing; it was said that they had been arrested or killed by the Japanese. When I went home to look after the house, I saw a nearby primary school surrounded by wire fencing. Out of curiosity, some other kids and I stood outside watching. There were many Chinese soldiers locked up in there, and when they saw us they would stab the desk with their small knives while shouting slogans, inciting us, small children, to resist. Such a fighting spirit and common hatred against the enemy has left an indelible impression on me.

English was included in the curriculum, but the Japanese replaced it with their language. The Japanese teacher was an old fogy from the last Qing dynasty who wore a pig tail and a cap. He was very old and had difficulty getting about and hearing. Because we students hated the Japanese so much, we refused to listen to his lectures. I once picked up a piece of chalk and drew a turtle on his back while he was writing on the blackboard.

I didn't expect Qi Ba and Qi Ma to be thinking about me at such a critical time, during the war of resistance against Japan, because they must have been very busy. But one day (I cannot remember the exact date), a stranger came to school to see me. He introduced himself as a cousin of mine and passed me a bag of biscuits. I asked for his name, but he would not tell me for security reasons; he only told me that he had been sent by Qi Ba and Qi Ma, and then left in a hurry. I never found out who he was, but some relatives told me that he could indeed have been a cousin of mine, who might have been killed or gone missing during the war.

In these two years, I overcame many difficulties and went to school in Shanghai. I said nothing about my family, so many of my teachers and classmates thought of me as an orphan. This experience led me to understand that life is not easy. Afterwards, I met Qi Ba, who believed that there were similarities between our childhoods. Due to the collapse of my extended family, I received less care from relatives than he had; hence, he felt sympathy for me and would take good care of me afterwards.

4. My Ordeal in the City of Gaoyou

In 1944, I finished junior high school in Shanghai and joined my family in Gaoyou, a city that would be liberated from the Japanese the following year. After the surrender of the Japanese the nationalist government moved back to Nanjing. Soon after, negotiations between the nationalists and the communists broke down and civil war broke out. The Kuomintang (KMT) started an endless bombing campaign in the northern Jiangsu area, which was near Nanjing but controlled by the communists. The bombings caused heavy damage to both lives and property. Hence, people in the region hated the KMT reactionaries with all their hearts.

People fled the city. I was then a first-year senior middle school student, and the majority of my classmates went to seek refuge with relatives in Shanghai and Zhenjiang. Only me, Xia Jiazhen, and a classmate called Song, who was lame in one leg, were left behind on the campus. We were all 14- or 15-year-old teenagers. We would often see the KMT bombers dropping bombs and shooting at the ground in broad daylight. During one air raid, the classroom walls were damaged and we crawled about on the ground to avoid being hit by bullets. Seeing bullets landing on the ground, we picked one up and saw that it had 'D.M' printed on it. It was said that such bullets were banned internationally, as their heads was poisoned; a mere scratch on the skin would cause death.

Wars are full of unforeseen and cruel consequences. On the way home that day, my classmate Xia Jiazhen was killed by a bomb. Under such dangerous circumstances, school came to a standstill. The New Fourth Army troops were still in the county. A few officers lived with us while we were still marked as members of an anti-Japanese family and received care from the local government and the troops.

Life in the liberated areas was very hard. Sometimes, when they did not have enough food, the civilians had to boil crushed corn cobs to feed themselves. Even though they all opposed the civil war, many displayed dauntless heroism in the face of the enemy. Once I saw with my own eyes some militias and soldiers shooting at low-flying enemy aircraft with their rifles. My stepmother played mahjong every day, taking no care but clearly biased against me. She was preparing to divorce my father, who lived somewhere far away; I had no idea where. In winter, I only had single-layer trousers to wear in the knee-deep snow, and my padded jacket was made by my grandmother, who cut up her own clothes for materials. I had chilblains on both my hands and my feet, and when spring came they turned into running sores, which were very painful and embarrassing, and left permanent scars.

I was always hungry and kept vomiting. At one point my half-brother, Erjun, was ill with typhoid fever. His mother was worried about becoming infected, so she asked me to give him his medicine. He recovered, but then I was struck down by the disease. I was isolated in a small room in the middle of the courtyard, but my stepmother did not call for a doctor to attend to me. Luckily, I recovered, but I was very weak. Jin, a cook with the army's kitchen staff garrisoned in our compound, could bear no more; he gave me some food that he had saved from his own ration, for which I was very grateful. One day, he carried me on his back to the public bathroom to have a bath; too weak to stand, I fell into the pool. I was unconscious and would have died if it were not for Jin, who carried me out of the room at once. Later, the troops made a strategic shift, leaving our city quite suddenly. The soldiers in our compound left too. The following day I went to the culture centre, where I met the director just coming out the door, blanket roll on his shoulder. He told me that the KMT troops would soon arrive, and urged me to find a safe place and to leave quickly.

5. Finding Qi Ba in Shanghai

In April or May of 1946, my father and stepmother's marriage broke down. She vented her anger on me and drove me out of the house. I was now homeless. My grandmother told me that my only way out was to go to Shanghai and find Qi Ba. She then pawned her clothes to pay for my travel expenses. She also gave me two gold rings, as compensation, because she had once used my scholarship for other purposes. I left home with an uncle who was four or five years older than me. Because the currencies were different in the liberated area and the area controlled by the nationalist government, we bought two chickens, planning to sell them after we entered the latter. My uncle was going to Nanjing, so when we parted at Zhenjiang, I gave him the two gold rings. Carrying the two chickens, I was ready to go to Shanghai.

However, I did not know what to do in the streets of Zhenjiang, as the day was getting darker. I had been planning to sleep in the street when someone hit me hard on the shoulder. Turning around, I exclaimed: "Good heavens! What a happy encounter!" It was Yang Ruxu, my classmate from senior middle school. After learning of my situation, he took me to a relative of a classmate's called Chen for the night. The owner of the house asked me where I was going. "Shanghai," I said, upon which he asked which relative I was going to see? I said: "Zhou Enlai". At once, he covered my mouth, saying that I should not reveal that name carelessly. He urged me to be careful, for my own safety. Only then did I realise that I was young and ignorant, and how grim the situation outside the liberated area was.

Although I knew Shanghai well, when I set foot in the city for the second time I was at a loss, not knowing where I could stay. I had no idea where Qi Ba was, nor did I know how to contact him. So I enlisted the help of my classmate Wang Dingwu (who would later become dean of the central institute of black metallurgy), who let me stay with his family. Seeing that I was alone and had no source of income, they found me a job in a factory washing medicine bottles, but I was turned down after the boss saw that I was too thin and weak.

Fortunately, before long, Mr Zhang Zhenbang, manager of the *Wen Hui Bao* newspaper, found me. Jia Daqing, Mr Zhang's nephew, was a classmate of mine; in addition, his eldest son was a member of the CPC underground, so as a progressive non-party person he sympathised with the revolution. Until today, I have no idea how Qi Ba found such a suitable person to make contact with me; it shows how solid the underground network was under Qi Ba's leadership. Mr Zhang handed me a letter from Qi Ba, the main gist of which was that I was to go to 107 rue Massenet to see Mr Chen Jiakang (one of the speakers from the CPC office in Shanghai).

6. Three Visits to Sir Zhou's Mansion

On the east side of pleasant, peaceful and secluded Sinan Road in Shanghai, which is lined by plane trees on both sides, stands a building numbered 73. The address was originally 107 rue Massenet, when the three-story Spanish-style villa was built in the 1920s. In 1946 it became the office of the CPC delegation in Shanghai.

After the victory over Japan in August 1945, the KMT betrayed the trust that existed between them and the CPC, intensifying their rule in the areas they controlled while making preparations for a full-scale attack on the liberated (CPC-controlled) areas. At this critical moment, civil war was about to break out. The nationalist government had returned to its capital, Nanjing, from Chongqing. In May 1946, in order to carry on with negotiations while also carrying out campaigns for peace and democracy inside the nationalist, government-controlled areas, Qi Ba led a CPC delegation to Meiyuan Xincun in Nanjing. Meantime, they were preparing to set up an office in Shanghai. They had to rent 107 rue Massenet as their office in General Zhou Enlai's name, because the KMT authorities refused to supply them with a house. The bronze number plate said 'GEN. CHOW EN-LAI'S RESIDENCE', but it was known to the outside as Sir Zhou's Mansion. From May 1946 to March 1947, Qi Ba and Qi Ma came to Shanghai many times and stayed in the villa. It was during these few months that I went to see Qi Ba three times, when he found time in his busy schedule to meet with me.

General Zhou Enlai's residence in rue Massenet, Shanghai.

Aibao, Qi Ba and Qi Ma

I received Qi Ba's letter in May 1946, so I accepted the arrangement and went to Sir Zhou's Mansion to meet Mr Chen Jiakang. After I entered the building, I immediately had an unusually warm feeling; it seemed to me I had been to this place before. After making some examinations, I found out the building nearby was the residence of Mei Lanfang (the Beijing opera master), the 'Western-style garden house' well known to people in Shanghai, where my father used to take me for visits when I was little. I now recalled that there were many plain clothes secret agents in the area. From the beginning to the end, those courageous communists, led by Qi Ba and Dong Biwu, stuck to their post and kept up the struggle with the KMT. In July of that same year, Qi Ba came to Shanghai from Nanjing. Chen Jiakang arranged for me, as well as for my brother Zhou Erjun, who had been living with our uncle Ma Shu-ang, to meet Qi Ba and Qi Ma. This was the second time I went to Sir Zhou's Mansion; however, it was my first time meeting Qi Ba since I had parted with him as a child. Because we were living in poverty, my brother and I were both in poor health. My brother had scabies on his head, while I had infected eyes. Qi Ma gave us some medicine, and they ended the meeting without saying anything else. However, Qi Ba made a deep impression on me. He was not tall and sturdy, like some books describe him, but of medium height, with the appearance of a refined diplomat but the bearing of a soldier. His brows were thick and his eyes were unusually bright, with large pupils. He had a wide upper lip and showed dignity when closing his lips, giving people the impression that he was a man with an inflexible will.

In September I was asked to meet him again, so I went to Sir Zhou's Mansion for the third time. Qi Ba talked to me alone this time, and our conversation lasted the whole morning. Only many years later did I find out that the situation was very tense at that point, and yet he still found time, which was so valuable to him, to talk to me.

During our conversation he asked about my grandmother. I told him about her time in Gaoyou with my stepmother's family. He also asked about my father and my stepmother, whose relationship had broken down, wanting to know my opinion on the matter. Although she had treated me badly, I did not make any spiteful comments about her because of my own misfortune; on the contrary, I told him that because I did not live with them, I had no idea what sort of problems they had. He was happy that I adopted the attitude of 'admitting what one really understands and what one does not know', praising my honesty. Mentioning my stepmother, he asked about her father, Ma Shijie. I told him what I had known of him: while going through the process of the land reform with him, I observed how he handed in land deeds and donated his collection of hydrological data of the grand canal, and noted how politely the local government officials received him. Qi Ba cared a lot about the liberated areas and wanted to know everything about them, so I told him everything I had seen and heard.

He then asked about my own situation. He showed much sympathy to me after I told him what had happened to me, and suggested that I go to Yan'an with him. Qi Ma overheard our conversation and came in to drag him out of the room. After a while, they returned. Qi Ba said: "Negotiations between the nationalists and the communists are in danger of breaking down, and the threat of a full-scale civil war is creating even more tension. You are young and in poor health, but you are good at your studies; so, can you finish senior middle school in Shanghai? We will pay for everything, leaving other problems to be solved in the future. You should study hard to enrich your mind with knowledge, getting yourself ready to greet the coming of victory."

At the time, I was indeed living in poverty. Dressed in a short, ragged gown, I tied my baggy trouser cuffs with strips of cloth. I was either barefoot or my toes poked out of my cotton shoes, which had big holes in them. "Seeing you makes me understand more about the people in the liberated areas. They are living in squalor," Qi Ba said, "and it is not easy for them to keep up their support for the front line. But you should know that we communists have no money. We serve the people. I believe you understand that the suit I am wearing is only for dealing with foreign affairs and meeting dignitaries from other countries. So, help from us will be limited, because our organisation needs to look after the children of our martyrs and pay their expenses. Anyway, we should avoid being suspected of favouring a relative. Yan'an has no middle schools, but we don't want you to miss the opportunity of receiving an education, let alone leave you to go on long-distance marches that your feeble body cannot handle." Young and impetuous, I said to him: "I've come to see you because my grandma asked me to. I don't want to rely on older family members who have succeeded at their jobs. Maybe someone from my stepmother's side has a mind to do so, but it is definitely not my way or my grandma's."

After I'd said these words, he asked me how much I would need to finish my schooling. Knowing that the communists had no money, I did not want to take up his offer, so I said nothing. A stalemate began developing until after lunch, when he asked me how I would arrange my studies. I then spoke my mind. I said that I would rather go to the state-run advanced agricultural vocational high school than a general middle school where the quality of teaching might be better, because state-run schools are free. He respected my choice, and withdrew quite a lot of money from an envelope he prepared for me, keeping some back for my daily expenses. He was very much moved by my decision, saying: "You are an honest child. What you've done is good!"

Their office was only divided from their bedroom by a curtain. On the wall of the office, there was a hand-drawn map of the military situation in the country. Qi Ba told me my father had worked in the office of the Central Committee of the CPC in Nanjing for a while, but had gone on to the liberated area in northern Jiangsu with Li Yimang. Pointing at the map, he said: "Your father may be in Huaiyin or Yancheng, but we don't know if he is still alive; he might be dead." That map on the wall left a deep impression on me. I can still remember it today: the whole map was covered with little red flags indicating the liberated areas, which also signified the impending victory of the revolution. As Qi Ba once said: "The people's century has arrived."

When our conversation was drawing to an end, he talked about the prose work *On the Love of Lotus* by Zhou Dunyi, expressing his hope that I would be like a lotus flower that grows out the mud but remains unsoiled, waiting for the arrival of victory. He also quoted the epigrams of Mencius to remind me that I should adopt them as criteria when examining myself during my growth: "Neither poverty nor lowly conditions can make him swerve from principle; neither riches nor honour can corrupt him; neither threats nor force can bend him." Afterwards, I learnt that Mencius' original epigram ran: "Neither riches nor honour can corrupt him; neither poverty nor lowly conditions can make him swerve from principle; neither threats nor force can bend him." Maybe it was because of my circumstances that he stressed the line "Neither poverty nor lowly conditions can make him swerve from principle", to encourage me to pull myself through my difficulties.

It was lunchtime when we ended our conversation. A young American army officer came by, so Qi Ba let me stay to have lunch with them. It was the first time I had seen an American serviceman at such close range. He was big, wearing a baseball cap and an army uniform. They did not talk about anything important; it seemed as if the officer had only come to pass on instructions from his superior. There was no interpreter and the two of them talked in English. Although I had learnt some English, I could not follow them. I was glad that Qi Ba had trust in me, allowing me to listen to their conversation. Recalling that incident now, I suppose this was my first ever 'foreign affairs' activity: attending a talk with a foreigner with my toes poking out of my shoes.

Relaxed and cheerful, we finished our lunch and my second meeting with Qi Ba and Qi Ma ended. Before I left, they gave me two quilts of theirs. Such a singular action showed the foresight of Qi Ba, who was clearly aware that after the breakdown of negotiations between the KMT and the CPC they had to close down the office in Shanghai. Not planning to return for a long stay, they gave me the quilts, which were essential to them. Also, if I remember correctly, he mentioned more than once that if civil war broke out, the results would be clear within a year and a half. Judging by the development of events, his prediction turned out to be correct. But due to the great disparity in strength between the armies of the communists and the KMT, few could make a precise forecast, even though there were still people who felt optimistic about the future of the revolution.

Qi Ba sent his chief security guard to escort me to safety. Because I was young and small, I had difficulty carrying the two quilts, so the guard carried them for me. I had no experience in dealing with being followed by secret agents, so before we left the guard told me to follow him closely and not to turn around. We walked and walked, finally stopping at the bank of the Huangpu river. The guard then told me that we had been followed, but that he had managed to throw them off, so I was safe now. He handed me the quilts and we parted.

Recalling now that Sir Zhou's Mansion was being watched by secret agents all year round, it was inevitable that I would be followed. They stopped following me only because I was young and in rags, thinking I was only a poor relative who had just received some relief supplies.

Sir Zhou's Mansion was like a beacon on a misty sea, shining out with great brilliance on the eve of China's liberation. To me, this meeting with Qi Ba had cemented my political orientation, and I was prepared to sacrifice my life at any time. From that moment on, Qi Ba has been an example for me on how to conduct myself in society; on how to forgive others, but be unsparing of oneself; on how to be dedicated, heart and soul, to the revolution and the people; on how to be honest and upright; and on how to deal with all things fairly. His lofty ideals, great character and down-to-earth style of working have been inexhaustible sources for me all my life. The way he treasured his blood relations is beyond description. Compared with thousands upon thousands of other young people, although I lost my mother in my infancy and then lived in poverty, I consider myself a very lucky man for having received personal teachings from such a great historical figure.

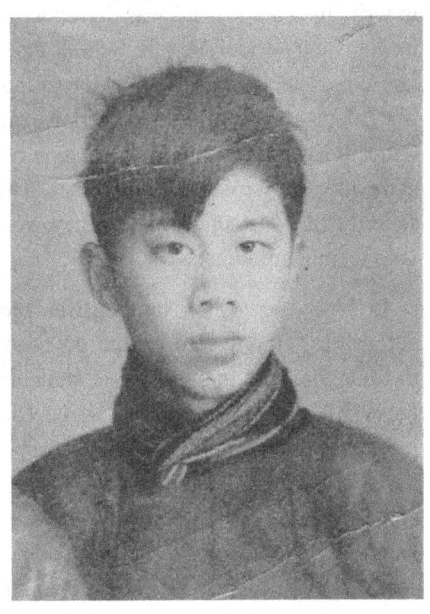

Zhou Erliu as a middle school student, 1947.

7. A Bayonet Digging into My Back

During the war of resistance against the Japanese, the nationalist government set up a few vocational schools in Chongqing, and the state-run advanced agricultural vocational school was one of them. After the war ended in 1945, the school moved to the city of Nantong in Jiangsu province and began to recruit students from Shanghai. All middle school graduates could apply. The cost of attendance was low, and every student would receive 23 litres of rice a month and was allowed to board at the school; therefore, I applied.

I was offered a place to study animal husbandry. However, at the registration office, they told me I needed a reference. I was very worried, because I had neither relatives nor friends in Shanghai whom I could ask to write me one. When I was driven to desperation, one of my schoolmates in Nanyang Model Middle School came to my help, although I did not know him personally. He was the grandson of Zhang Jian, who had won first place in the highest imperial examination towards the end of the Qing dynasty and who later became a well-known entrepreneur. Out of sympathy, he wrote me a reference. I then filled in the form, telling the school that I was an orphan so they would not suspect that I had relatives who were communists.

In 1948, the city of Nantong was about to be liberated, and the school authorities, empowered by the government, decided to move the school to Shanghai. On this issue, we students were divided into three groups: those who were against the move (this group was made up of some progressive students); those who supported the move (this group had a KMT background); and those who wanted to suspend schooling altogether and go home. The majority of the students in the first group had been listening to radio broadcasts from the Xinhua News Agency, which was run by the communists. We learnt from the radio that our school had a large quantity of machinery that would be useful to the future reconstruction of the liberated areas, but that the KMT authorities were trying to destroy it. The radio had called upon us students to protect the machinery, so we organised ourselves and started a campaign to protect the equipment. I then ran a bulletin, *Musheng*, and wrote an introduction to *Spring is Coming* to express that we were looking forward to the liberation. This article made me a suspected communist. The school undertook an investigation, only to find out that I was an orphan who had no other social contacts, so they gave it up.

Our campaign was unable to prevent us from moving, and before long we moved to the Gaoqiao area of Shanghai. We had our lectures in a local memorial temple, but these lectures existed in name only. Those who had families in Shanghai had gone home, while I and the students from the other provinces went to live with nearby peasant families. The People's Liberation Army (PLA) had successfully crossed the Yangtze river; they were quickly approaching the urban area of Shanghai and first met with battle at Gaoqiao, because it was a strategic gateway to the sea. The situation was tense and grim; gunshots and artillery thundered day and night, with the smoke of gunpowder filling the air across the area. The KMT army and police were desperately trying to hold on. At the time, we students were too young to know that we were in a place of strategic importance, but simply tried our best to protect the school and the machinery. Consequently, several dozens of us were arrested. We were locked up and given escorts, even when we went to the toilet. During the exchange of fire, the KMT army suffered heavy casualties and the mangled bodies of soldiers were to be seen everywhere. They then decided to let us students move the wounded soldiers and to put up slogans on walls in the streets. We objected to the order, so, by force, the policemen pointed their bayonets at our backs while the soldiers pointed theirs at the backs of the policemen. Like a string of fish we were pushed forward. I was near Wang Yongyi and Wang Yongying, two brothers. "You two run away and I'll cover you," Wang Yongyi quietly said to us. He then blocked the view of the policemen behind us and his brother and I ran towards a wall. While I was climbing, I said to myself: "Even if I die, I shall not do anything that will bring disgrace on Qi Ba." It still frightens me to recall it now. We students were unarmed, but the policemen were holding rifles with bayonets, and we could have died a violent death at any moment. We were very lucky that the policemen did not spot us, and that we were able to climb over the wall and run away.

We returned to school when it was getting dark. Some officers then said that it was pointless to keep us there, because it would only increase the number of unnecessary deaths. Hence, under the threat of bayonets, we were escorted to the urban area of Shanghai.

8. On the March to the Southwest with the PLA Second Field Army

After Shanghai was liberated in May 1949, I graduated from the advanced agricultural vocational school. I now had two options: to go to Beijing to meet Qi Ba and Qi Ma, apply to a university, and even go to the Soviet Union for further studies, or to answer the call of the student union and join the army.

At that time, I naively separated the revolution from the construction of the country, feeling that after the liberation we would not have the chance to implement any change. Therefore, I felt I had to take the opportunity to learn and steel myself for the revolution so I could contribute to it. Meanwhile, my brother Erjun had turned 16, and both my father and my uncle came to me and asked me to help him, because it was financially difficult to let him carry on with his middle school education. Hence, I decided to take him with me to join the army.

The task of the PLA Second Field Army – and their slogan – was to 'take the battlefields to the southwest and liberate the whole of China', so their destinations were Sichuan, Yunnan, Guizhou, Xikang and Tibet. In Nanjing, June 1949, I took my brother with me and we registered with the military and political college of the PLA Second Field Army. I was treated as a platoon leader. After the National Day on 1 October we left Nanjing. We marched to Zhengzhou, Xiaogan, Hankou, Changsha, and from west Hunan and east Sichuan we entered Chongqing. This 3,500km march was powerful and dynamic, filling us with enthusiasm throughout the journey. When we arrived in Zhengzhou, the local government and civilians rewarded us with steamed buns and cotton shoes. After we entered Hankou, we merged with the troops of the Fourth Field Army, and together we set off for Changsha. We spent some of the journey on trains, but because of the severe damage inflicted by KMT soldiers before they fled the city, some train carriages had no roof, and some did not even have walls, only a flat platform that passengers could easily fall off of. In this type of open train we had to spend 17 hours in the cold, and we were exhausted. In the suburbs of Changsha, one section of the rail track was damaged by secret agents, meaning our whole regiment had come within an inch of death. Afterwards, we marched on foot.

When we marched to east Sichuan through west Hunan, I was assigned an important task: taking charge of those left behind. They included the weak, the wounded and the sick, the women, and a small number of those whose minds were disturbed: about 30 to 40 people in total. It was hard to manage them, not to mention that many bandits and secret agents lived among the local inhabitants of minority nationalities, which added more uncertainty and danger to my job. If we were spotted by the enemy, isolated and far behind the main troops, the consequences would be beyond my imagination. We would be killed one by one. Under enormous pressure, I was thinking of how to bring everyone safely to our destination and rejoin the main forces. Then, at the crucial moment, a good idea occurred to me. I divided us into small groups, and after we had made camp at a certain spot we would go and tell the locals that we were the advance troops, coming to book accommodations for our main troops behind. Then, holding a piece of chalk in my hand, I drew circles on the houses and numbered them. The idea worked, giving the enemy the false impression that our main troops were indeed behind us. Hence, we could live in peace among our enemies. I breathed a deep sigh of relief after we caught up with the main troops.

At the time, our equipment was varied, but poor. Wearing worn-out uniforms, we lived a simple life. We needed to march in all weather conditions, so no one had the luxury to think about hygiene. Almost all of us had fleas all over our bodies, and we were therefore ordered to have our heads shaved. Yet we had the same spirit as the combat troops, relying on our firm faith and revolutionary optimism until we would finally achieve victory over the KMT. When we were in Chongqing, we didn't expect to find ourselves stationed in the old compound of the KMT's college of defence studies. I would often see KMT army officers who had defected and crossed over to the communists' side. Although they wore high-quality wool uniforms and leather shoes, they were expressionless. We, the people's army, would defeat them, even under inferior conditions, we thought to ourselves.

9. The Two Speeches by Liu Bocheng and Deng Xiaoping

During my studies at the Second Field Army's military and political college, I was lucky enough to listen to the lectures given by many senior officials of the Second Field Army. What impressed me most, and what I will never forget, was the one given by General (later Marshal) Liu Bocheng, the commander of the Second Field Army. That day, we were in our neat and simple uniforms, sitting on the ground in rows, carrying with us a small piece of tarpaulin in case of rain. "As for many of the young students present at the lecture today," Commander Liu said, "what is revolution? There is one simple sentence that can answer the question: that is, 'bury a white blade in somebody and pull out a red one'." Afterwards, whenever I mentioned this famous epigram to Qi Ba, he just couldn't stop laughing.

When Qi Ba talked to me about the Second Field Army of the PLA, he always said that these troops were good at fighting strategic battles that often determine their victory. He once mentioned the Shangdang campaign, saying that it had been a major battle of strategic importance and had played an important role in the development of the national situation. In the whole Second Field Army many lives had been sacrificed during the campaign, raising the curtain of our strategic counteroffensive. All soldiers had made a huge and historical contribution to this brilliant military success, in which commanders Liu Bocheng and Deng Xiaoping exercised skilled leadership, and their achievement will never be forgotten. With deep feeling, Qi Ba mentioned that he himself had once been the Red Army's general political commissar while General Liu Bocheng was chief of staff, who had made an outstanding contribution to the final victory of the Long March.

General Liu Bocheng followed Dr Sun Yat-sen and joined the Tongmenghui (the Chinese Revolutionary League). He then took part in the democratic revolution, joined the CPC, and participated in countless major and minor battles, becoming one of the few military theorists in China. He was both strict in commanding his troops and with himself, never drinking a drop of alcohol in his life. Among the PLA's senior military leaders, he was the one with the highest moral integrity and the strongest sense of organisational discipline; as an individual, he was a very cultivated gentleman. When I mentioned the above epigram to Qi Ba, he smiled, saying: "Your commander is good at using the most summary and vivid yet simple language for a soldier to understand, to express the meaning of as well as the requirements for joining the revolutionary ranks. It looks easy, but its form and use are inseparable from his long-term military life and experience, as well as his diligence in his studies and ability to summarise what he has learnt." But Qi Ba also pointed out that with large numbers of educated young people joining the army, delivering important ideas while only using language understood by uneducated soldiers–even if these ideas are vivid and touching, though not exhaustive–may not be sufficient to meet the requirements of the new situation. Humorously, he said that these educated young people joined the army, and that after a short training, if a soldier went to work at the forefront of the newly liberated areas, he would likely be wounded. For immediate treatment, he must have his head shaved; being a soldier with a clean-shaven head would take some mental struggle to accept, trifling though the matter was. As expected, in his speech, Commander Liu pointed out the disadvantage of keeping one's hair long both during combat and marches, and stressed the need for having a clean-shaven head.

It is more than half a century ago that Qi Ba said the above words to me, but at times, the amiable as well as insightful expression on his face flashes across my mind as if he spoke them yesterday, and I feel that I have gone back to the days when I was a young soldier. His profound understanding and consideration for his comrade-in-arms, General Liu Bocheng, once again evoke memories of the general who was like a strict father to me when I was in the army.

In those days, whenever a holiday came around, we new students would leave our compound and go to the city to do some shopping. In order to save time, some of us would take horse-drawn carts rather than walk. After Commander Liu became aware of this, he pointed it out in his speech:

"New recruits should learn from the veteran soldiers. As revolutionary military personnel, we must build up both physical strength and mental power. We must stand up to all tests, no matter if it is cold or warm, or if we have a full stomach or an empty one." He seriously criticised the few who took carts to town. "Although you have sung the school anthem of the Chinese people's anti-Japanese military and political college every day, you forgot the last line of the school motto, which is: 'We are the examples of the labourers.' So don't pick up the unhealthy habit of accepting things in words but never putting them into practice."

When I told Qi Ba about this, his face turned serious, and he said: "From this case, we can see that General Liu's strict teachings to you not only embody his great skill in commanding troops with consistent strictness, but also represents the care and regard shown to the younger generation by a veteran revolutionary. It also puts an important new question before the leaders of the party and the government; that is, after we are in power, how can we install higher-quality education among the younger generation? Meanwhile, in times of peace, how can we make the younger generation, through self-temperance, keep up the tradition of hard work and plain living when any slight ignorance will lead to untold trouble?"

Another event involving General Liu Bocheng that also left a deep impression on me took place in early October 1949, when the citizens of Nanjing enthusiastically celebrated the first National Day. The rain came down in sheets that day. General Liu, who was then over 50 years old, stood proudly reviewing the extensive parade (I was one of the marchers). Ignoring the downpour, he stood on the platform in Xin Jie Kou in his trim uniform, without an umbrella, raincoat, or rain cape, inspecting the army and the civilians. Many marchers were worried that he would catch cold, but were at the same time much moved by his firm revolutionary spirit. After I told Qi Ba about this, he said: "As the saying goes: 'A fine example has boundless power.' To the leading cadres of the party, the government and the army, after we are in power, it will be vital to maintain vigilance and continue to play an exemplary role. Commander Liu is such an example, and you should follow him. I myself also need to take extra caution and frequently pay attention to it: as the premier of a country, I must remember to always play a leading and exemplary role among the cadres and the common people."

Qi Ba and Deng Xiaoping both studied in France in the early 1920s. Deng Xiaoping was born in the same year as Qi Ma, six years junior to Qi Ba; hence, to Qi Ba, Deng Xiaoping was another 'little Deng', just like his wife, Deng Yingchao. The Chinese people habitually describe their relationship as not only like that between schoolmates, but like that between brothers. It was Deng Xiaoping who eventually took over the leadership from Qi Ba, so in the eyes of the common Chinese, they were the indispensable leaders of the Chinese revolution and construction. They were pragmatic, and upheld the general interests of the people.

The French branch of the Chinese communist Youth League meets in Paris. Zhou Enlai is the fourth in the front row from left. Deng Xiaoping is the third in the back row from the right.

During the Cultural Revolution, at a banquet held by Qi Ba and the Gang of Four for some foreign guests, the Gang of Four clearly stated that Deng Xiaoping was now the main Chinese leader, but that he was taking the capitalist road and must therefore be completely overthrown.

In response, Qi Ba repeatedly stated his position, emphasising that Deng Xiaoping could be reinstated in his former office even though he had made some mistakes. All guests, both Chinese and foreign, were astonished at the revelation of his stand on this issue. That he proclaimed his position without thinking indicated that it was not an easy one.

Here is a historical 'allusion' that I think will be interesting and provide us with food for thought, so I have decided to record it for the reader. Before the Second Field Army troops left Nanjing and marched to the southwestern region, Deng Xiaoping gave us, the brigade trainees, a party lecture in which he called on us to pass 'the three tests': the military test, the land-reform test and the socialism test.

The military test meant that the scale of military actions in the southwest would be not as large as the Huaihai campaign, but that we still needed to wipe out or reorganise the several million KMT troops that remained, and prevent them from fleeing to Taiwan or foreign countries to continue their resistance efforts. Meanwhile, because of the many large and small victories we gained over the KMT troops, many of the regional KMT armies revolted and crossed over to our side, so we needed to educate and remold the majority of them. In his speech, Deng Xiaoping proposed that if the vast southwestern border regions were stabilised, it could assist the healthy development of the national situation. Southwest China has a varied topography and the region has had an uneven development of communities and people. We suffered some casualties in countless small conflicts; however, the speech Deng Xiaoping gave before we left Nanjing had mentally prepared us not to be afraid of death, but instead to dare to fight in complicated circumstances. Hence, we won the final victory after several years' skirmishes all over the region.

The second test was the land-reform test. Large numbers of academy trainees had been to middle school, and some even to college, for professional training. Recruiting them had pumped new blood into the troops, providing local governments with cadres after they were transferred to civilian work. Many of them came from a family of landlords or rich peasants. However, the land reform was a major social reform, through which the government mobilised the poor and lower middle-class peasants to build a new political power base and to develop the local economy. The situation made many young cadres face a significant political problem. They needed to answer the call of the Central Committee and uphold the position of peasants and actively carry out reforms. If they chose to do the opposite, they would be disciplined and might be ordered to leave the army. Because Deng Xiaoping had given early warning in his speech about the issue, heightening our awareness of the need to support the land reform, these young soldiers could work with local citizens to carry out reforms, which would lay a solid social foundation on which to establish the new government.

The third test was the socialism test. In his speech, Deng Xiaoping only talked in a summary fashion about the socialist reform, saying that the further it developed and the more time passed, we as revolutionary cadres and military personnel would come across many problems which we could not foresee; hence, we had to be mentally prepared to deal with them. When my report to Qi Ba came to this point, he asked me, interested: "Did your commissar give a detailed account of this issue?" I tried my best to remember, but, strictly according to according to facts, I told him that he had not given us a detailed account on how to pass the socialism test successfully. As if absorbed in thought, he nodded his head.

It is impossible for people to predict precisely what will happen in the future, but it is vital to stick to one's principles and faith and make the necessary preparations, and this issue requires further discussion. As a member of the younger generation, I well understand and have sympathy for these two great leaders and historical figures, especially regarding the misfortunes they met with during the Cultural Revolution. Nevertheless, they enjoyed the trust, love and esteem of all Chinese people. It was only because of their remarkable leadership that the Chinese people could make it through numerous difficulties and were able to amend their direction and continue to march along the road of victory. Together we cherish the memory of all the historical contributions these two old men made to the country and the people. We are forever grateful.

10. I Become Acting Director of the Grain Bureau

When I entered the newly liberated area, to temper myself, I asked to go back to one of the grassroots units, where conditions were toughest. After my request was granted, I was assigned to work with the Military Control Commission in Wutongqiao, in Leshan prefecture, to take control of the banks, escort cash transportation and salt transportation, and manage the people there and act as secretary to veteran Red Army men. I was later transferred to the city of Leshan, the administration centre, where I worked for a trade company and grain bureau. I was a section member of a grassroots unit until 1952. Because the director of the grain bureau was in poor health and the deputy director was illiterate, I was appointed by the commissioner to become director, taking charge of feeding six million people in 16 counties. I was 22 years old, and "young and fearless", as Qi Ba commented afterwards.

Zhou Erliu, acting director of the grain bureau of Leshan prefecture, Sichuan, 1952.

During this period, because I was constantly switching between jobs, I had no fixed address. Concerned, Qi Ba asked Zhu Hua, the manager of the Chongqing cotton, cotton yarn and cloth company (he was Qi Ba's chauffeur when he worked with the underground movement in Shanghai in 1920s), to pass on his request that I write to them, tell them what was going on and keep in touch with home. Knowing that he was the premier, who shouldered great responsibility and was kept very busy, I felt I shouldn't bother him, so I restrained my feelings and did not write to them.

The first job I took on in the newly liberated area was in Wutongqiao, a strategic salt industry town with a long history. It was located in an industrial area, so there were no banks. I was less than 20 years old and had been in school all that time, hence I was a bit immature. Although at the time the development in Sichuan province was lagging behind that of the other regions in the country, the bank staff wore suits and glasses with gold frames, thinking highly of themselves. I was rather thin and small, like a child; after the long-distance march I had an enormous appetite, and furthermore I wore an old and faded uniform. In short, I was nothing like a high-ranking official who came to take over the running of the bank. They couldn't help but smile with closed lips behind my back. When I first arrived, they were puffed up with arrogance. Although they restrained themselves somewhat, from the way they talked I could sense that they had adopted a wait-and-see attitude. Later they realised that I was educated, had been to the well-known Shanghai Nanyang Model Middle School, and that my Chinese and even my English were good enough to work with some of the university graduates, and they changed their attitude at once.

When I began managing human affairs, I set up a few rules for myself: the first one was to go out for food with people less often. Not going out with them at all was not beneficial to my job, so I had to go sometimes, but I had to be the one who paid the bill – otherwise I would not go. The second rule was that society was not very stable so soon after the liberation, so whenever the daily cash was put in storage I voluntarily carried my gun and went to escort the truck, because it needed to pass a river and there were some dangerous elements there that were very difficult to guard against during the journey. The third rule was to be a professional at work. I tried to learn and act. I was young, so I learnt quickly, and tried to make continuous efforts to gain their confidence and have a say in the decision making. The fourth was to ensure that people stayed employed, so I combined looking into details of their past with an element of trust. Their backgrounds were complicated and some Red Army veterans were illiterate, so I often did both the managing and the physical work myself. I had to make sure they were not hiding anything, but we gave them our full confidence when we assigned them jobs. Therefore I had a good relationship with some of the better-educated staff members from the previous government, who said that I had thoroughly implemented the policy of serving the people, and had both a man's natural kindness and the ability to tackle the practical work.

At the time, in the newly liberated area, the production of grain and cereal was a matter of prime importance. Facing the complicated local situation, I found some methods that gave good results. When many regions in Sichuan had grain shortages, the processes of purchasing and supplying grain were quite stable in Leshan. For this I was made a model worker, and was assigned to give a talk in Chengdu, the capital of Sichuan. Qi Ba was very interested in what I had done, and he asked me to write a report on this specific topic for him to read.

During the days and nights of marching to the southwestern region, I threw myself into my work in the mountains, the border regions, and the newly liberated areas. The experience toughened me, and I will forever remember this unforgettable period of time. I am grateful to all my comrades-in-arms. In those days, as far as I was concerned, although nobody knew that I was a relative of Zhou Enlai, deep down I had the motive and determination that no matter what difficulties I was facing, I should not disappoint Qi Ba in his kind guidance and expectations. Especially after I learnt that he not only cared about the development of his relations' younger generation, but also paid special attention to the pioneering work that was being done in the newly liberated areas, my determination grew even stronger.

11. I Am Admitted to Nankai University and My Relation to Qi Ba Is Exposed

In 1954, I passed the university entrance examination and was admitted to Nankai University. Functionaries were allowed to take the examination, but the quota for our prefecture was only two people. I had been working as the acting director of the grain bureau and had attended a meeting with the leading party group in the finance and economics department of the prefecture, so the director of the Pingshan county grain bureau phoned me to say that it was unprofitable for me to go to university. But I liked studying very much, and after I had communicated with Zhu Hua in Chongqing I won support from Qi Ba, so I applied.

But Nankai University, a key university, was not the one I had applied to. Seeing as my English scores were higher than 80 per cent, I was among the most successful candidates in the southwest region. Also, I had work experience, so they offered me a work-study programme at the economics department. In 1954, I began my studies at Nankai University, where an incident happened at the end of the year.

The creek nearby was a natural border for the university, but when it froze during severe winters, people walked on it to reach the campus. One day, we heard the noise of glass being smashed. Running out, we found that somebody had smashed the window of the assembly hall. I then led a group of classmates in chasing the person who had done it, but we failed to catch him: the man had fled across the frozen creek. Meantime, some reactionary slogans were found on the walls of the toilets in the teaching building belonging to the physics department. I did not see them myself, because I was a student in the economics department, which was in a separate building, but I was told that these slogans had been wiped off by the university security guards to stop panic from spreading among the students and teachers.

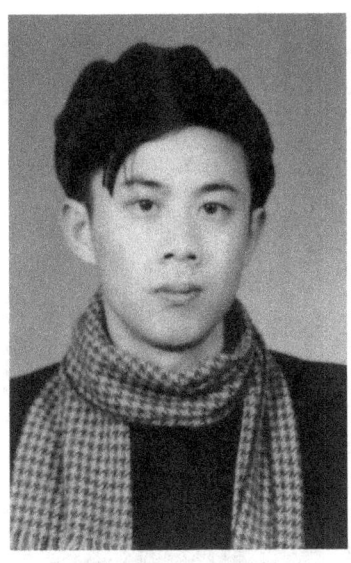

Mid-1950s: Zhou Erliu, a student at Nankai University.

During the winter holiday, Qi Ba asked me to give him an account of my university life, so I told him about this incident. "We are a new government; that evil elements from the old society are trying to sabotage things is to be expected, and not at all surprising. We need to look at how to deal with the problem," he said. He then asked me what I thought of the slogans in the toilets. I had a long think, and then said: "It's not proper just to wipe them off. We should expose this sabotage, showing everybody that the university is not pure: it is just like anywhere else. We need to maintain sharp vigilance. Security work should not only be carried out by a few specialised personnel, but also by everyone taking an active part." "What you said is right," he said.

Before long, the country held a conference on university security. Qi Ba gave a speech, and said: "My nephew is studying at Nankai University, and he is dumb. When he saw some reactionary slogans, he did not call everyone to come over and look, which could have sharpened their vigilance and helped to solve the case, thus closing the loophole in management and preventing the sabotage from being repeated. Instead, he wiped them off at once, because he was worried that it would cause panic among students and staff. So the future of national security appears to lie in integrating authority, cadres of specialised personnel, and the public, and this integration should bring any issues to the attention of related departments."

After I heard his speech, I complained to Qi Ma, saying that I did not want my relationship to them to be exposed. "Your Qi Ba has once again inconvenienced you," said Qi Ma. "He was overjoyed after you talked to him about the incident at your university, and he accidentally exposed your relationship to us. When he is dealing with issues like this, he always behaves in this way. He was not willing to directly criticise the personnel of the Tianjin municipal council and his old school, so you'll have to put up with it, which I'm sure you will understand."

Winter, 1954: Zhou Erliu at Nankai University.

People would then often ask me: "Does Nankai University really have a student who is the nephew of Zhou Enlai?" I told them that I did not know the details, never exposing my relation to Qi Ba. But after I returned to university, Mr Liu Piyun (before he took up the position of president of Nankai University, he was deputy director of the administrative office of south Sichuan, and my superior) called me to his office. He criticised me 'relentlessly', saying: "You have worked under my leadership for a long time, and now you are also my student, but you go so far as not to tell me about your relationship to the premier?" He then smiled and said: "What 'punishment' do you think you deserve?" And I was then 'hunted down and seized', and ever since, both the leaders of the Tianjin municipal council and the security bureau have made it a rule that I report regularly about my whereabouts while taking care of my own safety.

Many years later, a large number of people who had worked at the Ministry of Public Security would bring up this topic with me, holding the view that the gist of the premier's directive regarding security work was one of the most enduring guiding principles issued to many related departments, but they didn't know that I was involved in making it a guiding principle.

12. The Interesting Interpretation of My Name, 'Zhou Erliu'

My name has always been Zhou Erliu. It has never been changed, nor is it my own choice. My father, my grandfather and I all have names that include rarely used Chinese characters. This is probably because my grandfather was a scholar, who liked to use the rarely used characters to show that we were different from the rest, but it has brought me much unnecessary trouble in my life; for instance, when applying for scholarships or state funding that was essential for my education and my survival, it frequently happened that my name was misspelt, and I often panicked, afraid that I had failed to secure the money.

As early as 1946, Qi Ba told me that my father, about whom I had had no news for many years, might have died in the war. Hence, for many years I wasn't supported by my father – on the contrary, from 1946 to 1964, the expenses Qi Ba and Qi Ma supplied was the only income I had. Before the liberation, I had to declare that both my parents had died, and I was supported by my classmates. When I started working, according to the rules, I had to fill in forms giving my family origin and source of income in the three years before 1949, which would decide my family background. I did not want to tell them that I was a relative of Premier Zhou Enlai and that he nurtured me, so from the time I was in the university and for many years afterwards I did not own up about my relationship to Qi Ba. I mentioned nothing about my family in the forms, but filled in the column under family origin with 'urban poor'. Hence, I was humorously called 'a mega fool' by my teachers and the senior fellow students.

By accident, Qi Ma found out what I had filled in on the form, so she joked: "In our party we have already had a Li Yimang [*yimang* literally means 'a scoundrel'], who was the vice minister of the International Liaison Department of the Central Committee, and I'm not expecting there to be a Zhou Erliu in our family. An 'urban poor' is a person who has no regular income. Erliu, Erliu… it sounds like *erliuzi* ['idler'], said by a Northerner." Qi Ba overheard what she was saying, and said in a serious tone: "How can you talk to a child like that? He is a boy of great self-respect. He neither intends to benefit from his association with us, nor does he want to gives us a bad impression, which is a good thing. Do you know the meaning of the character *liu* in his name?" he asked her. Seeing that she was thinking, he carried on: "You can find it in the dictionary. It means 'fine gold'." After he had spoken these words, with a smiling face, Qi Ma cleverly said to me: "Erliu, in the future, no matter what setbacks or frustrations you suffer, you should always bear your name in mind." "Aibao," Qi Ba then said to me at once, "no matter what difficulties and grievances you suffer in your life, you should keep firmly your name in mind and take the whole picture into account. I believe fine gold will glitter sooner or later."

At this later time, I still keep firmly in mind that Qi Ba saved me from embarrassment in time, and moreover gave my name a more positive explanation. Qi Ba and Qi Ma were strict with me, and their outstanding personalities have exerted an influence on me, leading me to put other people's interests ahead of my own, take the whole picture into account, seek no personal privileges, and not give myself airs for being related to an official. Hence, I have always been low-key, and have never mentioned that I am a relative of Zhou Enlai when filling out forms. My family's older generation and the veteran revolutionaries were aware of what I had done. After the founding of new China, I joined the party and the army, and I tempered myself in the company of others. I did the hardest work, but whenever we were given a wage increase, I always put others' interests before my own.

I have gone through a lot with Qi Ba and Qi Ma, and I have also heard their teachings in person. During the Cultural Revolution, the Gang of Four seized every opportunity to frame Qi Ba. Qi Ma knew that I was honest and frank by nature, so she deliberately asked me to come see her. "Aibao," she said, "now is the most difficult and also the most dangerous time for your Qi Ba. Because of your relation to us, your life might be in danger, and of all our relatives you may be the first to be affected. Make the right assessment of the situation, so if necessary you can also follow other people in denouncing your Qi Ba..." Of course I would never, ever do such a thing. Every time I saw them in a dangerous situation and they could do nothing about it, while at the same time trying to protect me in such an exceptional way, I was both moved and sad; all sorts of emotions would well up in my mind and my feelings for them became stronger.

The Family's Cultural Relics and Qi Ba and Qi Ma's Letters (Part Two)

1. Qi Ba's Letter from Chongqing (1939)

The contents of the letter are as follows:

20th June,

Dear brother Run,

It has been two years since we parted and I miss you very much. I was greatly relieved to receive your letter in the spring. I came and settled in Chongqing last year, and my father also came via Guiyang and he is living with me in the country, as the houses in the city have been damaged. Today is my father's birthday; besides the celebrations, we are talking about you. Is dear Er Ma in good health?

Yours,

brother Luan.

PS: Your Qi Sao* passes her regards to Er Bomu. Please pass my regards to the nephews.

* literally 'seventh sister-in-law'.

After the war with Japan started, and as the nationalist government was cooperating with the communists, Qi Ba spent most of his time in Chongqing, the city that was established as a second capital besides Nanjing. This letter was sent to Shanghai from Chongqing, and the recipient was brother Run, who is my father: Zhou Enzhu.

It seems like a simple family correspondence: 'brother Luan' reporting to 'brother Run' and 'Er Ma' that his father had gone to Chongqing via Guiyang. The main contents of the letter are the safe family reunion: a few words expressing affection between relatives or talking about a family's daily life; hence, it attracted no attention from anyone. Here, 'Er Ma' and 'Er Bomu' are the same person, namely my father's birth mother, Cheng Yizhen. Qi Ba used to affectionately call her 'Er Ma'. 'Brother Luan' is Qi

Ba's pet name; 'Da Luan' for short. 'Qi Sao' is Deng Yingchao, and the 'PS' means she will not write a letter herself, and is just passing on her regards in this one. However, it is a letter worth analysing and understanding. The key point is that Qi Ba's father, Zhou Yineng, had been united with his son in Chongqing, and they were celebrating his seventieth birthday: a happy occasion, because such a peaceful reunion was expected by my family.

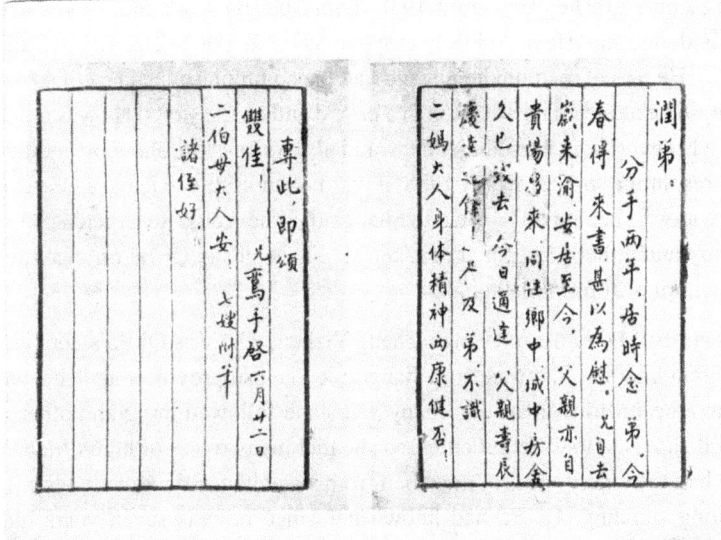

Zhou Enlai's letter, sent from Chongqing to Zhou Enzhu in Shanghai, 1939. For the full translation, see above.

When we received the letter, my family had moved to Joffre Lane in Avenue Joffre (now Huaihai Lane, Huaihai Road). In my memory, from 1931 onwards, my family in Shanghai moved house more than 10 times. Besides that, we were living in straitened circumstances, which forced us to move to cheaper lodgings. Our main reason for moving house was to try and avoid prosecution by the Japanese, the puppet government, the KMT, and the military police and the secret agents in the concessions. In those days, whenever my father came home late, my old grandmother would be fretful and worried, even shedding private tears.

In 1938, we lived in Huayuan Lane, Route Père Robert (now Ruijin

Erlu) in the French Concession, and Qi Yeye lived with us. We then saw him off to Wuhan to join his son; from there, he would go to the rear area in the southwest region. Qi Yeye was a kind and sincere elder. He was my grandfather's cousin, and when they were young they lived in the same compound in both Shoaxing and Huaian. My grandfather died early, in 1921, in Shanghai, and Qi Yeye lived with my family in Shanghai, Yangzhou and Zhenjiang until 1938, doing liaison work for his son and the underground. He had closely cropped hair and wore a cotton gown and shoes. He was of medium height and had the common appearance of an old man, so he attracted no attention in a crowd and on the street. He was quiet, but whenever there was danger he would always be calm, showing courage and resolution. In the year of 1938, it was not advisable to leave a 60-year-old widower behind on his own in Shanghai, as he would be targeted by the enemy and either persecuted or taken as a hostage, so Qi Ba arranged for his withdrawal from Shanghai.

The 'Er Ma' in the letter was Cheng Yizhen, who was Qi Ba's aunt and my grandmother. She was from Jiangdu in Jiangsu province, and she was quite a beautiful woman. For many years she followed my grandfather, a private adviser, to different cities, so she met many wives of high officials. She had the dignified air of a woman from a wealthy and influential family of long standing. Qi Ba had known her since he was seven years old, and she liked him very much. Qi Ba and Qi Ma cared for her with great solicitude. They congratulated her on her birthday each year, for 60 years, until her death at 90 years old.

My father, Zhou Enzhu, was the youngest and also the smallest of his generation. His pet name was Da Huan, and he was ten years junior to Qi Ba. When he was six, my family began to shelter Qi Ba, and Qi Ba then cared for him like an older brother, washing his face for him, giving him toys and illustrated storybooks, explaining the classic book *The Romance of the Three Kingdoms* to him, teaching him English and helping him with his exercises. Since his childhood, my father had frequently been ill, so he was weak. In addition, he suffered an impairment in his left ear. After he grew up, he went to Datong University in Shanghai, and also became an early graduate of the Shanghai Law School. However, he did not follow a legal career. He was fond of the Beijing opera, and he became an amateur performer of the Mei Lanfang style. He was also engaged in the literature and arts sectors in the liberated areas. Because he was closely associated with Shen Junru, Shi Liang and Mei Langfang, when he was in Chongqing Qi Ba arranged for him to work with department three of the defence ministry, which was under the charge of Guo Moruo, to liaise with related notable figures in both judicial circles and the world of literature and art. He was to guide them to join the anti-Japanese national united front. General (later Marshal) Ye Jianying received him and arranged his accommodation in Chongqing. His first job was to receive Lady He Xiangning, who had returned to the mainland from Hong Kong, but due to a lung disease he suffered from he was unable to carry on doing similar work for a long time afterwards.

Qi Ba wrote this letter in a neat and regular script, different from his usual running cursive, in order to show his respect and his filial attitude and feelings to a member of the older generation. All his life, he continued to dismiss the ridiculous rumour that communists turn their backs on their own flesh and blood; on the contrary, he attached great importance to the traditional virtue of 'respecting the aged and loving the young', and he practised what he preached. Upon examination, the letter shows that the handwriting is identical to that of the inscription on the Monument to the People's Heroes in Tiananmen Square.

When writing to family members, he frequently changed his signatures, either signing off as 'brother Lai', 'brother Luan' or 'seventh brother'. The letters would not be delivered by a postman, but by some non-party personage. All of this shows his active engagement in his underground work as well as his versatility.

2. Qi Ba's Letter from before He Returned to Nanjing from Chongqing (1946)

In 1946 my father recovered from his long illness, but his marriage to his wife, Ma Shunyi, had broken down, so they were in the process of divorcing. He had originally planned to go to Chongqing and ask Qi Ba to find him a job, but Qi Ba knew that the Japanese had surrendered and the nationalist government would soon move their capital back to Nanjing. As members of the communists' negotiating team, he and Qi Ma would follow the government; besides, if negotiations between the nationalists and the communists broke down, civil war would be unavoidable, so he wrote this letter to my father, explaining his concerns.

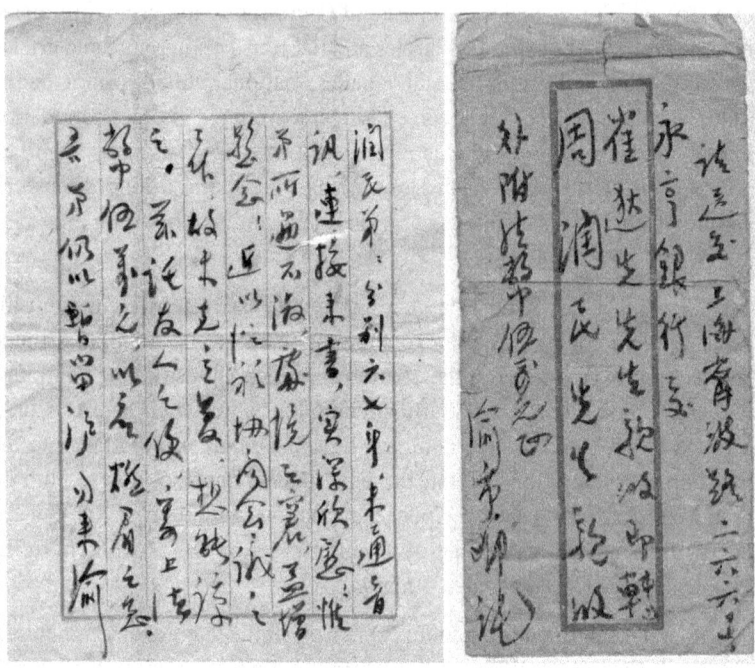

The first page of Zhou Enlai's letter to Zhou Enzhu in Shanghai, written before he moved back to Nanjing from Chongqing, 1946. For the full translation, see Appendix 3.

'Runmin' is my father's courtesy name. The lines "Your wife is not kind and gentle, and you are in an awkward predicament that increases my worries about you" refer to my father's second wife, Ma Shunyi, whom he married after the death of his first wife. Their marriage had been in trouble for a long time. Her behaviour was crude and monstrous; she would ceaselessly beat and scolded him at the slightest provocation. Unwilling to endure more, he left home to avoid being bullied and humiliated. Because she had sold all the family property and was in possession of the remaining cash, he was in dire straits and had to go to his cousin for help. Qi Ba, in accordance with the time-honoured (underground) routine, used Qi Ma's name, saying: "I will send you 50,000 fabi in cash [paper currency issued by the KMT government, from 1935 onwards] at the convenience of a friend, for your extremely urgent needs." At the same time, he advised: "You should stay in Shanghai for the time being – don't come to Chongqing. You may come when the country regains some stability, but right now you may have to find yourself a place to stay in Shanghai." These words show that he was a kind man, full of sentiment, who attached importance to blood relations and helping the weak. As a communist, he had always been honest, upright and self-disciplined, as well as strict with his relatives; yet he truly had no extra cash to help his cousin. Also, there was the country's complicated situation to consider, busy as it was setting up a political conference involving the cooperation of all parties and the office of the CPC delegation moving to Nanjing; therefore, it would be better to discuss the matter afterwards. On the other hand, the breakdown of negotiations between the nationalists and the communists could happen quickly and might then be followed by civil war, so it would be better to send 'brother Run' directly to the liberated area to work.

He also mentioned that he was very happy to learn from 'little uncle' Cheng Shaoqin that my grandmother was well, and he asked my father to pass his regards to her. Ever since the death of my grandfather, in 1921, to 1962, when she died, he never ceased sending his regards to her.

Things turned out to be exactly as Qi Ba had foreseen, so, on the eve of civil war, he resolutely sent my father to the liberated area in the regions Jiangsu and Anhui to work with chairman Li Yimang. Before my father left Nanjing, he had been working in the office of the CPC delegation in Meiyuan Xincun, as a secretary.

3. Qi Ba's Letter from Nanjing (1946)

After the victory of the anti-Japanese war, the KMT betrayed the trust of the CPC and tore apart the peace agreement between them, commencing an all-out attack on the liberated areas. In order to carry on with negotiations, as well as to launch campaigns to fight for peace and democracy, Qi Ba led the CPC delegation from Chongqing to Meiyuan Xincun, in Nanjing, in May 1946, making active efforts to prepare to set up an office in Shanghai.

At that time, I journeyed to Shanghai on my own to find Qi Ba. This trip was arranged by my grandmother. However, Qi Ba was in Nanjing, busy negotiating with the KMT. I was young and had no knowledge of this situation, but the worst thing for me was that I did not know where Qi Ba was and how I could contact him. So I wandered around aimlessly in Shanghai for several days, until my classmate Jia Daqiing found me. He was the nephew of Zhang Zhenbang, the manager of the *Wen Hui Bao* newspaper and a non-party democrat. In his home, he handed me Qi Ba's letter.

May 1946

Dear Aibao,

We both miss you. How is everything going?

We are in Nanjing and currently very busy. Sometime later we will come to Shanghai to meet you. After you have read this letter, go at once to see Mr Chen Jiakang in 107 rue Massenet. He will arrange for you to meet us, and then we can have a good talk.

Yours sincerely,

Qi Ba and Qi Ma

Holding this letter, I immediately went to Sir Zhou's Mansion, where Mr Chen received me. We then discussed the date on which I would meet Qi Ba and Qi Ma.

The way the letter was delivered as well as its contents showed that Qi Ba had been considerate in making arrangements, even though he was very busy. To me, young and ignorant, this letter, received at the right time, proved to me the tender care and affection that exists between blood relations. I can put it this way: it was the beginning of my future political journey.

Part Three

Part Three

The Years of National Construction

The most distinctive principle of Qi Ba's philosophy was that of 'seeking common ground while reserving differences'. All his life, guided by this philosophy, he carried it out steadily and in varied ways.

By his own recollection, he grew up in a big, declining feudal family. He had been to an old-style private school where he had gained knowledge about ideas that had existed since ancient times, as well as experiences summed up by our forefathers and the ideas that followed, such as: 'A gentleman gets along with others, but does not necessarily agree with them; a small man agrees with others, but does not get along with them.' To me, this ideology of his is inseparable from his worldview; that is, the Chinese traditional philosophy, the 'non-polar and yet supreme polarity' of our ancestor Zhou Dunyi, which sees the whole world as an integral whole and all things in a process of endless transformation.

Afterwards, he went to Nankai Middle School and then to university to study. He also went to Japan, France, Germany and England to study, to work and to observe. He compared the similarities and differences between China and those foreign countries. During this process, his own ideas about this philosophy gradually took shape, and it was established after trials and tests.

To use the language of the common people: this philosophy is based on the view that the world is an integral whole but pluralistic; planet Earth is a member of the whole universe, while the humans living on it have different cultures. And as for its political and practical value, under the guidance of this philosophy, Qi Ba was able to deal correctly with the relationship between the communists and the KMT.

In 1924, Dr Sun Yat-sen accepted the proposal of the CPC and the Comintern for cooperation between the communists and the nationalists. He agreed that members of the CPC and the socialist Youth League could join the KMT on an individual basis. He formulated three policies of alliance: one with Russia, one with the communists, and one to help the peasants and workers, and reorganised the KMT. In August of that same year, Qi Ba returned to Guangzhou from Europe. He was head of both the political department of the Huangpu Military Academy and the First Army of the National Revolutionary Army. His ideas about this philosophy matured during the following conflicts with the nationalists, particularly during the period of the first alliance between the CPC and the KMT and the split that followed. While working with the United Front, he learnt from experience that adopting a correct attitude towards the cooperation and the subsequent break between the KMT and the CPC would be impossible without the guidance and practice of this ideology: the destiny of China hinged on the outcome of adopting the correct attitude. When the CPC joined the Northern Expedition, it was to conform to the historical trend of the times and seek common ground, but the disruptive activities of the KMT seriously damaged the principle of this ideology, bringing suffering and misfortune to the country and the people. Therefore, Qi Ba took the lead and initiated the Nanchang uprising.

In 1936, after the Xi'an Incident, which made the overall situation favourable to a war of resistance against Japan, he and others helped to bring about cooperation between the nationalists and the communists for the second time. The principles of his ideology were once again successfully put into practice.

However, soon after the victory over Japan in 1945, the KMT ignored the desires and the voices of the people, who were looking forward to peace, and started a full-scale civil war that resulted in the second breakdown of cooperation between the KMT and the CPC, and, in the end, lost them the war and forced them to withdraw to Taiwan. When new China was founded, the CPC cooperated with the democratic parties and key figures in various circles to set up the people's government. One may well say that it was the most successful example of his ideology being put into practice.

Looking back at past events, from the lengthy armed struggles to the KMT military personnel who took various stances, Qi Ba adopted the following principle: 'Whether one joins the revolution early or later on, all are equally welcome.' This policy helped to bring large numbers of KMT military officers and men to revolt or to lay down their weapons. He approved of the contributions some of them had made during the anti-Japanese war, which helped to convince these officers and men to join him. For example, of the outstanding KMT generals, many were graduates from the Huangpu Military Academy and former students of Qi Ba's. They couldn't help feeling ashamed in front of their teacher, but to put them at ease, Qi Ba said to them: "I should say that I am not a good teacher, because I haven't fulfilled my responsibility. I should have guided you to walk on the right path earlier." Such an attitude of being strict with himself and lenient with others received overall praise and support.

Regarding his economic work, the conversations I had with Qi Ba as well as the ones with Mr Xu Dixin, a scholar and a long-term supporter of Qi Ba, informed me that in those years, Premier Zhou Enlai had tentative ideas about the economy, thinking that the period of the new democratic revolution should be reasonably extended and that our country's transition to socialism should not be hurried. Qi Ba's main concern was that China's industry was backward at the time. The country was mainly agricultural, with a large number of people working as small producers. Science and technology were at a low level. For these reasons, several economic elements had firmly taken root in our economy. Economic countermeasures would have to take into consideration the overall development of the country and society, as well as the various basic interests of all aspects of life. Following demand and the manufacturers' capacities, the government then made arrangements for rationed production while encouraging consumers to spend.

In terms of culture, Qi Ba agreed with the following policy: to 'let a hundred flowers blossom, and a hundred schools of thought contend.' He paid special attention to attaching equal importance to autonomy and tolerance. He respected academic freedom and did not agree with confusing differences in opinion when it came to political questions. He practiced what he advocated, maintaining contact with many scientists and artists as if he was their good teacher and helpful friend.

As for the aspect of diplomacy, he put forward, for the first time, the Five Principles of Peaceful Coexistence that would win support from prime ministers Nehru of India and U Nu of Burma. The Five Principles of Peaceful Coexistence have been a universally acknowledged historical contribution to the twentieth century, and the guiding principle is undoubtedly that of 'seeking common ground while reserving differences.'

1. Conversations About Social Issues

1.1. The Family Origins and Political Convictions

During my years at university, in order to learn more about the work taking place on a primary level, Qi Ba often asked me to write something for him to read. He would comment on what I had written and then throw it in the bin. A short article of mine still remains fresh in my memory. It was entitled *Middle Peasantization*. He was glad that I had broken new ground, but another article, commenting on the relationship of class origins to the quality of higher education, was subject to harsh criticism from him.

My viewpoint was very naïve then, because in the early years after the founding of new China the majority of university students were from middle- or upper-class families, and it was hard for some of them not to feel disturbed by the social changes. So, I wrongly thought that increasing the number of students from workers' and peasants' families would automatically raise the teaching quality of the universities.

After Qi Ba had read my article, he pointed out straightaway that my viewpoint was wrong, because the number of students from workers' or peasants' families who had been able to finish middle school and enter university before the liberation was very small. These people could not meet the state's and society's demands of quality and talent. Besides, students could not choose their family origins; this was an objective fact.

Therefore, no matter what background they had, the political orientation they pursued and the quality of their labour ought to be more important.

As for family origins, Qi Ba once said to me that firstly, there is class status, because it exists objectively; secondly, there is no class status, because one's class status is not his own choice; thirdly, how one is doing is more important than his class status, as this can fully stimulate the people's initiative, which is favourable to the unity of the Chinese people.

In the early days of new China, many university students came from reprehensible family backgrounds. Because they were young and ignorant, some of them even joined the KMT's youth organisation; however, they were not guilty of any crimes. Some of them became suspected reactionaries only because they had made contact with members of the KMT's Youth League. Qi Ba said to me: "In some cases, we need to make a concrete analysis of their conditions, dealing with different things or people in different ways. At that time, the KMT still controlled the central government; thus, people couldn't help thinking that the KMT were the rightful rulers. Young students in the large cities controlled by the KMT did not have any opportunity to find out what was truly happening in the liberated areas. Moreover, the KMT issued lots of twisted propaganda, which hindered them in understanding the CPC's policies correctly. As for the victory over Japan, people easily mistook the KMT as the only anti-Japanese force, which helped add to expectations about or illusions surrounding the KMT. Besides, there were countless ties among the middle- and upper-class families, and so on and so forth. So, it will take some time for them to understand us and then to have faith in us. It is understandable, because they are young and haven't yet gained any life experience. I believe the majority of them are patriots and believe in the truth, so, sooner or later, they and we will be one family. We must treat them with well-meant prudence, rather than handle the issue as we would like to."

History bears out that Qi Ba's stand on this issue, which was also the stand of many high-ranking officials within the party, such as Marshal Chen Yi, is correct. Anything opposite would certainly dampen the enthusiasm of many people.

I had the honour of listening to Qi Ba's teachings in person, so I would try my best to carry out his ideas in my work. In the following decades, many of my fellow students had problems with their family background, more or less, but I treated each of them as my equal while giving them timely help, making them feel warm-hearted. Many of them have become pillars of society and the state. At times, when we had a happy reunion, we would talk about the past, and together we would think of Qi Ba, with deep regard for his guidance and foresight.

In Qi Ba's office, besides the ordinary book shelves, one was specifically for journals. It was filled with all sorts of periodical publications, and the *China Youth* was always in a place easy to pick up, showing that the very busy premier paid great attention to the growth of the younger generation. Because I was in a work-study programme, I used to be a member of my university's Youth League committee, working concurrently as a student counsellor for the economics department and the foreign languages department, a secretary of the general Youth League branch, and president of the student union. Qi Ba would find time to ask me about my work, and subsequently offer suggestions.

Firstly, he was very concerned that members of the Youth League should maintain their vanguard role, and often said that young people have active minds, are susceptible to ideas and think a lot. He said that many of our forefathers were, from a young age, able to absorb a wide range of advanced ideas, which some of them used to nourish their minds and develop their own creative ideas. So if the Youth League organisation wanted to maintain its advanced nature, the very issue was to have an advanced ideology and be able to inspire, to assist, to guide and to unite the youthful masses, protecting their creativity while encouraging them to make great efforts to walk at the forefront of the times.

Secondly, one's youth is the most precious period for growth and development, so one of the most vital tasks for the Youth League organisations, especially those in the higher education sector, is to guide young students in making great efforts to develop themselves in an all-round way — ie, morally, intellectually and physically — because they are the future of our nation. Therefore, Qi Ba stressed that we should not make our students look like those frail scholars in a feudal society, but to help every one of them to gain a strong, healthy body through physical training. The traditional Chinese way of educating is to make large numbers of students take up the bad habit of neglecting manual labour. North Americans pay much more attention to this, and the young people in that country attach importance to the issue themselves; therefore, in China, we should also pay attention to the students' development in using their hands.

We should differentiate between universities and middle and primary schools. University students will develop into more mature young people, so we need to make sure to train their capacity to learn and work independently. Either we give all students a solid academic foundation, or we teach the individual who has creative potential in accordance with their aptitude. We should try our best to provide what they need and even regard each one as an individual case when giving support. In short, we must preserve the initiative of the young students, not to restrain them as we please.

Thirdly, we should encourage young students to get on well with one another: pooling everyone's wisdom is better than indulging in self-admiration and cutting oneself off from the masses. Scholars tend to scorn each other, which can easily make intellectuals incompatible with each other, but self-isolation is not a good thing. If it is hard to bring about harmony between the intellectuals and the workers and peasants, a job will sometimes not get done. In short, Qi Ba encouraged the intellectuals to mix with the working people and help them become knowledgeable, ultimately abolishing the antithesis between mental and manual labour. This is a lofty ideal, and we should not neglect it or misuse it. At that time, there was too much labour activity on university campuses, which held up teaching as well as studying. Both the teaching staff and the students complained about this, particularly the students, who thought that too little time was being spent on learning, which would affect their professional studies. This made them worried that they would not meet the standard after graduation and be unable to take on the jobs assigned to them.

Looking back now, Qi Ba and Marshal Chen Yi were aware of this long ago. They fully understood the problem and showed sympathy towards these reasonable complaints. It was only because of the social restrictions at the time that this problem was not easily solved.

I have been working in the higher education sector and as a youth worker for a long time. I have benefited from Qi Ba's teachings all my life, so in the following decade, I tried my best to prevent many university lecturers and students from being harmed by associating with various political movements. Consequently, I became a target of criticism from those who were ultra-left in their thinking. They kept in touch with me, giving me positive appraisals as well as gratitude for helping them. They regarded me as a man who would not let Premier Zhou Enlai down.

1.2. The National Minority Autonomy System

Qi Ba had a fervent passion for the ethnic minorities living in China. A young Uygur man once said that Zhou Enlai was always like a kind father to them, who sympathised with their historical experiences, who opposed any discrimination, who cared about them and helped to bring economic and cultural developments to their region.

Qi Ba believed that China was a multinational country. Dealing correctly with the problem of nationality was a major issue, relating to the future and destiny as well as the basic interests of people of all nationalities in China. China's national basis is formed by the Han, who have a large population and a more developed economy and culture, though they live in a relatively small area; on the contrary, the minority nationalities comprise fewer people and have less-developed cultures, but they live in vast areas with abundant natural resources. These so-called vast territories and abundant resources need to be made use of, which is not possible without cooperation between the Han and the other minorities. Meanwhile, areas inhabited by multi-ethnic groups are to be seen everywhere. In short, if the Han and the minority nationalities cooperate, it will be beneficial to both sides; if not, it will harm them both. So, the only correct way is to conform to the actual situation in China and to establish a system of regional autonomy for ethnic minorities, which means that different nationalities living together in the same region can maintain their national autonomic rights, rather than separate them through a federal system or install a regional republic system and copy other countries' models. Historical development has proven that Qi Ba has made a unique contribution to tackle China's nationality problem at its source.

At the inauguration of the autonomous region of Guangxi Zhuang, Qi Ba said: "Giving an ethnic minority this kind of regional autonomy makes for the correct combination of economic and political elements. It will not only allow the people inhabiting the region to enjoy the right of autonomy, but also the ethnic groups. From a large population's nationality to a small population's nationality, from a large region's inhabitants to a small region's inhabitants, almost everyone has their own autonomous unit and is fully enjoying their rights as an autonomous ethnic minority. The implementation of such a system is an unprecedented undertaking."

I was deeply influenced by Qi Ba, and I love the people of the ethnic minorities from the bottom of my heart. I have been to almost every region they inhabit; I have taken foreign guests to these regions to increase their popularity and cultivate mutual understanding, and to seek more development opportunities for them. They include: the region inhabited by the Miao as well as the Han in west Hunan, east Sichuan and Guizhou; the border region of Yunnan, represented by the Dai; the region bordering Sichuan and Yunnan, where the Yi reside; the Xilingele region, inhabited by the Mongols in Inner Mongolia; the vast area from Turpan to Urumqi in the Xinjiang Uygur Autonomous Region, represented by the Uygur and the Kazakhs; from Lhasa, Dangxiong county, to the border with Nepal in the Tibet Autonomous Region, the outstretched so-called 'Front Tibet' and 'Back Tibet', inhabited by the Tibetans; the region in Qinghai, inhabited by the Tibetans and the Hui; the mountain area inhabited by the Li people on the island of Hainan; and even the area populated by the Gaoshan in Taiwan. For three of the above trips I compiled an account of what I had seen and heard, and presented it to Qi Ba.

I wrote the first report in 1954. It was about the Miao living in west Hunan, east Sichuan and the border region of Guizhou, and the Yi living in Leibo, Mabian and Ebian counties in the minor Liangshan region in southwest Sichuan, near the border of Yunnan province.

I wrote the second one in 1965. This account was about the Tibetans inhabiting the region stretching from Lhasa and Shigatse to Nelamu county, bordering Nepal, and the Monpa, whose population was comparatively small.

I wrote the third one in 1975, when I went to visit the herdsmen and my cousin Zhou Bingjian, who had moved to the Xilingele steppe in Inner Mongolia to live and work after graduating from middle school.

My first report was quite long and divided into two parts. It was mainly about the journey I had made with the troops of the Second Field Army and what I had seen and heard in the regions of west Hunan, east Sichuan and the border region of Guizhou, an area disenfranchised by three provincial governments. The capital was Jishou, and the regional population was mainly made up of the Miao, as well as some Han and Tujia. The western Hunan region had picturesque mountains, but was very humid. Many local farmers planted rice as well as corn on the hilly land. The areas in east Sichuan and bordering Guizhou were desolate and barren, and the locals generally planted corn. Hilly land and high-rising cliffs dominated this area. In the feudal dynasties of past ages, due to the complicated geographical conditions, it had been difficult for administrators to reach the region. In the early 1950s, bandits, miscellaneous troops and local despots lorded over districts in the region. Because these lawless people fled to the hills, army troops sent to the region found it difficult to carry out their work. After the founding of new China, the local governments first needed to carry out a campaign of clearing out the bandits and opposing local despots on all levels, which included reductions in rent for land and interest on loans as well as land reform. Mobilising the masses was necessary for the newborn political powers to be firmly established. In those days, poverty-stricken Miao and Han were to be seen everywhere in the region; they did not have enough to eat and wear. Some utterly destitute women stood by the roadside, naked, with babies in their arms. Passing troops would give these women their own uniforms, though a soldier usually only had one uniform. They carried a heavy load of cartridges and a rice bag; many of them had only one padded jacket, wearing it inside out when on the march but turning it over when reaching a town in order to show neatness and hygiene. Moreover, the wretched sight of the locals, too horrible to look at, made them feel awkward when they had nothing more to give them. They had to report to the higher authorities to solve this problem. Because they had been living together for centuries, it was hard to spot any differences between the features and languages of some of the Miao and Han.

At the time, the party and the army enjoyed a good reputation nationwide, except for occasional malicious rumours from the enemy. What had spread wider were the stories of the fine style of the PLA and the party's policies — particularly the land reform policy, which had struck a chord deep in the hearts of the people. Because of the complicated geographical features and social conditions, the locals were hesitant to go near the army and civilian workers. If they made contact with us, they were risking their lives. At night, lanterns were scattered in the hills like will-o'-the-wisps; at times we could see armed robbers, ready to act. In areas where there were numerous valleys, when there was thunder, or the crack of a whip, the deafening noise could be heard miles away. Late at night, the howls of the wolves sounded like lots of women crying about their misfortunes. We were absolutely terrified by this sound.

Afterwards, I was assigned the task of taking one platoon of soldiers to escort at least 700 prisoners from five counties who were serving a sentence of reform through labour in the forests in Mabian and Ebian counties: their task was to transport the corn, which was laid up in warehouses due to poor means of transportation, to supply the army and the cities. Before we set off, we decided to leave our guns behind, worried that they would get stolen or lost in the valleys or forests, which could have serious consequences if they were used by bad people. But how to manage several hundred prisoners without a gun? I was just over 20 years old at the time. "The young are fearless," as the saying goes, and so we set off without demurring. Moreover, I found a way to manage these prisoners. I divided them into different squads, selecting the ones who had committed less-severe crimes, had a better attitude and were better educated as squad or platoon leaders, letting them manage themselves. I would give them admonitory talks, praising good behaviour while criticising the bad. In the beginning, when I talked to them, I called them "comrades"; later, when realising it was not proper to address them thus, I changed it to "activists". Qi Ba would laugh when I told him about this later.

The Mabian and Ebian regions had been wild and uncivilised since ancient times, making it easy for people to catch subtropical diseases there. There, deep in the mountains, lived the Yi, the owners of the forests, and their slaves. The humidity level was so high that not only could it cause newcomers to become lost in the woods, but a grenade being set off could cause torrential rainfall. We were in the depths of the mountains and valleys, and when we were passing through, the earth cracked under the scorching sunlight while torrents of water would rush down the streams in a split second — so powerful, they surged onward like ten thousand horses galloping, with whirlpools of all sizes swirling around. Anyone who fell into the water would have no chance of coming out alive. One time, the floods came out of nowhere; luckily, there was a peddler beside me. He hit me on the right shoulder with his bamboo pole. Aware of what was happening, I held the pole while he pulled me out the swirling water. Sometimes, after we had been climbing over seemingly endless hills, a lake appeared in front of our eyes. Seeing this small piece of level ground, we felt that we were in a fairyland.

The population of Mabian county numbered around three thousand — small, but with a complicated background. Some made a living by trading weaponry and opium; hence, the area was full of the smell of gunpowder. After innumerable hardships, we managed to transport all the corn to the town by carrying bags on our shoulders, completing our mission.

Yet some regions were very rich in underground natural resources. With the development of other democratic reforms after the land reform, as well as the new economic policy on transportation and the enforcement of various policies by the new government, the local troublemakers were finally chased off. We then helped to build a long-term friendship between the Han and the Yi and the Han and the Miao, as well as other ethnic groups. Tremendous changes have taken place in these regions in recent years, mirroring what Qi Ba said of his ideals and ambitions before his death: he wanted to turn these regions into heavens on earth, where the land would be shared by all nationalities, the economy would develop energetically, businesses would prosper, and people's lives would get better and better.

Qi Ba fully understood the history and reality of life in these regions. He notably showed sympathy to the ethnic minorities who had suffered throughout history, proposing that the Han people, who have a large population, should do more to help the minority groups develop faster; this can be seen as 'repaying a debt' or 'apologizing', which would benefit national unity while being consistent with the truth. Even if the enemy tried to sow discord among minority groups, it would be hard for them to have their way. We should have faith in the awareness of the people belonging to ethnic minorities — no need to be too afraid of the enemy stirring up trouble. Of course, we must maintain our vigilance, intensify our education and consolidate the nation: these are the fundamental deeds we must perform. Those of us who belong to the Han should play an exemplary role, but we must get rid of the Han's chauvinism. The minority nationalities should combine national and socialist sentiments. Do not commit the mistake of sticking to narrow, local nationalism; respect and pay attention to national sentiments, but do not exclude other nationalities. In addition, we need to train the minority cadres; the ratio of the deputies to the National People's Congress (NPC) must match the ratio of the population, combining unity with restriction. The purpose is to make the Han cadres unite with the minority cadres, dedicating themselves long-term to the construction and development of the remote areas. Their hard work, sacrifices and historical contributions should all be acknowledged.

In 1970s, it was rare for a foreign delegation to visit an autonomous minority region in China, so a visit like that had its own special significance. In 1975, Qi Ba had attended a visit from the Maori delegation of New Zealand to the Inner Mongolia Autonomous Region. At the time, I was director of the Chinese People's Association for Friendship with Foreign Countries (CPAFFC), so I was the one who arranged where they would go after leaving Beijing. I was thinking of taking them to Inner Mongolia, as well as some other ethnic minority regions. Coincidentally, my aunt Wang Shiqin gave me some ideas. During the Cultural Revolution, my uncle Zhou Enshou had been arrested and subjected to an investigation, but a conclusion had not yet been reached. His children lived all over the country, and his wife was home alone in Beijing. She missed her children, particularly her youngest daughter, Zhou Bingjian (whom we all called 'Little Six'). She was in Inner Mongolia, living with the local herdsmen. Her mother was worried about her and asked me if I could arrange for the Maori delegation to go there. I thought it was a good idea, and after the government of the Inner Mongolia Autonomous Region granted us permission, we were allowed to visit Xilinhot, in the Xilingol League, as well as Hohhot. For a long time, Qi Ba had been putting his energy into giving the Mongols living inside China equal treatment, and he had been paying a good deal of attention to the issue of autonomy. As early as 23 April 1947, he personally drew up the directive on Inner Mongolian Autonomy by the Central Committee of the CPC, defining regulations for the establishment of the Inner Mongolia Autonomous Region and its relationship to the liberated area, as well as the party's work, construction of power and military struggles. In May of that same year, the Inner Mongolia Autonomous Region was created. Since then, the party has gained valuable practical experience in creating policies on the regional autonomy of ethnic minorities, which have evoked widespread positive reactions from all other ethnic groups in China.

First, I led the Maori delegation on a visit to Hohhot. We went to factories that showed a picture of prosperity, and also visited some traditional temples, where we viewed many valuable historical relics. After leaving Hohhot, we paid a visit to the tomb of Wang Zhaojun. The leaders of the autonomous region especially recommended that we see the grassland, so we went to the vast and beautiful steppe of Xilingele.

Xilingele means 'river on a ridge' in Mongolian, and the landscape is considerably flat and open. The vast, natural grassland could bring tourists to the region in abundance, but we went there during the Cultural Revolution, when transportation was very difficult and the standard of living was low there. Arranged by the local government, my cousin Little Six came to meet us. You can imagine how hard it was for her and me to see each other on the vast grassland. I was very excited when I saw her, almost jumping out to call to her. She was very excited to see me too. I thought she

The Years of National Construction

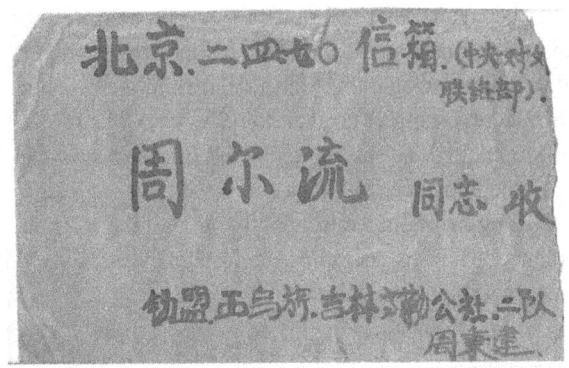

**A letter from Zhou Bingjian to Zhou Erliu.
For the full translation, see Appendix 4.**

might be the secretary of her Youth League branch, because she led a cavalry unit of militia from the white clouds far away, galloping single file towards the platform where the Maori delegation were seated. People on the platform were getting excited. Little Six, who was in the lead, might have been too excited, as she suddenly fell off her horse, causing a loud scream from the audience. Just then she turned over and jumped back on the horse, leading her mounted troops 'flying' past the rostrum, cheered on by the audience. All of us, including the foreign guests, gave this mounted troop the warmest welcome and the utmost respect.

The Maoris, the herders of Inner Mongolia, Zhou Erliu (second in the front row from the left) and Zhou Bingjian (third in the front row from the left).

Afterwards, Little Six talked to me about her days and nights on the steppe. As a Han girl from the capital of the country living on this vast grassland, she enjoyed the spectacular landscape, but experienced all the hardships of nomadic life. Fortunately, she had not let Qi Ba and Qi Ma down. In a short period of time, she had grown up from a young girl to a steppe soldier worthy of the name. At first glance, I could not tell her apart from the native Mongolian girls, because there was no difference between her and them. There were several bloody cuts on her ruddy cheeks, which made us adults feel sorry for her. As a senior member of the family, I was very proud of her. Meanwhile, I was thinking that I would give Qi Ba,

Qi Ma and aunt Shiqin a detailed account of our meeting. Later, Qi Ma discussed this with me and applauded what Little Six was doing on the Xilingele grassland. On Qi Ba's behalf, she said to me: "Our party and the state have always cared about the unity and progress of the Han nationals and all the other nationalities in the Inner Mongolia Autonomous Region. Well done to Little Six; she hasn't disappointed the older generation. You, the older cousin, who made the arrangement, should also be rewarded, so this trip has been well worthwhile. It is rare for a foreign ethnic minority delegation to visit the autonomous regions of our ethnic minorities. We will have accumulated a wealth of experience from this visit. We have learnt from each other, which will benefit both sides and will also increase our understanding of foreign delegations in relation to our party's nationality policy. The premier always reminds us not to forget the lessons of the degeneration and decadence of the 'children of the Eight Banners', and his warning has definitely influenced Little Six. He will be very happy about that. He also hopes to hear more such lovely stories. The unity between the Han and the Mongolians is very important, and the significance of the stabilisation of the northern border should not be overlooked."

"On my trip, I heard the news," I then cut in, "that universities in the Inner Mongolia Autonomous Region have taken on more Mongolian than Han students." "The cooperation between the Mongols and the Han has created a new understanding," she smiled, and then said: "Together we care for and nurture our younger generations. Let national unity and cooperation pass from generation to generation, to enhance the quality of all nationalities. It is quite an important job, and only by doing it will you live up to the requirements and expectations of your uncle."

1.3. Heart-to-Heart Communication during a Cultural Exchange

After Wang Zhangli (my wife) and I graduated from university, we did not begin working in the foreign ministry right away, because we wanted to avoid being suspected of getting the job because we were related to Premier Zhou Enlai. We took the jobs assigned to us, and both of us became engaged in external cultural exchanges.

Throughout his life, Qi Ba spent quite a lot of time talking to us about our work, and we are, and were, grateful for his teachings. During his conversations with me, he once said that a foreign cultural exchange was different from exchanges in politics, economics and other social projects, but that they were all part of foreign relations on the same course in history. These different parts naturally have their distinguishing features: thus, a political exchange emphasises connections in cooperative exchanges between the governments of different countries; 'seeking common ground while reserving differences' is the most important guiding principle for this relationship. The characteristics of an economic exchange are to strive for equality and mutual benefit. And as for a cultural exchange, one of the basic, noted features is, in a sense, to engage in flexible and diverse mutual understanding and communication between human beings.

As for methods, a cultural exchange, including education, science and the humanities, naturally needs to be flexible, diverse and rich in content. In short, a foreign cultural exchange can serve as an assessment preceding a political visit, a simultaneous action, or a post-visit supplementary action. It can be an exchange of friendship and cooperation between governments. It can also be a non-governmental exchange, with vast numbers of participants from different nationalities, and the forms can be semi-governmental, person-to-person or commercial. Intellectual communication, ideological communication and even soul communication between nationalities will come into being, and these positive results can also be turned into a common spiritual wealth or treasure for all humankind. Qi Ba even pointed out that a foreign cultural exchange can be sustained independently of the will of governments. It is a form of mass participation that is effective and has a long-term significance. This kind of exchange is for the feelings of the people, for those who have varied beliefs about the value of understanding and communicating with each other, and in the long process of history it can become wealth for the mind that human beings commonly possess.

So it is fortunate that I am in the foreign cultural exchange branch. Qi Ba wished for me not to follow those people who only paid attention to politics and businesses but did not have enough understanding of foreign cultural exchanges.

As for the extent of an exchange, on the one hand, according to necessity and possibility, our plans can be limited but clear; on the other hand, when the conditions are right, it is recommended to expand the size of the exchange to achieve a greater impact. Qi Ba's teachings to us on this topic can be summed up as follows:

1) As for the methods and channels of a foreign cultural exchange, we should pay full attention to the basic national conditions and customs of the target country, making flexible selections and applications;

2) As for the contents and projects, according to the aims of UNESCO, these should include education, science and culture, and this diversity would give us more space to develop our work;

3) We must try to gather as many participants as possible on both sides; ie, it is essential to take into consideration the extensive nature and participation of large masses of people;

4) We must pay attention to another feature of a cultural exchange, that is: it should have a lasting influence wherever it reaches. The Chinese people sometimes humorously call the so-called committee for cultural relations with foreign countries (CCFRC) the second foreign ministry. It is not an official term, but if the committee has done a good job along with the foreign ministry, the two can indeed complement each other.

Qi Ba used his belief in 'seeking common ground while reserving differences' to deal with pluralistic cultures. When handling a complicated situation, he went beyond the similarities and differences of states, nationalities, parties and ideologies; hence, he enjoyed the love and support of people around the world, which was natural and not at all surprising.

2. Qi Ba's Reflections During the Early Post-Liberation Period

2.1. Opposing Excessive Actions in the Land Reform Movement

As early as 1946, when Qi Ba had just met me, a 15-year-old middle school student in Shanghai, he asked me about land reform and mass movements in the liberated area of northern Jiangsu. During our conversation, he said that it had not been enough just to initiate the reform — the political awareness of the people needed to be raised too. In this respect, the leading role of our party ought not to be abandoned. We were to fully implement the party's policies on land reform, and care should be taken to conquer the erroneous tendency of running counter to the policy of the party, or it would bring harm to the revolutionary cause. In the liberated areas, we were to unite people of all social strata, consolidating political power and developing economy and culture side by side to resist the invasion of the KMT troops. Because of the war, large numbers of displaced people from the liberated areas had poured into the areas controlled by the nationalists, including Shanghai. Some of them said something about people getting beaten up or other incidents that ran counter to the party's policy in the land reform movement, which could cause city people to doubt or even misunderstand our policy within the liberated areas. Hence, we had to prevent improper behaviour in order to avoid any unnecessary misunderstandings.

Qi Ba was always a practical and realistic man. He paid close attention to make sure the policies of the party were properly implemented and any erroneous tendencies in our work put right in time. From our conversations, I learnt that he thought the situation in the area near Shanghai, south of the lower reaches of the Yangtze river, was quite different from that in many 'pure' agricultural areas in China. In this region, many city residents still possessed, more or less, land inherited from their ancestors, and the land reform movement would affect their economic interests. But they lived and worked in the cities or towns, and their main income came not from farming, but from other resources. Moreover, since the democratic revolution, Dr Sun Yat-sen had been advocating the socialist proposition of 'land to the tiller', which struck a chord deep in the hearts of the people. Therefore, these city dwellers, after we had patiently explained the extent of the communists' land reform to them, could understand us, so our work could be completed in time. However, it was hard for them to accept the excessive actions that led to abuse of people's dignity and even caused bodily harm. But when I accompanied my grandfather, Ma Shijie, to the town hall of the city of Gaoyou to hand in his land deeds, I did not witness any cases like that. Qi Ba was very happy after hearing my account, thinking that it had proved the importance of the proper implementation of policies. Around this time, he made suggestions to the Central Committee regarding the excessive actions committed during the land reform movement in the liberated areas. In May 1946, he sent a telegram to the Central Committee: "Recently, cities like Shanghai, Nanjing and Chongqing have all received letters, all mentioning, in one voice, the excessive actions during the campaign to expose and criticise landlords in north Jiangsu. Most of the people who wrote the letters have a good opinion of us, so we cannot just reply to them saying that the movement is in the early stages, making these excessive actions unavoidable." He then suggested: "The people in north Jiangsu can carry out the movement in a moderate manner, so that we can win over the middle and upper classes." On 19 July, the Central Committee sent him and Dong Biwu a telegram, saying: "Only the implementation of 'land to the tiller' can lay a solid foundation for national democratisation and industrialisation. Only the land belonging to the major traitors will be confiscated, but we should adopt some other reasonable methods in accordance with the spirit of Dr Sun Yat-san; for example, buying and paying according to an arranged price. The excessive actions are isolated cases, which are hard to avoid. Please inform the democratic league of China about the CPC's land reform policy."

On 17 February 1950, Qi Ba drafted a telegram, jointly signed by Mao Zedong. It was sent to Liu Shaoqi: "Last November, concerning the land reform in south Jiangsu, during a meeting with the Political Bureau, we mentioned that the issue of the rich peasants has to be handled with great care, because it does not only affect them, but the national bourgeoisie as well. Therefore, there should be some differences between the decrees of land reform in south Jiangsu and in the north. As for the 1933 documents and the land law of 1947, they also must be altered."

2.2. Vigilance for the Ultra-Left 'Valorous Elements'

Some years later, when Qi Ba talked to me, a university student, about land reform in the southwest region, he also spoke of some other issues.

He said that in the early stages of the land reform movement it was hard to avoid certain flukes. So-called 'valorous elements' or even 'saboteurs' were frequently undertaking reactionary or ultra-leftist actions to violate the party's policies, and these actions were not easy for the cadres and masses to distinguish from real party policy. On the contrary; some honest and prudent people had concerns, but they were slow to take action and needed the cadres to do more to inspire them. I would come to have a more profound understanding of Qi Ba's words when I took part in all sorts of mass movements later on.

The leading cadres must be good at seeing through the 'valorous elements' in an ultra-leftist operation. They must not only stop their actions in time, but also prevent them from misleading the masses and disrupting the correct implementation of policies. They must prevent these elements from being regarded as activists and sneaking into the cadre ranks, or even being put in an important position to shoulder the responsibility of leadership, which in the long run could cause great damage from within. As far as I know, on 20 July 1948, Qi Ba drafted a directive to the East China Bureau on behalf of the Central Committee, which said: "When putting on key demonstrations for land reform as well as consolidation of the party, we should put together the cadres who have been trained and who are quite sure they can do the job. Work is to start simultaneously in one or several counties under the prefecture level. After they have gained experience, the work should then spread to other regions. We should not carry out the work in a scattered or isolated fashion, in order to prevent the saboteurs from inciting their so-called 'spontaneous movement'." The above records are not only a historical testimony, but also a reflection of Qi Ba's consistent ideological style — that is, seeking truth and being pragmatic. More often than not, he dared to defy the gossip, conscientiously speaking out from a sense of justice and offering suggestions based on facts.

2.3. Safeguarding the Interests of Newborn Middle-Class Peasants

After the land reform, large numbers of middle-class peasants emerged among the population of the countryside. According to regular practice in those years, Qi Ba asked me to write him a report on this topic for reference.

In my report, I stressed that this was a normal phenomenon, and that the numerous middle-class peasants were people for us to unite and rely on.

The emergence of the middle-class peasants was a major social change that resulted from the completion of the land reform. Poor and lower-middle-class peasants took the initiative in production on the land they possessed, which led to an increase in agricultural and sideline products, particularly grain. As a result, surplus grain was available besides that which individual farming families consumed themselves. In order to obtain cash or to regulate the demand for grain, farmers often looked at the change in the market and then decided if they would sell their surplus grain, waiting for the highest bid. Thus, some areas received insufficient stocks, and it became difficult to supply the market. But it was normal for a farmer to sell surplus grain based on the changes of the market, and the government could not resort to coercive administrative actions or even deprive the farmers their due rights. This required us to spare no trouble to implement measures of scientifically calculated price control, which considered the interests of production, transportation and sales. For this, Qi Ba was very happy with me, saying: "All those years, the Soviet Union often magnified the 'middle-class peasant problem', fearing that newly rich peasants would tend towards capitalism at any moment. But if you can think and act in this way, it seems that you really are 'young and fearless'!"

But we can never blindly model ourselves on the actions of foreign countries; we simply have to regard the varied nature of selling grain as the unpredictable cause that sparks market fluctuations, thus making many local governments crudely cut off the connection between farmer and market, which will affect their initiative regarding production and selling. In particular, we should be careful not to cause a shortage of supply, and also try to avoid damping the farmers' initiative while producing and selling, because this may cause problems with sales, which in turn could cause instability in some areas.

2.4. Respecting Market Regularity, Complying with the Change in Supply and Demand

The newborn powers managed the grain supply, a job relating to the basic life support of every household. We could never let our guard down, or it would affect social stability, as well as the trust the people had in the new authorities. Qi Ba attached great importance to this issue and repeatedly took up the matter personally, even taking part in some related calculations.

From 1949, when I joined the army, to 1954, when I went to university, I worked various frontline jobs in the southwest. Qi Ba thought me a young idealist who did not pursue personal interests and had left the leading bodies voluntarily, instead choosing to work at a primary level. I had gained some understanding of the work and construction in the newly liberated areas that Qi Ba was interested in. During my first winter holiday after I'd left university, he let me stay in his residence for the convenience of being able to talk to me. He asked me to "talk about every experience, not missing a single one". He was trying to learn more about specific cases from me, which was his usual style of working.

In 1952, I took on the position of acting director of the grain bureau in Leshan prefecture, Sichuan. To solve the grain problem in the newly liberated areas, at the very beginning the new authorities had to send armed troops to the countryside to impose grain levies, appealing to the village heads or township leaders installed by the previous government to do the job. We needed to avoid armed attacks and robberies by KMT underground forces or local bandits, and, in addition, make sure we had enough grain to supply to the city residents, the army and the staff from the governmental organisations, which in itself was not a small issue. The situation changed with the development of the land reform, as grain from Sichuan could now supply the whole country besides the province itself. Sichuan is one of the biggest producers of grain in China, and one of the sources that play a decisive role in the country's grain production. Many problems relating to production, supply, sales, storage and processing, as well as the numerous intermediate links, did not permit any negligence; hence, I didn't dare to be slack about my work.

At the time, I was leading a team to work with a chosen primary-level unit in the countryside to gain first-hand experience. I found out that the formerly poor and lower-middle-class peasants had surplus grain after they had been given land. Their initiatives for production had paid off and they had already become middle-class peasants from an economic point of view. Thus, after paying the grain levies and keeping a small amount for self-consumption, they could sell the remaining grain at the market.

The policy of monopolising, purchasing and marketing had not been implemented at the time. The problem of purchasing and marketing the grain of tens of thousands of middle-class peasants did not only affect the regional economy, but also the country's state of preparation against war and natural disasters. If it wasn't dealt with properly, social stability would be in jeopardy — particularly the consolidation of the new regional authorities. But the surplus grain was scattered everywhere, and farmers were waiting for the price to go up, predicting that this situation would cause new economic problems; hence, after I returned to the city, I increased the stock. Meanwhile, through organisations on the basic level we explained to the citizens that there had been an increase in grain production and that the stock in the state warehouses could guarantee a basic supply, while regulating the market and making different products available could give us extra supplies. Thus, there was no need to panic.

Besides this, I implemented a series of measures to deal with the problem of a rush to buy stocks. For example, I called together the grain-processing manufacturers and the retailers, telling them that we would oppose any unlawful hoarding and speculation, making clear what their social responsibilities were. Therefore, when the other regions in Sichuan experienced a temporary grain shortage after an increase in production, we in Leshan district had a rather stable grain supply and a good social order. For this achievement, I was invited to give a speech in Chengdu. In my speech, I pointed out that we could not simply apply coercive administrative measures to middle-class peasants besides those mentioned above; we could also calculate and formulate reasonable prices for grain, so as to benefit from our control of the market.

2.5. Let the People's Hands Lead the Market

It was not easy to keep supplying grain to the huge population in the early stages of new China. Qi Ba once said to me: "Monopolising the purchase of grain and marketing it is an action we must take to prevent the grain shortage from causing social unease. It will only be applied for a certain period of time. In addition, we must improve research on market control and implement price control. In the long run, when there is a large increase in grain production and sufficient surplus for the market, the government needs to adjust to the new situation, stop the monopolisation of purchasing and marketing policies, and make changes to related policies and actions."

I understood Qi Ba's thoughts; he meant that monopolising the economy is not a long-term solution. The country's progress and the improvements to the people's livelihoods are inseparable from the supply of grain. It is a pity that the country had been through many social upheavals already, which made his plans hard to be realised at the time and went against his original intentions. They also made him mentally and physically exhausted. Numerous cadres and people, including his relatives, like me, showed him heartfelt sympathy, trust, understanding and support.

Regarding the market economy, he raised some heuristic questions about the elementary knowledge of economics I had picked up at university. For example, he once asked me: "In the West, there is a widespread theory that says the market economy is an invisible hand that has certain authority. Do you think this is right?" Thinking that he must have a profound understanding of the subject, I replied in an exploratory manner: "It is not an invisible hand. There are too many hands participating in the market, making it difficult to see the problem clearly. Moreover, some large commercial interests do not want people to be aware of any problems." Qi Ba was very happy with what I had said, saying that this was what he was thinking and that one day, in the future, the people would lead the market, and it would be a day worth celebrating!

Even today, I am still deeply moved by what he said. No matter how many theories the ancients left to us or imported from foreign countries, we must combine them with the reality of our own country. We can approach economic theories practically and realistically, but we should not follow them blindly or take a one-sided approach.

The noted Chinese economist Xu Dixin associated with me for many years during his lifetime. He was an outstanding scholar who worked directly at Qi Ba's side. He once said to me that in the early period of new China, Qi Ba came up with an important economic theory: namely, that it was better to extend the life of the new democratic society. I myself had the same impression. Qi Ba asked me many times about the situation in the newly liberated areas, the border areas and the mountain areas where the ethnic minorities lived. As a result, he thought that the diversity among economic elements should be perpetuated. Combined with my practical work, he pointed out that by economic means such as regional, wholesale, retail, and even seasonal price differences, varied economic elements could be regulated to achieve a balanced development of the country and society. In this way, the development would be more reasonable and beneficial to the improvement of people's lives and society as a whole.

3. Around the Time of the Great Leap Forward

3.1. Playing Ping-Pong with Qi Ba

In 1956, I played an unusual game of ping-pong with Qi Ba. The reason I call it 'unusual' is because I had received a notice from my university asking me to go to West Flower Hall to play ping-pong with him. Later, I found out that this game had taken place under special circumstances. As premier of a large country, it was difficult for him to find time to do something only for pleasure. However, it was by no means a rare occasion, due to the advice of his secretary, Xu Ming, that he should get more physical exercise for the sake of his health.

I was then both happy and nervous. Happy, because there were not many opportunities like this, to play ping-pong with Qi Ba, a high official as well as a member of the older generation; nervous, because I knew that he had fallen from horseback when he was in Yan'an and badly injured his right arm. He hadn't received any immediate medical attention, and although he had gone to the Soviet Union for treatment, his right arm was a bit bent and he was unable to wave as he wanted. Back then, I was young and lacking in life experience, wrongly thinking that the 50-year-old premier was 'getting on in years' — if he fell to the ground by accident, I would have committed an unforgivable error. Hence, I exchanged my fast attacks for a slow defence during the game.

Zhou Enlai playing ping-pong.

Qi Ba smartly noticed my change in pace: "The aim for our contest should be 'seeking to win but not seeking to be stable'." Smiling, he said to me: "Young people are generally eager to succeed, so they are short-tempered. If you tried to win on the basis of stability, it could be a big step towards toughening your character. You've come to help me to keep fit, while I help you to steel your attitude: here's a way to satisfy both sides."

Probably because he was not nimble with his right arm, his skills seemed average; however, from the beginning to the end, he was full of vigour and in high spirits. This friendly game made me feel that he was very happy to play with me. While playing, he would smile and say something light, which relaxed my tense nerves at once, and we ended our game without a hitch.

The room was small and without decorations. There was only the one table, making people feel like it was absolutely empty. The equipment could not even compare to that of an ordinary university. Qi Ba wore a normal Chinese tunic suit rather than sportswear. From this small instance, I once again understood that simplicity was the daily standard that he had been following for a long time as the head of a large country.

I later learnt that this game had an underlying political reason. Qi Ba had been opposing the blind, high speed of the country's economic development, the so-called opposition to a rushed advance. It was a normal and correct attitude, but met with severe criticism, as some people regarded him as "only 50 metres short" of being a rightist. He was ready to resign from his office. His secretary was worried that the premier, though always magnanimous and tolerant, giving no thought to personal gain, had become like a high-speed car driving on a motorway: if it stops abruptly, the car will turn over and the driver will get injured both physically and mentally. So, his secretary persuaded Qi Ba to take a break and play some ping-pong.

3.2. "I Speak as My Conscience Dictates"

In 1956, according to Hu Qiaomu's reminiscences, on all fronts and in all provinces and cities, people in the Chinese countryside followed the spirit of Mao Zedong's new tide of socialism and began to speed up and expand the previously made plans, increasing guidance for the budget. In the last 10 days of April, during a meeting of the Political Bureau held in Yiniantang hall in Zhongnanhai, Mao Zedong put forward a supplementary budget on capital construction for 1956, which was met with opposition by the people attending the meeting. Qi Ba made most of the speeches, insisting that supplementing a budget would cause tension in the supply of materials, increase the urban population and bring in a series of problems. Mao Zedong persisted in his opinion and announced the meeting adjourned. Afterwards, Qi Ba went to see Mao Zedong, saying: "I spoke as my conscience dictated," and it angered Mao Zedong very much.

Qi Ba had talked to me about the institutional reform of the economic management. In the first few years after the founding of new China, the highly centralised economic management played an important role in the recovery of the national economy, as well as in its large-scale economic construction. However, it also exposed some of its disadvantages. From March to April of 1956, Qi Ba spent a lot of energy studying this problem. Between May and August, he held a state conference. When he had edited the draft of his speech, he pointed out that the disadvantages of too much centralisation should be addressed, so in his speech he said: "Giving free range to the initiatives of local authorities is an important condition for our socialist construction. Currently, we have achieved a decisive victory in our country's socialist transformation. The democratic dictatorship of the people has become even stronger, which makes it necessary and also possible for us to adopt the principle that under unified leadership, managing at different levels and in line with the local conditions, we can further divide the central and the local administrative functions and powers in order to improve the administrative system of our country, and to bring the initiative of the common people into full play."

He also pointed out the issue of applying the law of value more effectively. He said: "Under the leadership of the centralised market of the state and in a planned way, we are going to establish some free markets. Within certain limits, they will produce and market products all by themselves. For some consumer goods we will practice selective purchasing. For all commodities we will grade and fix prices accordingly. These measures will not do any damage, but play a complementary role to the unified market of the country."

3.3. To Be More 'Leftist' or More 'Rightist'?

Qi Ba once asked Mr Fan Ruoyu (a Marxist theorist) to find him the source of the following quotation by Karl Marx: "Mankind thus inevitably sets itself only such tasks as it is able to solve, since closer examination will always show that the problem itself arises only when the material conditions for its solution are already present or at least in the course of formation." Mr Fan told him that it was from the preface to *A Contribution to the Critique of Political Economy*.

In this spirit, the eighth National Congress stipulated the policy for the country's construction as follows: "In order to develop our country from a backward agricultural country into an advanced industrial country, we must allow three five-year plans, or even more time, to build our industry up to become a basically complete system. The realisation of this target will be decided by whether we can actually produce, not by a high output. For a country this size, a slight slump in the increase of quantity will not hamper the realisation of a primarily complete industrial system."

Qi Ba explained: "After all, any country, when building socialism, needs a bit of independent capacity, particularly a country like China. Otherwise, when the wind rustles the leaves, no other countries will come to help us. In a country this size, all aspects are required to cooperate properly with one another. It is unfeasible that economic development only takes place in a single sector, so the speed will be lower. Take iron and steel, for example; our tentative plan is to set our target for the third five-year plan at 20 to 25 million tons. We might surpass the target if we do a good job. But we cannot set the target at 30 million tons, because if we do, the other quarters must catch up. As we often say: 'Hang both feet in the air, and disorder arises underneath.' It will cause difficulties in making overall arrangements, while the agricultural and light industries will be affected too, and as a consequence the target has to come down."

Then he took a clear-cut stand on the issue: "The plan and policies for next year must ensure certain areas are prioritised. Some areas have consumed too many resources, so they need to shrink a bit, but this does not mean that there is no focal point. Overall, we should downsize, otherwise we will wobble, which will affect our currency, goods, materials, labour and wages. We should be aware not to let happen in China what has happened in Poznán in Poland, where 100,000 people, or even more, took to the streets to present a petition. This is a serious problem." He also talked about the domestic economic policy, based on his observations of the overall international situation. He said: "When we worked out the first five-year plan, the Korean war was still going on, so we had to step up our efforts to create heavy industry and a national defence industry. After the armistice in 1953, we needed to have a look at the situation in the whole world. After the Geneva conference at the end of last year and the Bandung conference at the beginning of this year, we slowly sensed a relaxation in the international situation. Under such circumstances, we are planning for this year and the next to slow down the development of the defence industry; some of the production will be reduced, and that is a very natural thing to do."

To show his determination, he said, resolutely and decisively: "Imagine: there will probably be a period of peace that allows us to build a comprehensive industrial complex. This would be the best situation for us, and we will base our policy on this. But we also need to prepare for another possibility: the outbreak of war. This is decided by seeing if the enemy wants to take a risk. If war breaks out within 12 years, how is it going to be? Doesn't that mean we've made a mistake? If war breaks out and we are short of arms and munition, or if after we mobilise the reservists we find that we have no arms to equip them, then everyone will shriek and complain. However, at least we'd only commit such an error once. When it happens, we can redeem our sins and atone for our crimes by doing good deeds. I only have this method; otherwise we would simply hesitate at the crossroads, walking eastward several steps and then returning to walk several steps westward. If we gather all the equipment and funds to invest in the defence industry, thus producing fewer other products, so that people's livelihoods will not improve, tension will be high on all sides. But if arms have been produced and there is no war, we cannot eat those cannons and guns. Manufacturing too many bullets would turn out to be a disadvantage, so we must make the right decision."

On the same day, Liu Shaoqi expressed his opinion about the proportions and pace of the economic construction in his speech. "We should pay attention to this question," he said, "that is, the accumulation of capital for state and society. How many funds should we reserve for current investment, and how many for future investment? The proportion of funds towards the development of heavy and light industries and agriculture, as well as the speed of our industrial construction, should be put on a safe and reliable base. What could be safe and reliable? The common people will not go into the streets and create a disturbance while they are happy and enthusiastic. Yesterday, comrade Chen Yun also favoured the idea that we should slow down a bit, for a year or two… slow down for one year in every five, and it will be safer; that is to say, it will be a bit rightist. Which is better? A bit rightist or a bit leftist? Yesterday, some comrades said that even if we slow down a bit or become a bit rightist, it is still possible to make changes. If it is a bit excessive and a bit leftist, it won't be possible to make any changes."

Under the guidance of the 1957 national economy plan, the national economy developed healthily. The total output of industry, agriculture and state revenue was rising steadily, and the country basically realised a balance between state revenue, commodities and credit. The stabilisation of the market had been ensured, making 1957 the best year for economic construction since the founding of new China. Towards the end of the year, the country had surpassed the economic target of the first five-year plan by a large margin. A good position for the economic construction of the second five-year plan presented itself before all the people in the country.

3.4. How to Approach the Struggle within the Party and Avoid Being Privileged

After the eighth National Congress of the CPC in 1956, Qi Ma felt tired and was in poor health. She needed a rest, so Qi Ba called me in. "Have the party's solutions been relayed to you? Are you taking part in the study?" he asked me. "No, they haven't been relayed to the cadres of my rank." As usual, he stopped discussing the subject with me. Then he asked me if I had anything to tell him or if I needed his help, so I talked about a topic related to myself.

At university, I disagreed with what my department had done, feeling that some of their measures were not in keeping with the regulations of the party constitution. Furthermore, from what I saw and heard, such problems were quite common in the basic working units. Naively, I thought I could write to the NPC, hoping to bring it to the attention of the Central Committee, thus solving the problems in order to benefit the implementation of the work of the party and, in return, winning support for the party from the masses. But I never imagined that my letter would be passed on to my department, naturally causing the people involved to bear resentment against me. Their reactions put me under a lot of pressure and led me to believe that there would be no more places I could write to, making it difficult to undertake my daily activities.

After my confession, Qi Ba gently breathed a sigh, then talked to me about some matters of principle regarding the struggles within the party. They are as follows:

1) The party and society are inseparable;

2) Pay attention to and adopt an appropriate attitude towards the struggles within the party;

3) Attach importance to sound self-development, overcoming shortcomings immediately in order to check erroneous ideas at the outset;

4) Pay attention to the relationship between the party and the masses;

5) Guard against the leading group's day-to-day privileges.

The following is my recollection of the points above, one by one:

Firstly, the party and society are inseparable. Qi Ba was talking to me, a young intellectual who was simple and enthusiastic but lacking in political and social experience, and who was also part of his family's younger generation. Hence, he discussed the subject in a casual manner.

He said that young intellectuals are generally high in spirits, but lacking in experience. When they look at a problem, they often substitute political enthusiasm for objective reality. They rely on their book knowledge to observe complicated social phenomena, so it is easy for them to idealise the party. When they meet with some unreasonable realities or suffer setbacks, being unable to stick to their principles, they will feel dispirited and be at a loss as to what to do.

In fact, not only are the party and society inseparable, but the party is also an important component of society. Its vanguard role reflects the need to not only absorb society's progressive individuals, but also to prevent bad elements or even dissidents from being absorbed into the party in order to maintain purity. The same importance applies to keeping one's own advancement on the moral path and ideological line. Only in this way can the party truly be a guide for the masses. Only through continuously carrying forward good points and overcoming shortcomings, and making unceasing efforts to make the party itself healthy and further its development, can it put itself in an invincible position.

The party needs to absorb nutrients from society and constantly get rid of the bad influences that have already infiltrated. Such work is independent of man's will and has never ceased, even for a day. Therefore, the struggle within the party is not only a reflection of objective reality but also of having a wider social base outside the party organisation itself. Sometimes even the interior of the Central Committee cannot keep out of the affair.

Secondly, we must pay attention and adopt an appropriate attitude towards the struggles within the party. As stated above, the party organisation is an important component of society. Inner-party struggles have objective social foundations and are inseparable from assorted ideological struggles in society. They have their social and historical sources, and we need to adopt a correct attitude towards their occurrence as well as their development, and handle them carefully and skilfully. By doing so we will be able to preserve the party's vanguard role. It is impossible for the party to undergo any spontaneous developments; once it meets with a significant problem, it will bring disadvantages or destructive effects to its own development, as well as society's. As party members, any problem between an individual and the organisation or with the other members should be in line with the attitude mentioned above: it should be handled with them with skill and correctness.

Thirdly, we must attach importance to healthy self-development and to checking erroneous ideas at the outset. Our party achieved an absolute leading position after the nationwide establishment of the new political power. It can use the power it has to do good deeds for the people, leading the masses to propel history forward. Any carelessness will bring great harm to the interests of the people and the development of society. Hence, as the party in power, we must check erroneous ideas at the outset, make no move without careful thought and make no careless decisions, nor act presumptuously while strictly doing what we can to put an end to becoming privileged.

Fourthly, we must attach importance to the relations between the party and the common people. During the period of revolution, and particularly during the war, the vanguard role of the party organisation and its members was usually to take the lead and not fear death. But in a time of peace, and as a result of being in power for a long period of time, it is even more important to preserve both the vanguard and exemplary roles of party members. We must be modest and prudent, and on guard against arrogance and rashness.

I remember Qi Ba once severely criticised his secretary of many years, because he had re-laid Qi Ba's wooden floor. Though it was a trivial matter, Qi Ba thought of the exemplary role the leader of the country must play. If the premier took the lead, the other ministers would surely follow in redecorating their offices or residences, leading to a large cost compared to the national economic situation; hence, he treated the matter with gravity. Accepting privileges would damage the relations between the party and the masses, and, by gradual accumulation, form a gravely unhealthy relationship between them, which would affect the effectiveness of the party's rule as well as its position, and would also affect the progress and development of the country, even to the extent of causing social instability.

Fifthly, we must prevent the leader of the ruling party from receiving privileges. Because of their different needs in work and life, they have already received rather favourable treatment from the government, which can be understood and supported by the public. However, because there is a lack of effective supervision by the masses from top to bottom, some individuals among the leaders abuse their power for their own interests. The nature of this problem has become very serious. If more leaders do the same, the masses will confront the privileged class who have violated their basic rights, and the situation will get out of hand.

As I recall, Qi Ba once said to me that when he went to the Soviet Union, he witnessed many similar situations, which made him worried that the danger the leaders of the Soviet Union faced was not only the result of long-term ignorance of the ideological work of the party members and the masses. The basic problem was that the gradually privileged leaders would seriously clash with the people. It was a worrying situation, and furthermore, it would become more precarious in the future. Later, after experiencing ups and downs, the party finally disintegrated; indeed, one must admire Qi Ba's wisdom and foresight that still calls for deep thought from us today.

The two-line struggle involved the directions in which the party and the country were developing. It was a major issue of principle. During the war of liberation, we could have achieved complete military victory, or we could have seized state power and built a new power base. It involved the life and death of the party itself. After we had achieved victory, the question remained whether the power could be consolidated and if we could maintain the long-term stability of the country. Hence, the struggle between these two directions was also an important political choice every party member had to make at the critical moment. Such a struggle requires that everyone adopt a serious attitude, never lowering our guard. Besides, the party seeks a healthy development, which also involves the party leading the people of the country to choose the right direction; that is to say, it's in every family's basic interest. But according to the grave historical lessons the party has learnt, the two-line struggle is also a complicated issue, and it involves two aspects. The first is that we must strictly distinguish between two categories of contradictions, be good to the comrades who possess different opinions or have committed mistakes, and allow them to correct their errors. Being correct once does not mean we will always be correct. We should not be carried away by our achievements to avoid committing new errors. The second aspect is that we must make scientific, historical and thorough investigations, distinguishing right from wrong. The reason for this is that the wrong opinions sometimes get the upper hand, and in such circumstances the party must correct them to avoid wronging an innocent person, which will cause greater loss to our work and people. A party with vitality can easily correct its mistakes. When uniting people within and outside the party who hold different opinions, the only criterion for judging right from wrong is practice, so we must draw a clear distinction between these two, as well as between the two categories of contradictions, and do our best to avoid hurting ourselves.

To correctly identify these problems, one does not only need to make a subjective effort, but also to keep an open mind and remain unbiased. This subjective effort entails calmly and objectively analysing both domestic and international situations when these problems occur and their specific environments; only by doing that can we draw a reasonable conclusion. If a party can correctly handle the two-line struggle, it should not only keep track of current developments, but also look backwards and forwards and take into consideration the overall gain and loss.

In short, as far as I know, although Qi Ba had been aware of two-line struggles among the highest leaders over a long time and was even wronged several times himself, which shouldn't have happened to him, it appeared that he was able to uphold a selfless attitude, knowing what's what and keeping an open mind, thus helping the party to endure. He set high demands for himself and had the same expectations and requirements for later generations and younger party members.

3.5. Can Sulphuric Acid Billow in a Plant?

During the period of the Great Leap Forward, the grand mass-movement of launching high-yield satellites took place nationwide, quite the opposite of today's scientific outlook on development as advocated by the party centre. The unfortunate result was a huge waste of both human and material resources. Under the circumstances, neither the institutions of higher learning nor the foreign languages department of Nankai University, which had the lowest number of students, could stay out of the matter.

One of the projects connected to the launching of the so-called high-yield satellites, initiated by a small number of people in our university, was to set up a sulphuric acid plant using local methods of production. Some individuals even advertised, without evidence, that this project had yielded good results, advertising with slogans such as 'sulphuric acid billowing everywhere', boasting about high-yield sulphuric acid that didn't exist. Because the equipment used in the local methods was not up to standard, although the young male and female students were working day and night, the vicissitudes of the chemical industry ensured they were short of both the necessary equipment and the knowledge for the technical operations. Therefore, not only did they fail to gather any sulphuric acid, but the mother liquor also evaporated due to overheating. The surrounding area was filled with an unbearable stink, so people began avoiding it. The experiments also caused health problems to the students working there. At that moment, Liu Zhucai, party secretary and administrative assistant of the foreign languages department, asked me to take over leadership of the factory, requiring me to reverse the situation as soon as possible. I worked very hard for several days, and my padded jacket became covered in burn marks from splashes of acid. Once, I was working in the factory when I suddenly felt a sharp pain near my eye. Luckily we had a doctor close by, and he washed my eye with water. Afterwards he told me that if there had been any delay, the consequences would have been very severe. Then it occurred to me that I could ask the technicians at the regular sulphuric acid factory for help.

I reported this to Qi Ba. He agreed with me, saying: "In a big, modern factory, even engineers who are equipped with professional knowledge need to cooperate with experienced master workers. In addition, you are all young students of the arts, who lack the experience of working in a factory. It's no good for you to work blindly like this; you should know that safety during production is not a small thing, but a matter concerning the health of your students. The party and the state care a lot about the students' smooth development. Even the students' parents would not shut their eyes to this matter."

I took his point seriously and quickly asked for help from a large factory. They sent us several master workers, and we first improved the local methods. We put a catalyst and other accessories inside a large earthenware vat. Then the master workers gave us an on-the-spot demonstration, and we were finally able to produce some sulphuric acid. Comrade Liu breathed a sigh of relief, and he has been a close fellow student of mine ever since.

Qi Ba told me that the university should re-examine this project, as a factory run in a similar way would produce very little, and it was hard to guarantee the quality of the product. As there was a low safety margin and the project was causing environmental pollution, the university should dismantle it as soon as possible. What happened later proved what Qi Ba had said, and in the end the university dismantled this project they had blindly started.

In those years, Qi Ba also wrote and gave speeches to oppose the so-called spontaneity of the spontaneous mass movement, but he was criticised for being "only 50 metres short" of being a rightist. However, facts speak louder than words. With the support of the other leaders, Qi Ba put forward ideas according to the policy of 'regulating, consolidating, substantiating and improving', and after several years' efforts, the economic situation in China finally recovered.

3.6. An Innovative Experiment Comes to a Premature End

Today, everyone knows that Qi Ba held firmly to the principle of seeking truth from facts and that he opposed the policy of putting undue emphasis on high-speed development in those years. However, after Chairman Mao

Zedong personally initiated the Great Leap Forward and the party centre made the decision as well, the masses were mobilized. Just as before, Qi Ba had to comply with the organisational principle to actively patronize it. Besides, he paid attention to guiding the country properly, making some practical achievements while reducing unnecessary losses, trying to discover new things and giving these the requested support. As I recall and understand it, China's situation dictated that this was the only feasible course of action and attitude a mature and conscientious politician could choose.

In 1958, I was still studying at Nankai University, and concurrently held the position of secretary of the general Youth League branch. Meanwhile, I was elected chairperson of the student union of the foreign languages department. The period between 1958 and 1960 was the time of the Great Leap Forward; but at the same time, the movement of technological innovation and revolution, mechanisation, semi-mechanisation, automation and semi-automation had begun. During these two years, several things happened to my department: one of them was the trial production of electrical audio-visual equipment and the application of it. At the time, classes were suspended and the students caught up in the revolution, and universities were giving priority to physical labour. I was assigned the task of undertaking some scientific projects and presenting them as gifts to the party and the country. As a student of the arts, especially language, I thought about it over and over again, feeling that I should design a most useful and applicable device and name it 'the audio-visual support instruction'. Not knowing if this kind of facility already existed at home or abroad, I prepared to carry out this innovative experiment.

One of my guiding ideas was to try and make an electrically operated item. Teachers and students should be able to operate it with ease, even if they had received no training; my idea was to make it by hand and let it become our assistant during future studies, to raise our level of efficiency — not to replace the teachers, but so they could complement each other. Studying a foreign language at home is different from studying it in a native country, so I wanted my equipment to enable us to improve our teaching and learning environment. With students able to train themselves with regard to listening and watching, we could improve our listening, speaking, writing and translation skills.

I carefully selected around 20 students from different years: male, female, old (the mature and higher-grade students) and young (the first-year students). The key members were two former army radio operators (their knowledge and technique on the subject were only basic), while the other students were assigned different jobs according to their character and skills. For example, Ms Chu Xiuyun only had an ordinary interest in studying a language, but she was able to sit down and extensively study the scientific background that had no connection with the foreign language she was studying. Despite the conditions — she was lacking sufficient technical data and outside help — she succeeded in making a tape for recording after repeated research and tests. The two former army radio operators led us to use relays and 16 mm film to record a film in a foreign language, which could be replayed or paused. The pictures presented different scenes, while the characters in the film delivered the spoken language. They also used an ordinary intercom to enable students to practice speaking at a distance.

After more than 70 days and nights, we finally had a result, and all of us were very excited about it. The whole department liked and supported this set of audio-visual support instructions. Later, the leaders of Hebei province and the city of Tianjin heard about its success, and we were asked to give a presentation at the university.

I reported this to Qi Ba and he was very happy. He praised the efforts of his old school. "It's good to win the support of your university," he said to me. "If there are science students at the university or at other universities, as well as people from businesses that can take part, you can make an even greater achievement."

Unfortunately, I then fell ill and had to rest up for a while. After the smelting of iron and the laughable experiments in the development of 'high-yield satellites' in the agricultural sector failed one after another, the project of my audio-visual support instructions was also cancelled. After Qi Ba learnt about it, he was very sorry. "What a pity!" he would say repeatedly.

In fact, Qi Ba would express his objections to some projects, whether or not they were related to scientific research or production, if they were done recklessly; but if they had already been approved by the Central Committee, or if the public had been mobilised to carry them out, he could only lead them properly, trying to achieve as much as he could while reducing unnecessary loss and waste. He once said to me: "No matter if it is scientific research, or an industrial or agricultural activity — we all need to be serious, making no move without carefully thinking it over. But after we have started, if we create something from nothing, we should protect, support and lead the enthusiasm of the leaders and the people. If we put a full stop to the campaign, then we'll be committing another mistake and causing another loss to the party and the people. This requires us to summarise our mistakes, so we can learn a lesson from previous errors."

Under the circumstances, Qi Ba would go against the current and persist in dealing with the affairs of the party and country in a responsible and scientific manner. This showed a spirit that was worthwhile for us later generations to adopt. Such thoughts about respecting the scientific rules of development do not only exemplify the guiding ideas of the time, but also give enlightenment and imbue the scientific outlook on development as it is promoted today, as well as any future work, with a warning role. It doesn't matter if it is the leaders' request or the people's spontaneous initiative; this creative endeavour should be protected, especially newly developed items, which should be given more support, but still it needs to be dealt with scientifically, and we must analyse its advantages and disadvantages. Once it is put into effect, we must treasure the human and material resources. During testing, we must make corrections or adjustments. We should not act arbitrarily by either pushing it or cancelling it — that is not consistent with the requirements of the scientific outlook on development.

3.7. Qi Ba Returns to His Alma Mater, Nankai University

Walking into the campus of Nankai University on the banks of the beautiful Mati lake, where the lotus flowers bloom, one can see a monument of Qi Ba. Under his bust, a sentence is inscribed that he wrote to his classmates studying in Japan, when he was young: "I am indeed in love with Nankai." It is a vivid portrait of Qi Ba and shows that he was a man full of affection. The emotions expressed by the premier were always broad and sincere, not

The Years of National Construction

only to his relatives, but also to revolutionary military personnel, veteran cadres, old friends in the world of literature and art, workers and peasants, people from ethnic minority groups, his former classmates, relatives and friends from his hometown, many foreign friends, and, of course, his old school and university.

As I recall, during the 1950s he returned to his old university three times. He usually used his holiday time to visit Tianjin city, his second hometown, where he would visit his old university: Nankai University. When he visited it in May in 1957, I was a student there, so I would like to give a brief account of this visit.

Having a strong sense of principle, Qi Ba did not inform me of his visit in advance, so I, like everybody else, waited for his arrival with excitement. Qi Ma came too, but she remained at the back of the group, so except for the entourage, few people knew that she had come too. During this short tour, Qi Ba visited the library, the chemistry department, the foreign languages department, the lecture rooms, the laboratories, the student dormitories and the dining halls. Wherever he went, people were exhilarated, warmly greeting him and reluctantly saying farewell when the tour had ended.

During the visit, Qi Ba said to the reporters that he could not control how they were going to report what he said, but that they must respect his opinion on how they were to report his comments. To avoid any unnecessary influence on society, they should not report some of his words as they pleased. That is Qi Ba, respecting reporters while being discreet in both word and deed himself.

In one of the science laboratories, when he was told that some of the experiments they did had reached the international level and some of the achievements in the scientific research had been number one in the entire world, he said: "Don't say 'number one' so often. We do not have a full picture of the situation [of science] in the whole world, so we'd better have fewer words but more action. When you genuinely achieve the position of number one in the world, the government will join you in promoting it."

When he walked into the student dormitory, seeing eight students sharing one room with one big desk, he went to measure the length of the table and found it only had space for four students at the same time. He

The monument on the campus of Nankai University. The inscription reads: "I am indeed in love with Nankai."

asked at once what they were going to do with the other four. When told that they could go to the library, he then felt at ease. He said that we would slowly improve our conditions, reducing the number of students to a room to six or four. From this, we can see that he had a down-to-earth style of working and cared deeply for students.

In the dining hall, he asked the chefs about the preparation of the meals. He bought two steamed corn buns with money and a grain coupon, and then started to eat with relish.

He then gave a short speech to the staff and students on the small square on the east side of the administrative building. Humorously, but with a matter-of-fact attitude, he talked about the "big multiplication and division". He said that our country had a large population, and if each person consumed even a little bit more, a large number of materials would be consumed by the whole country; and in production, if each person contributed more, multiplying the numbers of the population, the output would be greatly increased. On the contrary, if we divided the natural resources or material supplies over this huge population, each of us would get less on average. He explained this profound idea in simple terms, vividly describing to us the basic national conditions that we could not ignore.

1959, Zhou Enlai visiting his alma mater, Nankai University. The man on his immediate right is the party secretary of the university, Gao Yangyun.

He went to the toilet and found that the lids for the water tanks had gone missing. Guessing that they had probably been taken to produce iron and steel, he said that we should not smelt iron and steel without thinking. If we were to smelt useful materials into scrap iron, that would really be a shame.

At the time, the Great Leap Forward was underway. Regarding the speed of the development, he insisted that the country should be realistic. For this he was unfairly criticised, and he was even forced to criticise himself. However, when he was at his old school, he stuck to his principle of being true to facts, using simple language to express his appeal that matched his usual pragmatic attitude towards the matter he was observing, showing in

Zhou Enlai having lunch in the staff canteen at Nankai University.

all respects his noble character as a great statesman who was not going to be restrained by brief gains and losses.

In the foreign languages department, he asked a female student to read a passage from the text book aloud. She was shy, so the premier encouraged her. He corrected her wrong pronunciations, showing her how to pronounce them correctly. When he heard that the students usually had five lectures in the morning, he proposed that the number of lectures be reduced to four, thinking that the students were spending too much time studying and that fatigue could affect their efficiency. In the dining hall, he told the students that, for their health, they must spend three quarters of an hour eating their meals.

Premier Zhou Enlai cared about the students; thus, when he returned to his old university, it was as if he was once again part of the harmonious community of his youth.

After the visit ended and he returned to the hotel, the security people at the university asked me to go to the hotel to meet him. When we were having a meal, I sat with chief security guard Cheng Yuangong and the other guards. "The food the premier eats at home is much simpler than the food here," Cheng said. In fact, the food in the hotel was very ordinary. Because I would often go to West Flower Hall and have meals with Qi Ba and Qi Ma, I knew that their life was no different from that of ordinary people.

Later, during my holiday from university, I went to see Qi Ba and Qi Ma. He asked me about the teachers' and students' reactions regarding his visit. I gave him a brief account of the news that I had heard directly or indirectly. He gave me a stare, then smiled and said: "I am certain that there is one thing you haven't said clearly." I could make neither head nor tail of what he was saying, wondering what I had missed. "There must have been someone saying that me eating steamed corn buns in the dining hall only happens once in a while; mere pretense." Oh, this is what he means, I realised, and was relieved.

Yes, I had heard a comment like that. Because I had paid no attention to it, I had forgotten to tell Qi Ba. This shows that he had a good understanding of the masses, and did not only lead by example but also communicated with the ordinary people, adopting their way of thinking. Furthermore, he didn't like to hear the 'gossip' that flattered or went in another direction, but didn't correspond with facts.

3.8. In Doubt, But No One Dares to Speak the Truth

In 1958, the whole country was involved in the Great Leap Forward. Some people were overexcited, and on all fronts, particularly in agriculture, they praised the launching of the high-yield satellites, claiming that they had produced an unbelievable astronomical device and record-breaking results. The Xinli village commune in Tianjin were this fanatic; they went so far as to make a model plot where the rice produce had allegedly reached over five million grams per mu (1 mu = 666.6 m^2). This was a ridiculous amount, running counter to all scientific theories, but some party leaders believed it. For example, Lin Biao called some generals in Beijing to go to Tianjin to visit, to learn and to liberate their thoughts. At the time, someone even said: "How bold people are — how much output the land will produce!"

Under such circumstances, we students also took action without delay. We rushed to Xinli to see the rice paddy. Indeed, we saw that the rice in the model plot was so densely planted that air had to be blown over it to give the plants some oxygen. Someone said that if you put a small child on top of the rice plant, it would not fall to the ground. Allegedly, the leader of the commune had suggested that rice be planted on top of the reeds, and he once reported to Chairman Mao to give the following suggestions: building a small canal that allowed 3,000-ton ships to sail along, and then planting grapes on both sides of the canal so people would lick their lips over the sweet sparkling grapes densely hanging on the trellises. On the deck of the ship, people would only need to lie down on their back and raise their heads to eat these grapes without any effort.

In the West Flower Hall, when I related these odd things to Qi Ba, he frowned and sighed deeply: "After your words, I feel sad." He then turned around and asked me: "Do you believe in such record-breaking results?" "Of course I have my doubts," I said to him, "but no one dares to speak the truth. But some individual villagers privately told us that the rice was not planted in that field, but moved from the other fields. Because the plants are too close to each other, air has to be blown across, or the rice will begin rotting very soon." Qi Ba replied: "They spoke the truth. Even you, a young man who grew up in the city, does not believe this scene, nor can you tolerate it; so how can we convince the people who work directly on the land, the broad masses in the countryside, of the party's correct guidance?"

All his life, Qi Ba often said: "One must act as his conscience dictates." He was deeply worried about the consequences of the blind and fanatic, going against the laws of science. As expected, examples of boasting and exaggeration appeared in many places around the country — "we have had an extremely good harvest and everyone eats for free", etc — resulting in an exceptional historical error: the three-year period of difficulties that had a tremendous effect on the country. It's obvious that this so-called natural disaster was actually the result of the people's tendency to boast and exaggerate, which, led by the wrong policies, caused unavoidable repercussions. Meantime, it resulted in a lamentable example from which we must draw a lesson.

3.9. I Visit the 'Chinese Miracles'

After I graduated from university and began working in the Committee for Cultural Relations with Foreign Countries and the International Liaison Department of the Central Committee (ILD), I had the opportunity to accompany Qi Ba to receive foreign guests, and afterwards I would take the foreign guests to visit different cities. The few places that were open to foreigners, such as the Anshan iron and steel company, Daqing and Dazhai, had just been inspected by Qi Ba. Whenever he went, he was more than glad to listen to the genuine opinions of the local cadres and the visiting foreigners. Some of these comments, even today, have a practical and immediate significance, as well as a warning value.

1. The Development Strategy of the Anshan Iron and Steel Company (AISC)

My special regard for the Anshan iron and steel company was directly influenced by Qi Ba, and also resulted from the accumulation of my emotions after frequently taking foreign guests to the place. I helped AISC become twinned with the city of Sheffield in England and won scholarships for two technicians from AISC to go to Sheffield to learn how to tackle environmental problems using technology. In addition, I helped to bring about the exchange visits of the mayors of the two cities.

Zhou Enlai talking with the workers at the Anshan iron and steel company.

When I began studying economics at university, I took a course called *Industry and Technology*. Some of the material discussed the technology of smelting steel. Qi Ba had talked to me about AISC. His general idea was that AISC was a milestone in the "most vital of the vital parts" of the socialist industrialisation. The historical contributions the workers made deserved a big reward from the whole country. Coincidentally, my middle school classmate Wang Dingwu was once the dean of the central designing institute of black metallurgy. He was also the deputy chief engineer of the Baoshan iron and steel company in Shanghai. The best in the business, he was the person to whom I made my inquiries about obtaining information on smelting steel.

Since the founding of new China, AISC has been the prime base for China's steel industry. As early as February and March 1950, China signed an agreement with the Soviet Union for a loan to the People's Republic of China (PRC), as well as a protocol for the Soviet Union to give technical aid to the PRC upon the resumed production and transformation of AISC. In 1952, the party centre gathered the forces of the whole country to resume the production and the transformation of AISC, calling it "the key job of key jobs". On 21 December 1953, Qi Ba visited the site, and he wrote down: "The going into operation of the heavy rolling mill, the seamless tubing mill and the number seven iron-smelting furnace signals the victory of our country's socialist industrial construction. Congratulations to the staff of the Anshan iron and steel cooperation for this great achievement. I hope you will make even greater contributions to the socialist industrialisation under the teachings of Chairman Mao." In fact, it only took one year for these three projects to be set up and become operative. In the following years, 1955, 1956, 1960 and 1962, Qi Ba again went to inspect AISC. In the first and second phases of the project, he saw to matters personally, from the equipment supply to the working rate, and helped to solve problems. Wearing old cotton clothes and shoes, his presence brought warmth and care to the hearts of the workers. By shaking the greasy hands of the workers working at the blast furnace, he made them feel valued, as if he was not the leader of the country but one of them.

Under Qi Ba's encouragement, the workers produced 30 million tons

The Years of National Construction

of steel in 1956, successfully solving the shortage. Qi Ba took a personal interest in deploying groups of university graduates to AISC, encouraging workers and technical personnel to try hard to master new techniques and, during the learning process, catch up with and even surpass international advanced standards. Between 1960 and 1962, because of the errors that occurred during the Great Leap Forward as well as natural disasters, the country met with many difficulties. Moreover, the Soviet Union terminated the contracts and stopped the aid while withdrawing their experts working in China. The international blockade made the situation worse; it really was one disaster after another. During this difficult time, it was Qi Ba who went to AISC to encourage the cadres and workers to withstand the pressure. Finally, the company overcame the difficulties, and through self-reliance achieved a quicker development.

I remember when I went to AISC with the foreign guests and I listened to the cadres' and workers' lengthy and illustrative comments about Qi Ba's commitment to AISC, which moved not only the Chinese, but also the foreign guests. It allowed them to have a comprehensive understanding of the unyielding integrity of the Chinese, which increased their confidence in the future development of China as well as the possibilities for cooperation between China and foreign countries.

But in those years, in the city of Anshan, chimneys arose in great numbers, spewing black smoke and flares. As we lacked knowledge about environmental protection at the time, we ignored the hidden problem of pollution.

Another problem with AISC was that an enterprise of this scale was usually built like a society in miniature. The development level was different from that in existing local communities; therefore, two districts with two different lifestyles were formed. The two neighbouring communities lacked the necessary means of communication and could not form a cooperative relationship. The increasing working population of AISC had to solve issues of employment and livelihood of the surplus people within the cooperation, sometimes losing contact with the need for its own development and turning itself into an overstaffed enterprise. I remember that at the time, some leaders of AISC told me that they only needed 170,000 staff members, but had had to expand to 400,000. The workshops and the branch of the cooperation existed in name only, which would inevitably affect the management and the efficiency. Meantime, nearby communities could not benefit from the development of the enterprise. All of these issues could easily lead to new social problems.

After Qi Ba learnt of the abovementioned problems, he was lost in thought. But due to the circumstances at the time, many accumulated problems could not be solved in one day, and obviously time was needed to solve these problems completely. When I was working at Beijing University, I wrote a research plan on how to solve this, a decision inspired in part by Qi Ba's teachings.

2. The Dazhai Development Strategy

In the 1960s, 'in agriculture, learn from Dazhai' was a household slogan issued by the party and the state. In December 1962, in his government work report for the third NPC, Qi Ba commended Dazhai as an advanced example of the country's agriculture for the first time.

Zhou Enlai in Dazhai, 1965.

The Years of National Construction

Dazhai was a brigade in the Dazhai commune in Xiyang County, Shanxi province. As it was barren and mountainous, with poor soil, all planting was done scattered along the valleys and on slopes. Led by Chen Yonggui, the locals carried out construction on the farmland and turned 4,700 small patches into 2,900 areas of high-yield farmland that would ensure a stable production despite droughts or excessive rain. Their essential experience lay in building terraces on the mountain slopes, with each terrace having a 1m-deep layer of rich organic soil. The soil could hold moisture and fertiliser, thus becoming drought resistant and a moisture reserve: a 'sponge field'. After an investigation by the minister of agriculture, Liao Luyan, who had been sent by Qi Ba, it was reckoned that this kind of sponge field had a general scientific significance, as it brought about a great advance in dry-land farming. After minister Liao returned to Beijing, he wrote a report to Qi Ba and Chairman Mao. Chairman Mao at once praised Dazhai and Chen Yonggui: "A marvellous deed has been done in the backward valleys."

Qi Ba once summarised the Dazhai farming construction, saying: "The Dazhai brigade adheres to the principle of putting politics in command and being in the lead in their thoughts, self-reliance, and ability to build up an enterprise through arduous work. The communist principles of loving the country, loving the collective — all of these are more than worthy of recommendation." In order to prevent and stop the practice of boasting and exaggerating, he purposefully initiated a discussion about Dazhai with the North China Bureau and the Shanxi provincial government, sending out people to measure the land and check the output of grain. They confirmed that Dazhai had a land area of 796.69 mu and was producing 404,500g of grain per mu on average, which was above the average yield in the Yangtze river basin. In May 1965, Qi Ba and Li Xianlian accompanied some guests from Albania to visit Dazhai. They took a helicopter, but the bumpy ride consumed a lot of Qi Ba's energy. After arriving at the destination and taking a short break, they began to inspect the hills, covering 40km in one round trip. With the scorching sun directly overhead, as well as the heatwave, even the young people found it difficult to continue walking in the hills, but Qi Ba walked the whole journey without a straw hat and with enthusiasm.

He paid special attention to the way the Dazhai people had tackled the *langwozhang* ('wolf den'). There was a local saying: "The mention of *langwozhang* reminds me of the mountains, the hungry wolves and the rocks." After Qi Ba learnt that the *langwozhang* gully was a small-scale example of how the Dazhai people combat nature, he highly praised the arduous fighting spirit of the local people. On their second trip to Dazhai, Qi Ma went along especially to visit the *langwozhang* gully. In order to learn how the Chinese people braved the elements to carry out construction works through their own efforts, Qi Ba often advised foreign visitors to go to Dazhai to get a first-hand experience. This experience would enhance their understanding of China, and furthermore would assist in the development of a mutual friendship. My wife and I had the opportunity to follow in Qi Ba and Qi Ma's footsteps. We accompanied some foreign visitors to Dazhai, where we met the vice premier at the time, Chen Yonggui, and his young successor, Ms Guo Fenglian. All visitors, both Chinese and foreign, without exception, were touched by the fighting spirit of the Dazhai people.

Today, however, it is obvious that the Dazhai development strategy needs to be amended to suit the current reality; all the same, we should continue to carry on its spirit. Even if in those years, Qi Ba clearly believed that everyone should have their own Dazhai, and not be identical.

On the November 13 and 15 in 1971, Qi Ba received the Hinton family from the US, comprised of Carmelita, William, Joanne, Joan and Erwin Engst, and others. When talking about Dazhai, Qi Ba said to the guests: "We hope that every province and every county has their own Dazhai. People shouldn't think that they must travel for a thousand miles to find magic." To counter the saying that the Dazhai are selfless, he pointed out: "Don't speak in absolutes — first in public, then to yourself. This is the way to do things that everyone should learn." I remember how he harshly attacked the question of egalitarianism in distribution: "As for the issue of distribution according to labour, now we have the principle of 'four of the same'*. And here is another one that can be added: to do easy or difficult things is the same. None of these help to mobilise the initiative of the workers and staff

---

* ie, to do more and to do less is the same; to do good and bad is the same; to be able and unable to do something is the same; and to do or not to do something is the same.

members, nor to control their number. I think the following saying is right: 'It is necessary to have a reward system'." This, like all of Qi Ba's other teachings, left deep marks in my mind.

In the 1980s, when China's open-door policy was in its initial stage, guided by the principle of seeking truth from facts that Qi Ba had preached and practiced all his life, Professor Fei Xiaotong and I put forward the policy of adopting measures that suit local conditions: to have diverse strategies, to make adjustments according to the situation, and not to allow the opportunity for the country's economic development to slip. I believe this policy, on the whole, meets the essence of the directives Qi Ba issued during his lifetime, and can stand the test of time.

3.10. The Taiwan Issue

The famous English journalist F. Greene has mentioned his interview with Qi Ba, as well as Qi Ba's unforgettable, wonderful speech, to me many times.

Taiwan is a domestic issue for China, and the Chinese people should decide how to settle it. However, a country's so-called international interference policy makes it more complicated to settle the issue. Mr Greene, besides his full understanding of this principle and the Chinese government's stand on this issue, was most interested in when Taiwan would be liberated. Qi Ba's reply, which was humorous but not without seriousness, was beyond his expectations. "You are younger than me," Qi Ba said to him, "but why are you more impatient? We have enough patience to solve this problem, and it must be in the basic interests of those on both sides of the Taiwan Strait to solve the issue of China's unification in a peaceful way. Any unjustifiable outside interference will meet with complete defeat."

Mr Greene was filled with gratitude and admiration for the foresight and optimism of the Chinese leaders. He believed that if the other international leaders were to have the same foresight and broad mind as the Chinese leaders, many vital international disputes could be solved simply by keeping the basic interests of the people in mind. What he said reminds me of the conversations I had with Qi Ba about the Taiwan issue.

My Uncle Zhou Enlai

As early as the 1940s, during my studies at the advanced agricultural school, I had the chance to do some fieldwork in Taiwan. After Qi Ba learnt about this, he was very interested in my trip. He asked me to tell him what I had seen and heard while I was there.

During the summer holiday of 1948, a teacher from Guangdong province, who had a relative in Taiwan who ran a farm, found us an opportunity to undertake some fieldwork at several farms and research centres in the cities of Danshui and Tainan, in Taiwan. Such opportunities were rare, so we treasured the trip very much. The organisers also found us a cargo ship that would take us to the island for free. It was only a small ship, and we slept on the upper deck. It was summer time; the heat from the engine was unbearably hot, while the sulphurous smoke from the chimney landed on us, making our faces as black as charcoal. We looked at each other and smiled, seeking joy amidst sorrow. The memory reminds me of the description of Ms Bing Xin in her prose work *Fanxin*, when she is lying on her back on the deck watching the stars, a scene pleasing to both the eyes and the mind. There was a great difference between the poet's imagination and the reality we poor students found ourselves in, but our optimistic outlook on life was the same. Sixty years have passed quickly, and only the people involved will remember the taste of hardship. Through what I had heard with my own ears and seen with my own eyes, I had gained a tentative knowledge and understanding of the local people's life and work. Internationally, Taiwan was called *Formosa*, which means 'beautiful island'. The island was densely forested, the streams were clear, and beautiful hills and rivers were to be seen everywhere. At the time, the locals mainly worked the land and their standard of living was average. As it had been under Japanese rule for a long time, the industry on the island was not yet fully developed.

There was an interesting episode during this trip. Because people were under the wrong impression that I was an orphan in rags, some classmates refused to allow me to come along. The money for this trip came from what I had saved from the money Qi Ba had given me. So after I told Qi Ba of my little secret, he couldn't help laughing at my childish and honest words. Later, when I was at university, I had the chance to tell Qi Ba about my sketchy impression of Taiwan. I thought that Taiwan had been a Japanese colony for many years. The roads and the elementary education facilities were common, but higher education, particularly courses relating to politics and law, was plagued by severe restrictions. In general, Taiwan was only a base to supply farm products and human resources for Japan to start wars of aggression. However, it is now an inseparable territory of the motherland, so it is indeed necessary that it will return one day so we can realise the reunification of China, or it will affect the integrity, the safety and the development of the whole country.

When our conversation reached this point, Qi Ba said: "The islands in our coastal waters are like the pearl necklaces or brooches we wear, so we must not allow anyone else to snatch them from us or to harm them. The islands of Taiwan and Hainan are like two eyes for us. They are indispensable parts of the body — we cannot do without them, even for a moment. It is a matter of life and death, so how can we tolerate others to have a hand in the matter and sabotage the unification of China?"

To this day, I remember this statement vividly and I am still much moved by what he said. However, what has made us resentful is that there are still people all over the world who have a hidden agenda, saying that Taiwan is an "unsinkable aircraft carrier", and who attempt to make it into a military outpost to spy on China, or a base to invade and occupy us.

Throughout history, Spain, the Netherlands and Japan have occupied Taiwan on and off. Though surely its strategic location in the coastal area and in the Pacific Ocean was what made the invaders hanker after it, the key reason for Taiwan's repeated invasion and occupation was its lack of national strength. Moreover, communication and interaction between the people on both sides also needed to be improved. International factors still play a large role in the final settlement of the Taiwan issue, which we must pay attention to and solve appropriately.

When Qi Ba talked about the direction of Taiwan's economic development, he said that Taiwan's natural and agricultural resources were mutually complementary with those of mainland China. But unfortunately, the Taiwanese authorities chose to follow the Americans in all aspects —

especially in their economy, which was dependent on the US. To make use of local workers, open up the local market and also raise the economic strength that could be used to compete with the mainland, the Americans hastened along the industrialisation of Taiwan, meanwhile forcing it to open up its market to US goods, especially agricultural products. Because in the US farming is usually large in scale and intensively managed, this has made it hard for Taiwan to compete. Besides, the decrease in farming land will make it difficult for Taiwan to increase its crops, even to gradually decrease production. So its agricultural development has become restrained, or even gone into decline. Some individual products may never be able to recover after the setbacks, or their decline will reach a point that is unbearable to describe. All these measures will unbalance the development of Taiwan's economy, which will exacerbate social problems between the urban and rural areas and increase its dependence on the US. As a consequence, Taiwan's independence will diminish. However, if it reunites with the mainland, the economies of both sides will complement one another, which will be extremely beneficial to the balanced development of Taiwan, and it would suit the basic interests of people on both sides of the Taiwan Strait.

Qi Ba also paid close attention to Taiwan's peaceful land reform. He told me that the KMT learnt a serious lesson after their defeat on the mainland. Pushed by the Americans, they achieved peaceful land reform in Taiwan, meaning they freed the labour forces in the countryside while investing scattered capital into various industries. Such measures are feasible only to a certain extent.

The abovementioned talk between Qi Ba and myself took place in the 1950s. Fifty years have passed, but what he foresaw then has been proved by today's reality.

There is one more interesting anecdote relating to this unforgettable conversation between Qi Ba and I. When he talked about Taiwan's rich agricultural resources, he asked me if I knew the saying 'A B C R S T'. I was familiar with the way he posed this question: he was trying to inspire me to think and broaden my knowledge. So, after some thought, I replied: "The B is for banana, the C is for camphor, the R is for rice, the S is for sugar, the T is for tea," but what the A stood for I still did not know, even after thinking hard. Qi Ba was already very happy with my answers, and, seeing I was embarrassed and deep in thought, he smiled and said: "The A is for 'ananas'. As it is often called a 'pineapple' in English, it didn't come to your mind." I then added that, although I had been in Taiwan only for a short while, I knew that the locals pronounce 'pineapple' as *ong lai* in the south Fujian dialect. Qi Ba said to me: "It seems the examiner and the student each have their strong points; we have reached a draw!"

After I began working, Qi Ba talked to me about Taiwan several times. When he became terminally ill, he called Luo Qingchang to his sick bed, urging him not to forget about his old friends in Taiwan. Seeing how much he cared about Taiwan stirred the deep feeling among compatriots that blood is thicker than water, and moved us all to tears. After Qi Ba's funeral on 15 January 1976, Qi Ma received us relatives, Qi Ba's staff and the related medical personnel in the Great Hall of the People, having specially chosen the Taiwan room. After the downfall of the Gang of Four, the Central Committee arranged for Qi Ma to take charge of the work relating to Taiwan. None of this was a coincidence; it was inseparable from Qi Ba's exceptional concerns about Taiwan during his lifetime. Working hard for the well-being of the people on both sides of the Taiwan Strait, he had devoted himself to the great cause of maintaining and striving for the peaceful unification of China.

4. "I Raise My Hat to Salute Intellectuals"

4.1. Chen Lao Zong Solves My 'Ideological Problem'

During the first stages of the post-liberation period, it was commonly understood in society that intellectuals were brain-workers. However, after the rise of the anti-rightists and other political movements, people began to mistake intellectuals in general for bourgeois intellectuals, stressing the need for physical labour and ideological remoulding. Many university students, particularly the mature ones, found it difficult to accept this and felt massive political and mental pressure, because the majority of them were members of the party and the Youth League. Many of them had been either cadres or military personnel, but now they were suddenly being called

Marshal Chen Yi.

bourgeois intellectuals. Furthermore, countless political movements had had an effect on normal teaching schedules, with classes often being suspended for revolutionary activities; therefore, some of the mature students were forced to give up studying halfway through a term and go to work instead. I myself was also thinking about discontinuing my studies at university.

After I told Qi Ba and Qi Ma about this, they took it very seriously and tried hard to understand why I was thinking that way, trying to straighten it out. During the winter holiday between 1959 to 1960 and on the eve of Chinese New Year, I was with my younger brother Zhou Erjun's family, who, along with his wife Deng Zaijun, had just been transferred to work in Beijing. Suddenly there was a phone call for me, asking for me only to go to building 18 of the Diaoyutai state guesthouse to attend an important banquet. I would be picked up by Qi Ba's chauffeur, master Yang. After I arrived, I discovered that building 18 was a small, Korean-style building with a solemn, elegantly decorated interior. Around a very big round table sat many members of Qi Ba's staff. I was aware that this was a family-style new year's dinner. The food was nothing special, but the cordial atmosphere made it a memorable experience.

The hosts, of course, were Qi Ba and Qi Ma, but several special guests attended. Two of them were my cousin Zhou Erhui and his girlfriend from Wuxi. According to Qi Ba, she was a university student from a worker's family. Another unusual guest, who was sitting beside me, jokingly mumbled in a thick Sichuan accent: "I thought, it must be an important get-together that would require me to come on New Year's Eve. It is a gathering for your own family. Anyway, now that I am here, I will simply eat." Raising my head, I saw that it was Marshal Chen Yi, or Chen *Lao*

Zong*. I learnt afterwards that Qi Ba and Qi Ma had had several intentions for holding this 'family banquet'. Firstly, to express their gratitude for the staff's hard work during the year. Secondly, to welcome Zhou Erhui and express their support during their first meeting with his girlfriend, who had had a long journey to Beijing. And thirdly, to let Marshal Chen Yi solve the problem of my erroneous thinking.

After we had finished our meal, I went to say goodbye to Qi Ba. Only he and Marshal Chen Yi were in the restroom. When I entered, out of curiosity, Marshal Chen Yi came up to me and started to measure our respective heights. Although he was of medium height, similar to me and Qi Ba, his exceptional temperament made people feel at once as though he was tall and sturdy. Noble in appearance, he did indeed have the extraordinary qualities of a born commander. When he saw me wearing my Nankai University badge, he turned to Qi Ba and asked: "Who is this young man?" Qi Ba smiled and said: "His name is Zhou Erliu. The character *liu* is written a bit oddly, but it has nothing to do with him — it was the elder generation's custom. His pet name is Aibao, and I've known him since the day he was born. He is a student at Nankai University, and he is having some problems. So, one of the reasons we asked you to come today is to talk to him and try to help him solve his problems." "What are your problems? Tell me and let me see if I can help you," Marshal Chen Yi said to me, holding my hand.

"I am in a work-study programme," I replied hurriedly, "and I have studied economics before, but I am currently studying English language and literature. I have three problems with my thinking: firstly, I was a young revolutionary in the military and a cadre before I came to university, and I never imagined that I would become a bourgeois intellectual. Some of my classmates have already left university. I raise this question not just for me, but as a general social problem worth paying attention to." Young and impetuous, frank and honest by nature, without thinking twice, I spoke what had been on my mind. "But it is not going to remain small if the trouble is getting bigger." Marshal Chen Yi cut in, and his words were even more direct: "This will turn into a political issue — a line issue.

---

* used with a surname as an affectionate form of address to a general or high-ranking commander of the PLA

Because we have begun the construction, we must be certain on whom we can depend." "Secondly," I went on, "I am also the person in charge of my university's student union. Too much labour and too many social activities are happening on campus. Although I have gained full marks in all my subjects and was a model student in Tianjin, in fact I've spent too little time on my studies. I worry that I will be labelled as someone who is professionally competent but not politically conscious, so, mentally, I feel confused and miserable, because if the situation carries on like this, I might eventually become that very person, and feel I have wasted my time at university. And thirdly, Qi Ba and Qi Ma have asked me to go to see my grandmother in Shanghai every holiday, but the cost for the return journey is too expensive. They paid me back the fare for the trips, which put a financial burden on them. I feel uneasy about this, so I would like to go to work and earn the money to pay for these journeys myself."

After I finished speaking, Marshal Chen Yi cheerfully explained to me: "Firstly, both the premier and I think that the majority of intellectuals are an important and integral part of the working population. This was decided in the social climate of old China, which was semi-feudal and semi-colonial. The majority of the intellectuals who had patriotic feelings adopted an anti-imperialist and anti-feudal stand. In new China, with the social development and changes we've had, we have trained many young and new types of intellectuals who were less influential in the old society, but who are ready to work hard for the security and the construction of the country. Secondly, the historical process of change in society after the liberation also proved that the old and the new intellectuals, like the working people of the whole country under the leadership of the party, are happy to join hands for the creation of a better future. Intellectuals in general have no property — what's more, they do not own the means of production. We have muddled up their actual class by giving them the rank of bourgeois, which will inevitably hurt their initiative. This is obviously wrong. But unfortunately, now, in both society and the party, there are some people who are extraordinarily leftist in their thinking. I do hope these people will turn round and give up this incorrect position, which confuses right and wrong and has affected the relationship between the intellectuals and the party. As to the issue of the relationship between study and work, of course students must put their studies first. Labour is absolutely necessary, but there shouldn't be too much of it, or it will affect their studies and the loss will outweigh the gain. As to the question of your financial burden — your uncle and aunt are happy to help you, so you should not feel uneasy about it. I think you should carry on with your studies until you graduate. That will be the best way to show your gratitude to them for their care and for helping you."

He then turned to Qi Ba and said: "I think your nephew is very capable of pondering a problem. He will not be the sort of person who just follows the crowd. From his temperament and experience, I think he will be suitable for a position in the foreign affairs department or some other government department. I welcome him to the foreign ministry to work."

"This will depend on the dispensation of the organisation, as well as his own efforts. As our nephew, it will be hard for him to avoid being linked with us," Qi Ba said to Chen Yi. Then Qi Ba turned to me and said, "We can see that the mass of intellectuals, including the majority of the new and old ones, are feeling oppressed, or regard it as a heavy burden that the label of bourgeois intellectual has been put on them. It looks as though it is urgent to rid them of this label. Our relationship with the intellectuals needs careful and skilful handling. Starting with the guiding ideology, the party must revise its erroneous judgment of the intellectuals' class. You are lucky that Marshal Chen Yi can teach you in person. I hope you will live up to our expectations and requirements and study hard, exercise caution in speech and conduct, and do your best in your work."

The words of these two great elders have been engraved on my mind all my life. In the following years I was lucky to have several opportunities to see Marshal Chen Yi, but I never sought to engage in personal conversation with him, because, after all, he was in a high position and a very busy man. Though I was very grateful for his teachings, I did not want to disturb him while he was working whenever I saw him.

4.2. "Today, I Raise My Hat to Salute You!"

I only found out after the Guangzhou conference in 1962 that Qi Ba and Marshal Chen Yi had once again made an effort to rid the Chinese intellectuals of the label of bourgeois intellectuals. Giving a speech entitled *On the Question of Intellectuals* during the conference, Qi Ba gave a further theoretical exposition about the historical status and role of Chinese intellectuals, confirming the basic transformation and great progress the Chinese intelligentsia underwent after the founding of new China.

Due to his busy schedule, he had to return to Beijing before the conference ended, but he entrusted Marshal Chen Yi to pass on his 'salute to the intellectuals' to the delegates. Sonorously and forcefully, Marshal Chen Yi said: "You are the scientists of the people, of socialism, of the proletarians and of the revolution. The label of 'bourgeois' must be removed from you. Today, I raise my hat to salute to you all!"

His words, as well as Qi Ba's, won heartfelt support from the intellectuals and the people of the country. In September of that same year, around the time the 10th plenary session of the eighth Central Committee was

In March 1962, in his *Report on the Work of the Government,* Zhou Enlai pointed out that the intellectuals in China were labouring people who should not be regarded as bourgeois intellectuals.

being held, the question of the 'left' intellectual was growing more urgent. Someone even said to some of the bourgeois intellectuals: "Although their body has come to our side, their soul refuses to move; but for some, even their body has yet come to our side." Such sayings were contrary to Qi Ba and Marshal Chen Yi's correct appraisal of the class of the intellectuals. Ever since then, and up until the time of the Cultural Revolution, the situation grew worse and many intellectuals suffered persecution. Qi Ba and Marshal Chen Yi were censured, which had a major impact on their situation. Feeling guilty, I believed it might have been because of me.

Until the downfall of the Gang of Four and after the end of the Cultural Revolution, Deng Xiaoping proposed that "the majority of intellectuals are already intellectuals among the working people; therefore, we can say that they are already part of the working class itself". Only then did we realise how the essence of Qui Ba's speeches had been continued and developed. Qi Ba and Chen Yi's historical contribution, braving hardship and dangers to plead on people's behalf, has received wide and unanimous public approval.

Mr Xu Maijing, the author of the poem *Song of Prisoners*, told me that a scholar reported Marshal Chen Yi's speech during the Guangzhou conference to the vice premier, Lu Dingyi, who then passed it onto Chairman Mao Zedong. Hence, Qi Ba again had to clarify his view to Chairman Mao, while reaffirming that what he said had been approved of by the Central Committee, making it necessary to restate it at the Guangzhou conference. Many years later, Lu Dingyi wrote a commemoration upon Qi Ba's death. His descendant sorted out his writings and had them published. In his article, he wrote:

> (Frederick) Engels once said: "A large class, like a great nation, never learns better or quicker than by undergoing the consequences of its own mistakes." Only by admitting his mistakes, analysing them seriously and then correcting them can a party be great. Don't be frightened! Premier (Zhou) was the first comrade in the party who was brave enough to criticise himself. I witnessed him do it more than a dozen times; yet he still enjoyed the highest prestige in the party and the most profound trust of the people. I had not taken a clear stance on

the issue of the class of the intellectuals, even though I did advocate to strictly separate academic issues from political; hence, I had a leftist understanding of it. It was Premier Zhou Enlai who taught me a lesson. He used political conduct, rather than his personal worldview — considering only whom to serve — as the only standard to determine the class of the intellectuals, thus putting into practice another guiding principle of his: 'Let a hundred flowers bloom, and a hundred schools of thought contend.'

4.3. The *Shiwu Guan* Opera Becomes a Model

On 18 May 1956, the *People's Daily* published an editorial: *A Discussion on the One Play that Has Brought a Genre of Drama Back to Life*. It praised the Kunqu opera *Shiwu Guan* ('*Fifteen Strings of Coins*') for being a good example of the policy for drama reform to 'let a hundred flowers bloom and new things emerge from the old'. In that same year, the opera was made into a film, and it quickly became popular all over the country.

Qi Ba asked me to go to see the play. "You probably don't know," he said, "that your grandfather was a very good performer of the South Kunqu opera. In old China performing an opera was not only a hobby, but an artistic accomplishment widely advocated by scholars; your grandfather was one of the best at the time. Also, your father learnt Beijing opera with grand master Mei Lanfang, and he slowly became a well-known amateur performer of the Mei Lanfang style in Shanghai. He once performed on stage in the liberated area, and it was said that the audience liked his performance very much. In short, he was an opera fiend. I myself have also acted in dramas. Your grandparents came to watch me playing a female role. It seems that all our family members like the arts. You should go to the theatre often, because seeing plays can broaden your vision and knowledge while making you a connoisseur of theatre."

Hence, when the *Shiwu Guan* opera troupe came to Tianjin, I bought a ticket and went to see it. Because I knew the Shanghai dialect, I felt very touched when I watched it. I was absorbed by the complicated plot, which made a deep impression on me. It featured a butcher, You Hulu, who was excessively fond of drinking and loved money; Lou Ashu, who was a gambling addict; Guo Yuzhi, a fatuous county magistrate who settled a murder case; and the prefecture chief, Kuang Zhong, who pleaded on behalf of the people. Through three different views of the murder case (the county magistrate's, the prefecture chief's and the governor of Jiangnan's), the play vividly portrayed the characters and at the same time exposed the decadent habits of local officials in a feudal society, satirising the fact that a miscarriage of justice does people great harm, and singing the praises of prefecture chief Kuang Zhong, who upheld justice while bringing the people enlightenment.

Later, when I was with Qi Ba, he talked about the opera. He said that both the Shanghai and Shoaxing dialects belonged to the Taihu family of languages, so it was no surprise that I felt deeply about hearing that dialect when I watched the play. I then imitated the tune that had been played when Lou Ashu came on stage. Qi Ba laughed loudly, saying my imitation was rather good.

Later, as Huang Yuan, the director of the cultural bureau in Zhejiang province at the time, remembers it, in 1956 the Feng Kun opera troupe in Zhejiang adapted the traditional Kunqu opera *Shuang Xiong Meng* ('*A Dream of the Twin Bears*') for *Shiwu Guan*, and they were encouraged by the leaders of the culture ministry, such as Tian Han, Sha Wenhan and Lin Mohan. After the play had first been performed in Beijing, it caused a stir in the city. Luo Ruiqing, the minister of public security, called it "a play about public security", and recommended it to Chairman Mao. On 4 May 1956, Chairman Mao watched the play from his residential compound. Huang Yuan in Zhejiang received a phone call from the troupe, telling him: "Chairman Mao watched the play and he thought it was very good. He clapped his hands, and his hands were above his head."

1956 was an important year, but the year before was packed with notable events as well. In 1955, the country launched a campaign for agricultural collectivisation and the socialist transformation of industry and commerce. A movement for the elimination of counter-revolutionaries started in July. Its main purpose was to eliminate hidden reactionaries. A large number of cases had accumulated during the campaign, and figuring out the best way to handle the screenings, the investigations and the trials was a test for the politicians and how well they could handle a case, but affected cadres of all ranks. Under these circumstances, Chairman Mao proposed to try the cases based on facts, while correcting mistakes whenever they are discovered. He called for investigations and research, while opposing subjectivism. *Shiwu Guan* proved a good match with the political and social atmosphere: an excellent example of a work of art getting involved in reality.

One month after Chairman Mao watched the play, on May 2, he gave his famous speech: "Let a hundred flowers blossom, and a hundred schools of thought contend." And when Minister Lu Dingyi of the culture ministry conveyed the instruction of Chairman Mao's instruction to the cadres, he gave the opera *Shiwu Guan* as an example of weeding through the old to bring forth the new. On 17 May, in the Huairentang hall of the central government compound Zhongnanhai, Qi Ba held a seminar for the people of the Ministry of Culture and the dramatists association, especially for the opera *Shiwu Guan*; such an event was unprecedented. Qi Ba spoke for an hour and a half. The following day, the *People's Daily* published an editorial that roused the enthusiasm of the opera's audience.

"This one play has brought the genre of drama back to life," was one of Qi Ba's comments after he saw the opera himself. He said to me: "This play is rich with human feeling and has both a rather high ideological level and artistic quality. It has brought back to life an old genre of drama that is almost close to death, and, moreover, makes the classic Kunqu opera shine with new, dazzling splendour. It proves that historical dramas can also play a realistic, educational role. *Shiwu Guan* has set a good example for us to continue carrying out the policy of 'letting a hundred flowers blossom, and weed through the old to bring out the new'. It is a successful example for people involved in theatre to expand the organisation, writing and direction of classic drama. It can be played as a Kunqu opera, but also as other types of drama." Qi Ba also said: "We mustn't lose the excellent Chinese traditional culture. For us to build a socialist culture, besides carrying on our own excellent cultural traditions, we need to make an effort to assimilate elements from advanced foreign cultures and integrate them into our own national culture." In addition, creations made by the masses need to be respected, and this should not be ignored.

Afterwards, I became engaged in foreign cultural exchanges, and for many years, whenever my job had a direct connection with traditional Chinese culture and arts, I would recall what Qi Ba had said to me. His dialectic exposition to traditional culture guided my work, the opera *Shiwu Guan* constantly reminding me not to commit subjectivist errors.

4.4. Recording History Truthfully

From my close relationship to Qi Ba and Qi Ma, I knew very well that they always approached historical research, as well as related material, with a serious attitude, being scrupulous about every detail.

I remember once, in the early years of new China, the Tianjin party committee sent some historical data (photos and written materials) to Qi Ba and Qi Ma to examine (Professor Liu Yan, a veteran underground party member in Tianjin, once the director of Zhou Enlai's research centre at Nankai University, was the man who handled the matter. He himself mentioned this in his related writings). They thought it presented a good chance to train me as a young cadre; hence, they requested that I come to their residence to see these items. They picked up several objects and gave me a detailed demonstration on how to sift through and handle them, improving my ability to appraise cultural relics.

I remember that among the objects there was an ordinary photo of them, without anything in the background. They told me about a principle regarding such photos: all items that had nothing to do with history but came from private lives should not be selected as historical data, much less be put on show to the public. Another photo had been taken when Qi Ba was in France. In the photograph, he is alone, standing at the entrance of a building. There was nothing else in the photo, but the building was the office for the Youth League. Because the photo was connected to real historical events, it could be listed as historical data. But the original caption of the photo said that the building was the location of the party office, so Qi Ba said: "The museum should correct the illustration to tally with the actual situation."

On that day, Qi Ba also said to me: "The president of Nankai University, Mr Zhang Boling, was a very good educator. He and I maintained a good and friendly relationship teacher-student relationship for a long time. However, in those years he was keen to expel progressive students, and during the May Fourth Movement in 1919 he even ripped out the part of the page where my name appeared, because I had been arrested by the reactionaries for being a student representative. Under the circumstances, he had to behave in this way for the sake of the university as well as for his own safety, which was understandable. This is a true historical situation. Mentioning it will not harm his reputation, but it can help future readers to gain a deep understanding of the real circumstances at the time." "We Chinese sometimes adopt some incorrect or wrong practices when keeping records or to studying history," he went on. "We often conceal the truth for those we respect, or for one's own relatives and the deceased. We deliberately cover up their faults and advertise their merits, thinking we should not speak ill of the dead. None of these are good habits. When we undertake historical research, we must respect the facts. We must stick to our principles and hold ourselves responsible to history; hence, facts must be made known to the public. We should take a serious and responsible attitude towards our ancestors, as well as to modern people and later generations. We should never infer, imagine, twist or make up historical events to serve the people of today. We must educate the cadres and the masses so that together they can adopt a responsible attitude towards history. Our ancient historians could, heedless of their own personal safety, take a risk and write impartially. We modern people should do more to record history scientifically and study the real facts. Any thoughts and actions arising from personal considerations should be avoided."

4.5. Qi Ba's Interesting Remarks on Basic Training for English Students

Around the time I attended Nankai University, China looked at Russia as a model. The university stopped teaching English and began teaching Russian instead. I had learnt English during my childhood in Shanghai, but when I applied to university, I was unable to take any courses in English.

In 1956, after Qi Ba and other related personnel had been promoted, the higher learning institutions in the country began to pay attention to the English language. As a result, Nankai University reintroduced English courses. Because my English was better than that of my peers in the work-study programme, I was transferred to the foreign languages department to study English.

When I first registered, I didn't tell Qi Ba and Qi Ma that I was applying at Nankai University, nor did the university have any idea that I was the nephew of Premier Zhou Enlai. After Qi Ba and Qi Ma found out that I had been admitted to their old university, they were so happy that they organised a dinner to celebrate. In the 1950s, there were few university students in China. Of my generation of the Zhou family, only Zhou Erhui and I went to university. As Zhou Erhui was in poor health, it was comparatively easier for me to study. Hence, Qi Ba and Qi Ma paid much attention to my studies, especially after I had been transferred to the foreign languages department. Qi Ba talked to me several times about the importance of learning a foreign language, giving me the opportunity to listen to his idiomatic English. When I accompanied him to the cinema to watch some foreign films, I noticed that he needed no interpreters when watching an English film, only when watching films in other languages.

In 1959, Qi Ba visited Nankai University. He made sure to visit the foreign languages department, talking with the students and helping them with their pronunciation. I remember him often saying to me that it is better to learn a language when you're young. After he switched schools, from the northeast to Tianjin, he found out that English was a hard language to learn. Some years later he went to England, and when he first arrived in London, he had difficulty speaking English. But after years of practice he could speak it fluently, and his English was no different from that of people who had studied it as their major, and even had a unique quality. About this, he would sometimes say jokingly: "Everything comes to him who waits: studying and practising produces the best results."

I graduated ahead of schedule and became director of the teaching and research section of my department. Qi Ba was uneasy after he found out about this. He said to me: "Teaching English includes pronunciation, grammar and vocabulary…" And I found out his knowledge about teaching English hardly fell short of that of professional teachers. He also taught me some creative teaching methods. He said that, excepting linguistic professionals, who do research on pronunciation, grammar and vocabulary, teaching was a medium to express ideas to general language users; hence, I should lay the stress on practice. The Chinese and foreigners have their own ways of thinking and expressing their thoughts, feelings and wishes, so when we are learning a foreign language we must pay attention to how we can accurately express our thoughts and ensure that what we have said is easily understood and accepted. In addition, Qi Ba emphasised that when we practice another language (in the classroom), teachers should encourage students to express ideas, stories, or even completed scenes, meanwhile paying attention to improving their all-round capacities in listening, speaking, reading, writing and translating. I found his viewpoint to have a guiding significance during my language teaching, particularly the emphasis on the comprehensive application of the language — much better than simply reciting words or tests.

He also discussed the usage of various words with me. He said that we Chinese habitually put one word in different places to create different objectives of expression, but a foreigner uses different expressions with different objectives, using different words. For example, when we Chinese say *changchang*, the intention is not very clear; but the English equivalent could be either of various terms: 'occasionally', 'used to', 'usually', 'often', 'frequently', 'constantly', or 'always', to name a few. I only learnt to use these words in the classroom, but Qi Ba spoke from his own learning experience. He could reach this kind of a conclusion about the use of words without deferring to good teachers at school; it was inseparable from his competence in learning and summing up what he had learnt.

Once, I accompanied Qi Ba to receive some foreign guests. The interpreters were the chief interpreter of the foreign ministry, Mr Ji Chaozhu, and the senior interpreter of the ILD, Ms Lao Yuanhui. Both of them were respectable interpreters. While translating the conversations between Qi Ba and the foreign guests, both of them used the phrase 'as well as'. After the reception had ended, Qi Ba suddenly asked the two interpreters: "Do you know the exact meaning of 'as well as', and how to use it?" Neither of them knew how to reply, because they only used the words but had not done any research on why they should use them in such and such a way. As I had taught some English at university, I had paid attention to the correct usage of words. I replied: "It means 'in addition to'." Qi Ba was quite satisfied with my answer. In this moment, I felt even more that Qi Ba did not only have a solid foundation in the English language, but also the ability to demonstrate a rigorous approach to learning it, never regarding himself as infallible.

I also noticed that although he, like me, had a southern accent when he speaking standard Chinese, his English pronunciation was quite precise and elegant. His education had only reached university level, and English was not his major, but he could discern, from a teacher's viewpoint and while using language that was concise and to the point, the regular pattern of a language while finding ways to practice it. I admired him greatly. Qi Ba also said to me: "When we learn things, we should not only learn from books, but also from the common people and, repeatedly, through practice."

4.6. The Soulmate of Translators and Interpreters

Before the Cultural Revolution, according to the rules, interpreters would stand aside when a group photo was taken. Since the beginning of the Cultural Revolution, when receiving foreign guests of importance, the names of the interpreters were included in the list of names for the reception, and they were allowed to join the group in pictures that would be published in newspapers and magazines. The protocol for how to treat an interpreter differed from person to person, occasion to occasion and status to status. Such a change was at least agreed upon by Qi Ba. Although at the time the political climate was leaning to the left, the change showed that Qi Ba had paid attention to the interpreters because they were indispensable in foreign affairs activities, and because their hard work, role and contribution deserved genuine recognition by the government and society.

As for the interpreters themselves, Qi Ba once pointed out: "A qualified and outstanding interpreter needs to meet at least three requirements. First, they must have a clear-cut political stance, especially those who interpret during foreign affairs activities. This is a universally recognised, must-have requirement for an interpreter. Second, they must have a very high level in understanding foreign languages, and be able to precisely communicate the ideas and opinions of both sides. If they interpret something wrongly, the consequence that may result will be hard to recover from. Third, they must have extensive knowledge of and be able to deal with all sorts of topics, as during an exchange of opinions, the conversation will not only involve the subject at hand. Besides the meetings and negotiations themselves, all sorts of topics will be covered before and afterwards, such as history, astronomy, geography, current events, leisure, and names of people and places visited; these conversations embrace everything and always turn to unexpected subjects." Thus, the third point is very important, which is what Qi Ba emphasised.

Sometimes, both sides — hosts and guests — need to know each other's situation, so when Qi Ba introduced the topic of the current situation in China, he maintained that he would not exaggerate our merits and say nothing about our shortcomings. True to his word, he never gave diplomatic answers, but spoke honestly. Also, Qi Ba took care, more than the other Chinese leaders, to learn about the other countries' strong points. For example, as the history of new China was rather short and the country's pension system was not very refined, he paid a lot of attention to some of the other countries' pension systems and their application. When introducing foreigners to China, he always urged the other Chinese not to conceal our shortcomings from our guests.

To interpreters, Qi Ba was a soulmate and close friend. He understood the hardships of their work and would give them time to make necessary preparations in advance. "Some people think that an interpreter can interpret everything, no matter the subject, which is not correct. Some leaders and reception personnel do not communicate with the interpreters beforehand, so that, being underprepared, the interpreters' work will be of a lower quality, or sometimes they will inevitably interpret something wrongly." These were not only his words, but also his actions, and they encouraged the interpreters enormously. In those days, he showed much respect and approval towards Ji Chaozhu and Lao Yuanhui, so that it would allow these two most senior interpreters to be brave enough to take on responsibilities without worrying too much. When an interpreter made a mistake in their interpretation, he would not correct or criticise him or her on the spot if it was not necessary, but inform the related department as well as the interpreter to remedy it. Once, when an important Chinese leader was receiving some foreign guests, he mentioned a historical fact to the guests. His interpreter had only been working as an interpreter for a short time and knew little about history and international affairs. Consequently, the interpreter made some errors. No one noticed but Qi Ba, because he had a wide range of knowledge and he was familiar with the topic. Thinking that he could point it out afterwards, he did not say anything, knowing that if he did, he might embarrass or the interpreter and create a misunderstanding. He spoke to the related department and the interpreter himself after the reception had ended, asking them to seek an appropriate opportunity to correct the mistake, and told the foreign guests about the genuine historical fact.

Qi Ba usually used his broad range of knowledge to help, complement and improve interpretations, also setting an example for the interpreters. To him, interpretation meant mutual communication between different nationalities. The quality of the job not only depended on precision,

In 1973, Zhou Erliu (second from the right in the second row) accompanying Zhou Enlai to receive visitors from New Zealand. Lao Yuanhui is second in the second row from the left. Ji Chaozhu is third in the second row from the left.

but sometimes required some artistic input. To some cadres working in the foreign affairs office who lacked experience, interpreters provided assistance, and their role was to complement and adjust on the spot, thereby contributing to the work of the whole reception. When Ji Chaozhu and Lao Yuanhui interpreted, they made some necessary adjustments to logic and grammar at times in order to fully convey the original meanings of the Chinese leaders, which Qi Ba often approved of and encouraged.

People used to call Qi Ba's residence 'West Flower Hall in Zhongnanhai', but actually, West Flower Hall is a grand hall where Qi Ba officially received guests from both China and foreign countries. Qi Ba and Qi Ma lived in the back of the hall, where there was a bedroom, an office for Qi Ba, offices for the staff, a kitchen and a small drawing room. In this drawing room, a film projector had been fixed to the wall, which Qi Ba and Qi Ma used to play films in their spare time. The staff and their children, as well as several acquaintances, were also allowed to watch films there, and I was lucky enough to be one of them.

Little Bell was a colour film, jointly made by China and France (in the 1960s), and I can still vaguely remember the main storyline: the monkey king from the Chinese fairy tale makes friends with French children. As the film was in French, a simultaneous interpreter was needed. Because many Chinese and French flowers, plants and trees were mentioned in the film, the task of interpreting was not easy, unless the interpreter had grown up in both China and France and had an extensive knowledge of flowers and plants. Naturally, such an interpreter was hard to find.

Qi Ba looked very happy after watching the film. He asked me to say something about it, so I gave him my opinion. "After the meal, both you and the interpreter are to stay," he said to me and the interpreter, and smiled. When we had finished eating, we took a walk in the courtyard. Pointing at the flowers and trees, Qi Ba requested the interpreter to find out how to say their names in both Chinese and French, so that in the future, when guests came, the interpreter could tell them the correct names in both languages. Qi Ba then said that officials must cooperate with interpreters and do some 'homework' beforehand, so that interpreters could be better prepared, as no interpreter could know how to interpret everything. After he had spoken,

The Years of National Construction

I suddenly realised that this was Qi Ba's concern for me, and was another higher and stricter requirement he made of me. His method of teaching was heuristic, using living examples and giving demonstrations. He never used force-feeding teaching methods or took things as they came, or made comments at will without giving specific guidance or help. No wonder people at the foreign ministry often said that the premier's teachings were both strict and kind. Even his criticism was welcome, because he either set them a high standard or convinced them with reason, and even came up with solutions or detailed arrangements. In short, people were completely convinced, feeling it an honour to be criticised by him, because the more criticism they received from him meant the greater progress they could make.

To Qi Ba, an interpreter's training was a long-term task. It should start as early as possible and not be interrupted; it is not something that can be done hastily. During the Cultural Revolution, because of the emphasis that was laid on manual labour, many teachers and students at institutes of foreign languages also needed to go to the countryside to work in the fields. Qi Ba asked these institutes not to stop teaching English and made them guarantee to give students time to study, in order to meet the demand for interpreters after the end of the Cultural Revolution.

I will never forget how much Qi Ba cared for the female interpreter Zheng Lingyu, who used to be a child labourer and who died in her prime. Zheng Lingyu was born into the Wang family in Huzhou, in Zhejiang province. Her birth father worked in a silk mill, and her mother was a housewife. They had six children. After the Japanese invasion, her father was beaten up by the Japanese for no reason and the family was forced to move to Shanghai. As they were too poor to feed their children, the infant Lingyu was adopted by the Zheng family, a worker couple who liked the baby girl very much and changed her surname, Wang, into Zheng, treating her like their own child. Unfortunately, both her adopted parents died of disease, one after the other. She found a job in a cotton mill and became a child labourer, making her own living. After Suzhou was liberated, the workers' union sent her to study at a local school on an accelerated education programme, and she graduated with honours. She was good at working both in the factory and at school, and was admitted as a party member. After finishing middle school at the end of 1950, she passed the university entrance examination and went to study Indonesian in the oriental languages department at Beijing University. After graduating, she was assigned to work for the ILD. When the Indonesian president Sukarno visited China, she was Zhou Enlai's interpreter. She liked her work very much and her superiors were very happy with her. During her years at Beijing University, she was honoured as a national model student and her merits were on put show in related exhibitions. After graduating, she proved exemplary at her work, which was noted by her superiors. She was loved by her colleagues, who showed sympathy for her unfortunate past, and later found her birth parents in Shanghai.

Around 1960, I was helping with the university's exhibitions for the national model students and I found many testimonies written about her. When I went to see Qi Ba and Qi Ma, I told Qi Ba about her and her exemplary deeds. Qi Ba at once asked me to take his car. I found her in her dormitory and then took her up to West Flower Hall. Qi Ba asked me and Wang Zhangli (my wife) to attend his conversation with Zheng Lingyu, because, not long before this, Liu Shaoqi had collected the opinions of people from all walks of life in his book *How to Be a Good Communist*, and Zheng Lingyu had been recommended. Naturally we discussed the book during our conversation. We all thought that the paragraph about *shen du* ('taking care of oneself when alone') was well worth studying and putting into practice. Qi Ba pointed out that Zheng and I had both been friendless and uncared for in our childhoods, but that we could take care of ourselves. He stressed that the principle of *shen du* was not foreign in origin; Marx and Lenin did not mention it in their works. It was the cream of the Chinese traditional philosophy of self-cultivation, making comrade Liu Shaoqi quite right to include it.

Zheng Lingyu was very grateful for Qi Ba's care and encouragement, and after their meeting she worked even harder. But Heaven does not follow the will of humans — in a routine health check she was found to have stomach cancer. During her childhood she had lived in straitened circumstances, and had often had an upset stomach. Restricted by conditions at the time and young and eager to do well in everything, she had ignored the disease for too long. She bravely faced her lot in life and struggled with her illness tenaciously. Qi Ba also worried about her condition, which was a great consolation to her. Unhappily, she passed away after two years of treatment. Qi Ba's care and help for Zheng made me realise that he did not care only for certain individuals, but that he felt compassion for the people en masse. It was a display of a great communist's sincere and lofty sentiments and sympathy.

4.7. A Search Spanning Half a Century

In the 1990s, my wife Wang Zhangli and I returned to her hometown Huzhou to search for the Jia Ye Tang library, a major historic and cultural site under state protection. The trip was not an ordinary one, but fulfilled a long-cherished wish of ours. Qi Ba had asked us to go because he wanted us to understand our own hometown and thus pay attention to protecting culture and heritage. At the end of the 1950s, when Qi Ba met Wang Zhangli for the first time, he asked about her family, where she was from, where she was born, her parents' occupations, and so on. When he found out that she was from Huzhou in Zhejiang, though born in Shanghai, he smiled and said: "So we are fellow townspeople. I am originally from Shaoxing in Zhejiang. The silk industry in Huzhou is well developed, and it is also the city where the traditional inkbrush comes from, the *Hubi*, which is well known in China." The more he talked, the happier he became. He talked about the scenery of the region, which is in the area south of the lower reaches of the Yangtze river, as well as local customs. He even mentioned the private libraries in Ningbo and Huzhou, and especially the Jia Ye Tang library. He told us that it was located in the ancient town of Nanxun. The writer Lu Xun once humorously called the library owner, Liu Chenggan, "the dumb one". What Qi Ba said made us curious, because we knew nothing about it, even though we were from that region. Qi Ba said that we should go when we had the chance. For many years we didn't have the opportunity to fulfill Qi Ba's wish; however, we kept it in mind. At the time, we were amazed by his wide range of knowledge, because he knew a lot about this library that few people knew about. Only half a century later, after we had visited the site ourselves, did we learn about the library's background.

My Uncle Zhou Enlai

The library and the local village of Xiao Lian Zhuang face each other across a river in the ancient town of Nanxun. The library's name comes from a plaque, presented by the Xuantong Emperor (1908-1911) of the Qing dynasty, inscribed with the words *qin ruo jia ye* (literally 'admiring your fine enterprise'). It was indeed fine: the whole compound is made up of gardens and groups of buildings. It is the largest of all private libraries in China and has the biggest collections and finest block-printed books. It covers an area of 1.3 hectares, and the floor measures 1,936m^2. The buildings have two storeys and combine Western style with Chinese tradition. The structures were so in harmony with the pleasant smell of ink that people were amazed. Another astounding fact is that the library has a collection of 600,000 volumes, each one rich in content. There are block-printed editions from the Song dynasty, as well as woodblock-printing editions of *The Records of the Grand Scribe, The History of Former Han, The History of Later Han* and *The Records of the Three Kingdoms*. There are 42 volumes of the Yongle encyclopaedia, the lost copies of the *Imperial Collection of Four*, and manuscripts by those who have a literary reputation or are distinguished men. The library also has the imperial academy edition of the *Twenty-One Histories* from the North and South Song dynasties, the Jiguge edition of the *Seventeen Histories* from the Ming dynasty, the Wuying Palace edition of the *Twenty-Four Histories,* the 1912 handwritten copy of the *Veritable Records of the Qing Dynasty* (1644-1911), *The Complete Collection of Tang-Period Prose and Literature* and *The Complete Tang Poems*, as well as others.

Besides the huge collection of books, the layout of the buildings is impressive too. Books are neatly arranged according to categories and readers can easily find what they want. The architects have integrated the structure and function to such perfection that the whole experience is pleasant to both the mind and the eye. The following guidelines were adhered to when building this library:

> *A library ought to be tall. Each room should be wide and clean. The compound should be surrounded by high walls and far away from residential areas. Water sources should be close to the buildings and supplied with a drainage system. Windows should be open for air and sunlight.*

The Years of National Construction

This library was built in the 1920s. Its owner was Liu Chenggan, who was a successful candidate in the imperial examination at county level towards the end of the Qing dynasty. As I mentioned previously, Lu Xun once called him "the dumb one", apparently thinking he was not doing any decent work as a businessman, but in fact praising him for being well-read and dedicated to his collection of books. However, since its foundation, the library had suffered from banditry and the Japanese invasion of the country. Books had been looted and scattered everywhere, and at one point the fate of the library looked very grim. Before the liberation, Qi Ba, who had just entered Beijing with the Central Committee, gave instructions to the troops marching south of the lower reaches of the Yangtze river who were under the command of Chen Yi, asking them to take special care to protect the library. Surprisingly, Qi Ba had given them its exact location. Chen Yi then sent a battalion to guard the spot and he also paid a personal visit to the compound.

According to the staff, the library has made a special contribution to a foreign affairs-related matter. They supplied historical data regarding the border between China and India. This was the only physical evidence available and proved to be a substantial piece of testimony, favourable to China, in the settlement of the border dispute with India.

This once again proved that Qi Ba's instructions to protect the library were extremely important, timely and indispensable. Despite the chaos of war, he still cared about cultural matters and could come up with a detailed arrangement to protect a library. All of this shows his foresight and meticulous attention to his work as the housekeeper of new China, which is a rare occupation in this world and fills people with respect and even wonder.

Here I have copied Qi Ba's letter to the central propaganda department. It verifies the trials and tribulations of the Jia Ye Tang library, that treasure house of culture, as well as the great fortune they experienced during a terrible time.

Draw up a telegram for the following two affairs that will be authorised for dispatch by Director Yang. My original notes should be kept in the central propaganda department.

Request the People's Liberation Army to give special protection to:

1. The Liu's Jia Ye Tang Library in Nanxun (between Wu Xing and Wu Jiang, to the south of Lake Tai).

2. The Pushan monastery in Taiyuan, which has the collection of Chinese Buddhist encyclopaedia printed in the Kaibao period of the North Song dynasty, as well as part two of the Song edition set (the Qi Sha edition).

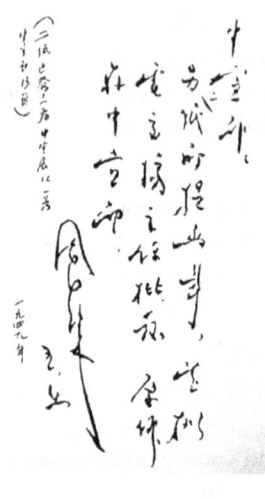
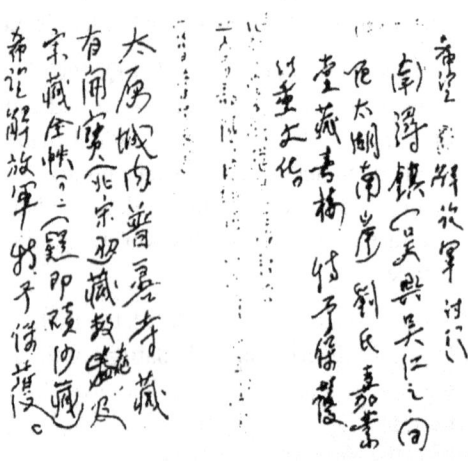

Zhou Enlai's letter to the central propaganda department.
For the full translation, see above.

The Family's Cultural Relics and Qi Ba and Qi Ma's Letters (Part Three)

1. Qi Ma's Letter from Beijing (1956)

In 1956, Nankai University decided to reintroduce English courses in the foreign languages department. Qi Ba followed this development closely, thinking that whether it was only for the time being or would continue in the future, the country would need more and more people who knew a foreign language, particularly English. He even regarded the popularisation of English education as a necessary part of enhancing the nation's qualities.

I have liked English since my childhood. After I finished middle school, I studied very hard and gradually laid a foundation to teach myself the language. So when I applied to Nankai University, I got pretty high marks on my English test, which would turn into my forte. The university thought they needed a secretary for the general Youth League branch as well as a mentor for the newly established English section; therefore, I was a suitable candidate.

At the time, I had been enrolled in the work-study programme in the economics department for two years. During that time I worked for the basic level of the Youth League and also as a mentor. I had received the highest marks for all my courses and had been made an exemplary student in Tianjin, but I thought I had spent too little time on my studies. Furthermore, my income as a part-time cadre was low. When I went to Shanghai to see my grandmother, Qi Ba had to pay for my travels. For all these reasons I let the university know that I would like to finish my studies ahead of time, so that I could begin earning my own living.

I wrote to Qi Ba about this matter, and he called for a family meeting at once. Four people attended: Qi Ba, Qi Ma, my uncle Zhou Tongyu, and my aunt Wang Shiqin. After discussing the matter, they put forward some suggestions, and Qi Ma wrote me the following letter:

Morning, 13th July

Dear Erliu,

We have received your letter. It's only a couple of days before the closing ceremony of the People's Congress, so we are very busy. I am mentally and physically tired. Regarding the matter you mentioned in your letter, I had a fly-by family meeting with your Qi Ba and your uncle Tongyu and his wife, your aunt. We discussed your problem, and are of the same opinion about the matter. Uncle Tongyu will talk to you, so you are to go to his house as soon as possible. He was at your home in Shanghai not long ago, so he can tell you about your dad and your grandma's current situations. When you arrive at his house, you should phone comrade Cheng Yuangong or comrade Zhang Yuan.

Your Qi Ba is in good health.

Regards,

Qi Ma

Nine people in total are mentioned in the letter. Besides the family members, Cheng Yuangong was Qi Ba's chief guard, while Zhang Yuan was Qi Ma's secretary. The term 'fly-by family meeting' originated from the term 'fly-by gathering', used by Qi Ba and Qi Ma during their revolutionary actions and underground work in the city. During such gatherings, people often quickly appeared and swiftly dispersed. Qi Ma used the term to indicate that the family meeting had been a very short one. The letter is about whether or not I should carry on with my studies at university. Qi Ma asked me to go to see uncle Tongyu after receiving her letter.

I travelled to Beijing and went to see uncle Tongyu. He told me that all of them shared the same view: that it was inappropriate for me to end my studies now, because our country would soon need many people who were equipped with foreign language skills. Moreover, there were only two university students in the family at the time and I was doing very well with my studies, so I had the potential to do even better. Qi Ba was hoping that at least one of the family members of the younger generation would be trained as a professional working for the country's foreign affairs. Therefore, It would not be right for me to quit my studies halfway through. They hoped that I would accept the university's arrangement to study English.

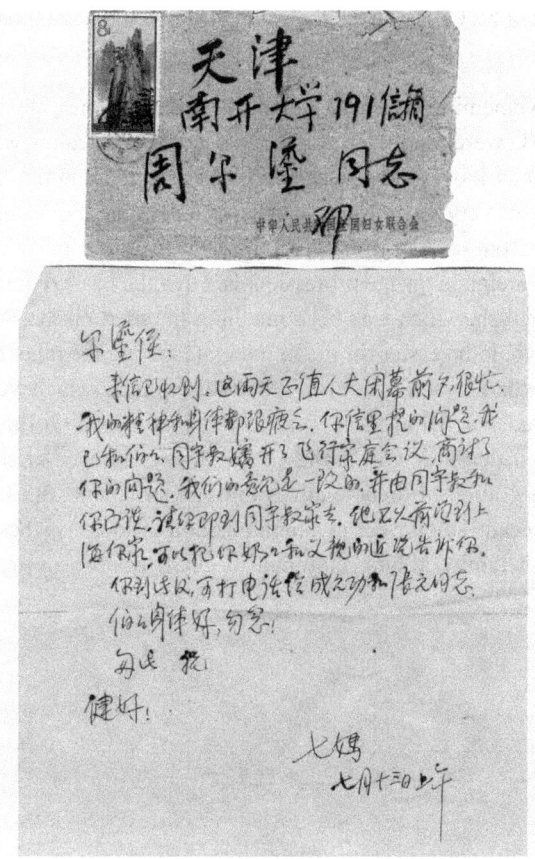

**Deng Yingchao's letter to Zhou Erliu, 13 July 1956.
For the full translation, see above.**

Regarding my financial problems, Qi Ba would continue to support me by withdrawing money from his salary. As such, I followed their advice and started studying English in the renewed English language section, meanwhile working as a mentor as well as a secretary of the general Youth League branch of the foreign languages department.

My father, Zhou Enzhu, was in Shanghai at the time. He had spent most of his life travelling around the country, so my time with him was precious. My personal affairs, like studying, living, working, and even my wedding were attended by Qi Ba himself, while Qi Ma would sometimes take part in discussions.

The abovementioned case as well as the letter demonstrate that both Qi Ba and Qi Ma were discreet in words and deed. When dealing with matters, they always took every tiny detail into consideration and put the national interest above everything else when making a decision. For example, in my case, at the front of their minds was the fact that the country would soon need more foreign language professionals. I met the basic requirements for studying English, which was not something imposed on me. As a mature student, it would be easier for me to integrate among the other students by being a mentor. I myself have always been disciplined, which would benefit the other students. All of these were factors that helped Qi Ba and Qi Ma to make their decision. Qi Ba and Qi Ma always showed affection to the younger generation of their relatives through strictness. But I personally think that because they were in a high position in society, when they were dealing with family affairs, they had to guard against any malpractices

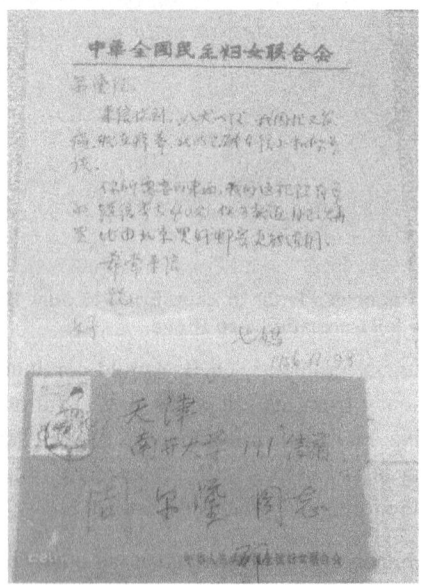

Deng Yingchao's letter to Zhou Erliu, 28 November 1956. For the full translation, see Appendix 5.

gradually creeping in and remained concerned about the reaction of the masses. Hence, I never wrote to them or visited them often, even if I missed them very much, for which I apologised. Yet Qi Ba often said to me: "There should be affection between relatives. In order to lighten the burden on the state, we try our best to give you financial help. But we also encourage you to become self-reliant, so we have strict requirements for you. In short, we will help you, but we will also stop you from being dependent or feeling privileged. I will be more than happy to see you playing a leading role among the masses. I believe you will understand and respect what we have done for you."

Usually, Qi Ma would cut in: "As premier, your Qi Ba is very busy. I need to lighten his burden, so I will do more than him to look after you. Anyway, I am serving the people — you are our relative, but you are one of the people, too!" She would laugh and then say to me: "As for you, your Qi Ba began having conversations with you when you were young. I will do more to look after your personal life. This is how we share the work. I hope you will understand this and cherish our training, and the expectations we place on you."

Although it is a short letter, it has influenced me in my ideological development, my life and my choice of work, and the mental strength it gives me is inexhaustible.

2. Four Precious Presents

2.1. The Inauguration Outfit

The inauguration of the PRC on 1 October 1949 was an extremely important day in Chinese history. The leadership of the Central Committee of the CPC and the other democratic parties took the matter seriously: they made every delegate, including Chairman Mao Zedong, a new wool Chinese tunic suit, except for Qi Ba, who attended the grand ceremony in his ordinary dark reddish-yellow khaki outfit. His secretary, He Qian, was trying to persuade him to get a new wool outfit, so, beating around the bush, he said: "This outfit fits you very well, but it is made of ordinary material. If it had been made of wool, you would look much smarter." The other

Zhou Enlai wearing his suit to the inauguration of the PRC.

staff also whispered about him being persuaded to get a new wool tunic suit. "This khaki outfit is good enough," Qi Ba said to his secretary and the other staff. "Why must I wear wool? We have just come to power. We have inherited the awful mess left behind by the KMT. There are many things waiting to be done, so we must build up the country through thrift and hard work. We should spend the money we have saved on the construction and improvement of the people's livelihoods. I am the country's first appointed premier, so I must play an exemplary role to justify the great trust placed in me by the party and the people."

Of course, he knew the importance of his own image at the inauguration ceremony. On the day the ceremony was held in Tiananmen Square, Qi Ba looked dignified and graceful in his ordinary khaki Chinese tunic suit.

When I started going to Nankai University in 1954, I was short of money. As I was enrolled in a work-study programme and needed to travel to Shanghai to see my grandmother during winter and summer holidays,

I had no extra money to buy new clothes. Seeing that I was of a similar height and build as Qi Ba, besides giving me the money, Qi Ma found some old clothes of his and then gave them to me to wear. In the winter holiday of 1954, Qi Ba and Qi Ma saw that I did not to have enough clothes to wear, so they gave me the dark reddish-yellow khaki Chinese tunic suit. Qi Ba had worn this suit on almost all occasions — in his office, when playing ping-pong with me, or at the dinner table. So when I was given the suit, I was grateful, but didn't think about it any further.

In those days, university students generally wore blue or grey clothes. To avoid giving the impression that I was showing off my clothes and to make the suit dirt-resistant, I dyed it a dark blue colour. Qi Ba and Qi Ma praised me for what I had done. "You have even thought of changing the colour of this old suit," they said. "This is to turn the old into the new, while not cutting yourself off from the masses. What you've done is great!" With the passage of time, the suit became worn out.

In 1976, Qi Ba passed away, and the relevant department of the central government began gathering information about Qi Ba's staff. They came to me for the suit, and only then did I realise the suit I had dyed and worn out was the suit that Qi Ba had worn for the inauguration of the PRC.

Today, whenever I think of it, I am deeply regretful and unable to forgive myself for what I did to his suit. What a valuable item it was! Qi Ba gave a memento like this to a relative without telling him the story behind it, his only motivation being to "let the poor student wear it, and let it serve its proper purpose!" How well this reflects Qi Ba's great virtue: he was a simple, thrifty and noble man.

2.2 The Xibaipo Army Uniform

During April and May of 1948, Chairman Mao Zedong, Qi Ba and the other Central Committee leaders moved their headquarters to the Xibaipo area of Shijiazhuang. Qi Ba was then vice chairman of the Central Committee and concurrently held the post of general secretary of the Central Military Commission.

In this rather shabby civilian house, Qi Ba assisted Chairman Mao in commanding the Liaoshen, Pingjin and Huaihai military campaigns. These three campaigns would become the largest in human history, both in scale and in the number of participants. Qi Ba drafted over 20 telegrams a day, which were then sent to the battlefields all over the country.

At the time, like the other leaders, he wore an informal grey cotton army uniform supplied to him by the local military base. In this simple uniform, and in that smallest of headquarters, he devised campaign strategies and meticulously commanded the three campaigns, which turned the war in favour of the communists. Victory over the whole country was just around the corner. This uniform revealed a solemn historical fact: that a genuine victory is decided by the will of the people, not by material conditions.

This uniform had been preserved by his security guards until New Year's Eve of 1960. I attended the annual New Year's Eve dinner Qi Ba held for his staff at the Diaoyutai state guesthouse. When we had finished our meal, the guards took out some of Qi Ba's souvenirs and handed them to Erhui's girlfriend. She planned to take them to Nanjing for the exhibition at the Meiyuan Xincun museum. Qi Ba knew that I was short of clothing, but he still asked his guards to bring in this valuable uniform, which came as a surprise to me.

I could not help but notice that the guard was reluctant to hand me the uniform, which was neatly folded. "There aren't many mementos left," he said to Qi Ba. "Only two items are important. One is this uniform, and the other one is the whip you were using when you fell off your horse and got injured in Yan'an. I suggest that we keep these two items for a more

Zhou Enlai's Xibaipo army uniform.

important occasion in the future." "This poor student has no more clothes to wear," Qi Ba said to the guard. "Give him this set of clothes, letting all things serve their proper purpose." Pleasantly surprised, I took them from the hands of the guard. Qi Ma and Marshal Chen Yi, who was also at 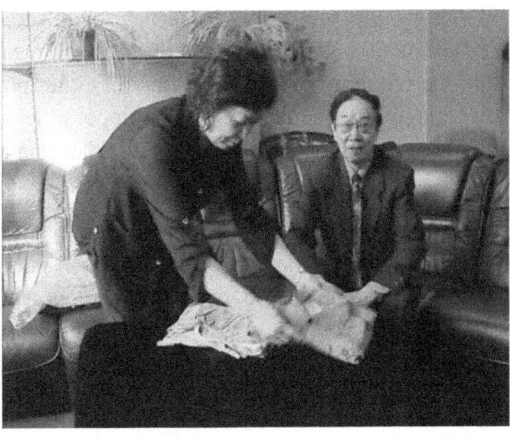 the dinner, congratulated me on me receiving such an important gift from Qi Ba.

Then Qi Ba asked Qi Ma to take me for a walk around the compound of the guesthouse. Qi Ma jokingly said to me: "I have become the honourable wife of the premier of a country, and I am also the person in charge of the All-China Women's Federation. Today, I can walk around the compound of a state hotel for the first time, all because of you. And you are even luckier, because you have received a set of clothing, which is very significant."

At the time, I was indeed short of clothing. But I only wore this valuable uniform for several days, because Qi Ba ordered me to; I then took it off and kept it in a suitcase from that moment on. People say: "A leopard leaves behind its skin when it dies. A man has a reputation to leave to posterity when he dies." Some people would rack their brains, not thinking of the party or the people and stopping at nothing in order to gain fame, fortune and power. But Qi Ba never put his individual interests first. For major issues, as with all previous struggles within the party, he acted in all cases in the interests of the party, the state and the nation, never taking his own personal power and position into consideration. Minor issues, as when he gave me souvenirs of significant importance, he regarded as "letting all things serve their proper purpose". This simple phrase mirrors his noble character and lofty persona.

Among the souvenirs Qi Ba has given me, there are many items of revolutionary significance, like the uniform mentioned above. Because he told me nothing of their importance, I either put the clothes on or passed them to other people. It is now impossible to recover these precious revolutionary mementos, and I regret what I have done.

Except for withdrawing money from his salary or giving clothes to his relatives, Qi Ba left no property to his family after his death. He gave his all to the state, the nation and the party. He left his will on his death bed: there would be no tomb and no tombstone, and his ashes must be scattered on the land, rivers and lakes of the motherland. However, Qi Ba, with his noble character, remains as a tall monument of intellectual wealth in the hearts of his relatives and the people.

2.3. A Tin of Peanuts

In 1960, all of China found itself in a time of so-called natural and man-made calamities. In Tianjin, there was an insufficient supply of food — most of all in the universities, among the young people who consumed more food than those in other age groups. Meantime, the mass-movement of technical innovation was underway at my university, which encouraged students to work day and night to get results in the shortest possible time. I was put in charge of the experimental equipment for the electrical audio-visual support instruction. After more than 70 days' work, to our surprise, we had successfully made a 16mm film projector. Physically exhausted, we were celebrating our success when a warehouse near the railway station caught fire. Many warehouse workers and some other people became badly burnt when they tried to put the fire out. The hospitals needed large quantities of blood, so the majority of students answered the call and went to the blood collection centre to donate blood. I was rejected because I was underweight, due to malnutrition. I was a person who always tried to play an exemplary role, so I ran a few miles back to my dormitory to put on a padded jacket and trousers as well as heavy boots. Now my weight was just over the required 50kg, and I ended up donating 200cc of blood. After I had donated the blood, I returned to the university at once to continue with the experiments for the technical innovation campaign.

To a healthy person, donating blood is a normal thing. But because I was severely undernourished, I was feeling tired and had a slight oedema even

The Years of National Construction

My wedding present from Zhou Enlai: a can of peanuts.

before I had made my donation. That night I became out of breath and was sent to hospital by my roommates. I had severe oedema, and the reading for albumin (x-protein) was only half of what was considered average. Hence, I had to stay in hospital and receive treatment, but I couldn't afford the hospital fee, which was Rmb50 per month. So I went back to my dormitory, planning to rest up at university while my classmate Miss Wang Zhangli (she was my girlfriend then) looked after me. To avoid any gossip from those who knew nothing about our relationship, Wang Zhangli and I decided to get married.

In October 1960, when I became engaged to Wang Zhangli, Qi Ba was absent because he was busy working. We had our photo taken at West Flower Hall to mark the occasion. Qi Ma was there, as well as my brother Zhou Erjun and his wife. Qi Ma thought that the arrangement in the photo didn't show that it was me and Wang Zhangli getting engaged. She asked the photographer (the security guard) to take another one after Wang Zhangli and I stood on either side of her. Qi Ma then took up the camera and took a photo of my wife and me.

October 1960. Zhou Erliu and Wang Zhangli's engagement photo with Deng Yingchao in the West Flower Hall, Beijing. Zhou Erliu's brother and sister-in-law, Zhou Erjun and Deng Zaijun, are on Deng Yingchao's left.

At the time we got married, life necessities were scarce in China. The local deputies of the NPC granted us permission to buy a quilt (with a cotton cover) and a honeycomb briquette stove.

We had nothing besides the daily necessities. After Qi Ba and Qi Ma found out about our situation, they asked my wife to go to see them, and she went. They gave her Rmb100 in cash and some sweets. Qi Ba then picked up a tin of Ma Ling peanuts, and handed it to my wife as our wedding gift. "Right now, our country is in economic difficulties. Materials are scarce. There is no need to give guests any sweets, so you can let them share this

Zhou Erliu and Wang Zhangli's engagement photo, taken by Deng Yingchao.

tin of peanuts. The ties of friendship weigh heavier than the materiality of a courteous reception." He then urged her: "Sell the empty tin to the nearby recycling station after the peanuts are gone." When we first went to see Qi Ba and Qi Ma after our engagement, Qi Ba told us: "You don't need to buy sweets for your wedding; one tin of peanuts will be enough for the guests." I originally interpreted it as a metaphor to teach us to share the comforts and hardships of the common people in this period of economic difficulties, never thinking that Qi Ba would fulfil his 'promise'.

This time, when Qi Ma saw my wife, she asked her: "Why have you and Erliu chosen this time to get married, when he is so ill?" Qi Ba cut in and said: "You don't understand. This must be because Aibao became very weak after donating blood. He needs somebody to look after him. Zhangli is a young girl, and it would cause a misunderstanding if she looked after him. It is not suitable to explain this to everybody, so they simply got married. Do not blame the children." Zhangli was a quiet and shy girl, and Qi Ba's words moved her to tears.

I did not follow Qi Ba's instructions, so I kept that tin for over 50 years. I put my August First military badge in it, hoping the tin would become an heirloom for my descendants and a tool for their self-education, or be collected by a museum for the audiences to understand the hardships in the early years of the construction of new China.

Around this time, my tutor, Professor Yang Shanquan, brought me the only hen his family kept. It would lay eggs while keeping me company during the day, while my wife attended her classes. A hen embodies the friendship between a teacher and his student during extremely difficult times, and it also represents a teacher's care and love to his student. I was malnourished, and so was the hen. She would occasionally lay an egg to give me a treat. One day I let it out in the courtyard, and somebody tried to snatch her. Her leg was broken and she died soon after.

The first time I stayed in hospital for treatment, many of my fellow patients were cadres from the districts of Tianjin. Considering the living conditions in hospital were not very good, they would use all sorts of excuses to go home to rest. One of my ward mates was minister of the organisation department of a district in Tianjin, who had to stay in hospital because of the poor conditions at home. He did not know I was an ordinary mature student, but thought I was the relative of a high-level official because I often asked to go home to rest, for which he was quite displeased with me. Meantime, my home was burgled. The municipal security department thought we had lots of property, or even confidential documents, so they cordoned off the area while searching my house. After ending the search, they all laughed, saying: "You are as poor as a church mouse." One policeman was touched, and tearfully said to me: "Little Zhou, seeing your house, which contains nothing but a quilt and a honeycomb briquette stove, we are again reminded of how strict Premier Zhou is with himself." My displeased ward mate apologised to me after he learnt the truth about me staying at home rather than in hospital, saying that we Chinese are proud and lucky to have Premier Zhou Enlai.

2.4. An Old Wool Coat

Qi Ba gave me the outer layer of an old wool jacket. This wool jacket had once had a leather lining, but as leather was expensive, it was inappropriate to give it to a student. I cut off the tattered edges and made myself a wool coat with a corduroy lining. Qi Ma praised me for my work. At the time, I had no idea that this was the coat Qi Ba had worn when he attended the negotiations between the KMT and the CPC in October 1945, until Qi Ma told me about it. This coat should have been listed as an important cultural relic. Fortunately, it has been kept until today, although it has been washed many times.

3. The Lost Cultural Relics

3.1. A Pair of Cotton Shoes

In 1958, all of China surged towards an emulation of socialist labour. Initiated by Qi Ba, building of the Shisanling reservoir began in Beijing. The leaders of the Central Committee, as well as the state, led cadres of all levels to take part in the labour on the building site. Despite his bad right arm (injured during the war), his preoccupation with his daily work, and his age (60 years old), Qi Ba led the ministers and directors of the state organisations, as well as the cadres, directly under the flag of the Central Committee. This group, comprising a total of 300 people, went to work at the reservoir building site. On 15 June, he wrote a report to Chairman Mao Zedong about the ongoing work.

The wool coat Zhou Enlai wore during the negotiations between the nationalists and the communists

Today, the photo from the news report shows us Qi Ba pulling a cart of soil. If you examine the photo closely, you can see that he was wearing a pair of ordinary cotton shoes. Later, more and more people joined in to help build the reservoir. University students from Beijing and Tianjin also took part. When I arrived in Beijing, I went to see Qi Ba and Qi Ma, wearing

1958, taken at the Shisanling reservoir building site. The cotton shoes Zhou Enlai is wearing would be given to Zhou Erliu.

my boots. Qi Ma was concerned and asked me to change my shoes. She found the cotton shoes that Qi Ba had worn when working on the reservoir. "It will be interesting for two generations to wear the same pair of shoes to the building site of the Shisanling reservoir." I knew that they did not have much surplus material for themselves, so I declined the shoes. "Well, do you think this pair of cotton shoes is not good enough for a university student?" Qi Ma glared at me. "Don't mock Aibao," Qi Ba cut in. With a smile on his face, he said: "Aibao has a poor physique. His body weight is probably below average, so his boots might help him when he digs his spade into the soil. It can also stop him slipping and falling when he pushes his cart up and down the mound."

I was very touched by what they had said, and felt very warm. Later, while working, I switched between the two pairs of shoes. I feel very lucky that I still have one picture in which I am wearing the cotton shoes and working alongside the other students. However, one of my classmates took my shoes without telling me. He later threw them away when they were worn out.

3.2. A Pocket Watch

In 1954, Qi Ba attended the Geneva conference. His chief security guard, Cheng Yuangong, went with him. All the staff used their pocket money to bring some souvenirs and articles for daily use. Cheng Yuangong bought himself an Omega pocket watch. But after they returned home, all the security guards sooner or later owned a watch, so the pocket watch was kept in a drawer or lent to other people to use.

I was a part-time student at the time. Life was inconvenient without a watch, but my savings from my income could not buy me a new watch. Qi Ba and Qi Ma felt sorry for me, and at the same time, they felt the situation was awkward. Firstly, if they were to give me a watch, it should not be too expensive; secondly, they did not have an extra watch for a gentleman (Qi Ma had an old watch, but it was for ladies); thirdly, they did not have any extra money to buy me a new one.

Qi Ma found a solution. She went to discuss this with Cheng Yuangong and swapped his pocket watch for her lady's watch. From then on until the 1960s, I carried that pocket watch. In those days, I always had it with me, either because I had no money to buy myself a new watch or because I was attached to it. Whenever I wore it abroad, other people, including customs clerks, thought it was too old-fashioned. However, they did not know about its political significance or its travelling history.

In addition, at the time, I had no idea of its material value. When the watch needed repairing, I did not know if it could be done in Beijing, so I gave it to a relative in Shanghai. He didn't manage to get it to work, so he sold it to somebody else. I have regretted this all my life, and Cheng Yuangong also felt very sorry about the loss of the watch.

This pocket watch had a special significance. All their lives, Qi Ba and Qi Ma had been honest and clean, while loving to help the others. They did not have any extra money to buy their relative a new watch, but they were full of affection for their family. Thinking it inconvenient for me to be without a watch, they found a way to help me by swapping somebody else's pocket watch. This shows that Qi Ba, Qi Ma and their guards were as close as family members. This pocket watch connected all of us. We were all part of a new type of big family, and the watch symbolised the care and love Qi Ba and Qi Ma had for me and the people around them.

Part Four

The Years of the Cultural Revolution

In the early days of the Cultural Revolution, Qi Ba felt that he could not keep on top of the situation. The Cultural Revolution, which lasted from 1966 to 1976, brought disastrous civil strife. It was wrongly initiated by the country's leader and was exploited by counterrevolutionary cliques. It brought calamity to the party, the state and all nationalities in the country. During those 10 difficult years, Qi Ba endured humiliation, ignored the limits of a normal mental and physical workload as well as the huge political risk, and worked for the safety of the whole country. He worked hard to shore up the shaky and dangerous situation. Just as he said: "If I do not go through hell, who will? If I do not go through the sea of bitterness, who will?" He gave his all until his heart ceased to beat.

During those years, he did his best to seek common ground with the complicated contradictory political forces, trying to limit the damage inflicted on the country from the top to the lowest level by the ultra-leftist ideologists. With the firm and persistent spirit of a man of great courage who looks like a coward, or like a wise and far-sighted man who appears slow-witted, he led the Chinese people to reduce their losses while promoting the country's effective strength, bypassing hidden reefs, steering the ship on the right course. He had won the understanding and trust of hundreds of millions of Chinese people. His death aroused their grief and indignation.

In 1965, Chairman Mao Zedong issued a directive "to attack the people in authority who are the capitalist-roaders within the party." (A capitalist-roader is a person in power who takes the capitalist road, a political label often pinned on cadres by the Red Guards during the Cultural Revolution.)

Then he said to some regional leaders: "How are you going to fare if revisionism appears in the Central Committee?" These were dangerous hints that, in fact, Mao Zedong was ready to launch the Cultural Revolution.

However, Qi Ba merely had the feeling that the divergence of views between Mao Zedong and the other leaders of the centre might become more and more tense, although not likely to result in unusual political upheavals. In his address to the reception on the National Day in 1965, Qi Ba emphasised: "Now, the people of our country are looking forward to a glorious future. Full of confidence, we are greeting the third five-year plan, which will start in 1966."

In November of that same year, the *Wen Hui Bao* newspaper in Shanghai published an article by Yao Wenyuan, *Review of the New Historical Drama, Hai Rui Dismissed from the Office*. It openly criticised Wu Han, the author of the drama, who was also deputy mayor of Beijing and a noted historian. This scheme was designed by Jiang Qing and Kang Sheng, and it shocked the whole country. However, Qi Ba knew nothing about it at the time, and he agreed with Peng Zhen that the issue of Wu Han was not a political but an academic one. An academic issue must adhere to the policy of 'letting a hundred flowers blossom, and a hundred schools of thought contend.' At the beginning of 1966, Mao Zedong decided to bring down Peng Zhen, Lu Dingyi, Luo Ruiqing and Yang Shangkun. On 16 May 1966, the Central Committee dispatched a notice: "Figures like Khrushchev are sleeping beside us, which must be brought to the notice of party branches at all levels." Around this time, Qi Ba's main concern was arranging drought relief throughout the country, as well as sending aid to Xingtai, which had been hit by an earthquake. He even thought: "The Chinese Khrushchev-like revisionists have already been ferreted out."

On 25 May 1966, as plotted by Kang Sheng and his wife Cao Yi-ou, Nie Yuanzi and seven others of the philosophy department of Beijing University put up a poster, which said, in big characters: 'What exactly have Song Shuo, Lu Ping and Peng Peiyun done for the Cultural Revolution?', attacking the party branch of Beijing University and the Beijing municipal committee, which was practising revisionism. But they met with resistance from many members of staff and students. Because there were foreign students from dozens of countries at Beijing University, Qi Ba instructed the university to act with great care when engaging with the movements, and to take note that there was a difference between domestic and foreign ideologies. After Nie's poster was put up, that same night Qi Ba sent the North China Bureau of the Central Committee, the foreign affairs office under the State Council and the leading cadres of the higher learning ministry to Beijing University. They criticised Nie and the others for breaching the principle stipulated by the Central Committee and messing up the centre's plans. They repeated the instructions of the Central Committee, saying there was a difference between domestic and foreign entities, which must be strictly observed. After Kang Sheng learnt of the abovementioned situation, he went behind Liu Shaoqi and Deng Xiaoping's backs, who were taking charge of the work of the Central Committee, and secretly reported the contents of Nie's poster to Mao Zedong, who was in another part of the country. On 1 June, Mao Zedong instructed Kang Sheng and Chen Boda to let the Xinhua news agency radiobroadcast the contents of Nie's poster and publish them in the press nationwide. The night after the broadcast, Chen Yi asked Qi Ba: "Why did you not inform us in advance about such an important matter?" Qi Ba replied: "I myself was informed by Kang Sheng only shortly before the broadcast. He told me that the contents of Nie's poster would be broadcast to the whole country by Radio Central."

1. My Confusion and Bitter Experiences

1.1. The Work Groups and the Two-Line Struggle

The Central Committee was quite worried about the quickly spreading chaos and unrest in the movement, and was hoping to keep it within certain bounds. The leaders in charge of the daily work of the Central Committee were Liu Shaoqi and Deng Xiaoping. In the first 10 days of June, they decided to send 'work groups' to universities and some middle schools in Beijing. In addition, from the end of May to the early days of June, they sent them to the general offices of *People's Daily* and Beijing University. All these had been originally approved by Mao Zedong himself; however, 'rebel groups' then clashed with the 'work groups', leading more and more of the latter to be driven out by the former.

Early in June, facing charges made by Liu Shaoqi, the members of the standing committee of the Political Bureau made the decision to send work groups to universities and middle schools in Beijing. Zhang Yan, the director of the foreign affairs office under the State Council, went to the Beijing Second Foreign Languages Institute (BSFLI) to guide the movement. Because he did not handle the situation properly, many people from the BSFLI as well as the foreign cultural liaison committee complained about him. During this period, people in charge of the party branches and administration and teachers in many universities and middle schools were indiscriminately criticised and denounced at public meetings. 'Big character posters' began appearing all over the place. Some individuals committed suicide by jumping off buildings.

In the early stages of the Cultural Revolution, in 1966, the issue of the work groups was an important problem, involving many departments and organisations, as well as the cadres and the masses. At the time, to the majority of the leaders of the Central Committee, it seemed like veteran revolutionaries were encountering a new issue, and they did not know what to do.

On 18 July, Mao Zedong returned to Beijing. Jiang Qing, Kang Sheng and Chen Boda wrote him a false report about the work groups, imposing all sorts of charges on them. From then on, Mao Zedong regarded the role the work groups were playing as a negative one that obstructed the movement. He changed his opinion about dispatching them. On the 28th of July, the reorganised Beijing municipal committee made the decision to withdraw the work groups from all universities and middle schools in Beijing. The following day, they announced the withdrawal of all work groups from all departments and organisations. Later, Mao Zedong criticised the dispatching of work groups as having been a mistake in orientation, which brought unprecedented pressure upon many party organisations. The vast numbers of party members and the masses felt insecure, not knowing what to do. In the resulting, extremely awkward situation, many people were criticised and denounced in public meetings for being work group members.

1.2. The First Time I Write to Qi Ba about Political Issues

My wife, Wang Zhangli, and I were originally sent out to work for the Chinese Embassy in Sweden by the CCRFC. Because the newly founded BSFLI was short of teachers, we were temporarily sent there to work. Wang Zhangli was still in the countryside in Shanxi for the Four Cleanups Movement, so I went alone to report for duty at the end of April and the beginning of May. At the time, affected by the situation at home and abroad, some of the teachers who had been involved in previous political movements harboured resentment. Without any reason, they began to attack the newly set up party branch of the BSFLI for being "dilapidated". What they said obviously did not tally with the actual situation; it was an extremely inappropriate charge.

The BSFLI had only been set up shortly before. All party members among the teaching staff and students were from different organisations in Beijing, such as the CCRFC, the Xinhua news agency, the first institute of foreign languages and some other broadcasting organisations and press associations. They only worked together for a short while, either not knowing each other very well or having previously collaborated unsuccessfully. The accusations made by some individual members of staff naturally caused discontent with the majority of the teachers and students, especially the young ones. Hence, they stood up to explain as well as to reject these wrong charges. The atmosphere was not tense then.

At the time, the majority of the members of the work groups were students from the cadre training section. Middle-aged or young, coming from all over the country, they had been chosen and sent to Beijing to be trained as cadres. They all had a certain level of ability to judge what was right and what was wrong. Because they knew about the BSFLI's circumstances, it was very natural for them to support the teachers and students in refuting the accusations. So, when some of the young people, being unsophisticated and simply striving to make progress, found overnight that they had committed directional and ideological mistakes, they were all shocked and terrified.

At this moment, Director Zhang Yan of the foreign affairs office controlled by the State Council heard something through the grapevine, and he came to the BSFLI. Having arrived, he openly expressed his support for the so-called rebel groups, showing a negative attitude towards the new party committee of the BSFLI. The party secretary, who had just been transferred to Beijing, then rounded up many party and Youth League members to go out to protest, even calling on them to get ready to die in defense of the party committee of the BSFLI; consequently, two opposing factions emerged.

My personal feeling then was that on both sides, it was unavoidable that good and bad people would be thrown together. On one hand, the two factions had different principles; on the other, their actions had nothing to do with principles, but were committed only for factional reasons. Usually, on such occasions, all sorts of elements in society took part. As for the issue of the divergence of views and struggles related to the party's Central Committee involvement in the factional struggle, it was hard for the masses in the primary units to know the truth.

I regarded the movement in the foreign affairs sector as inseparable from Qi Ba and Chen Yi's leadership. Furthermore, I felt that I must leave behind all considerations of personal gain or loss, speaking and acting with caution. I had to avoid accidentally doing something harmful to Qi Ba and Chen Yi, no matter how small a mistake, and being taken advantage of by bad people. At that time, somebody from the rebel groups spread the word that Zhou Enlai was close to and trusted Zhang Yan. But I felt that Zhang's words and actions were not in keeping with the spirit of Qi Ba's directives. After struggling with this for some time, worried that the chaos would endanger the capital's safety and under the requirements of the masses of the BSFLI, I wrote Qi Ba a letter (regarding a political issue) for the first time in my life, in which I brought up my doubts about Zhang's negative attitude towards the party committee of the BSFLI.

In my letter, I briefly gave an account of the movements involving the BSFLI, raising some questions. The letter was written mainly in the hope that Qi Ba would catch on quickly and keep abreast of the situation in the BSFLI after the arrival of Director Zhang.

Qi Ba was away on a trip abroad, so I received a reply from Qi Ma. From her letter, I could see that she had got the gist of the Central Committee (ie, the Central Committee directed by Liu Shaoqi and Deng Xiaoping), requiring me to follow Zhang Yan as a leader. At once, I sensed there was a big difference between this movement and the movements we had seen before. There were different opinions in the Central Committee. Qi Ma knew very little about the circumstances, while Qi Ba would likely end up in a difficult situation. Hence, I decided to join neither of the two factions; nor would I have any private contact with the heads of the BSFLI, only secretly keeping in touch with some individuals who were reliable and whom I knew very well. I would report to Qi Ba about the situation within the BSFLI. At the time, somebody wanted me to be director of the revolutionary committee of the BSFLI. In order to avoid becoming involved in any factional struggle, I found an excuse: I needed to go to Shanghai to visit a relative who was seriously ill. Soon, Qi Ba returned to Beijing from overseas. Just as I expected, he came to the BSFLI, viewing the posters and talking to the people to learn about the situation of the movement. Although he was at an advanced age and his health was not as good as in previous years, he immersed himself in the masses and became one of them. The only difference was that in his conversations with them, he explained two points: firstly, although it was he who had given permission to set up the BSFLI, he had forgotten about it. The hidden meaning of this was that his visit to the BSFLI was not a special occasion, but only a pretext to learn about developments in the foreign affairs sector, to be investigated and reviewed further. Secondly, as he pointed out, comrades Zhang Yan and Chen Yi might know each other, but he himself had not recommended Zhang, much less appointed him, to guide the movement in the BSFLI, making it clear that he knew little about Zhang.

Therefore, I was relieved. It was clear that he had understood my intentions in writing to him: I had hoped his visit would clarify that he had no personal relations with Zhang Yan and put a stop to the rumours circulated by people with ulterior motives, because they were trying to incite the students, who were unaware of the facts, to take a sceptical attitude to Qi Ba.

Qi Ba had been to the campus of the BSFLI near Tongxian county five to six times. I thought I could console myself, because my feelings about and understanding of Qi Ba's precarious and difficult situation tallied with the actual circumstances. As such, it was necessary for me, in my own way, to keep reporting to him about related circumstances. I would do what little I could, living up to Qi Ba's long-time training and teachings. Between 1971 and 1974, when I made contact with a few of the heads, some of my actions and opinions were approved by Qi Ba and Qi Ma. Qi Ba often said: "Act as one's conscience dictates." Throughout my life, I think I have encouraged myself using the same motto.

On 24 July 1966, regarding the issue of dispatching work groups, Qi Ba wrote a letter to Liu Shaoqi and Deng Xiaoping. The contents were as follows:

To Liu Shaoqi and Deng Xiaoping, regarding the dispatching of the work groups (24th July, 1966)

4 PM, 24th July

Comrades Shaoqi and Xiaoping:

Regarding the matter we talked about last night, having considered it over and over again and read some more documents, I think the different opinions mainly originated from the appraisal of the situation and the understanding of the issues. The others are not primary factors. So it is better not to talk about it any more, because our views are not the same.

In Beijing, the dispatching of work groups has its universality and necessity. However, what happens to each individual group at the work unit has its specific characteristics. Therefore, this requires us to make an on-the-spot investigation and a concrete analysis.

Working relationships must be addressed clearly, with specific rules put in place; otherwise, it will be difficult to carry out the work.

This morning I went to the institute of foreign languages to view the big character posters in order to gain some perceptual knowledge.

The Years of the Cultural Revolution

Sorry for my hurried report.

With high respect!

Zhou Enlai

This letter shows us that in both his life and work, Qi Ba always upheld the principle of seeking truth from facts. He thought that different work units and work groups operated under specific conditions, making it necessary to perform an on-the-spot investigation and make a concrete analysis, not to act carelessly or at one's will. Even if he did not know the so-called truth or was aware of certain wrong inclinations that had been plotted or manipulated by Jiang Qing, Kang Sheng and the like, or even of things that had confused truth and falsehood, he still tried his best to analyse a problem concretely and made efforts to solve it. By actually acting on this, he tried to benefit the populace and to recover any losses incurred by the masses.

To this day, I also think that the individual organisations or work units had their own situations, as the level of each work group was varied; hence, we should uphold the principle of making a solid analysis of a problem to such an extent that, in the end, we can reasonably solve a particular issue. We should never do things again as they happened during the Cultural Revolution, such as drawing a line between the people, confusing right and wrong, or standing facts on their head, much less create opposing groups among the masses.

1.3. My Visit to a Foreign Country with Wu Han Is Suspended

Wu Han.

Wu Han was a famous Chinese historian who had worked at the universities of Yanjing and Qinghua. After the founding of new China in 1949, he became deputy mayor of Beijing, an academic member of the philosophy and social science committee of the Chinese Academy of Sciences, and president of the Beijing history society. He was the man who had directed the excavation of the Dingling tomb, one of 13 Ming-dynasty tombs found at a site in Beijing. He advocated the spirit of daring to speak the truth, and had written a couple of articles, such as *Hai Rui Scolds the Emperor*, and in 1960 he wrote the historical drama *Hai Rui Dismissed from the Office*.

In early 1965, I accompanied a group of more than 50 members from the Song-and-Dance Ensemble of the Tibetan military command to Nepal. This visit to our neighbouring country, south of the Himalayas, was a great success, so the leaders of the Tibet Autonomous Region were planning to reward me for my hard work. As I had gained some experience during the trip, the CCRFC arranged for me to go to Nepal with the Chinese friendship delegation once more. This visit lasted from the end of September to the beginning of October, when the Nepalese Nepal-China Friendship Association organised a celebration for the Chinese National Day. Wu Han would be president of the Chinese delegation, while I would be his secretary. But for some reasons, we didn't leave as planned.

In November 1965, Yao Wenyuan published a newspaper article, *Review of the New Historical Drama, Hai Rui Dismissed from the Office*, accusing the play of being an anti-party, anti-socialist "poisonous weed" that was trying to reverse the party's verdict of Peng Dehuai. In 1966, criticism of the drama became a prelude to the Cultural Revolution.

Only after the sudden outbreak of the Cultural Revolution did I realise that, because of this play, Wu Han had become a counterrevolutionary, declared guilty of wantonly vilifying the leader and scheming to seize power. In fact, within the party, opinions about the play were varied. Initially, Qi Ba and Peng Zhen regarded it as not a political but an academic issue. However, Qi Ba was unable to even fend for himself at the time, and the author, Wu Han, had become mentally and physically exhausted. He was arrested in March 1968 and died of persecution on November 11, 1969. In 1978, after the third plenary session of the eleventh Central Committee of the CPC, he was rehabilitated, and his ashes were allowed to be buried in the Babaoshan revolutionary cemetery in Beijing. Although I did not know Mr Wu at all and had only met him once, for a discussion about the trip abroad, I was forced to give a full account of my meeting with him. Because I was young and did not have enough political experience, I hardly slept during those days, laden with anxiety. As I was unable to clarify whether or not I had taken part in the so-called scheme, I felt I might be connected with it and meet with unexpected consequences. Afterwards, Qi Ma told me that she and Qi Ba had been worried about me. This shows that during the Cultural Revolution, unjust charges or verdicts appeared one after another, and as a result, everyone felt insecure.

Qi Ba once told me that he had heard Peng Zhen say, jokingly: "Working for of our party is like driving a car. The driver is holding the wheel. He turns left, then right, and eventually ends up on the right course." In the 1980s, I was invited to visit the Linfen area in Shanxi province, where I chanced upon one of Peng Zhen's nephews. He confirmed that he had been told about the above metaphor.

1965, the Tibet Song-and-Dance Ensemble performing in Nepal. The picture was taken at the Chinese Embassy in Kathmandu. The Chinese foreign minister, Marshal Chen Yi, sits in the middle of the second row. Zhou Erliu is second from the left in the front row.

2. Qi Ba and the Other Leaders

2.1. Chen Yi

After the Cultural Revolution had taken place, my wife and I received a notice from Qi Ma, asking us to pay attention to things happening at the lower levels. Hence, we went to watch the public criticising of Chen Yi. On 11 August 1967, the contact centre for criticising Chen Yi, which had been knocked together by the 'overthrowing faction' from the foreign ministry and the Beijing Institute of Foreign Languages, held a meeting to criticise and denounce Chen Yi in the Great Hall of the People. Qi Ba accompanied Chen Yi to the meeting. The Red Guards held Chen Yi tightly and fiercely, with his arms behind his back and his head forced to bow low, which put the slightly overweight Chen Yi in agony. Qi Ba, seeing this scene, called out loudly at once: "You cannot treat Chen Lao Zong in this way. If you do, you'd better trample on me as well." Later, because the soldiers interfered, the Red Guards ended the denunciation meeting.

In fact, in the early stages of the Cultural Revolution, Wang Li, Guan Feng and Qi Benyu intervened in foreign affairs without authorisation. Although Chen Yi was head of the foreign ministry, he had already become a target of criticism. In the period around 1967, three incidents took place involving the foreign affairs sector. Firstly, Yao Zhongming seized power; secondly, Chen Yi was denounced; and thirdly, the Red Guards burnt down the British Representative Office in Beijing. At the time, Qi Ba repeatedly appealed for a stop to be put to any disorder in the foreign affairs sector, and to stop any changes being made to foreign affairs policies. He further requested that there be differentiation between home and international policies, but he was ignored by the rebel groups. Wang, Guan and Qi had the trust of Mao Zedong; however, these three incidents were an embarrassment to Mao. Qi Ba denounced the ultra-leftist trend and proposed to reorganise the foreign ministry, but this incurred the displeasure of Mao Zedong, who openly commented on Qi Ba's proposal as being leftist in form but rightist in essence.

Chen Yi and Qi Ba were intimate comrades-in-arms during their long military careers. When the first Afro-Asian conference was held in Bandung, Indonesia, in 1955, the Chinese foreign minister Chen Yi attended. This conference was very successful. When the delegates voted for the second Afro-Asian conference to be held in Algeria, Chen Yi voted

Zhou Enlai and He Long.

in favour, although he knew nothing about the coup that had just taken place in that country. But one African official lodged a protest, saying that the behaviour of the rebels should not be encouraged. Qi Ba agreed with this African official, so he criticised Chen Yi for exposing his position before he had formed a clear understanding of the situation. Chen Yi accepted this criticism and withdrew his support.

On another occasion, Ho Chi Minh, Qi Ba and Chen Yi met in a cave hotel in Guangzhou, built by Tao Zhu, for a rest. Qi Ba arranged for Ho Chi Minh to have the best room. Considering that Chen Yi wasn't in good health, Qi Ba asked him to take another room with better conditions, and Chen Yi happily accepted. Many years later, when the hotel staff mentioned this to me, they said with great emotion that the mutual respect among the three leaders of China and Vietnam had naturally demonstrated their intimate and comradely, as well as brotherly, relationship.

2.2. He Long

Marshal He Long was assistant commandant of the Second Field Army of the PLA during the war of liberation, but we were not to meet. When Qi Ba asked me about the commanders of the Second Field Army, I told him that I had met Liu Bocheng, Deng Xiaoping, Li Da and Song Renqiong, as I had attended their lectures. As for He Long, I had only heard that after the liberation of Sichuan, he had been concerned about the scenic spot of Mount Emei, ordering it to be protected. In addition, he was in charge of the building of the southwest auditorium. After I said this, Qi Ba smiled and said: "How could some people say that the veteran comrades in our army are only military men? Soon after the liberation of the southwest, He Long cared about the protection and construction of scenic Mount Emei. Isn't he adept with both the pen and the sword? He Long is sure to be able to develop his ability to the fullest. He has done a popular and good deed."

Whenever the August First Nanchang uprising was mentioned, Qi Ba would tell the staff of the museums, especially the researchers and the guides, that the troops led by He Long formed the main force behind the success of the uprising. He would give a broad overview of He Long's life, who, heedless of his personal safety, resolutely joined the revolution when the party was facing the most difficulties. Thus, the historical contributions he made should be remembered by future generations.

In 1967, for He Long's safety, Qi Ba arranged for him to stay temporarily at West Flower Hall. At the time, I would often go to Fuyou Street, where West Flower Hall was situated, to observe the situation. I saw that the Red Guards had set up tents, and the whole compound was so closely besieged that not a drop of water could have trickled through. Anti-Zhou Enlai posters were everywhere, some of them demanding the removal of Qi Ba from his office as premier. The Red Guards even read out the text on the posters through loudspeakers. Under these circumstances, Qi Ba clearly felt that West Flower Hall was not a safe place, so he transferred He Long to the protection of the army. He didn't expect that the army was at the time actually under the control of Lin Biao, to a certain extent. Qi Ba's original intention was to protect He Long, but unluckily He Long failed to escape disaster, which became one of Qi Ba's biggest regrets in his life.

2.3. Peng Dehuai

During the Cultural Revolution, Marshal Peng Dehuai had been in prison for eight years. He was subjected to endless criticism, denunciations and investigations, and was subjected to merciless mental torture there.

In the spring of 1973, Peng Dehuai suffered from rectal carcinoma, passing blood in his stool. His whole body had collapsed. Because the cancer cells were spreading, he was in unbearable pain. The prison wardens tried to send him to Fuwai hospital, but met with rejection. When they contacted the First Division Hospital of the Beijing garrison, they were rejected there, too.

I happened to accompany a foreign visitor to see a doctor in the 301 general hospital of the PLA. I met Chen Yi in the reception hall. He knew the foreign visitor from a long time ago, but he only shook his hand out of courtesy (no conversation took place). At once, some hospital staff came up to me, blaming me for my carelessness, which allowed Chen Yi, who was labelled a member of the February Countercurrent, to make contact with the foreigner. Luckily, the hospital director was making his way towards us. Leaving no doubt about his intentions, he signalled the staff to leave. I knew what he meant: it was an accidental encounter, and there was no need to make a mountain out of a molehill and complicate the situation. The staff turned away and my mind was set at ease. It seemed that the hospital director knew about me and trusted me, so we began to chat. He couldn't help mentioning the fact that Peng Dehuai wanted to come to hospital for cancer treatment.

Sympathetically, he said that it was already a very unfortunate thing to have been reduced in his military rank from Marshal to the army level. The medical personnel in the hospital wanted to take him in, but unexpectedly, the chief of staff, Huang Yongsheng, was strongly against them doing so, saying that he would not come for treatment if Peng was in this hospital. The director was under huge pressure and did not know what to do. Luckily, Qi Ba soon learnt of this and gave the following instructions: "No conclusion has yet been reached on the problem of Peng Dehuai, but we must pay attention to his disease and give him treatment." Hence, Peng went and received treatment at the 301 hospital. Under the circumstances, this was all Qi Ba could do for Peng Dehuai, even though he had repeatedly requested Qi Ba to announce his rehabilitation.

2.4. Lin Biao

"Lin Biao was a fourth-term student at Huangpu Military Academy. I am very happy that he will be taking up the post of the vice premier." This is what Qi Ba said during one of our talks in 1956. He called me, as well as his third younger brother, Zhou Enshou, in for a meeting at his residence. As our conversation had something to do with his brother, Qi Ba asked his niece, Zhou Enshou's daughter, to make herself scarce. When Qi Ba talked about how his brother was doing in the early years of the revolution, he said: "Zhou Enshou and Lin Biao were both fourth-term students at Huangpu Military Academy. Lin Biao is now taking the post of vice premier. History has proven that he persevered during the revolution and has made an outstanding contribution to it. I am very glad about that." At the time, I felt that Qi Ba thought highly of his student. But during the Cultural Revolution, after Lin Biao was confirmed as Chairman Mao's successor, the military representative of my work unit, who was from a certain air force academy and a subordinate of Lin Biao's, made things very difficult for me for many years, because I was a member of Zhou Enlai's younger generation.

After the Lin Biao Incident, someone spread the rumour that it was Qi Ba who had ordered Lin Biao's private plane to be shot down. Qi Ba said: "I have no direct leadership position in the military; where would I get the power to order military personnel to shoot down the private plane of our party's vice chairman?"

2.5. Li Fuchun

As early as 1919, Li Fuchun also went to France to study while doing some part-time work. He joined the Chinese Youth League in 1921 and the party in 1922, returning to China in 1925. Since taking part in the Northern Expedition, he had been Qi Ba's intimate comrade-in-arms. His wife, Cai Chang, was one of the country's female leaders, along with Qi Ma. The two women had been working together for a long time. After the founding of the PRC, Li Fuchun concurrently became vice premier, director of the planning commission, secretary of the secretariat of the Central Committee of the CPC, and a member of the standing committee of the Political Bureau, working directly under the leadership of Qi Ba.

In 1975, when I accompanied a foreign guest to Beijing hospital for treatment, Li Fuchun was there for treatment of his lung cancer. Despite the fact that he was the vice premier, as he was regarded as a member of the February Countercurrent, he only held that position notionally. The hospital staff thought that although he was in a high position, he was honest and modest, so they respected him very much and assigned him a nurse, who used to be the chief nurse, to look after him. According to regulations, she checked on him every two hours. Because the hospital had no screen monitors at the time, he died choking on his own mucous during one of the two-hour intervals.

According to the doctors and nurses, one thing that he couldn't get off his mind before he died was Qi Ba's health. He said: "I don't know how Zhou Enlai is. I'm worried about his condition, and I hope it will not get any worse. The development of the Chinese economy will not go well without Zhou Enlai, especially in times of difficulty." The reason he said this was because he was in charge of the national economy when Qi Ba was the notional premier, and he was expected to come up with countermeasures to free the country from its difficult economic position. He then put forward a policy of reorganisation, consolidation and improvement, and went to discuss it with Qi Ba. After some thought, Qi Ba changed it to readjustment, consolidation, substantiation and improvement. Afterwards, the policy was approved and put into effect, and the country's economy could finally extricate itself from a difficult position. Therefore, on his sick bed, Li still could not forget the huge contribution that Qi Ba had made to China's economic development, thinking that Qi Ba's economic policy had played a guiding role in China's long-term development.

2.6. Zhang Xiruo

Zhang Xiruo was a famous Chinese patriot and non-party democrat. He served as education minister, president of the foreign affairs association and director of the international liaison committee, and also in other leading positions. Before 1949, Mr Zhang had opposed the dictatorship of Chiang Kai-shek, openly calling for him to resign. During the meeting of the first political consultative conference, prevailing despite the many dissenting views, he suggested the new regime be called the People's Republic of China. In 1980, the well-known Beijing University jurist Professor Wang Tieya told me that because of the negative impact the Cultural Revolution had had on the juridical system of China, he was worried that the Chinese jurisprudence circle would be short of qualified successors. Meantime, Professor Wang mentioned that of those belonging to the older generation, he had the greatest esteem for Zhang Xiruo, who had been a mentor figure in the Chinese jurisprudence circle. Mr Zhang's thesis, written in 1931, *The Origin of the French Declaration of the Rights of Man and of the Citizen (1789)*, was very high in academic value.

Zhang Xiruo died in 1973. Before he died, he was in Beijing hospital for treatment. By chance, the foreign guest whom I accompanied to the hospital was in the ward just next to his, which I had not expected. Without informing me or the hospital, he freely walked into the ward and began to speak in English with the foreign patient. Frankly, he told him that he was suffering from heart disease, and might not live long. I had to introduce him to my foreign guest. After they had had a short conversation, he turned to me, asking me who I was. After I told him my name and introduced myself briefly, he happily said to the foreign guest: "This young man is my subordinate, whose name has long been familiar to me but whose face I have never seen." What he said was true. In 1960s, he was the director of the CCRFC and I was one of the staff members. He was a noble senior executive while I was an ordinary cadre, so it was simply not appropriate for me to chat with him directly. But now, at this very moment, in hospital, he wanted to have a chat with me. For the last few decades, the contents of our conversation have remained fresh in my memory, as I did not dare forget them.

He mentioned an important past event to me. In May 1957, he was invited to attend a symposium for the democratic parties and non-party democrats, held by the United Front Work Department (UWFD) of the Central Committee. During the symposium, he made a speech about anti-dogmatism, as well as the deviations that existed in the work of the party and the state. His speech could be summarised as follows: "We crave greatness and success, seek instant benefits, hold past traditions in scorn, and make a fetish of the future." Then he gave a detailed explanation. 'We crave greatness and success' means that we think socialism is grand, and no matter what the people's livelihoods are or what consumers need, we need large-scale solutions to satisfy our craving for size. When we 'seek instant benefits', it appears that we put emphasis on achieving rapid results and use quick methods to achieve long-term goals. When we 'hold past traditions in scorn', it means that many people ignore historical factors, copying foreign dogmas for any and all ends and treating many things left over from history as feudal remnants that must be done away with. And when we 'make a fetish of the future', it means that we think everything in the future will be great and all future developments will happen at the same speed.

On that day, many non-party democrats were labelled rightists due to their 'inappropriate' speeches. At first, it was hard for him to escape being labelled, which he only achieved because Qi Ba gave him his full support. He then carried on working as president of the Chinese People's Institute of Foreign Affairs, which was under the direct leadership of Qi

Ba. It was said that Mao Zedong was not happy at all with what Zhang had said, but he still thought that "Zhang Xiruo was a good man". During our conversation, Mr Zhang also mentioned that Qi Ba had once been regarded as only 50 metres short of a rightist, and had even been pressured to resign. The Chinese people regarded Qi Ba as China's general housekeeper, but sometimes he was powerless, making it indeed hard to act according to principles. It seems that it was easy for Qi Ba to provide protection to the non-party personnel, but much harder to provide the same protection to comrades within the party. In short, the benefits I gained from Qi Ba's wisdom, courage and insight appeared during my conversation with Mr Zhang, and have stayed with me for the last few decades.

3. US President Richard Nixon Visits China

In the early 1970s, when the Cultural Revolution was gradually entering its later stage, through the coordination of different quarters, China and the US began a series of secret negotiations; however, the ping-pong diplomacy was out in the open. On 21 February 1972, US president Richard Nixon and his party finally crossed the Pacific Ocean and arrived in Beijing, embarking upon a seven-day historical visit to China. They were welcomed by Premier Zhou Enlai and the other Chinese leaders. During his visit, President Nixon met Chairman Mao Zedong and talked with Premier Zhou Enlai. The two sides exchanged views on international situations and the Sino-American relationship. They emphatically discussed the issues of Indochina and Taiwan. On February 28, the two countries signed the Joint Communiqué of the United States of America and the People's Republic of China in Shanghai, which had a milestone significance and declared to the whole world the normalisation of relations between China and the US. From then on, the Sino-American relationship entered a new historical era, which laid the foundation for the future development of relations between the two countries.

3.1. The Foreign Ministry and the Ministry of Public Security's Joint Circular

Before 1966, I worked with the CCRFC, whose director was Zhang

Xiruo. After the Cultural Revolution started in 1966, this organisation was closed down and its staff members were reassigned. My wife and I had been appointed to work at the Chinese Embassy in Sweden, and we were ready to go. But I was required to work temporarily at the BSFLI, which was under the management of the CCRFC. Soon after my arrival, all staff members were sent to the May Seventh Cadre School in Xinyang, in Henan province, to take up farm work. Because the military representative at the farm had joined the Gang of Four and Lin Biao's clique, I suffered unjustifiable persecution from 1969 to 1971, and the treatment I received showed a complete lack of justice. Generally speaking, in this two-year period, the two main activities I took part in were manual labour and receiving criticism. Yet Qi Ba had already given directives that the training of talented foreign-language speakers must not be abandoned; hence, I still received a small amount of teaching. At the farm, my position was company commander, but after I returned to Beijing at the end of 1971, I reassumed my previous position as department director. Soon after I returned to Beijing, I was transferred to the ILD, of which Geng Biao was the minister. He was a distinguished strategist and diplomat, and it was he who withstood pressure while resolutely implementing the cadre policy of the party, redressing cases in which people were unjustly, falsely or wrongly charged or sentenced. As a result, a large number of cadres were called back from the farms and allowed to reassume their previous jobs.

Before I had time to go to report for duty, the education ministry appointed me to translate the UNESCO constitution for the United Nations. During this period, I was suddenly notified by the foreign ministry and the Ministry of Public Security to take part in the reception for President Richard Nixon of the US. Feeling odd, I thought: "How could I be useful there?"

But I had to obey the decisions of the government organisations, so after I finished my translation, I went to the foreign ministry to report for duty. I then found out that my job was to accompany the American media crew members and the security personnel of the White House. I had done culture-related jobs before, so I had experience with accompanying people from the press and the media, but I was surprised that I was also to accompany White House security guards. Soon I understood why. One of the main directors of the White House security force had begun his life as a professor. He had regular features and refined manners, and standing at just over 1.70m tall among the strapping security fellows, he didn't seem like a man who had served in the army. In this case, it was a matter of course for me to accompany him. Recalling it now, I believe the reason Qi Ba ignored his usual practice of not giving the impression he favoured his relatives and arranged for me to take part in President Nixon's reception was that he regarded China's domestic situation during the Cultural Revolution as complicated, and he was preparing for any and all contingencies.

Before President Nixon's arrival, I was sent to the Beijing hotel to check on the preparations. The old lift had been dismantled, so we had to use the temporary lift for construction workers to get to the rooftop. The lift was very simple and crude, built out of a few pieces of wooden board with air blowing in from all directions, and people felt unsafe when it began to ascend. After I got to the top, I was told that Qi Ba, who was at an advanced age and not in good health, had taken the same lift to the rooftop to examine the security conditions for the reception of the American president. Many cadres had praised Premier Zhou Enlai for his thoughtfulness. My companions and I felt that this praise was very true.

3.2. Qi Ba Is Unaware that He Is Seriously Ill

In fact, there was nothing specific for me to do, and my work with the security people was in name only. My most important job was to accompany the minister of the Chinese organisation ministry while he attended the state banquet for President Nixon. Before it started, parties from both sides neatly lined up in two rows. Premier Zhou Enlai shook hands with the American guests, one after another, while President Nixon, Mrs Nixon, US Secretary of State William Rogers, President Nixon's national security adviser, Dr Henry Kissinger, and others shook hands with the Chinese personnel. The Chinese welcome committee consisted of some of the leading cadres, non-party democrats and senior intellectuals, as well as the KMT generals who had come over to the communists' side. Both President Nixon and Dr Kissinger were healthy and strong. Their cheeks were flushed, probably from excitement.

The Years of the Cultural Revolution

Qi Ba accompanied President Nixon, Mrs Nixon and Dr Kissinger to sit at the head table. The PLA army band began to play 'America the Beautiful', a famous American song. This song was personally selected by Qi Ba. He told the band that this song had been played at President Nixon's

Zhou Enlai greeting Richard Nixon at the airport, Beijing.

My Uncle Zhou Enlai

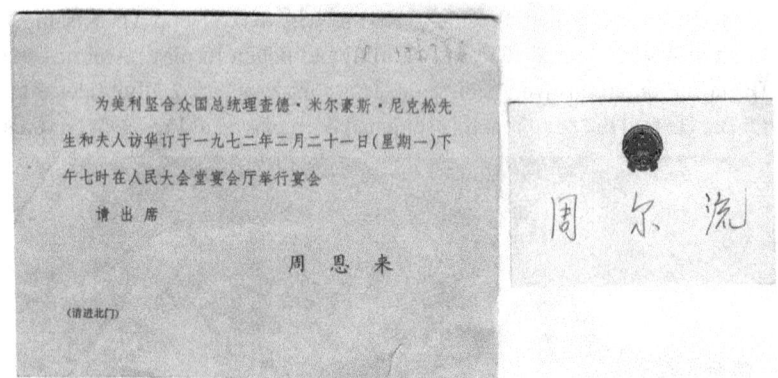

The invitation for Richard Nixon's welcome banquet. "Zhou Enlai invites you to the state banquet for the visiting president of the United States of America, Mr & Mrs Richard Milhous Nixon. February 21, 1972. 7 PM. Banquet Hall, the Great Hall of the People (please use the north entrance)." On the back of the card: "Zhou Erliu".

inauguration in 1969, and as he was a music expert, we chose this piece of music to emphasise the friendship between the Chinese and American people while making him feel at home. When this warm and cheerful scene was broadcast live on television across the US, it sparked reverberations among the American people. When Mr Nixon wrote his memoirs in his old age, this scene was still fresh in his mind. "After the toasts, the orchestra played 'America the Beautiful', and I remarked that this was one of the songs I had chosen for my inauguration in 1969." (p.34, *The Memoirs of Richard Nixon, Vol 2*, Warner Books, 1979)

After the hosts and the guests were seated, Qi Ba toasted the guests: "President Nixon's visit to our country at the invitation of the Chinese government provides the leaders of the two countries with the opportunity to meet in person, promote the normalisation of relations between them and exchange views on questions that are of concern to both sides. This is a positive move, corresponding with the desire of the Chinese and American peoples, and an unprecedented event in the history of relations between China and the US."

"The American people are a great people. The Chinese people are a great people. The peoples of our two countries have always been friendly to each other. But owing to reasons known to all, contact between the two was suspended for over 20 years. Now, through the common efforts of China and the US, the gate to friendly contact has finally reopened. We hope that, through a frank exchange of views between our two sides to gain a clearer notion of our differences and make efforts to find common ground, a new start can be made in the relations between our two countries." Qi Ba's speech was constantly interrupted by applause.

Then President Nixon toasted: "...So, let us, in next five days, start a long march together, not in lockstep, but on different roads leading to the same goal: the goal of building a world structure of peace and justice, in which all may stand together with equal dignity and in which each nation, large or small, has a right to determine its own form of government, free of outside interference or domination...

"There is no reason for us to be enemies. Neither of us seeks the territory of the other; neither of us seeks domination over the other; neither of us seeks to stretch out our hands and rule the world.

"Chairman Mao has written, 'So many deeds cry out to be done, and always urgently. The world rolls on. Time passes. Ten thousand years are too long. Seize the day, seize the hour.

"This is the hour, this is the day for our two peoples to rise to the heights of greatness that can build a new and better world."

After the speeches, Qi Ba proposed toasts to every member of the American delegation. It was well known that Qi Ba could drink. I learnt later that at the time, he had already begun passing blood with his urine and become thinner. The doctors had told him to drink less while making sure to rest properly, but with great willpower, he could still work hard. After the American guests left China, Qi Ba told me that drinking that amount of liquor would have been nothing to him in the past.

3.3. Qi Ba's Chopsticks and President Nixon's Wine Glass

In order to give the American guests a good reception, the standard for the state banquet was unusually high. It included nine cold dishes, six hot dishes, seven assorted desserts, fruit and wine. At the dinner table, the

American guests sitting on either side of me were the 'professor' and a 26-year-old security guard, who was 2m tall. Seeing me raise my head to look at him, he told me that he was not the tallest among them; when necessary, they could form a wall of bodies to shield their president. I noticed that many of the guards were nervous, all following the professor in raising their glasses or to starting to eat, worried that they might commit a breach of etiquette. Before they came to this mysterious country, they had been given some training on how to use chopsticks, so they could manage to pick up the food. However, the clumsiness of the guards still aroused some well-intentioned laughter, though the president could use the chopsticks with ease.

The professor was very polite. Refined in manner, he spoke softly. I understood more of Qi Ba's intentions in asking me to attend the reception. The professor asked me what I did, and I told him that I was a teacher. However, he couldn't tell me precisely what he was did, so I stopped asking, thinking he might be an intelligence or security officer. He asked if all the people sitting at the table were in the same business — he meant working in security. As soon as I finished translating the sentence, the minister of the organisation department said yes, nodding his head. I was a little embarrassed, but I couldn't explain much. Afterwards, the American guests told me that they knew that the minister and I had no experience with this diplomatic aspect of their visit. Seemingly, they had done a good job in gathering intelligence. They apologised to me for any misunderstandings. Also, they offered their gratitude for receiving a reception of such a high standard in Beijing.

When the banquet came to an end, one thing impressed me very much. Without being commanded or directed to do so, all the security guards from both sides stood up and charged towards the platform to guard their own leader. Amazed, the minister of the organisation department and I were moved by their spirit of dashing ahead regardless of their own safety. Our table was number 18, a spot from where it was easy for the security guards to keep a lookout and to get near the head table; it seemed that it had been arranged just so by both sides.

When the banquet ended, the Chinese were busy taking photos. None

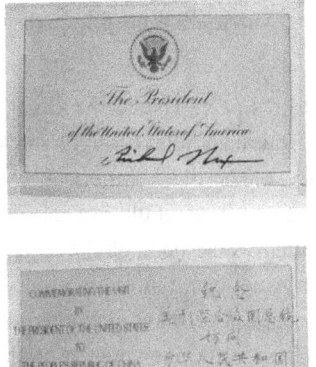

Presents from Richard Nixon during his China visit.

of us paid any attention to the items left on the table, because we had not been told that we could take them as souvenirs. But the Americans took everything with them, from the wine glasses to the menus — someone even took away the chopsticks Qi Ba had used. Later, the foreign ministry made up for our lack of souvenirs, and I received a crystal wine glass imprinted with the US presidential seal and a name card in a Perspex pocket, signed by President Richard Nixon. These are gifts of significance, and I have kept them with me till today. It was said that Qi Ba approved of the souvenirs, as they were memorable, yet cost little.

3.4. The Week that Changed the World

To report on the president's China visit, the Americans sent along a strong publicity team with a large amount of equipment, to record the daily news conference and the live broadcast back home to the US.

While I was busy receiving the American media, I met a black member of the television staff. He told me that his wife was Chinese and living overseas, so he had a strong appreciation for China. He was excited to have been able to come to China with the president, but also he felt that by reporting on it he was shouldering a grave responsibility. He was very nice and extremely conscientious in his work, which left a deep impression on me.

On 24 February, President Nixon and his party visited the Great Wall. According to the arrangements, the American television broadcasting van was to be driven by a Chinese driver. The black American was not happy with this at all, saying that Chinese drivers could not manage the van because they lacked the experience and would damage the equipment. He insisted that the van be driven by an American. I strongly argued with him, and in the end, he gave in. But I could never have imagined that on the trip to the Badaling section of the Great Wall, one antenna on the van would touch a farmer's house and break off. The Chinese driver panicked and didn't know what to do. The American was furious after he learnt of the incident. He was so angry that he banged his fists on the reception counter and smashed the glass.

Then I spoke to him, insisting that no one had wanted an accident like that to happen, and that we were trying to sort it out and making sure it would not affect their broadcast. "But," I said, "it was impolite for you to behave in such a way, and you ought to pay for the glass you damaged. However, now that the Chinese and the Americans are friends, we won't ask you to pay." After I had said this, he slowly calmed down.

To be honest, I appreciated the Americans' working spirit very much. On that day, though it was snowing heavily, both men and women crawled on the ground without hesitation in order to catch the historical scenes with their cameras. They also admired our work efficiency. As it had snowed the night before, a thick layer of snow covered the streets and roads in Beijing. In order to allow the American president and his party to reach the Great Wall smoothly, Qi Ba gave instructions to the Beijing municipal council to mobilise more than 100,000 Beijing citizens to sweep away the snow on the roads leading to the Great Wall overnight. At the time, China had no snow ploughs. The job of clearing away the snow depended on manpower only.

Hence, the Americans were amazed to see the clean streets and roads.

Some guests said that, as seeing is believing, "the socialist system does have some advantages." President Nixon also thought it unimaginable, saying that it was impossible in the US to mobilise that many people in one night. After he had climbed onto the beacon tower of the Great Wall, he excitedly said to Marshal Ye Jianying, who was accompanying him, that he was also a "true man".

Qi Ba was very objective. Throughout his life, he maintained that we should let foreigners see both China's good and bad sides and not cover up anything that was not so good. When they were climbing the Great Wall on that very cold day, Qi Ba saw some little girls rubber band skipping in their jumpers, which was too obviously staged by some organisation. He was not very happy with it. When he accompanied the American guests to a hospital to witness the procedure of acupuncture anaesthesia, the guests thought it was amazing, and they all gave their thumbs up. But Qi Ba calmly said to the other Chinese that we should tell the guests about the scientific principle behind the acupuncture. Meanwhile, we should do more research ourselves, and we should never exaggerate the importance of this traditional method, because some operations cannot be done with acupuncture anaesthesia.

At the last banquet held before he left China, President Nixon said in his toast that his seven-day visit to China could be called "the week that changed the world". History has proven that what he said was very right. It is said that after he returned home, President Nixon indicated that if China had not had Mao Zedong, the revolutionary flames might not have been kindled, but that without Zhou Enlai the revolution would have burnt out, and only the ashes would have remained.

3.5. The Five Principles of Peaceful Coexistence and the Shanghai Communiqué

On 28 February 1972, during President Richard Nixon's visit, China and the US published the Joint Communiqué of the United States of America and the People's Republic of China, also known as the Shanghai Communiqué. The principles that should be followed by both China and the US to normalise their relationship are, in fact, the Five Principles of Peaceful Coexistence, which were developed by Qi Ba in the 1950s. Besides being just and usable, they also have a great vitality, to which the development of the world's history is entrusted.

The Shanghai Communiqué distinctively showed the aim of 'seeking common ground while reserving differences', Qi Ba's philosophy and its creative application. It reflects his understanding of the complicated world and his policy of how to deal with international relations in a correct way. The communiqué clarified the principles that would guide China and the US in their long-term relationship, setting out the divergence of both sides while restricting the use of force when settling disputes. These did not only give guidance as to how the world's largest and most-developed country, the US, and the largest developing country, China, can do their best to coexist peacefully and seek mutual development, but also provided a creative basis as well as a diplomatic example for all other countries in the world to follow. I remember Deng Xiaoping once commented on this. His point was that for many years in history, the fundamental, general and specific policies that have proven effective in the long run must be the Five Principles of Peaceful Coexistence.

After 1972, I was lucky enough to hear comments made by some senior officials working in the foreign affairs sector, such as Geng Biao, Wu Xueqian, Huang Zhen, Wang Bingnan and Huan Xiang, as well as the grand masters Fei Xiaotong, Lei Jieqiong and Ji Xianlin. They all agreed that the Five Principles of Peaceful Coexistence had made a huge contribution to peace and development in the world.

As a person working in the foreign affairs sector, I am very lucky to have experienced such a once-in-a-lifetime event as the visit to China by US president Richard Nixon. In my remaining years, I have been recording bits of the actual facts that would be beneficial to both the Chinese and the Americans, as well as humankind, to leave behind a conscientious and responsible synopsis for future generations.

3.6. The Story of the Maotai Liquor

During the banquets he held for foreign visitors, Qi Ba would eat while talking or making toasts, and the atmosphere would generally be relaxed. Whenever he casually interposed a remark, he was, in fact, using the opportunity to introduce things with Chinese characteristics or customs of localities to foreign visitors. Such remarks were usually extensive and they played a role in enhancing the foreign visitors' understanding of and friendship with China.

Maotai liquor is the most distinguished representative of Chinese spirits. Whether a guest was visiting China for the first time or had been to China many times before, during a banquet, it was natural to talk about Maotai, the liquor they were drinking. Qi Ba would then cleverly connect the liquor with the Long March, because it was based on his own experiences. His vivid descriptions often made the visitors highly enthusiastic.

He said that in those days, when the Red Army had entered Guizhou province, they soon reached the region of Zunyi. For many generals and soldiers, this was the first time they had been to the region and they knew nothing about local customs and specialities. The local Maotai liquor was then not so well known as it is today. After a long trek, drinking Maotai was an opportunity for the exhausted army personnel to taste something new. At the start, many of them couldn't drink it, but they soon got used to it and would not tire of drinking it. To wounded soldiers, it was either a disinfectant or a stimulant. They would buy it until the liquor was sold out, and only the distiller's grains were left at the bottom of the containers. After the Red Army left Guizhou, the distillers could no longer make Maotai of the same quality as before. The newly brewed Maotai did not have the same flavour as the old.

Jokingly, the local people would say: "The Maotai liquor has become an inseparable companion and comrade-in-arms to the Red Army. They took with them the genuine flavour of the liquor when they left. The fascinating liquor has lost its former wonder." But fourteen years later, the PLA garrisoned the region. Because the liquor had been accumulating at the bottom of the distillers' containers for the last decade, the flavour of the new liquor had even surpassed the flavour of the past. Happily and also jokingly, the locals said: "The Red Army took away with them the Maotai of the past. After a long separation, the PLA has brought back home a brand new flavour of Maotai." Then Qi Ba would turn the conversation to his old comrade-in-arms Marshal Liu Bocheng, saying: "This well-known strategist, theoretician and illustrious hero was not the same as the majority of the generals and the soldiers. He touched no spirits, which aroused sympathy in all the others, because wines did not appeal to him." Qi Ba's words either aroused reminiscence or a kind-hearted, clear-sighted comparison, which gives a rough idea of his artistic diplomatic style.

4. Qi Ba and the Gang of Four

4.1. Criticise Lin, Criticise Confucius and Criticise the Duke of Zhou

During the Cultural Revolution, the Gang of Four regarded Qi Ba as an obstacle: hard to bypass on their way to usurp the party leadership and seize state power. Their dislike reached such an extent that they stopped at nothing to attack him, and they even did it in front of foreign visitors. One of their most used tricks was to misuse historical stories, using the past to satirise the present. I personally witnessed this on one occasion and I profoundly feel that it is necessary to recall it.

On 18 January 1974, Chairman Mao Zedong approved the joint recommendation of Jiang Qing and Wang Hongwen, and ordered the publication of *Lin Biao and the Doctrine of Confucius and Mencius*, an article compiled by the Great Criticism Group of the Beijing and Qinghua Universities, in that year's number-one document of the Central Committee. Thus, a campaign to 'Criticise Lin, Criticise Confucius' was launched throughout the country.

Right from the beginning, this movement was unusually ferocious and surreptitious, trailing a strong smell of gunpowder. Jiang Qing behaved as if she was acting on the emperor's orders, assuming the air of being in charge of the campaign and commanding the politburo. On one hand, she frequently wrote letters in her own name, sent out material and called together the mobilisation meetings. On the other hand, she sent the members of her gang and her followers to stir up trouble at many places. All over the country the rebel groups were roused into action without delay, and once again they formed factions and began uncovering and struggling against the local representative figures of the restorationist forces. They tried to use this opportunity to spearhead their criticism of Qi Ba.

In those years, one professor at a certain university wrote an article, which was titled *Confucius Put Shaozheng Mao to Death*. According to historical facts, Confucius had had Shaozheng Mao killed, and the earliest record of this can be found in the *Youzuo* by Xunzi, which lists the crimes of Shaozheng Mao as follows: "[He] was extremely knowledgeable, but had malicious intentions; acted wickedly, but was unwilling to repent; resorted to sophistry; actively followed, with interest, the dark side of society; followed and spread unorthodox ideas." In addition, in Xunzi's *The Twelve Evil Men*, it says that Shaozheng Mao "acted wickedly, but was unwilling to repent; concealed faults and glossed over wrongs; resorted to schemes and intrigues; was skilled in debate, but argued in an unreasonable manner, and all these behaviours have been forbidden since ancient times." Anyway, the crimes of Shaozheng Mao listed in these two articles are similar. Then, in the chapter titled 'The Hereditary House of Confucius' in *The Records of the Grand Scribe* by Sima Qian, it said: "After Confucius became acting prime minister of the Lu state, he sentenced Shaozheng Mao, a senior official, to death. His crime was that he was against the administration." But, historically, no conclusion was reached on whether or not Confucius had had Shaozheng Mao killed, because there were many questionable aspects to the matter. Later generations called the incident into question as well. But after the ignorant Jiang Qing found out about the article, she at once went to the professor and asked for copies. Afterwards, she brazenly violated diplomatic protocol and handed the copies to visiting foreigners, vainly attempting to spread the contents overseas. Trying to imitate what had been done by Confucius to Shaozheng Mao in the old days, she wanted to make Qi Ba a 'present-day Confucius' and bring him down from his office.

To enlarge the effect, she instructed the article to be duplicated, so that foreign visitors would distribute them to other people after they returned home. After I learnt of this, I asked my work unit at once to send a car to the professor, and I got hold of about 50 copies, which I secretly burnt at home. I completely disregarded my own safety, nor did I tell my wife about it. At the time, not everyone in the foreign affairs sector had studied these historical stories. Jiang's behaviour, acting as if she had found a treasure while giving these barely understandable Chinese articles to foreigners to read, aroused suspicion among the Chinese. People finally became aware of her motives. Her conduct, which showed an ignorance of history, exposed her intentions to make use of the movement to bring down Qi Ba once and for all, and once again made clear her political ambition.

Qi Ba was kept in the dark when the movement started. He knew nothing about being attacked with innuendo and the past being used to disparage the present. At the beginning of the year, he told Mao Zedong in his written report that it should be called the Criticise Lin and Rectify Campaign, not the Criticise Lin, Criticise Confucius Campaign. But from the force of the movement and the realisation that he had been pushed aside on the matter, he soon found out what was behind it. He had to prepare for the worst from this unfavourable political situation, getting ready to be attacked by name and at any moment. Under such circumstances, Qi Ba, who knew very well that it was hard to act against a trend, was fully aware that this movement was aimed at him to a great extent; he just deliberately did not lay bare the truth. To stop the Gang of Four from seizing power, he kept on doing his work, never retreating from his position. To prove this, I would like to quote what Qi Ba said to Geng Biao, minister of the ILD, who was called by name and criticised by the Gang of Four. "Other people are trying to bring you down, yet you simply stand still; they want to drive you away, yet you refuse to leave; they make things difficult for you, yet you do not die." This is my Qi Ba: combining the breadth of vision of a faithful and unyielding revolutionary and his wisdom for fighting an opponent.

Mr Nan Huaijin, the grand master of Chinese classics, used to work at Huangpu Military Academy. He had great esteem for Qi Ba and especially admired his facial features, saying that Qi Ba was a very good-looking man, and that I was the Zhou family descendant who resembled Qi Ba the most. He and I had several face-to-face conversations when he invited me to take charge of Taihu University in Wujinag district, Suzhou, in Jiangsu, but I declined his invitation. When he talked to me, he would refer to Qi Ba as the "duke of Zhou". He said that the historical duke of Zhou had been a very respectable man, who had had no wild political ambitions. Zhou Enlai, like the real duke of Zhou in ancient times, was a model political figure, rare in the history of China and even the world. Mr Nan jeered at the shamelessness and ignorance of the Gang of Four.

The Years of the Cultural Revolution

Zhou Erliu and Nan Huaijin.

4.2. The Photo that Stunned Viewers

During the Cultural Revolution, when secretaries and chairmen of Marxist-Leninist parties around the world visited China, many of them were received by Qi Ba. Ted Hill, the chairman of the communist party of Australia, came to China almost every year and had become a friend of Mao Zedong's. Mao Zedong's viewpoint that "war causes revolution, while revolution stops war" was uttered during one of his conversations with Mr Hill. The reception of these leaders generally took place in the Fujian room in the Great Hall of the People. Because these were all breakaway parties, they were small in size. In order to show that large and small parties were equal, after Wang Jiaxiang and Kang Sheng left their offices, Qi Ba, though very busy, had to receive the delegations himself. The members of the Gang of Four, including Zhang Chunqiao, Jiang Qing, Yao Wenyuan and Wang Hongwen, would also attend these meetings. The reception often began in the afternoon and went on until after the evening banquet. In those days, Qi Ba was in a very perilous situation: besides receiving the foreign visitors, he had to be on guard against the Gang of Four making trouble. They always attempted, through these foreign visitors, to initiate something that would have an international impact, stopping at nothing to hint at the outside world that Qi Ba's position was not secure.

In April 1974, Ted Hill visited China. When Qi Ba received him, there was a photo opportunity. The picture was to be published in the newspapers afterwards. In a normal situation and according to the diplomatic protocol, Qi Ba was a member of the standing committee of the Political Bureau and head of the government, which allowed him to stand in the middle of the front row. Except for the foreign visitors, the other Chinese would stand on either side of him or in the back rows according to their numbers and ranks.

As for myself, if there were fewer people, I would stand on either side of the row according to my rank. If there were more people, I would stand in the back row. Because I was a relative of Qi Ba's, I always chose to stand away from him to stop him from being accused of favouring a relative. On that day, I had already stationed myself on the left-hand side of the back row for hosts, but I didn't expect Jiang Qing to stand in the centre of the front row, where Qi Ba should have stood. Hence, Qi Ba had to move to the guest's left, which was just in front of me. This unexpected circumstance surprised me, and also made me rather indignant. Afterwards, the people working for the protocol department told me that the premier had showed a little politeness, so Jiang Qing had simply taken the central position in the front row.

The photo created a great stir both at home and abroad after it was published. It especially received close attention from the international community. The international press, such as *The Times* and *The Guardian* in the UK, published the photo with a review, saying that China was making readjustments in its cabinet and that Zhou Enlai would step down as premier, and that his position would be taken by Jiang Qing. This matter not only showed the mistake on our part, but also sent the wrong signal to the people both at home and abroad, which had a terrible political impact!

During the Cultural Revolution, because I kept in close contact with Qi Ba for my work, other family members were very worried about my safety,

The special photo taken in April 1974 (Geng Biao is first from the left in the first row. Zhou Erliu is second from the right in the second row).

1970s, Zhou Erliu (fourth from right) accompanying Zhou Enlai and Geng Biao (fifth from the right) while receiving guests from Australia. (Zhang Chunqiao is third from the left.)

Zhou Enlai receives a guest from Europe in the Hall of the People's Congress. (Geng Biao is third from the right in the front row. Zhou Erliu is second from the left in the back row.)

so they rarely spoke to me on the phone. But this time, Qi Ma phoned me up at once. "Erliu, you are always very cautious about matters like these; why did you stand so close to your Qi Ba this time? What happened?" she asked me eagerly. I explained to her what had happened and she heaved a gentle sigh on the other end of the phone, urging me to take care. Later, when she saw me, she discussed the situation at the time with me in confidence.

This photo has become a piece of historical evidence of the Gang of Four trying to usurp power. They never let slip any opportunity to defame Qi Ba. Once, during a banquet for foreign guests, Jiang Qing suddenly said to the guests with a straight face: "Dear friends, I must tell you — of all the Chinese hosts who are present today, only Premier Zhou has studied the books of the doctrine of Confucius and Mencius." At the time, the Criticise Lin, Criticise Confucius and Criticise the Duke of Zhou Campaign had reached a peak, and it was obvious that Jiang Qing was trying to tell the foreign guests that Zhou Enlai was a key target for criticism. The atmosphere became tense at once; the foreign guests stared at Qi Ba with wide eyes while their raised wine glasses hung in the air. Retaining his composure,

Qi Ba turned to the foreign guests and then to Zhang Chunqiao. "Have you read them?" he asked Zhang. He then turned to Jiang Qing and asked her: "Have you read them?" Shamelessly, both Zhang and Jiang said no. In a casual manner, Qi Ba said to the foreign guests: "Generally, in China, it is not just people like me, but those in the age group of Zhang and Jiang who have all read the books of the doctrine of Confucius and Mencius. The only difference is that during the May Fourth Movement in 1919, my young comrades-in-arms and I came up with the slogan 'Down with the Confucian shop'." On one hand, what Qi Ba was saying exposed the lies of the Gang of Four; on the other hand, it was evidence of the firm anti-feudal stand he had taken in his youth. In those days, the disgusting conduct of the Gang of Four had violated foreign affairs policy, and moreover, their misconduct turned out to be a major political error. At the time, we were very nervous and worried for Qi Ba, but he was calm and carried on talking to the foreign guests.

After the banquet finished, Qi Ba, who was in poor health, left the Fuijan room, carrying his brief case and walking with difficulty. I rushed to his side, and then heard him say to me in a soft voice: "We still need to continue to study and analyse the doctrines of Confucius and Mencius in a comprehensive, reasonable and scientific manner; thus, no change from the essence of my previous talks with you."

4.3. Zhang Chunqiao's Unreasonable Behaviour

Throughout his life, Qi Ba would often personally give banquets in honour of the leaders of fraternal parties; after the banquet, they would go on talking until midnight. Guests from Oceania usually came to China in their summer holidays, which would be around the Chinese New Year in winter.

As premier of the state and a member of the standing committee of the Political Bureau, receiving distinguished foreign guests was a serious and solemn activity for him. The conversations would be more extensive, cordial, friendly and sometimes even light-hearted. But, contrary to our expectations, the Gang of Four would once again make him the target of their attacks, in front of the guests.

I remember him asking about pensioners in Australia. The guests said that Australia had a small population, but that two million people were already receiving pensions in 1970; the ability to live out one's life in retirement was not only a major social issue, but to some extent could affect the results of the election. Qi Ba listened with rapt attention. But suddenly, the aloof Zhang Chunqiao opened his eyes. Rudely, he interrupted the guest and said: "We don't have these problems, because we are a socialist country." His arrogant words, along with his stern glance, made the guest confused, not knowing what to say or how to continue the conversation. Zhang privately felt that Qi Ba had raised an inappropriate question. After some silence, Qi Ba refuted Zhang's viewpoint. Straightforward, he said to him: "What you just said is not correct. After all, we are a young socialist country. That more and more people are receiving a pension is a social problem that needs to be seriously and carefully dealt with. It's necessary for us to make early preparations for it."

The foreign guest smiled, nodding his head, and the tense atmosphere changed back to normal. To our surprise, Qi Ba then said, jokingly: "I am from north Jiangsu and I am generally an honest man. But of those present today, Jiang Qing, Zhang Chunqiao and Wang Hongwen are all from Shandong province. People from that region are ferocious." He then laughed, softly, and began to talk about the other topics, seemingly as though nothing had happened. I couldn't help turning my eyes to the Gang of Four. They were embarrassed and they did not know what to say. The other Chinese smiled. It was exceptional for Qi Ba to make a joke in such a careless manner, and of course, he didn't mean that there was a big difference between people's characters in different regions.

4.4. The Truth of the Creation of the Ballet *Red Detachment of Women*

In the late seventies, the Gang of Four had been overthrown and the Cultural Revolution had been given an absolutely negative verdict. Under these circumstances, Lin Mohan, the former vice minister of the central publicity department, recounted to me how Jiang Qing had distorted history and claimed that she was the creator of the model operas. Bitterly resentful, Lin said to me: "It is a disgrace that Jiang Qing has claimed credit for other people's achievements. We should expose her lies and tell the public the truth." Specifically, he used the ballet *Red Detachment of Women* as an example to make clear that he was working under the direct leadership of Premier Zhou Enlai, receiving instructions from him and gathering writers and artists for the production. After a lot of hard work, they accomplished this pioneering task.

Unexpectedly, Wu Zuqiang, chairman of the China Federation of Literature and Art and former dean of the Central Conservatory of Music, contacted me in 2008 to give me an even more detailed account of the whole story.

As it turns out, at the beginning of 1964, to celebrate the upcoming 15th anniversary of the founding of the PRC, Qi Ba suggested that the key members of the world of literature and art produce, as quickly as possible, some good plays that would meet the requirements of being revolutionary, national and modern. As for ballet, the film *Daji and Her Fathers* was initially chosen and the leading group assembled. The group's leader was Li Chengxiang, who was also the writer and director of the Central Ballet Ensemble, while Wu was the deputy leader who would be in charge of the music of the play. Wu gathered five people (including young students) to form a composition team and began to compose music for the play. Having begun their work, they decided to abandon *Daji and Her Fathers* and chose the film *Red Detachment of Women* instead. This bold but creative idea received the support of Qi Ba and Lin Mohan. So, the group set off to the island of Hainan to experience the local life and gather materials for the ballet, which was to be based on local history. After six months' hard work (from March to September), based on the composition of 'The Anthem of the Detachment of Women', they finally succeeded in creating the ballet *Red Detachment of Women*. The ballet had six acts, including the overture and finale, and would last for two hours.

Qi Ba was the first central leader to give guidance to the creation of the ballet. He was also the first leader to see it. After the rehearsal, he was extremely happy, saying that it was beyond his imagination: a success that met the requirements of being revolutionary, national and popular. He recommended it to Chairman Mao and invited him to watch it in the small hall of the People's Congress. After seeing the ballet, Chairman Mao commented: "It is successful in its revolutionary scope, the orientation is correct, and it is a good work of art." He was happy to have his picture taken with the members of the stage crew. Qi Ba also encouraged the stage crew, and said to them: "It is successfully revolutionary and the creative direction is correct. It serves the workers, the peasants and the soldiers, and it serves socialism. It is good in an artistic sense." Afterwards, a special performance was given for Prince Norodom Sihanouk of Cambodia, who had made his home in China at the time.

Wu said that he had some major problems at the time. One of them appeared when the play was performed in the hall of the People's Congress and the Tianqiao theatre. He had to reduce the number of musicians by half, because the orchestra pits were too small. Although it was solved in the end, it was not easy for everyone involved. Like Lin Mohan, Wu also stressed: "Jiang Qing wilfully distorted history. It's a shame that she claimed credit for other people's achievements." Significantly, he spoke of his personal understanding of the event. He said that in those days, when Qi Ba stressed the principle of the arts being revolutionary, national and popular, he not only ratified the creative work of the artists who had created the play by combining a Western form of art with a theme taken from real life in China, but he also set up elaborate, well-conceived restrictions on the ultra-left trend of thought in literature and the arts in China at the time. People were particularly filled with admiration for Qi Ba because he had a premonition that Jiang Qing and the others would refute this greatest achievement in the arts in the 17 years since the founding of new China. Resourcefully, he invited Chairman Mao to watch the play. When Chairman Mao expressed his positive opinion, it stopped Jiang from interfering in the matter for the time being.

4.5. *The White-Haired Girl* Becomes *The Red-Haired Girl*

The White-Haired Girl is an opera known in every household in China. The plot was originally based on legends of a white-haired female immortal circulating in the border region of Shanxi, Chahar and Hebei provinces. The Lu Xun Academy of Fine Arts in Ya'an adopted the story as early as 1945 and turned it into a Western-style opera. They named it *The White-Haired Girl*.

In 1962, Zhou Enlai and Deng Yingchao watching the opera *The White-Haired Girl* in the China National Opera Theatre.

After 1949, *The White-Haired Girl* was adapted into a film, a Beijing opera and a dance version, all of which were successful and very popular in China. Each version had the same plot: the tenant peasant Yang Bailao is unable to pay the rent, and he is killed by his landlord, Huang Shiren. His daughter, Xi'er, cannot bear the landlord's insult, and she escapes to the mountains, where she lives for many years until the Eighth Army liberates the region. She regains her freedom, but her hair has turned white. She then becomes the white-haired female immortal from the local folk tales. But what is heartening is that in the end, *the white-haired girl* finally returns to the human world and is reborn. Although the means of artistic expression were varied, they all had the same theme. And it was this very theme — that of the old society turning a human into a ghost while the new society turns a ghost into a human — that made *The White-Haired Girl* so successful and popular. The artistic power of all forms had been approved of by the audience. Meanwhile, the play stirred up sympathy among the masses. I personally experienced a scene like that: in the theatre, several new soldiers from poor and lower-level peasant families became so emotional that they collapsed in the theatre. They had to be carried outside by their companions to be restored. Without a doubt, the power of the play can be transformed into an unmatched spiritual strength in our work and on the battlefield.

But people did not expect that Jiang Qing, who had wreaked havoc in literature and art circles, would attempt to carry out the so-called reform of the opera in the early stages of the Cultural Revolution. She made a bizarre change to the role of Xi'er after she escaped to the mountains. Although Xi'er possessed the spirit of revolt, she was young and weak. However, Jiang changed her role into that of a female political commissar of the Red Army. To show off her amazing achievement, she invited Qi Ba to watch the revised play in 1967. After seeing it, Qi Ba deflated Jiang's arrogant provocation with one sentence. To Jiang Qing and some of the stage crew members, as well as several audience members who had stayed behind, Qi Ba said: "This play is not *The White-Haired Girl*. It should have a new name. It should be called *The Red-Haired Girl*." He then excused himself, saying that he was very busy, and left the theatre, leaving the angry Jiang behind. During the adverse circumstances of the Cultural Revolution, Qi Ba was not always willing to show the arrogant and ignorant Jiang that he had been outdone by her. But many times, adhering to principles, he would cleverly expose Jiang's doings and pay her back.

Mr Xu Yizhang had returned to China from Indonesia, but he currently lives in the UK. He is an old friend of mine. In those years, he acted on orders and became one of the composers for the opera *The White-Haired Girl*. What happened that day left a deep impression on him. Even talking about it now still makes him sigh again and again.

5. The Last Days

5.1. My Last Reunion with Qi Ba

At the lunar new year celebrations of 1974, some members of the Zhou family had a last reunion with Qi Ba at West Flower Hall. My wife was abroad at the time, so I went with my daughter, Zhou Rong. The other family members included Zhou Bingde and her husband, Zhou Bingyi and her husband, Zhou Binghua and his wife, and Zhou Binghe. Qi Ma asked us to take our seats, and called for my daughter to sit beside her. Holding her hand, Qi Ma asked whose daughter she was. After learning that she was my daughter, Qi Ma then said: "I know, I know. She is that little girl who wears her key on her neck all day. Children from poor families learn to manage household affairs early. She can be our family's Li Tiemei." She then peeled a Laiyang pear for my daughter to eat. When Qi Ba's car arrived, we all went out to meet him. He shook hands with us and we celebrated the new year together.

Unexpectedly, Zhou Binghe suddenly asked Qi Ba why he had paused during his speech at the memorial service for Marshal He Long, inquiring if it was because he was too upset to deliver the memorial speech. I was very worried, feeling that Zhou Binghe was too young to think clearly for posing a question like that to Qi Ba, who himself was ill and would find it difficult to answer. As expected, after hesitating, Qi Ba explained: "My vision was blurred, so I had to take my glasses off. My speech was interrupted when I cleaned my glasses." As far as I know, Qi Ba had repeatedly bowed and apologised to the widow and He Long's other family members, which was enough evidence that he was apologetic and that he had the heart but lacked the power to save He Long.

Then Qi Ba walked to a different room and asked me to follow him. To save time, he talked to me while eating his lunch. It was a very simple meal: rice with soya sauce poured on top, two vegetable dishes and a bowl of clear soup. Here we discussed three things, which were his last urgent requests to me.

Before we said goodbye, Qi Ma said that most of their staff had gone home for the New Year holidays, so she would not keep us for supper. She then gave us the presents that she had prepared for us to take home.

5.2. Qi Ma's Special Words to Me

In the spring of 1974, Qi Ba was not only very ill, but also in dire peril politically. One day, Qi Ma dismissed the people around her and had a conversation with me, urging me to cooperate with them to prepare for the worst. I felt, in a sense, that this talk was their last prompt to me.

Generally, any long talks with me were always held by Qi Ba. Qi Ba and

Qi Ma had different timetables, so when Qi Ba talked to me after supper in his office, Qi Ma would go and rest for the night. Also, whenever Qi Ma had talked to me in the past, she had only talked about our daily lives; this time we talked about politics, which was quite unusual.

She phoned me as early as the autumn of 1971, after I had returned to Beijing from the farm in Henan province. She asked me about my time at the farm and my circumstances after returning to Beijing. She had learnt that I would be transferred to the ILD, and expressed relief that I was fit and congratulated me on my new job.

In 1972, after I finished working on the reception for US president Richard Nixon, she found out from the husband of one of my cousins, Shen Renhua, that a small tumor had been found on my chest, near the heart area. I wasn't sure what it was, nor did I know what had caused it. She told me that after she and Qi Ba had learnt about the tumor on my chest, they were a bit worried. They wanted me to go to hospital to have it checked out and arrange to get treatment as soon as possible. Soon I received a phone call from Dr Wu Weiran, the director of Beijing hospital. He asked me to come and see him. After the examination, the initial diagnosis concluded that it was a lipoma. The question was whether to leave it as it was or to remove it in an operation. Dr Wu asked me to consult with Qi Ma, and then the hospital would act according to our decision.

I went to see Qi Ma and she said: "It's quite odd how many physical similarities there are between you and your Qi Ba. His clothes, shoes and socks all fit you; besides, you both have the same AB blood type, and you have a good memory too. During the few years when the country was in dire circumstances, you suffered from edema as though your liver had been damaged, while your Qi Ba had suffered from hepatapostema during the Long March. Both of you have experienced some hardships, but I had never imagined that you two would grow the same lipoma on your bodies." She said this jokingly. "The lipoma on your uncle's back grows bigger each year, and it is now the size of a small hen egg. It seems that there is no need to remove it, so I don't think you need an operation either. Some lipomas do no harm."

I accepted her opinion and told Director Wu of our decision. I left this lipoma as it was and I have done nothing about it to this day. At the time, when I expressed my gratitude to Qi Ma as well as Director Wu, Qi Ma said: "Don't thank me. You should give credit for your hospital membership to the Beijing Hospital, and you know these doctors yourself."

In 1974, staying clear of her secretary and staff, Qi Ma phoned me in secret to come see her. She had a long talk with me that day. She asked me to tell her in detail about my experiences and my life during the Cultural Revolution. It seemed she had learnt of my condition. I told her that I had used my wife giving birth as an excuse to stay in Shanghai for a month. I had voluntarily given up my position as leader of the revolutionary committee at work. I had not joined any factional organisations, nor had I participated in any activities with them, except that I had persuaded the people of the rivalry factions to stop the violence. Of the Red Guards who supported Qi Ba, I would make contact with some of the more reliable individuals. Of those who opposed Qi Ba, I had tried to win over some individuals who were not core members of their faction. I had helped Qi Ba to clarify the misunderstanding that he had had a personal relationship with Zhang Yan, the director of the foreign affairs office under the State Council. Besides, at no point during these years had I given any thought to personal gains or losses, never seeking to benefit myself in either work or life. In some affairs that the masses didn't know the actual situation of, I preferred to suffer abuse than to explain. I always took the interests of the whole into account. I understood the perilous position Qi Ba was in and I acted accordingly. Qi Ma said to me that she and Qi Ba were pleased with what I had done in the last few years.

When I told Qi Ma for the first time what I thought of this movement, I mentioned Kang Sheng and Jiang Qing. As early as the 1950s, some servile followers of Kang Sheng made up charges against me, subjecting me, a young and naive university student at the time, to political persecution. Although she did not mention his name, Qi Ma said to me: "Your going to university was the result of all your own hard work and efforts. Your Qi Ba and I never exerted any influence on the matter. I was aware of it and I also had clear ideas about some of the issues. I told you in Tianjin that your Qi Ba and I would not have thought that we would become a burden on you. As our nephew, you haven't benefited from your relationship with us, but only endured disadvantages and harm. However, this is something with which you have to cope. Ever since the Cultural Revolution began, we were more or less aware of your suffering. But you should understand that almost everyone who was close to us has suffered; some of them have even been put in prison or executed, so dying a violent death is unavoidable when you join this movement. You and Zhangli have been working in the foreign affairs, culture and education sectors, which were the first areas to be affected. It seems that you will not only share our joys and sorrows, but also our fate. In the future, anything unexpected can happen, so I hope you are well prepared. When you married Zhangli, I told her that you must be prepared to die at any moment. You told me then that she had accepted this, so you two are faithful to each other. It's not easy for a person to think and act in this way in all one's life."

"As for your mentioning Kang Sheng," she carried on, "he's said that the work done in the foreign affairs sector has been more about making peace with imperialists, revisionists and reactionaries in every country, but less about giving support to the national liberation movement. And, acting on his own high principles, he accused the foreign affairs sector of having surrendered to the imperialists, the contemporary revisionists and the reactionaries to eliminate the national liberation movement. You told me that besides Wang Jiaxiang, he also attacked your Qi Ba. What you have said is correct. The Gang of Four has done the same. I cannot tell anyone else, but I must tell you. Jiang Qing is against your Qi Ba. It seems that she has wild ambitions and will not stop until she reaches her goal. I called you here today because I've had a long think. On the phone I could only say that I was asking you to come and read Zhou Ercui's letter, which was an excuse. I don't want my words to be recorded, because if they are, it will cause us trouble, as we are already being targeted by the Criticise Lin, Criticise Confucius and Criticise the Duke of Zhou Campaign, and even by the movement to criticise the capitulationism of Song Jiang. Just as you said, their target is your Qi Ba himself. The premier is now seriously ill, and still he has to endure such vicious slander and attacks. You have worked in the foreign affairs sector, so you understand him. You will be very angry about the unreasonable and unjust treatment he is receiving. Moreover, such misfortune may fall on you and your family too, which is one of the reasons your Qi Ba asked me to call you here. We hope that you are prepared for the worst. Your daughter is young and there are no adults to look after her, so the poor little girl has to look after herself, wearing the house key around her neck every day. She is a beautiful girl, and your son, with his thick eyebrows, is lovely too. If possible, you should send them to the south and ask your relatives to look after them. It's hard to tell what the situation in Beijing will be like, nor will we know how your Qi Ba's disease will develop."

I then complained to her about Kang Sheng for a while longer, but my complaints were certainly not directed at Kang himself. "The foreign affairs work has always been done under the collective leadership of the centre. Qi Ba is a man of strong principles. On all major issues, he has always asked Chairman Mao and the Central Committee for instructions. But Kang Sheng has inappropriately and unfairly criticised the work of the foreign affairs sector, so it is crystal clear whom he is targeting. The Central Committee decided that the May 16 Group* was a reactionary organization. Kang Sheng and company then departed from their normal behaviour and pushed the 'project team' to wilfully enlarge the number of members of the May 16 Group. This action resulted in many innocent people being wrongly charged, which led to the people who were unaware of the truth directing their discontent and misunderstanding at Qi Ba. If the number becomes absurdly astronomical, it may be that no one will be charged, which will obviously let the bad people off the hook. What's more, if I, a relative of Qi Ba's, could disintegrate the opposition and win them over, isolating the handful of bad people as much as possible, this could be the right thing to do."

After I had spoken, Qi Ma thought it over for a while. Then she said to

---

* On 16 May 1966, during a long meeting of the Central Committee of the CPC, a circular was issued that marked the beginning of the Cultural Revolution. The rebellious May 16 Group appeared in society while the Red Guards called themselves the 'May 16th Corps'. Incited by Jiang Qing and Kang Sheng, they directed a frenzied attack towards Qi Ba and vainly attempted to seize overall control of the foreign ministry, which led to the calamitous incident of the British office of the chargé d'affaires in Beijing burning down. Next, the Central Committee decided that the organisation was reactionary.

me: "What you've said is reasonable, and I will tell your Qi Ba about it. He once said that he didn't believe that there were that many May 16 elements. In the past, it was always your Qi Ba who talked to you regarding your work and politics. Now I am the one talking about these issues with you and I'm sure you'll understand the reason. There is a man called Mao Baozhong in your work place, who is in charge of the receptions of foreign guests. It is said that he is one of the leaders of the rebel group. I have observed that because Jiang Qing, Kang Sheng and company have thoroughly cut themselves off from the masses, some of the latter can still appreciate your Qi Ba's lofty character. Moreover, their future is precarious; hence, they may try and get close to us. I will inform Mao Baozhong that you will try and find a chance to talk to him. Humans should make fewer enemies. It is a good thing to convert an enemy into a friend and to have fewer people rooting against you. As the premier of a country, Qi Ba is engaged in many and diverse activities, making it unavoidable for him to commit errors. If he has committed a mistake, you could openly criticise him alongside the masses. Our talk today has that intention. We'll understand, and we won't blame you for it. After you go back to work, you should make contact with Mao Baozhong. In short, after our conversation today, you, your wife and all your other family members should prepare for any contingencies to avoid panicking in the future when bad things start to happen."

At once, I replied that we had begun to be ready to sacrifice our lives if necessary long ago, and that Qi Ba and Qi Ma could rest assured that we would never follow the crowd and echo other people's views or make wanton comments about them.

At this point during our conversation, Qi Ma took out a book: the *Grey Eminence* (the full title of the book is *Zhou Enlai: China's Grey Eminence*). "A friend from the foreign ministry brought us this book from abroad," she said. "It is said that some of the book's contents have been provided by a certain person. Jiang Qing and Kang Sheng may exploit these contents and make trouble for your Qi Ba, who is already in poor health. I hope that you can translate the related parts of the book as soon as possible and then send them to me. None of our staff know about the matter."

After I returned home, I finished the translation in a hurry. As expected,

Mao Baozhong sent people over to invite me to go to his home and have a talk. I considered it over and over again, thinking that it could easily cause a misunderstanding among the neighbours, so I did not reply to his invitation.

I sent my translation to Qi Ba and Qi Ma to read. At the time, we did not see any other anti-communist material written by the same person. It wasn't until the 1980s, through other relatives, friends and foreign scholars, as well as indirectly through my research in the libraries of the Hoover Institute on War, Revolution and Peace in the US, that I learnt that when Qi Ba was still alive, Ma Shunyi, my one-time stepmother, had spread many rumours attacking communism, new China, and even Qi Ba himself. It was quite a serious matter, and small wonder that Qi Ba was very upset at the time.

5.3. The Deeply Touching National Day Reception of 1974

In the autumn of 1974, as scheduled, I received an invitation to attend the National Day reception. I was both happy and worried. Happy, because the invitation card was signed by Qi Ba, which meant there was an improvement in his health and that he would attend the reception; worried, because he was still ill. If he insisted or even forced himself to go, it might be his last appearance on such a grand occasion. Under the circumstances, at a time when many reliable veteran cadres had been overthrown, he himself was not only very ill, but also in a perilous situation. Whether he lived or died could change the political situation in China, as well as the country's prospects.

I knew that Qi Ba himself also attached great importance to this occasion. He was hoping to use the opportunity to give some consolation to the people within or outside the party who had been persecuted during the Cultural Revolution. Though he had just had an operation, he still carefully read out the names of over 2,000 guests from his list. Having done so, he wrote overnight to Wang Hongwen, who was in charge of the day-to-day work of the politburo, suggesting to add the names of more representative personnel from all walks of life to the list.

On the evening of the 30 September, the National Day reception was

My Uncle Zhou Enlai

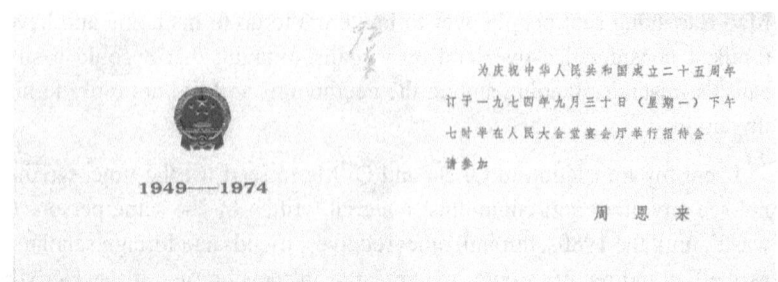

The invitation for the National Day banquet, 1974. "Zhou Enlai invites you to the National Day reception to celebrate the 25th anniversary of the founding of the People's Republic of China. September 30 (Monday) 1974. 7 PM. Banquet Hall, the Great Hall of the People."

held in the Great Hall of the People in a grand style. Delegates arrived in swarms, eagerly waiting to see Premier Zhou Enlai, who was ill and had been out of the public eye for some time. The delegates, including many foreign friends, filled the whole hall, which was brightly lit. I sat beside Mr Adler from England and Mr Coghlan from the US. They were well-known foreign friends who both had lung cancer, though the cancer was in remission after they had received treatment. Full of vitality, they watched the platform, waiting to see the premier who commanded love and reverence among them.

Qi Ba, whose face was thin, emerged. The delegates were simmering with excitement, standing up and waving to him enthusiastically. After he took his seat, the whole hall was silent, waiting to listen to his speech. At this point, Zhu De and Kang Sheng took their seats in wheelchairs. Qi Ba began to speak, and his voice was as sonorous as usual, which soothed the souls of the listeners who felt that the premier could make a full recovery from his disease.

Qi Ba's short toast was interrupted by warm applause ten times. After his speech had ended, everyone in the hall was filled with a feeling of immeasurable joy. From the bottom of their hearts, they cherished a feeling of great reverence for Premier Zhou, thinking that as long as Premier Zhou was there during a critical situation, there would still be hope for the state.

From a distance, I gazed at Qi Ba, who I hadn't seen for a long time and who was still looking ill. I couldn't help it, but my eyes were filled with tears. In my heart I prayed for his speedy recovery.

When the reception was nearing its end, the people in the hall couldn't sit still any longer. Many of them lost control of themselves, but they didn't care. Abandoning their usual formalities, they jumped on the tables and chairs to watch the premier's departure. Many of them hoped that he would walk very slowly, as they wanted to have a good look at him. Veteran Red Army soldiers, actors and actresses, cadres of the party and the government, cadres of the ethnic minority groups as well as foreign guests — no matter if they were male or female, old or young, in all languages they called out to and saluted the premier. Several people were muttering to themselves and I overheard a young foreign lady saying to herself while standing on top of the table: "How nice it would be if I could dance with Premier Zhou." But many veteran cadres and Red Army soldiers cried out: "Beloved premier, get some rest and take good care of yourself!" The two foreign friends beside me, Mr Adler and Mr Coghlan, were old friends of Qi Ba's. They were already 70 years old and in poor health, but they seemed to have forgotten their own illness and repeatedly urged the host to let the meeting end as soon as possible in order to not affect the premier's rest. In short, the hall that had a capacity of 10,000 people was suddenly permeated with a sea of revelations of people's true feelings about the good premier of the people.

Qi Ba's appearance was gratifying, and the whole country was talking about it afterwards. In general, people felt that Qi Ba's existence was a sort of check on the ultra-leftist ideological trend, as he represented the people's hopes for tomorrow. The warm atmosphere in the hall made it the ideal place for people to express their love and care for Qi Ba, because at that very moment, the Gang of Four was plotting the Criticise Lin, Criticise Confucius and Criticise the Duke of Zhou Campaign; but the exceptionally grand and special implications of the National Day reception showed the world that justice remained in the hearts of the people.

5.4. "This Cultural Revolution Has Cut Off 10 Years of My Life"

Qi Ba died, to our great sorrow, and the whole country wailed with grief. The funeral procession, which was unprecedentedly spectacular, shook

China and the world. After most of the grief had abated, I couldn't help recalling what he had said before he died: "This Cultural Revolution has cut off 10 years of my life." His words are not at all an exaggeration.

Many cadres and citizens in China, as well as many foreigners, wondered what would have happened if Qi Ba had received immediate and proper treatment after he being diagnosed with bladder cancer. I remember the relatives, staff and medical personnel listening to Qi Ma's speech in the Taiwan room of the Great Hall of the People, the main gist of which was that the doctors had tried their best, and others should not blame them. In this way, she, a widow as well as a politician, was trying to reassure the public, because it also concerned the stability of the country. Hence, under these circumstances, she had to say what she had to say.

However, many years later, she told me some of the real reasons for Qi Ba's death. Number one among them was the Cultural Revolution, because during the movement, large numbers of important state cadres, including the vice premiers, were recalled or subjected to persecution in succession. The task of handling state affairs had mainly fallen to Qi Ba, exhausting him and severely affecting his health, as he had overworked himself for a long time. Another reason was that the surgery took place too late. After the diagnosis, a medical team was formed, of which Wang Hongwen was the team leader. They decided that they would not tell Qi Ba about his actual condition for the time being, using conservative therapy instead.

However, Qi Ba's condition quickly worsened. They insisted on reporting it to the Central Committee and operating on Qi Ba. Meanwhile, Qi Ba himself found out about his condition and wrote to the Central Committee, also requesting an operation. But it was too late — the cancer cells had already spread. Many medical experts told me later that the bladder is like a bag. If it had been removed before the cancer cells had spread, under the medical conditions of the time, a bottle could have been attached to catch the urine, and although it would have been inconvenient, his life could have been saved.

Before Qi Ba was sent to the operation theatre, with his weak hand, he signed his name under his statement about the so-called Wu Hao Affair. This statement would clarify some facts about him in the future. Then, in front of everyone, he called out: "I am not a capitulator!" This was not only a grievous and indignant cry of protest, but the last call of a revolutionary who adhered to principles and justice.

6. Qi Ba Passes Away

6.1. The Funeral that Shook the World

In the afternoon of 8 January 1976, the deputy minister of the ILD, Feng Xian, unexpectedly phoned me and asked me to come to his home, saying he had something important to discuss with me. As I hurried to his house, I suddenly had the feeling that something ominous was going to happen. After I entered, I saw him standing, with a straight back, in front of Qi Ba's portrait. He called to me to come stand beside him and asked me to bow to the portrait three times. Then, in a solemn voice, he said: "Our beloved premier, your Qi Ba, has passed away." The news hit me like a thunderbolt. I felt dizzy. Worried that I might collapse, he rushed forward to grab my arms and let me sit down. Distressed, I was so overwhelmed with grief that I wished that I was dead. Tears rained down my cheeks uncontrollably while I was dying to shout out to the whole world: this is the worst tragedy in human history. We must denounce the brutality of the Gang of Four, who had been persecuting Qi Ba for a long time.

Qi Ba's serious illness was confidential, but mentally I had made some preparations, as Qi Ma had talked to me in late 1973 and early 1974 and mentioned that Qi Ba was seriously ill, emphasising that we should wait for the unexpected to happen. She showed me a prescription from a Chinese herbal doctor, giving me a hint of the seriousness of Qi Ba's condition while urging me to prepare for the worst and send my children to the south of the country. She said that if a major change happened, I could be the first family member to be affected. But I was still hoping that Qi Ba would recover from his illness.

In addition, at the time, I was in charge of the European department of the Ministry of Foreign Affairs. Towards the end of 1975, we were given a special assignment to translate some medical data from English, German and Swedish into Chinese. Although we hadn't been told which leader or which work unit these medical data would be for, I was very worried when I compared the foreign medical data to the prescription from the Chinese herbal doctor Qi Ma had shown me. Despite having made mental preparations, it still didn't prepare me for the fact that the news of Qi Ba's passing would come so soon.

While Feng Xian was trying to say some words of consolation, there was a phone call from Qi Ma's secretary. Ms Zhao Wei passed on Qi Ma's directive to inform the other relatives living in the other parts of the country, asking them to restrain their grief but carry on working, and not to come to Beijing for the funeral or to take part in any memorial services. I held back my tears, but I did not call for a car from my work unit at once. I waited until late at night to ask for a car, then went to the main post office to make some short phone calls to the many relatives who lived outside Beijing or who lived in Beijing but were on business trips. However, after giving it some thought, I developed a 'special arrangement' when making the phone calls. I did not use the direct telephone line between the central government and the local governments, which could quickly connect me to my relatives, but the phone line for civilians, because I hoped that after hearing the sad news on the radio or through some other channel, they would all want to come to Beijing. This would not have made me violate Qi Ma's directives, but still would have allowed them all to come to Beijing to say farewell and pay their last respects to Qi Ba. After I had done this, I finally felt at ease.

I then went to Beijing hospital. Of all the relatives of the younger generation, I was the only one who paid my respects to Qi Ba's remains in hospital twice. I saw a large, garage-like mortuary, empty and without any decorations. I saw Geng Biao and some other leaders from the foreign affairs sector, standing like guards at the bier, solemn and with a heavy heart. During the procession of the mourners, people from the foreign affairs sector frequently ran up to hug me, and we choked with sobs. One of them, I still recall, was Mr Zhang Baosheng, the Chinese ambassador to Mozambique.

On 11 January, when Qi Ba's remains were removed from the hospital, I saw that many cadres and ordinary people had spontaneously gathered

The Beijing citizens paying their last respects to the deceased Premier Zhou.

outside the main entrance of the hospital. Ignoring the security guards, they stood densely packed around the main entrance and pushed forward, hoping to see the remains of their beloved Premier Zhou Enlai for the last time. Because of the heinous crimes committed by the Gang of Four, the resentment and anger of the masses that had been accumulating for a long time reached a breaking point, like a volcano on the verge of exploding. We didn't know who made the decision that Qi Ba's remains were to be removed via the back entrance of the hospital.

I remember that Wang Hongwen, the vice chairman of the Central Committee of the CPC, rode in the first car before the hearse. The second car transported Wang Dongxing, a member of the politburo, who at the time was in charge of the forces of the central security guards. Qi Ma rode in the third car, and the fourth vehicle was a minibus that held a small number of family members, mainly the eldest sons of the various households of

Saying farewell to the premier in Changan Street.

the Zhou family. As the eldest son of the second household, I rode in this minibus. I was too heavy-hearted to notice the other family members, and I can only recall Zhou Bingde and Zhou Bingjian sitting in the vehicle. Tong Xiaopeng, the director of the office of the State Council, who had followed Qi Ba for a long time, was also squeezed into the fourth vehicle. The majority of the family members could not go to the Beijing hospital to see Qi Ba's remains, nor could they take the minibus to the Babaoshan revolutionary cemetery to pay their last respects to Qi Ba. They could only go to the public memorial service, which was held in the Beijing Working People's Cultural Palace, to express their grief.

When the minibus I was on left the back entrance of the Beijing hospital, inwardly I felt very angry, uneasy and worried. On one hand, I felt that the Gang of Four had made this arrangement to stop the public from being near the remains of Qi Ba, because they feared it when the public showed their love for Qi Ba and felt their own sorrow for his demise. They tried to steer clear of the public and rashly sent Qi Ba's remains to the cemetery. On the other hand, it was a very cold Sunday. The public didn't know that Qi Ba's remains had already been moved out of the hospital through the back entrance, so I was worried that the funeral would be a quiet one, with no public attending.

However, when the bier was slowly rolling down Changan Street, the scene outside took me by surprise: tens of thousands of people were densely packed into the street, from the Beijing hotel onwards, and slowly followed the bier. I felt gratified, and my spirit was elevated tremendously. I felt as though a load had been taken off my mind. Ignoring the cold weather and not fearing any obstructions from the Gang of Four and their lackeys, the Beijing citizens had spontaneously gathered in the heart of the capital, presenting an unprecedented and spectacular scene in human history.

The view, as well as the words to describe the view, will not only go down in history, but will also will be indelibly engraved on the memory of hundreds of millions of Chinese and people around the world. People from all social strata — men and women, old and young, workers, peasants, cadres, intellectuals, and even some foreigners — could be seen everywhere during the journey from the hospital to the cemetery. They drove in front of the bier, stopping at road crossings or bridges, standing on both sides of the street, bowing while taking off their hats to salute in the biting cold. Then they would drive on and do the same at the many more road crossings and bridges. Many cameramen climbed into lamp posts, flag poles and tree tops to take shots. When the bier procession was nearing Tiananmen Square, people who were standing along the street couldn't help but cry. Though I was inside the minibus, I could clearly hear their earthshaking wails. This spectacular scene continued for five km, right up to the cemetery. Afterwards, I heard many more touching stories regarding Qi Ba's death and the funeral. Several hundreds of workers from the Capital Iron and Steel Corporation and some other key enterprises in Beijing were against the cremation of the premier's remains. They had tried to stop the bier from entering the cemetery. The workers at the cemetery refused to press the button to start the cremation. The Belgian ambassador to China had ordered a wreath especially made for the funeral, and the wife of a counsellor of the Yugoslavian embassy in China had lost consciousness after hearing the sad news. A friend of mine in the foreign ministry, Ma Xiaoyan, told her

Muslim mother of the sad news, who nearly went blind from crying so much.

When the bier arrived at the cemetery, Luo Qingchang and the others carried the crystal coffin into the memorial hall, for which I admired them greatly. Following Qi Ma, the small congregation of relatives walked towards the coffin to pay their last respects to Qi Ba's remains. Having experienced all kinds of hardship, Qi Ba had grown very thin, but his face remained peaceful, unyielding and kind. Holding back our grief, we relatives went to stand beside Qi Ma one after another and looked at the remains of Qi Ba. At this moment, Qi Ma said, affectionately: "Let Xiao Chao pay her last respects to you." Then she turned around and said to us, the younger generation: "Let the children have a good look at you for the last time, and as much as they like!" I closely followed the crowd and lowered my body towards the coffin, trying to pay my last respects to Qi Ba. I had requested my wife and my daughter to remind me not to cry too much, not to let the tears blur my eyes. I had to hold my breath to have a good last look at Qi Ba, but I couldn't help crying while holding my breath, and said gently to his remains: "Dear Qi Ba, let me show my respect to you and say farewell for the last time." Before I could finish speaking, all the doors in the hall opened and in rushed a group of senior cadres. They all charged towards the coffin, pushing away the relatives. I was forcefully pushed aside by somebody. Turning around, I saw that it was Qiao Guanhua (the foreign minister at the time), who was very tall but comparatively thin. He lowered his body and his face touched the crystal coffin. He was a big guy, but he couldn't help weeping, his tears falling like rain.

I couldn't help but sigh inwardly. In those days and under those circumstances, someone had lost their integrity and gone so far as to follow the Gang of Four, not hesitating to 'do harm' to Premier Zhou, whom he owed a favour, in order to pursue his own interests. This was not only shameful, but also made it hard to escape the criticism of the masses and the denunciation of his own conscience. However, when he was still alive, the broad-minded Premier Zhou had fully understood these people's circumstances. He had forgiven them for what they had done to him. They had been his followers for many years, and had received personal training and guidance from Qi Ba. But during the Cultural Revolution, the circumstances had sometimes forced these people to pretend to make a clean break with Premier Zhou, which he understood. Even Qi Ba had said to me that if I ever met with difficulties in my work, I could go to them for help, which is enough evidence that Qi Ba was open-minded, magnanimous and selfless.

After the funeral, Qi Ma received the relatives, Qi Ba's staff and the medical staff in the Taiwan room of the Great Hall of the People. She stressed that the doctors had tried their best during their treatment of and care for Qi Ba, while Qi Ba himself had kept up a tenacious struggle against his illness. The final result was grief, a result the medical people never wanted to see. The doctors and nurses had used all of their healing efforts, and the strong-willed Qi Ba had fought dauntlessly against his illness. They had battled together to overcome the disease. Their fighting spirit and the friendly sentiment between the medical staff and the patient were expressions of extreme responsibility, which was highly commendable. The relatives and the staff working at the side of the premier should thank the doctors and the nurses for their efforts. They should not blame them, or be sceptical about their work. When Qi Ma was giving her speech to the large number of people, her secretary Zhao Wei saw that my wife and I were pushed away and made to sit in the very last row, at the back of the room. She then called us to come and sit in the front row. Qi Ma was speaking calmly, but when she saw us, she came up to us and shook hands with my wife, saying to her: "Zhangli, we haven't had the chance to have a good talk since you returned from the UK." When she said this, she choked with sobs and tears gushed from her eyes. My wife and I were unable to suppress our sobs either, feeling the incredible pain in our hearts. We sensed that Qi Ma's words to the people in the room had been both very considerate and timely. I understood that what she was saying was a necessary warning for us to stop the Gang of Four from making trouble. Of course, it was also the continuation of implementing the good customs handed down by Qi Ba, namely to observe the feelings of the public and to think matters over carefully. Qi Ma had chosen the Taiwan room to receive us and tell us that the premier's many unfinished causes would require us to work hard to be accomplished, and that we should cherish the memory of the good premier of the people by our actions.

6.2. The Gang of Four Falls from Power

Our beloved Premier Zhou passed away, to our great sorrow. Hundreds of millions of Chinese people were in deep grief, and memorial services in all forms were held nationwide, which was beyond the tolerance of the Gang of Four. They ruthlessly suppressed people who attended the memorial services, and the Gang's brutality caused the Tiananmen Incident on 5 April 1976, when a crowd of an unprecedented size gathered to protest. It is unnecessary for me to go into details, because the written recollections and accounts of the incident in newspapers at home and abroad are too many to count. At the time, night after night, my wife and I secretly went to Tiananmen Square to take part in the spontaneous memorial services and protests of the masses, but we never suspected that we were being followed by an individual from our work unit who had ulterior motives. He reported us to the leaders of the rebel group in our work unit. If the Gang of Four's plot to seize power had not been crushed so swiftly, we would have met with disaster, like the many revolutionaries among the masses.

Luckily, the Gang of Four was overthrown in October of that same year, and there was nationwide rejoicing at the news. Being in one mind and full of confidence, the Chinese people were to walk towards a prosperous future. I remember a certain leader, who at the time held the office of foreign minister, jumping on his bicycle and tracking me down at a friend's house to inform me that Geng Biao had asked me to go to the reviewing stand in Tiananmen Square. Geng Biao then passed on the instructions of Hua Guofeng and Ye Jianying that I was to be the sole relative of Qi Ba's to be invited to stand at the front of Tiananmen Square and join a million Beijing citizens celebrating the overthrow of the Gang of Four. I didn't know the details of the celebration, nor did I go to the viewing stand. It was clear that the first generation of the leaders attached importance to the people's practical conduct rather than the closeness of clansmen in the selection process.

In a flash, the joy of victory helped me to overcome all the diseases I was suffering from. A few days later, when I was having my eyes checked, the director of the Tongren hospital told me: "It seems that your glaucoma symptoms have gone, without any treatment." From the bottom of my heart,

I am very grateful to veteran cadre Geng Biao and the Chinese people, because we had leaders and people like them in the dark days when the reactionary forces were on the rise, which could have become history in the twinkling of an eye. Instead, the bright and joyous days had finally arrived.

End of the 1970s. Zhou Erliu accompanies Deng Yingchao at the reception for the European guests.

6.3. The Odd Behaviour of Cao Yi-ou, Kang Sheng's Widow

It was around March 1976 that guests from Oceania came to Beijing. They requested to see the widows of Zhou Enlai and Kang Sheng to express their condolences to their deceased husbands, so Qi Ma and Cao Yi-ou attended the reception banquet. At the time, due to the unclear political circumstances, the cadres and the people of the country were secretly very worried about the country's prospects.

It seemed Qi Ma had something on her mind. In front of the foreign guests, she talked about nothing serious, but she would engage in some small talk about the family's daily life and household affairs. For example, she said that she was getting old and starting to forget things, hence she had to leave different pairs of glasses in the living room, bedroom, kitchen and bathroom, in case she couldn't find a pair when she needed them. Laughing at herself, she seemed ill at ease, and her comments were off topic.

We Chinese who were present at the banquet inwardly felt sorry for her, because we knew that she had paid a lot of attention to learning about etiquette from Qi Ba, particularly with respect to foreign affairs. Generally, she would carefully read the information we sent regarding the reception in advance, and she would make the necessary preparations. So her performance aroused our imagination as well as our sympathy, feeling that there must be something on her mind that she was finding hard to disclose, so that she was only capable of dealing with the reception passively — not like other times, when she talked about serious topics or engaged in witty conversation with guests.

Meanwhile, Cao Yi-ou was behaving quite oddly. Hands trembling, she took out a headshot of her late husband from a pocket inside her jacket. Deadly serious and far too politely, she handed the portrait to the foreign guests. She then urged the interpreter to tell the foreign guests that this was the last portrait that had been made of Kang Sheng, and that she had especially brought it with her and would present it to the foreign guests to express her gratitude that they had come to China to convey their condolences for her deceased husband. She neither consulted the reception unit for her actions, nor did she inform Qi Ma beforehand. Taken by surprise, we felt that what she was doing was inappropriate.

During the banquet, I didn't expect that Qi Ma would carelessly turn to me and say: "Erliu, you should not just listen. You could also say something." When she said this, it seemed as though she was talking to a relative. However, it caught the attention of the paranoid Chao Yi-ou. When the banquet had ended, we saw the foreign guests off. When the vigilant Chao learnt that both Qi Ma and I had withdrawn from the hall, she went to obtain some information about me from the reception staff. After she found out that I was the nephew of Premier Zhou, she lost control of herself, shouting: "This person has been hiding in our work unit for a long time. It's a shame that even I wasn't aware of this." Afterwards, the other people told me about this, worried that Cao would do something harmful to me. I then told these kind-hearted comrades: "I have made sufficient mental preparations for the unexpected. I only wish that the leaders of the work unit won't be dragged into the matter."

Fortunately, in October of that year, the Gang of Four was overthrown. Like everyone else, I was overjoyed. I was experiencing the happiest moment of my life, feeling that I had regained my freedom. People would never again need to be anxious or worry about the tyranny of Kang Sheng or the Gang of Four and their ilk, wantonly committing crimes and even causing death to innocent people. It is a matter for rejoicing that the gang was finally swept onto the rubbish heap of history.

Ever since then, whenever I accompanied Qi Ma to receive foreign guests, she would return to her normal bearing, calm and solemn. Every now and then she would make some witty remarks during conversations with the foreign guests, which made us admire her — the widow of premier Zhou Enlai, who herself had experienced the Long March and who was a distinguished representative of Chinese women. Meanwhile, whenever we saw her, time and again she would direct our thoughts to Premier Zhou Enlai.

Part Five

Everlasting Memories

As far as I know, every male member of the Yi and En generations of the Zhou family has been of average stature. Both Qi Ba and his brother Zhou Enshou, as well as my father Zhou Enzhu, had the reputation of being very good-looking men. However, in real life, Zhou Enzhu was slightly shorter, while Zhou Enshou had been nicknamed 'Little Blackie' by relatives during his childhood for being dark-skinned; hence, the light complexions of Qi Ba and Zhou Enzhu stood out in the crowds.

Qi Ba was 170cm in height, comparatively tall compared to his siblings but not as tall as men from the northern region of China. On one occasion, he compared his height to my own. Smiling, he said that I was not a short man. With a most striking posture, he was well-proportioned in stature and stood straight. He had a heroic appearance. The two large eyes under the thick eyebrows would sometimes give people the impression that he had double-fold eyelids. When he focused his gaze on people or things surrounding him, his eyes were deep, bright and penetrating, but still warm and kind. Qi Ba's nose was straight. His lips were thin, and the upper lip was wide. When he bit his lips, he would pout slightly. All this, combined with his thick, frowning eyebrows and his piercing eyes, would impress people with his majestic appearance. In short, he had the bearing of a bright and brave soldier, yet his simple manner as well as the way he spoke gave people the impression that he was a scholar through and through. Personalities from all different walks of life as well as common people from China and abroad couldn't help but gasp in admiration after having met him.

One time, after a meal, despite the fact that he was very busy, he commented on my language and my dietary habits. "Both you and I are from the Jiangsu and Zhejiang provinces," he said to me. Our ancestors were from Shaoxing in Zhejiang, which was a historical, cultural city in the region of rivers and lakes, south of the lower reaches of the Yangtze river. Starting with my great-grandfather, many family members settled in Huaian in Jiangsu, which is north of the Yangtze river. Huaian is also a historical and cultural city, so the cultures of southern Jiangsu and northern Zhejiang and Shanghai, as well as the cultures of Anhui and Hubei provinces, have been developed within ourselves. Whether through language, diet or other habits and customs, the regional cultures have had an influence on us. For example, we would call the large, deep-fried meatballs braised with soya sauce and vegetables *shizitou*, *routuan* or *rouwanzi*, and a paternal grandfather *yaya* in the Shaoxing dialect, but *yeye* in the Huaian dialect. Because many members of the 'En' generation moved to the north of the Yellow river, and some even to the northeastern region, their language and dietary habits were not the same as those from the Jiangsu and Zhejiang regions. When Qi Ba spoke standard Chinese, excepting some northeastern influences, the main characteristics of his accent came from his hometown in northern Jiangsu, but I had more influences from south of the Yangtze river in mine. Despite living in Beijing for many years, when we spoke standard Chinese, we both sounded like southerners, using more of a dental than a retroflex sound, high in pitch and with a clear pronunciation.

Although Qi Ba always had the bearing of a soldier, when giving speeches, he would give people the impression of being a scholar or a man of letters, as well as a southerner. When he walked, his footsteps were light, not like people from the north, whose steps were usually heavy. Despite the fact that he had broken his right arm during the war, he could still move the arm to a large extent. The swift and wide movements of his arms and body made people feel that he was a man bubbling with enthusiasm. Coming straight from the heart, his sunny laughter was very natural. Hearty and heroic, his laughter, combined with his scholarly temperament, merged into an organic whole: not pretentious, but totally natural.

Qi Ba was also a man rich in feelings. There was one thing he had in common with his father: both cried easily. My grandmother told me this, laughing when she said it. Although I had never seen Qi Ba cry, there were indeed records that this had happened. For example, he cried when he learnt that Marshal He Long had died after being persecuted, and when he was informed about the September 13th Incident (the day Lin Biao died in a plane crash). I can recall an interesting scene of him 'crying' when family members jokingly imitated these 'crying scenes'. At the time we were just chatting, but suddenly we were talking about being apt to cry. "I am in the habit of crying," Qi Ba said to Qi Ma, and then began to imitate the sound of crying. He did not only imitate sobbing softly, but also loudly, which made everyone in the room burst into uproarious laughter.

Warm and sincere, Qi Ba was also a totally trustworthy man. He was a good teacher and a helpful friend on any occasion, and you could talk to him about what was on your mind without worrying that he would be offended. Conversations with him were sensible and free of vanity, and they would influence people involuntarily. His wide range of knowledge also made people feel that he was one of their colleagues. His vision seemed to be penetrating, making people feel that he understood things thoroughly, which would set their minds at ease and let them feel that there was no need to gloss over problems.

The way he went about his daily activities, such as eating, drinking and living, as well as wearing clothes, can be summed up in one sentence: "I am a commoner." Sometimes the demands he exerted on himself were too excessive; however, his dignified appearance was always in harmony with his clean and neat patch shirt. An aspect of his ideology was that, as one of the leaders of the ruling party, he should never forget about the hardships of ordinary people. He played a leading role in society and even paid attention to minor matters. All this had an imperceptible influence on me, the people surrounding him, and the general populace of China.

1. Zhou Enlai in the Minds of the Founders of the PRC

My broad life experience has turned me into a jack-of-all-trades, giving me the opportunity to encounter people from all professions at home and abroad. Among them were the founders of the PRC, and I was very touched by their genuine affection for Qi Ba. I think if one can be loved and admired both before and after his death, he must carry an inexhaustible intellectual wealth. This wealth, the result of his memorable choices in life, should be remembered and emulated by future generations.

1.1. General Yang Chengwu

On 8 October 1914, Yang Chengwu was born to an ordinary peasant family in Changting, Fujian province. When he was a student at the provincial Number 7 Middle School, the wave of revolution was sweeping through China. He chose to join the revolutionary ranks. In January 1929, he took part in a local armed insurrection in western Fujian, and in March 1930 he was placed in the third column of the Fourth Army of the Chinese Workers' and Peasants' Red Army (which existed from 1928 to 1937). He then joined the CPC.

Yang Chengwu.

I had heard Qi Ba and General Geng Biao talk about General Yang's heroic achievements as well as the historical contributions he had made, so I had long been an admirer of his. At one point, Qi Ba told me that during the counteroffensive to Chiang Kai-shek's Fourth Encirclement Campaign in the central base area, in 1932, the troops led by General Yang fought bravely and resourcefully and achieved a glorious victory over the enemy. Marshal Nie Rongzheng once praised General Yang for being a model regimental political commissar. Both Qi Ba and Geng Biao praised him for his bravery and skills in battle during the Long March. In May 1935, along with the regiment leader, General Wang Kaixiang, he commanded his troops to run 120km overnight to seize the Luding suspension bridge, which ensured the safe crossing of the Dadu river for the Red Army troops. During the anti-Japanese war (1937-1945), General Yang led his troops in a fight to resist enemy forces from five directions. Then, during the communist forces' Hundred Regiments Offensive, his troops killed Abe Norihide, lieutenant general of the Imperial Japanese Army. During the liberation war between 1946 and 1949, he took up the posts of column commander, army commander, and second political commissar of the Field Army. Throughout his military career, he commanded combat troops on the front line. He was also a deputy commanding officer of the military parade during the inauguration of the PRC. Subsequently, he was involved in supervising the National Day parade eight times.

During the Cultural Revolution, he was named the PLA's acting Chief of General Staff. He had followed Chairman Mao to inspect the areas north and south of the Yangtze river. Unfortunately, Lin Biao and the Gang of Four framed a case against him and Yu Lijin (the PLA's air force commissar) as well as Fu Congbi (commander of the Beijing Garrison Force). He was imprisoned for six years. His wife and his children were also thrown in prison and subjected to inhumane treatment. The miscarriage of justice in the case of 'Yang, Yu and Fu' moved people to tears. He returned to work after the case was readdressed. Qi Ba felt very bad about the treatment the three generals received, so he was very happy when they were rehabilitated. He had spoken highly of the historical contributions made by the generals.

According to General Yang, he had learnt what I was doing, as well as something about my character, through Qi Ba. Although I had first heard of him a long time ago, through Qi Ba and Geng Biao, it was not until the late 1970s that I had the chance to meet and talk to him. At the time, he was going to lead a Chinese delegation to visit some western European countries. I was invited to attend a briefing for the delegation about the customs of the countries they were going to visit and diplomatic etiquette. General Yang was brimming with energy and vitality, feeling very happy and proud to be able to represent the Chinese military personnel by visiting foreign countries after the Cultural Revolution.

When the seminar ended, he came to shake my hand, indicating that I stay behind. Then, in a sentimental tone, he told me about his suffering during the Cultural Revolution. When he came to the point where he had lost three family members (Qi Ba had apologised for this, as well as for his inability to stop it from happening), General Yang sighed with emotion. "The Cultural Revolution was an unprecedented catastrophe," he said, and continued: "The premier bore the responsibility as well as the blame, but in the tortuous and complicated circumstances, he did all he could to reduce the loss of human lives. Having made self-sacrifices and ready to go through hell, the premier risked being misunderstood and accused. He did his job with exceptional wisdom and great tenacity throughout the years until he was mentally and physically exhausted. The premier made a monumental contribution to the party and the state when they were both in a hopeless situation. He was the most indispensable man of our time. Of his own initiative, he offered me and my family an apology, assuming responsibility for the party and the state, which made people understand and esteem him even more. In the complicated circumstances during the Cultural Revolution, it was not that simple and straightforward to demonstrate conscientiousness and be reasonable."

"In those years," General Yang went on, "Lin Biao had been chosen by Chairman Mao as his successor, the chairman's right to do so having been written in the party constitution. Also, Lin was one of the premier's earliest students. Hence, when dealing with things regarding Lin, it wasn't convenient for the premier to advocate his point of view as he pleased. How can people like me wantonly blame him for my suffering?" the general asked. "The Chinese people love the premier and they are grateful to him, which is totally understandable. As for Lin Biao's death in an aircraft crash, somebody spread the rumour that it was the premier who ordered the aeroplane to be shot down. This is sheer nonsense. The premier was not in charge of military affairs, so how could he have ordered the shooting down of the vice chairman's private plane without the permission of the chairman and the Central Committee?"

During our conversation, General Yang recalled past instances of Qi Ba caring for and helping the growth of young revolutionary soldiers, who would take the premier as a role model, just like the veteran soldiers did. He mentioned that Qi Ba was one of the founders of the PLA, as well as the creator of the PLA's political department. The historical importance of the Nanchang uprising, during which the first shot against the KMT reactionaries had been fired, is known to all Chinese, but the premier never claimed credit for it. Although he never received a military rank, he will always be a field marshal in the hearts of the people and the PLA soldiers. During the Cultural Revolution, some members of the rebel groups went so far as to try to change the date of Army Day from 1 August (the date of the Nanchang uprising, led by Zhou Enlai) to 9 September (the date for the Autumn Harvest uprising, led by Mao Zedong), which even Chairman Mao himself was very angry about. Chairman Mao meant that the Nanchang uprising, a national event, had taken place before the Autumn Harvest uprising, which was a regional event. How could we change history as we please? We should never change it. We communists should be historical materialists.

General Yang emphasised that whenever the party and the state encountered any major misfortune, Zhou Enlai was always the one who stepped forward bravely to tide them over. During the 10-year Cultural Revolution, especially when the cadres of the older generation were 'overthrown' one after another, the country's economy was on the brink of collapse, and domestic troubles followed foreign invasions, it was Zhou Enlai, then in poor health, who had to bear the responsibility and the blame. He had made vigorous efforts to turn the tide. With great wisdom and courage, he was an impassable obstacle to the Gang of Four, who were trying to seize state power. In those days, he was an indispensable leader, and internationally he won the understanding and support of the people around the world, as well as the leaders of some countries, for his efforts towards the Chinese revolution and the construction of new China. The contribution Zhou Enlai made to China's history was unprecedented, and no other Chinese leaders could challenge him for the high praise he received from the international community. Therefore, it is not a false statement to say that the safety of all of China was dependent on the premier in those difficult days.

This conversation with General Yang was a long one. When it was over, he sent me to the elevator. Cordially, he said to me: "Little Zhou, I hope you take your uncle as your role model, working hard to equip yourself with skills and serve the people. Do not waste or fritter away your time."

1.2. Huang Zhen

Huang Zhen (1909-1989) was a talented general, artist and diplomat. Like Geng Biao, he was also a general diplomat for new China who had experienced the Long March. He was a very capable man who was treasured by Qi Ba. I had been his subordinate for some time, so I knew how much he esteemed and loved Qi Ba. In his work, he always acted on Qi Ba's ideas, which made me admire him.

Huang Zhen.

He was a legendary man. Born to a peasant family in Tongcheng county, Anhui province, he went to Shanghai to study painting in his early years. After graduation, he taught painting for a while, but he was sacked for his support of the progressive student movement. He then took part in the Ningdu uprising and joined the Red Army, beginning his life as a revolutionary. During the Long March, he wrote stage plays and songs, which became popular among the Red Army soldiers. He also painted, and his sketches and cartoons were so touching that they enhanced the morale of the troops. These paintings were later compiled in *An Album of Paintings of the Long March*. They became rare historical images of the Long March, as well as valuable works of art.

In 1946, during the negotiations between the nationalists and the communists, he was appointed chief representative of the regional executive team, bearing major general as his military rank and matching the KMT reactionaries blow for blow in their struggle. In July 1948, he was transferred to Xibaipo and worked in the political department of the military commission of the Central Committee. During this period, he oversaw the design of the flag for the PLA.

He was appointed Chinese ambassador to Hungary in 1950, and then moved on to become Chinese ambassador to Indonesia in 1954. When the first Asian-African conference was held in 1955 in Bandung, Indonesia, he personally guarded Premier Zhou Enlai, who was attending. The conference was a great success for Premier Zhou. In 1961, Huang returned to China and served as vice minister of the foreign ministry. In 1964, he was appointed Chinese ambassador to France. In 1973, he went to America to work as chairperson of the PRC's liaison office in the US, promoting mutual understanding and the normalisation of relations between the two. From 1977 onwards, he served concurrently as the first deputy head of the publicity department, minister and deputy party secretary of the Ministry of Culture, party secretary and director of the Committee for Cultural Relations with Foreign Countries, as well as standing committee member of the central advisory commission.

Before the Cultural Revolution, I worked with the Committee for Cultural Relations with Foreign Countries, which was shut down during the Cultural Revolution. Sometime around 1977, the organisation was reinstalled and Huang Zhen was appointed as its head. Some of the former staff members returned, and I was expected to return, too. As I was working for the ILD, he went to talk to my superiors. Thereafter, I was 'loaned out' to the Committee for Cultural Relations with Foreign Countries. I was in charge of the external cultural exchanges, films, international publicity, and other such things.

After he found out that my salary was far below what I ought to receive for the number of years I had been working, during a meeting of the party group, he used me as an example of Qi Ba's high requirements for relatives and a reminder to keep Qi Ba's teachings in mind, which was to be strict with oneself and broad-minded towards others. "During his life, the premier clearly stated that we should be strict with the children of the senior cadres, not turn them into idle and wasteful children from privileged families. From Zhou Erliu, we can see that the premier led by example to be strict with himself." In fact, Huang Zhen also made Premier Zhou his own role model, setting similar requirements for himself.

In 1973, before he went to the US to take up the post of director of the liaison office, the general service department of the foreign ministry was planning on applying for money to make him some new clothes. When he found out that this wasn't in keeping with the general rules, he stopped them. "Premier Zhou often paid out of his own pocket for clothes made for foreign trips. When I accompanied him to visit 14 countries in Asia and Africa, our comrades in the Chinese Embassy in Egypt saw that his shirt was patched. They wondered why the Chinese premier of 600 million people was wearing such a ragged shirt, and they would have liked to have given him some clothing vouchers to buy new ones. But the premier resolutely rejected them. So I should learn from Premier Zhou, and you will not report to the higher authorities for my suit." Afterwards, he bought himself a suit out of his own savings.

In 1980s, my wife and I were selected and dispatched by Huang Zhen to the UK, where I worked as a cultural counsellor in the Chinese Embassy, in charge of Sino-Anglo cultural exchanges and cooperation.

During our time in the UK, we actively pushed for the signing of an agreement for cultural cooperation between China and the UK. We made contacts in British political, diplomatic and cultural circles and sought friendly cooperation in multiple fields. We helped to bring the Royal Ballet, the London Festive Ballet (now the English National Ballet), the English National Ballet School, the Modern Dance School and others to China to give performances or to take part in a cultural exchange in some other way. Having won the support of the British deputy prime minister's wife, my wife secured scholarships for several Chinese children to come to the UK to study ballet. She also became a close friend of the chairperson of the National Federation of Women's Institutes.

But there were different opinions inside China regarding this procedure of sending children overseas to study ballet. Some were against the idea, thinking that it was a sheer waste of talent because many of them would not return and we were giving away our talent to other countries. Huang Zhen held a similar opinion, and the argument went on and on.

After I returned to China to report about my work in the UK, Huang Zhen discussed this matter with me. I stuck to my opinion, saying that China has a large population and that both opportunities and talented candidates are few. But judging from historical trends, it is natural for some of them not to come back. Even if they choose to stay overseas, their

Everlasting Memories

"Gloucestershire Echo" 6.9.84

Mr. Zhou Er Lui, Cultural Counsellor at the Chinese Embassy in London, with his wife and the Mayor, Coun. Gerry Bingham, in the Mayor's Parlour at the start of a two-day visit to Cheltenham.

The city of Weihaiwei is twinned with the English city of Cheltenham. Zhou Erliu and Wang Zhangli with the mayor of Cheltenham.

affection for their homeland will not be diminished. Meanwhile, they can play an active part in spreading Chinese influence internationally, which can enhance the social status of the overseas Chinese and help to push forward cultural exchanges between China and foreign countries. So, I held on to my view that we should encourage Chinese youngsters to go abroad to receive training. Huang Zhen nodded his head, then said to me: "It seems that Premier Zhou has influenced you a lot. You speak with foresight, so I agree with you."

A cultural counsellor's job is to engage in cultural exchanges, but for the other friendly exchanges, we also need to follow Qi Ba's teachings. With high-level leadership and the support of Huang Zhen and Wang Bingnan, I have helped to bring together 10 pairs of twin cities in China and the UK, which has sowed the seeds for a Sino-Anglo friendship and strengthened the foundation for the two peoples to understand each other.

Huang Zhen and I shared our affection for Qi Ba, so we felt particularly close to each other, which allowed me to freely put forward my different opinions regarding our work. For example, the pianist Fu Cong enjoyed a high reputation at home and abroad. He was well liked by his audience for naturally blending the charm of Chinese poems from the Tang dynasty with the music of Chopin. When he was invited to play in Taiwan, many people in mainland China boycotted this performance. But I thought that we should let him go. We can remind the artist not to be used by others for any political purposes, and still respect him and have faith in him. Afterwards, when the pianist was approached in Taiwan by some people to spread their anti-China propaganda, as expected, he sternly refused to cooperate with them.

1.3. Geng Biao

After Qi Ba's death, whether in a public meeting or a private conversation, Geng Biao said many times that Premier Zhou was an honest man who had never been fond of people boasting and currying favour with him, who had been a good leader and had always had the wellbeing of the people at heart. He also said that the premier was not only a good general manager of the country, but in fact had already been a good manager for the whole party, the army and the liberated areas before the founding of new China.

Geng Biao.

Geng Biao came from a poor peasant family and had been a coal miner in his early years. Although he did not have a higher academic background, he made no secret of his feelings towards Qi Ba and he would speak out about what he was thinking in a sincere and straightforward manner. He hated evil like an enemy and he bitterly despised the Gang of Four. He refused to shake hands with them; hence, under the circumstances, he was persecuted. In 1977, at a meeting for a whole team of cadres of a related organisation, he mentioned that he felt bad after he had been denounced in name by the Gang of Four. He went to see Premier Zhou in his residence, who then spoke these three sentences: "When other people are trying to bring you down, just stand still. When they want to drive you away, refuse to leave. When they make things difficult for you, do not die." It was this advice that made him understand the inflexible will and determination as well as the expectations and encouragement of the premier. They became his source of strength to carry on working and fighting under adverse circumstances. He finally understood that it had nothing to do with the interests of the individual, but with the safety and prospects of the state, into whose hands the power would fall. Though the premier was in poor health, he still earnestly practiced what he advocated, so Geng Biao thought that he mustn't retreat, but instead put up with the criticism and stand fast at his post until the final coming of victory.

He once told me, with tears in his eyes, that Qi Ba had been forced to criticise himself during the so-called campaign to denounce 'capitulationism'. In order to protect the other leaders and cadres, Qi Ba even took responsibility for historical errors that had nothing to do with himself. At the meeting, tears in their eyes, many cadres at ministerial level felt resentful about the treatment Qi Ba had received. "Didn't he act bravely for a just cause and save other people's lives at the risk of his own?" Geng Biao asked me.

During the Cultural Revolution, Geng Biao endured a lot of pressure from the Gang of Four because he had great esteem for Premier Zhou. Yet he had made a historical contribution to the complete crushing of the Gang of Four when Hua Guofeng and Ye Jianying sent him to the broadcasting institution to take control of the media, which played a role in consolidating the victory and stabilising the situation.

I got to know Geng Biao during the Cultural Revolution. From 1969 to 1971 I was in the May Seventh Cadre School in Henan to do manual labour. The military representative at the farm was a man from a certain air force organisation who was a follower of Lin Biao. For reasons I couldn't understand, he would find all sorts of excuses to punish me and give me a very hard time at the farm. This put me in a very difficult situation as well as in an extremely bad mood. I discussed my circumstances with my university classmate Lu Jingsheng, who was an ordinary cadre working with the ILD. He was very sympathetic to my plight, so he told Minister Geng Biao about my situation. Geng Biao didn't know me then, but he was unhappy about the treatment I had received and became concerned about me. Hence, in 1971 I was ordered to return to the ILD, and ever since then I have stayed in touch with him. It was around this time that US president Richard Nixon visited China, so I was dispatched to work for the foreign ministry until the reception work finished.

Qi Ba passed away on 8 January 1976. In March of that same year, some foreign guests came to China to express their condolences. Geng Biao then took some of the guests to the island of Hainan. I went too. We landed in Haikou and went on to visit the whole island. Our final stop was Tianya Haijiao in Sanya, a beautiful tourist resort with a beach with fine sand on the edge of the blue sea. The southern wind wafted gently, and the whole scene was like a wonderland. We all marvelled at the natural beauty. Then the foreign guests and the Chinese hosts were invited to board a boat to review the PLA Navy's South Sea Fleet. The warships were all lined up and presented a magnificent sight. Just at this moment, leaving his secretary and guards behind, Geng Biao lay down on his back on the beach. He then waved at me to come near him, which made me realise that he was going to use this unmonitored place of leisure to have an unusual discussion with me. So I took off my shoes, pretending I was going to swim, and ran in his direction. His secretary, a very kind man called Gao, whom I knew very well, also started to run. I knew that he was just putting on a show of joining me and Geng Biao.

Geng Biao asked me to lie on my back beside him. "Some things I can only tell you in this way, under the present circumstances," he said to me quietly. "You know that Premier Zhou was a man of principle and found himself in a precarious situation for years, so it wasn't convenient for me to talk to you directly in those days. Now he's finally left us. He was a great leader of the party and the state and he enjoyed the love of the people all over the country. He had a noble character. He conducted himself remarkably, but the Gang of Four regarded him as their biggest obstacle to supreme party leadership and state power. Now, with all my respect and admiration for the premier, I am taking a risk and telling you the truth. You'd better leave your present job and go, the farther away the better. Please understand me. In the present situation, I am unable to provide any protection for you because I cannot guarantee my own safety." He passed on to me the three sentences Qi Ba had said to him, and then said: "There may be a fundamental change in the situation very soon. When it happens, I will ask you to come back, but I hope you can understand me regarding the arrangements I am making now." What he said was so sudden, yet I still felt the warmth of his words. In an open and sincere manner, he was giving me advice. I understood his difficulties. It was for my safety that he had made this arrangement, so I expressed my understanding as well as my gratitude at once.

Geng Biao (middle) and Zhou Erliu (first from the left) in Hainan.

After I had returned to Beijing, but before I could find a safe place to go, my indignation for the Gang of Four and my worries for the country caused the pressure on my eyes to increase. My doctor told me that I might have glaucoma and could even go blind, so I stayed in Beijing to recuperate. Luckily, Geng Biao and the other leaders in the foreign affairs sector cared deeply for Qi Ba. They also knew that I was a faithful and reliable young cadre, so they didn't put any additional mental pressure on me, but bore the risk themselves.

1.4. Wang Bingnan

Wang Bingnan was Qi Ba's right-hand man. Trained by Qi Ba, he was the leading cadre in the Chinese foreign affairs sector, so he would follow Qi Ba all year round. Because I had once been director of the Chinese People's Association for Friendship with Foreign Countries (CPAFFC), I knew him very well. I genuinely felt that Qi Ba had influenced him a lot. He was strict with himself and would practice what he preached. He often went to work on foot and was kind and warm to others. Although he was of my father's generation, he often called me 'Little Zhou'.

He used to be vice minister of the foreign ministry and director of the CPAFFC. In his early years, he had gone to Japan and Germany to study. While in Germany, he took part in the anti-Japanese and national salvation movements organised by the Chinese in Europe, and he also engaged in some international liaison work. After he returned to China, the Central Committee sent him to Xi'an to win over General Yang Hucheng of the Northwest Army to ally themselves with the communists in the war with Japan. He worked meticulously and played an active part in General Yang's decision to cooperate with the communists. When the Xi'an Incident happened in 1936, he was a good assistant to Qi Ba in the peaceful settlement of this incident.

After the victory over Japan in 1945, he became Chairman Mao Zedong's secretary during the negotiations between the nationalists and the communists in Chongqing. He later became deputy secretary of the foreign affairs committee of the CPC as well as a speaker for the CPC delegation to Nanjing. He was instrumental in helping Qi Ba to introduce the CPC and extend its influence to the international world.

After the founding of the PRC, he was director general of the general office of the foreign ministry and assistant foreign minister, helping Qi Ba to organise the foreign ministry. In 1955, he was concurrently the Chinese ambassador to Poland and chief representative of China in the nine-year-long Sino-US ambassadorial talks. He returned to China in 1964 and took the position of vice minister of the foreign ministry. During the Cultural Revolution, he was framed and consequently subjected to persecution. In 1975, he began working again and became president of the CPAFFC.

In 1983, he led a six-member CPAFFC delegation to visit the UK, which included Dai Weiran and Yang Xianyi. The UK hosts were aware of Wang Bingnan's experiences, so they attached great importance to the

Zhou Enlai (first from the left), Wang Bingnan (middle) and Gong Peng (the woman in Cheongsam in the middle of the back row) with their foreign friends during the anti-Japanese war.

visit. The deputy leader of the House of Commons received them. Wang was already 70 years old by then and suffered from Parkinson's disease, so his hands would frequently shake, but he ignored his condition and carried out the work conscientiously, which moved many people emotionally. I accompanied them for the duration of their visit to the UK.

When in London, he insisted on visiting Karl Marx's grave. In 1848, Karl Marx published his *Communist Manifesto* in London, marking the birth of Marxism and the beginning of the communist movement. After his death, Karl Marx was buried at Highgate Cemetery in north London, and his grave became a shrine for communist revolutionaries. I fully understood the sentiments Wang Bingnan, a veteran revolutionary, felt towards Karl Marx, so I took him to the neat, solemn, and harmonious cemetery. The marble engraving on Karl Marx's grave reads: 'Workers of all lands unite.' In a dignified manner, Wang Bingnan bowed low three times to Karl Marx's bust. I was once again touched by his sincerity.

During his time in the UK, he was invited to the home of the chairperson of the Welsh branch of the Society for Anglo-Chinese Understanding, in a small town in Wales. Ignoring his health, he accepted the invitation with pleasure. He asked me and my wife to go with him. When we were there, he told me that he had something that he needed to talk to me personally about. I wasn't sure what important things he had to tell me. After thinking for a while, he slowly said to me: "In the history of China, talented and virtuous prime ministers have not been few in number, but only Premier Zhou has enjoyed such prestige both at home and abroad. He is China's number one prime minister, able and virtuous, and he will forever live in the hearts of the party and the Chinese people. During his lifetime he has met many foreign leaders, so no one else can match or surpass his influence in China and in foreign countries. In the hearts of the Chinese people, Premier Zhou stands highest in their respect, love and esteem." I knew that Wang had been secretary to the other central leaders, but these words, coming from his mouth, did shock me, making me understand more about his heartfelt respect for Qi Ba.

He then urged me, Qi Ba's younger relative, to carry out the premier's wishes, to implement his teachings and to carry forward the good traditions he founded. Though two decades have passed, the words of Wang Bingnan are still in my ears.

1.5. Wu Xueqian

Wu Xueqian was concurrently state councillor, foreign minister, vice premier and vice chairman of the Chinese People's Political Consultative Conference (CPPCC): another distinguished leader who worked on the foreign affairs frontline in China. He was born in Shanghai, where he had been involved in underground work for many years.

Wu Xueqian.

I first met him in the 1960s. Besides working in the same work unit, we were neighbours at home. At the time, I was living in Beijing in 4 Fuxing Road, unit 21, on the fourth floor, while he lived on the third floor; hence, jokingly, he said that I was his immediate superior. He was in charge of west Asian and African affairs at the CPAFFC, while I was the deputy director in charge of European and Australian affairs. But he was my senior in age.

Once, he asked me to come to his home. He told me that he had only found out recently that I had been a student at Shanghai Nanyang Model Middle School. Excitedly, he said that the school had been one of the bases for his underground work in Shanghai, meaning I had received material assistance from them at the time, but because I was young I had known nothing about it. "Contact between us is still scarce, and this should change," he remarked, smiling. I felt very warm at his words. He also commented that "we should have met before, but we meet now", indicating that knowing and meeting each other was a lucky event in both our lives.

Because he had been working in the foreign affairs sector for a long time, he had direct knowledge of Qi Ba's personality and capacity for work. Several times he talked about the influence of Qi Ba's people's diplomacy on him. He told me that Qi Ba had once said: "Diplomacy is carried out through the relationship between one country and another. But the basis is to influence people and win them over. It is a dialectic, and we must be clear about it."

In 1980, when I was appointed cultural counsellor for the Chinese Embassy in the UK, Wu Xueqian was the foreign minister. He talked to me a few times before and after I went to England. In our conversations, he told me in detail about the guiding ideology and principles for diplomatic work that Qi Ba put forward in the early stages of new China. The seven principles are:

1) To adhere to internationalism and oppose narrow nationalism;

2) To adhere to patriotism and oppose cosmopolitanism;

3) To adhere to collectivism and oppose individualism;

4) To adhere to a proletarian sense of discipline and oppose liberalism;

5) To adhere to democratic centralism and oppose bureaucracy;

6) To have a high degree of party spirit and oppose insufficiency of the political atmosphere;

7) To encourage living simply, working hard and being thrifty in order to oppose bourgeois extravagance and waste.

He also told me that Qi Ba had summarised his style of diplomatic work in the following, penetrating words: "Action corresponds with a standpoint; manner is compatible with status; have a sense of propriety when speaking, and etiquette will follow convention." People working in the diplomatic field must study these guiding and specific ideas conscientiously and carry them out in their practical work.

During the time when he worked for the ILD, he visited many African and west Asian countries and actively carried out the people's diplomacy. He visited more than 50 Asian, African and American countries when he was foreign minister. He quoted Qi Ba's words and said that the actual social conditions made Africa unsuited to socialism. He said that every time Qi Ba talked to African visitors, he would always mention that each country should deal with their national affairs on the basis of its national conditions, treating foreign policies as reference material only. When Qi Ba talked to foreign guests, he never humbled himself or showed disrespect, but convinced them through reasoning. He opposed both blind self-importance and improperly belittling oneself, but insisted upon being practical and realistic. The premier's lofty ideology and fine style should be learnt and carried out in all practical work, and also be handed down to future generations by the people working in foreign affairs.

Wu Xueqian had been in charge of the external work in Africa and west Asia for many years, feeling profoundly that Chinese involvement in foreign affairs was comparatively weak in these regions. It was Premier Zhou Enlai who put forward the necessary policies and had them put into practice. Generally, in this respect, working did not only mean pioneering, but also making considerable progress. In this connection, Wu listed Qi Ba's eight principles for giving foreign aid as follows:

1) Our government always provides foreign aid on the basis of equality and mutual benefit, never regarding such aid as a unilateral grant;

2) When our government provides foreign aid, we must strictly respect the sovereignty of the recipient country, never having strings attached or asking for special privileges;

3) Our government provides financial aid by giving a loan with either a low or no interest, and, when necessary, extends the deadline for repayment and makes it possible to lighten the recipient country's burden;

4) Our government's aim in providing aid is not to make the recipient country dependent on China, but to help them to be self-reliant and develop their economy independently;

5) The aid projects aim at making small investments that return quick profits, increasing income and accumulating capital for the recipient country;

6) Our government provides the best equipment and materials within its power and negotiates a price according to the international market. If the equipment provided by the Chinese government does not meet the negotiated standard and quality, the Chinese government guarantees its replacement;

7) When our government provides technical aid to a foreign country, we guarantee that the personnel of the recipient country can master said technology;

8) Experts sent by our government receive the same remuneration as experts in the recipient country, allowing no special claims or comforts.

Today, the diplomatic support and economic exchanges between China, other Asian countries and African countries has become well developed. But we, the future generation, should never forget the teachings of deceased leaders such as Premier Zhou Enlai. We must gain new insights through studying old materials, putting into practice what we have learnt, closely following the situation and making further advances while trying to achieve the best practical results. Of course, when studying the ideologies of the revolutionaries of older generations, we must consider their specific social and historical circumstances and the general level of understanding at the time. We should never carry out isolated evaluations and analyses. Only by doing this will we be able to grasp the essence of their ideology.

Wu Xueqian was a good and approachable leader who never forgot the people, on which point he and Qi Ba were very similar. From him, I saw that people working in the foreign affairs sector were not only rigorous in their work ethic, but that they highly esteemed Zhou Enlai, the founder of diplomacy for new China.

2. Qi Ba and His Chinese and Foreign Friends

2.1. Xu Beihong and Lao She

Qi Ba met Xu Beihong, who was studying oil painting in France, as early as 1924. They visited the Communards' Wall in Paris and had a photo taken to mark the occasion. Qi Ba thought highly of Xu Beihong's artistic talent and principled integrity. On 23 September 1953, Xu Beihong suffered from the recurrence of an old illness and died, aged only 61 years, during a meeting of the second representative assembly of national literary and art workers. "Xu Beihong's death is a tremendous loss that we will never recover from! How could we keep him in a meeting from morning to night when he was ill? Such a thing must never happen again." His voice trembling with deep grief, Qi Ba said this to Zhou Yang (the vice minister of the Ministry of Culture) and the others when he paid his last respects to the deceased Xu Beihong at Beijing hospital.

A painting by Xu Beihong.

Lao She.

During the Cultural Revolution, the writer Lao She was persecuted. The Red Guards had insulted his dignity, so he chose to commit suicide by jumping into the lake in Beihai park. After hearing the news, Qi Ba felt profound sorrow. He inquired about Lao She's death several times, concerned for his widow and other family members. When Qi Ba was ill, he once went to Beihai park to rest. Facing the lake, he asked the personnel beside him what day it was. It was 24 August, an ordinary day; but, with deep sorrow, Qi Ba told them that it was the day Lao She had killed himself by jumping into the lake.

2.2. Guo Moruo

Guo Moruo and Qi Ba were intimate friends in their early years. Guo had once worked under Qi Ba's direct leadership. From Qi Ba's remarks about Guo, I could tell that their friendship was a deep one, and it was Qi Ba who prompted Guo to join the party. He was a gifted scholar of our time and a great romantic poet, who had also made outstanding achievements in archaeology, palaeography and calligraphy. He was once president of the Chinese Academy of Sciences. Because of my job, I came into contact with him.

Xu Maijin was the author of the poem *Song of Prisoners*. He was in charge of the Xinhua Daily in Shanghai and had spent many years in the KMT prison in Suzhou. After 1949, he became director of the general office of the Ministry of Culture, and was thrown in prison again during the Cultural Revolution. He had made a huge contribution to the revolution, but his life was rough and rugged. However, he preserved the spirit of revolutionary optimism in spite of his misfortune.

Qi Ba once told me an interesting story involving Guo and Xu. During the peace talks between the nationalists and the communists in 1946, Guo poked fun at Xu by writing Xu a couplet. The first line was: "*Xu Xiangqian Xu Maijin Xuxu Xiangqian Maijin; Xu Maijin Xu Xiangqian Xuxu Maijin Xiangqian.*" So far, there has been no good second line for this couplet. The 'Xu Xiangqian' in the couplet was one of 10 PLA marshals who had founded the PRC. Hence, Xu Maijin and Xu Xiangqian: one civilian and one military man. It was very witty to have two famous men in that line of the couplet. Xu Maijin kept in close contact with me, and he confirmed that Guo's couplet was true.

Qi Ba and Guo both took an extensive interest in things that they usually didn't know much about. In the early 1970s, when the Maori delegation from New Zealand visited China, Guo accepted my suggestion to receive them. The Maori are an important ethnic group living in the South Pacific Ocean. The arrival of the Europeans and their plundering turned the Maoris in New Zealand and the Aborigines in Australia into minority groups. At the time, the Chinese knew very little about them, so we hoped to learn more from their visit. Qi Ba even wanted to know more about intermarriage between Maoris and Europeans, hoping to study it as a social problem of nationality. Guo had always had a great interest in civilisations around the world, so he received the guests with excitement despite his age (he was 80 years old) and health (he had heart problems). He told me that the pronunciation of the Maori language is close to Malay. Because these two peoples both live on islands in the South Pacific, they might have common ancestry.

After he learnt that some of the guests were good at singing and dancing and that one of them, a poet, could write in the native Maori language, he cheerfully requested the guests to perform for him. The Maori dance was loud and powerful, so we were worried that he would not be able to stand the excitement because of his heart condition. But he insisted that they dance. The guests were very happy and went to pick up their musical instruments from the hotel to put on a show. Guo was excited, so he suggested that both the hosts and guests sing the song *The East is Red* together. Hence, a striking scene took place when this 80-year-old scholar sang along with the six Maori guests as well as Ms Ding Xuesong, the former female Chinese ambassador.

Qi Ma told me afterwards that when Qi Ba saw this photo in the newspaper, he talked to her about it with great interest. He said that Guo either had a scholar's intellectual power or an artist's taste; in his old age, he displayed a young man's interests, which told us that Guo's poetic temperament and charming manners were as strong as they had been in the past.

During the banquet held in the hall of the People's Congress, in reply to Guo's invitation, I recited a poem:

> Untitled
>
> *Red banner, easterly wind, stars, moon and sky,*
> *Hospitable Guo Lao gave us a feast of poems to recite.*
> *China has a long history,*
> *With old affections and new friendships, we'll talk for*
> *ten thousand years.*

What is fascinating are Guo's remarks on the translation of his poems into foreign languages. He said that if a Chinese poem has been poorly translated into a foreign language, it is like Maotai liquor that has been turned into plain water; but if the translation is good, it will be like the Maotai has been turned into brandy, which tastes good to both the Chinese and foreign guests.

During the Cultural Revolution, both Qi Ba and Guo Moruo were under unnecessary torment and pressure. Two of Guo's sons died while persecuted. But as veteran revolutionaries, Qi Ba and Guo shared the same quality that had been formed during their long revolutionary careers. They always kept their revolutionary spirits young and worked hard and ceaselessly for the country's prosperity. When Qi Ba was dangerously ill and heard that Guo had attended a meeting to criticise the capitulationist Song Jiang, he sighed, saying that he was surprised by this act of Guo's. But when Qi Ba died on 8 January 1976, the memory of the past welled up in his heart. Grieving, Guo wrote a poem on 13 January to express his condolences and to recollect the profound friendship between them, spanning half a century, and his sincere esteem for Qi Ba.

A revolutionary pioneer, brilliant at running a country,
Five continents are grieving for the death of a giant star.
Flows of people rush to mourn,
Tears welled up in their eyes.
Prestige lies in the hearts of the people,
Brilliant achievements are immortal.
Your loyalty shines like the sun,
The Heavens and Earth grieve for your death.

After the Gang of Four was overthrown in October of that same year, the whole nation celebrated. Guo wrote another poem to express his excitement. In the same year, an old man, well over 80 years old, grieved for the death of the people's premier, and was also joyous about the overthrow of the Gang of Four. With a poet's romantic enthusiasm, he wrote twice to voice the aspirations of the people as well as his deep feelings towards Premier Zhou.

Thinking of Premier Zhou (to the tune of Nian Nu Jiao)

With one teacher, we united all our efforts for a common purpose. With one heart, we shared a common fate. Fifty years are like one day; we unceasingly carried on with our long march, leaping forward. Unified China, contending against two hegemonies. The Chinese and foreign people loved and esteemed you. When you died, they wept.

How did Wang, Zhang, Jiang and Yao form a gang? They slandered and wreaked havoc all over the country. Reactionary forces were ascendant, but one blow turned them to dust. You eliminated traitors from the party, rid people of the scourge, assuaged popular indignation. Together, loyal souls and living creatures celebrated all over the country.

2.3. Mei Lanfang

My father, Zhou Enzhu, was a close personal friend of Mei Lanfang, the grand master of Beijing opera. Qi Ba always urged my father to keep in contact with Mr Mei. In the 1930s, he used to take me with him to Mr Mei's house in Shanghai, where he would seek his advice on Beijing opera

Zhou Enzhu and Mei Lanfang at Mei Lanfang's residence in rue Massenet, Shanghai.

performances. We were short of money in those days. To show our respect to Mr Mei, my father had a special children's suit made that I could wear when we went to his house. When I was little, I had a fair complexion and slightly blonde hair, which made me look like a doll. Mr Mei liked me very

Mei Lanfang at home, explaining a play to Zhou Enzhu.

Zhou Enzhu and his granddaughter Zhou Rong with the Mei Lanfang family. In the front row, from the left: Mei Baoyue, Zhou Enzhu, Mrs Mei Lanfang (Fu Fangzhi). The girl in the arms of Mrs Mei is Zhou Rong. Mei Baojiu stands at the back.

Wang Zhangli (first from the left), Zhou Erliu (second from the left), and Zhou Rong (first from the right) with Mei Baojiu.

much. He was glad when I came and would give me apples to eat. With Mr Mei's guidance, my father could perform, independently, the operas *Susan Qijie, Wang Baoxun, Shen Tou Ci Tang, Yuzhou Feng*, and *Dayu Shajia*.

After the liberation in 1949, I once heard Qi Ba say to my father: "We must make sure that Mr Mei carries on playing the role that no one else can play, both in China and abroad. He is a national treasure and he deserves to be cared about and respected... Mr Cheng [Yanqiu] has pursued political progress, while Mr Mei has done the same. In this respect, they have done better than you." "I am ashamed of my inferiority," my father would say, again and again.

Extraordinarily, after Mei Lanfang's death, my father kept in touch with his family. In 1971, he took his granddaughter Zhou Rong to Mr Mei's former home and paid a visit to Mrs Mei and her children. To his surprise, when he entered the gate, he saw Mrs Mei kneeling on the ground, choking with tears because of the happy memories she had of her contact with Zhou Enlai's brother, as well as the bad memories she had of her family members being humiliated and her hair being shaved off by the Red Guards during the Cultural Revolution. Now that she saw my father, Zhou Enlai's cherished representative, she couldn't help recalling the memorable friendship between Mei Lanfang and Zhou Enlai's brother. Later, in 1981, Mr Mei's children Mei Baojiu and Mei Baoyue came to Shanghai to see my father, showing that they treasured and respected the deep affection that existed between the older generation, as well as the friendship between the Mei and the Zhou families that has extended to the younger generations.

2.4. Jin Shan

After Qi Ba died, some members of society said that he had had many adoptive sons and daughters. I was in constant contact with Qi Ba, but as I recall, these claims are not true. Qi Ba's bodyguards and secretaries can also attest that these were merely rumours. However, Qi Ba and Qi Ma did indeed have an adoptive daughter: Sun Weishi. I had met her and her husband Jin Shan many times at West Flower Hall. When I was with them, I felt I was with my sister and brother-in-law.

Jin Shan and Sun Weishi.

My Uncle Zhou Enlai

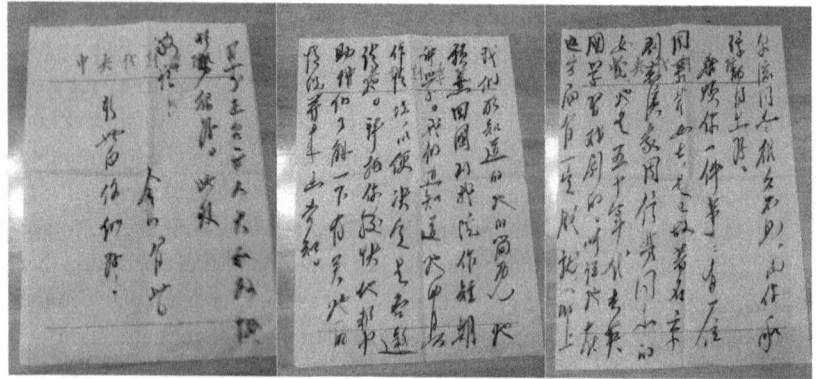

Jin Shan's letter to Zhou Erliu. For the full translation, see Appendix 6.

Both Sun Weishi and Jin Shan were famous artists in China. Jin was a party member, and he had been engaged in CPC underground work for many years. He had made some special contributions to the party. He had close relations with Du Yuesheng, the Shanghai gangmaster, and he even represented the KMT in their negotiations with the communists. At once, I was captivated by his fascinating life story.

In the 1950s, Jin Shan may have committed some errors in his work, about which I know no details. Qi Ba called Jin and Sun to his residence and had lunch with them. I was there that day, so Qi Ba asked me to join them for lunch. Jin was a very handsome man. He was different from the rest, as he wore his hair long and had the air of an artist. As Sun had spent many years in Russia, she had incorporated some Russian elements into the way she spoke and moved. In her *blazy* (the Russian word for 'long dress'), she showed a foreign trend in her appearance. They were a bit uneasy seeing me there. "Although Erliu is young, he always obeys what I say. He is discreet in word and deed, so there is no need to worry about him listening to our conversations," Qi Ba said to them.

That scene is still fresh in my mind. Looking ashamed, Jin Shan lowered his head and listened quietly while Sun looked at him with an expression of affection, concern and forgiveness. I had the feeling that she was a reasonable woman, not narrow-minded.

Because of my presence, Qi Ba didn't talk about any details. But he requested that Jin should genuinely learn a lesson, to treasure the foundation and the experiences he had accumulated. He should look forward to the future, make a fresh start and contribute more to the arts. Qi Ba mentioned that while grand masters of art are alive, they are usually regarded as national treasures. After they die, their surviving family members should be looked after by the government. If any of them possess skills handed down to them by the grand masters, we should support them. Then, in a mild manner, he said to Jin: "As long as you correct your mistakes, you will be fine. The key is the way in which you behave in the future. Pick yourself up from where you fell, the quicker the better. You must look forward." The expression on Qi Ba's face was so kind and his tone was so gentle that it made me feel that he was not a strict father, but a loving brother.

2.5. Israel Epstein

The American journalist and writer Israel Epstein became a Chinese national after 1949. He was chief editor of *China Construction* magazine. Qi Ba and Mr Epstein had got to know each other very well during the war of resistance against Japan.

Mr Epstein once said that during the Cultural Revolution, Chinese external publicity was full of extraordinary leftist, distorted, and even rude and harsh slogans. Premier Zhou strongly opposed such language and would from then on personally examine the final proofs of publication. He pointed out that some of the articles had simply been mechanically copied from domestic newspapers and journals. These articles advocated great-nation chauvinism, made us blow our own trumpet and forced our views on others without considering audiences overseas. Premier Zhou also instructed the magazine not to publish the photos Jiang Qing and Ye Qun had sent in. Later, after Lin Biao's downfall, Premier Zhou instructed the magazine editors: "The Gang of Four is not allowed to meddle with external publicity."

After the Xin An Jiang reservoir was built, commentators would tell visitors that it was the best reservoir in the world. Mr Epstein told us that he remembered Premier Zhou saying: "When we promote China to the outside world, we should never be boastful, nor make our deeds incredible, like saying that our attainments are all up to the most advanced level in the world. We must be true to facts. Some people don't have a clue what the most advanced level in the world is, but they just carry on saying things like the commentators at the reservoir. Yet when pressed by further questioning, they don't know what to say… So, when we encounter scenes like that, we should stop the commentators at once and correct them. The chairman thinks one should have the courage to admit one's mistake!"

2.6. Anna Louise Strong

In September 1958, 72-year-old Anna Louise Strong made her home in Beijing, moving there from America. In her own words, she said: "In September 1948, I started my return journey to China, thinking I might never leave again — but it took me 10 years to arrive!"

Touchingly, she had previously written about Yan'an in her articles. She said: "We are in the caves of Yan'an… Over here, there is no wealth or rank, nor a life of ease and comfort — only people who keep forging forward. They are prudent and have an international perspective. My heart was opened in Yan'an." The above description shows how much Strong treasured the days she spent in Yan'an.

In March 1947, Chairman Mao Zedong and Vice Chairman Zhou Enlai hosted a farewell dinner for Strong in the Yan'an cave. They told her: "You must leave Yan'an now, or you won't be able to leave at all. For the time being, you can't go with us to where we are going. But you have all the material about us you need. You can come back when we renew our contact with the world." When she asked when they would win the war, they replied: "In around two years." In 1948, she returned to the US with her manuscript for *The Chinese Conquer China*.

At the end of 1948, she was planning to enter the liberated Chinese city of Harbin through the Soviet Union. Four months later, she was refused a visa to leave Russia. On 14 February 1949, the Soviet authorities suddenly arrested her, accused her of being a spy and deported her through Poland. The Soviet Union withdrew this groundless accusation six years later, in February 1955. After struggling for another three years, she finally obtained

1946, Zhou Enlai with Anna L. Strong in Yan'an.

the government's permission to leave the US. In September 1958, again through Moscow, she arrived in Beijing.

While in China, she published *Letters from China*, which was distributed worldwide in five languages. Every time I paid her a visit, I would take some copies along and hand them to the Chinese and foreign personnel. *Letters from China* was well received by its readers. When I was at her house, I would often see her, though she was getting on in years, busy writing on her typewriter. She was full of vitality.

I once read some documents relating to Strong, and I was sceptical about the espionage charges held against her. I asked Qi Ba about it. He said that because she held different views, she had been wrongly charged as a secret agent. Such practices — disregarding principles while easily falling out and becoming enemies — were wrong and despicable. We Chinese were going to respect her and treat her well, which was the right thing for us to do.

2.7. Ma Haide

Ma Haide — originally George Hatem — was born on 26 September 1910 into a Lebanese-American family in Buffalo, New York. While at university, where he received his doctoral degree in medicine, he became acquainted with a student from China. From him, he learnt much about China, her ancient civilisation and her present-day poverty and backwardness. His strong curiosity about the country and his sense of duty as a doctor to cure sickness helped him make the decision to practice medicine in China. At that moment he was doing research on oriental tropical diseases, and China was an ideal spot for his research.

Zhou Enlai with Ma Haide in Yan'an.

In 1936, introduced by Soong Ching-ling (Mme Sun Yat-sen) and accompanied by the well-known American journalist Edgar Snow, he crossed the KMT lines and arrived in Yan'an. Having visited here, he decided to stay. He joined the Red Army, and in 1937 he joined the CPC. In Yan'an he learnt to speak standard Chinese, as well as the local dialect of the northern Shaanxi region. He then changed his American name, George Hatem, to a Chinese name, Ma Haide.

Dr Ma Haide and Qi Ba became very good friends. When Qi Ba fell from his horse and broke his right arm in Yan'an, doctor Ma Haide quickly called Ba Suhua and Ke Dihua, two other doctors from India. They held a group consultation on Qi Ba's treatment. Dr Ma Haide was very worried when he saw the fracture was not healing very well and that Qi Ba had suffered from muscular atrophy in his right arm. He tried to improve Qi Ba's condition in every possible way, but finally the Central Committee decided to send Qi Ba to the Soviet Union for treatment.

After Qi Ba's death, Dr Ma Haide once treated the lipoma on my back. He told me that it was non-cancerous and that I did not need to worry. Interestingly, he said to me: "A lipoma also grew on Premier Zhou's back. The two of you also have the same blood type, AB — a surprising similarity between two generations." What he said was amazingly similar to what Qi Ma had told me, which made me feel that he knew Qi Ba very well.

2.8. Rewi Alley

Rewi Alley was born in New Zealand in 1897. He came to Shanghai in 1927 and worked in the Shanghai Municipal Council of the International Settlement. When in Shanghai, he observed what it was like to live in semi-colonial China, and pledged to join the Chinese people in their fight for the transformation of old China. Rewi Alley, Ma Haide and Agnes Smedley joined the first foreign Marxist-Leninist Study Group in Shanghai, and made contact with the CPC. After the anti-Japanese war broke out in 1937, Rewi Alley and Edgar Snow set up the International Commission for the Promotion of Chinese Industrial Cooperatives, to manufacture both goods for daily use and military supplies. While doing this, his footsteps covered more than half of China. Before Wuhan fell into Japanese hands, Alley met Qi Ba, who was to give him a lot of help.

Zhou Enlai with Rewi Alley.

After 1949, Alley settled in Beijing. He never married and had no relatives in China. A girl in New Zealand had loved him for more than 10 years, and wanted him to return to get married. Knowing that his endeavours lay in China, he didn't go back to New Zealand to marry her.

Qi Ba was concerned about this and tried to introduce Alley to a Chinese girl. But Alley rejected her, saying that he was too old for marriage. In fact, his mind was on his adoptive Chinese children, some of whom had grown up and could make their own contributions to state and society. Qi Ba once said to me: "You grew up in Shanghai, so you should know Hardoon Road (now Tongren Road), whose name records a piece of the history of the old Shanghai concessions. Silas Aaron Hardoon was a wealthy businessman of Jewish origin. He lived in China for many years. Not only did he own much property, but he also adopted many Chinese boys as his adoptive sons. It is said that after Hardoon's death these adoptive sons started a fight about property inheritance. But Rewi Alley had shared comforts and hardships with many Chinese revolutionaries, and, considering that he might die for the revolution, didn't marry, but chose to adopt many Chinese children and raise them so that he had children and grandchildren. Some of these children have turned into capable cadres. This shows that even international friends, such as Rewi Alley, can turn themselves into respectable members of the Chinese revolutionary ranks through constant efforts. We really must learn from his spirit of persistent and selfless devotion."

2.9. Edward Heath

The former British prime minister Edward Heath was an old friend, whom the Chinese people are familiar with. He talked with Premier Zhou on many occasions, and they respected each other's views and talents. They established a rather unique kind of friendship that can only exist among great statesmen whose social systems and political convictions are different.

In 1982, internationally renowned violinist and 'citizen of the world' Yehudi Menuhin invited Mr Heath to attend a

Former British prime minister Edward Heath.

concert he was holding for the Chinese child prodigy and violinist Jin Li in the small town of Folkstone, England. After the concert, Mr Heath and I talked about Qi Ba's funny remarks. Mr Heath recalled that he had once asked Premier Zhou a question: "What exactly is the difference between the Chinese and the Taiwanese?" Without a thought, Qi Ba replied: "The Chinese in Taiwan and the Chinese on the mainland are all Chinese. Generally, there is no difference between them. The only difference is that both of them want to lead the unification of China." When he said this, Mr Heath threw back his head and couldn't help laughing.

2.10. Felix Greene

Famous British journalist Felix Greene was received by Premier Zhou several times. He also produced a documentary film about Deng Xiaoping. He accompanied the British field marshal Bernard Montgomery to visit Premier Zhou, and he also cooperated with Premier Zhou for the return of Li Zongren, the former acting president of the nationalist government, to mainland China.

Mr and Mrs Greene with Zhou Erliu and Wang Zhangli.

When he first went to China in the 1950s, he brought a mini tape recorder with him. It was an item commonly used by reporters, but he was stopped at customs in Guangzhou airport because they suspected him of being a spy. Later, he would often remark that the customs personnel, in this case, should not be blamed. He said that it had happened because China knew little of the outside world at the time, but that, luckily, the country had a good leader — Zhou Enlai — who had a broad perspective. He believed that China would gradually pursue a policy of reform and open the door to the outside world; then the Chinese people would learn to understand other cultures, temper themselves through contact with other countries, and raise the management standard.

In the 1980s, Mr Greene was diagnosed with prostate cancer. When I went to see him, he made sure to record our conversations. To cherish Premier Zhou's memory, he said during the recording: "What is unforgettable is that no tiny detail escaped his attention. For example, at a very busy reception meeting where Premier Zhou was to hold a presentation, due to a small operation, I was wearing a soft slipper on one foot, which I believed no one else had noticed. At the time Premier Zhou said nothing, but the next day people from his office came, asking me what was wrong with my foot and if I had received any treatment. They also brought me a pair of very comfortable cotton shoes. To me, personally, Zhou Enlai was not only a great Chinese statesman, but also an internationalist who was kind-hearted and often cared for and helped his foreign friends."

2.11. Dai Ailian

During the years in which I was engaged in external cultural exchanges, I never forgot what Qi Ba had said: "We must skilfully handle our relationship with intellectuals." My association with the famous Chinese dancer Ms Dai Ailian (1916-2006) is an example of how I put this into practice.

Ms Dai Ailian's life story is quite legendary. Her ancestral home was in Xinhui county, Guangdong province. She herself was born in Trinidad and Tobago in the West Indies. She began dancing at the age of five and practised ballet from the age of 10. When she was 14, she went to England to continue her studies under Margaret Craske, then went to study modern dance in the studio of Mary Wigman. She once proposed a theory of combining ballet with modern dance in order to "integrate more closely the movement of the body and one's inner feelings".

In her old age, I accompanied her to the British Royal Dance School to unveil a bust of herself, which was a great and special honour. When the school praised her as a distinguished Chinese dancer who had made great progress for dance in China, she said: "The honour belongs to my country." These words come from the bottom of this overseas Chinese woman's heart, and can also be seen as a true portrait of the close links between her life and the fate of China.

As early as 1937, when the anti-Japanese war broke out, she took part in benefit performances in London, raising money for the Hong Kong-based China Defense League led by Soong Ching Ling, whom she would meet in Hong Kong in 1940. In 1941, after the attack on Pearl Harbour, she travelled to mainland China via Macao and returned to wartime China, using her dancing to promote resistance against Japan. She then created the famous dance routines *The Story of Guerrilla Forces, Air Raids and Longing for Home.*

Wang Zhangli, Dai Ailian and Zhou Erliu.

In 1942, she moved to Chongqing. She set up a dance group in educator Tao Xingzhi's school and gave dancing lessons in multiple locations, and directly received care and help from Qi Ba and Qi Ma from that moment on. It was under Qi Ba's guidance that Dai collected folk songs and operas and created dance routines based on folk traditions: *Spring Outing, Ganzi Ancient Dance, Luoluo Love Songs, The Moon of the Miao People*, and others, causing a sensation in Chongqing.

After the liberation in 1949, she travelled around the country and created more famous dance routines: *Building Our Country, Dove of Peace, Flying Apsaras* and *The Dance of Lotus Flowers*. By now, she had become China's most influential dancer.

Qi Ba talked to me and my wife about Dai Ailian. He said that as Dai had been born and grown up in foreign countries, she could express herself in English better than in Chinese. Foreign influences on her diet and wardrobe were so great that it would be not easy for her to get used to life in China. Qi Ba urged us to respect the fact that Dai had grown up overseas, and at times we talked to her in English.

I was closely associated with Ms Dai, and my wife Wang Zhangli and I had been to her home many times. She lived in a Huaqiao apartment in the Baiwanzhuang district in Beijing. After entering her house, we noticed that there was nothing but a small gym, which was fitted with a huge mirror on the wall. In this gym, she practiced, created and taught, and she never ceased dancing all her life.

Ms Dai had an independent, straight, optimistic, vivacious and inflexible attitude to life. She lived on her own all the time, and liked to do everything she could manage. Once, my wife and I stayed for a meal, talking while we were eating. When we were talking about dance, she stood up, excited, and danced a piece for us. Watching her dance, we couldn't believe that she was already over 50 years of age: she was so quick in her movements, so fit for her age and so high in spirits.

Dai Ailian is called 'the mother of Chinese modern dance'. When she stood on the podium to be honoured, her first thought was of her country, which moved me very much. As cultural counsellor of the Chinese embassy in the UK, I then said to the audience: "In the early stages of the development of Chinese modern dance, it was the education Ms Dai received in England that laid the foundation for her dancing career, which enabled her to integrate Chinese dance into Western dance. At that moment, dancing began to develop in China. China treasures her talent, and the contribution Ms Dai has made to Chinese dancing is unequalled."

3. The Painters Who Cherished the Premier's Memory

3.1. Wu Biduan

Mr Wu Biduan was a famous Chinese woodblock painter. On the first anniversary of Qi Ba's death, he created *Portrait of Zhou Enlai*. This outstanding painting was an excellent likeness both in spirit and in appearance. It was very popular in China and abroad, and many books, magazines and autograph books, such as *The Selected Works of Zhou Enlai*, used it as their cover photo. Qi Ma also liked the painting very much, and she invited Mr Wu to West Flower Hall to express her personal gratitude.

There are many paintings of Qi Ba, but few of them are as extraordinary as Mr Wu's. The reason he could produce such a remarkably lifelike portrait is that besides his extraordinary artistic accomplishments, he had met Qi Ba several times in real life. Other painters didn't have his luck.

Mr Wu had experienced life's hardships in his childhood. Because of the Japanese invasion, he had wandered from Shanghai to Chongqing, destitute, an Oliver Twist in the true sense of the term. But he was lucky that a wartime nursery school took him in in 1938, and then sent him to the Chongqing Yucai School, founded by educator Tao Xingzhi, to study painting. Qi Ba and Qi Ma had been to this school many times to give speeches to the students. When the 12-year-old Wu asked for an autograph from Qi Ma, she wrote down the words, "Outdo your master", urging him to study hard.

After the victory over Japan in 1945, he was lucky again to be transferred to work at the secretariat of the CPC's Central Committee office, which had just been set up in Chongqing. His job was to read newspapers and pick up important information for Qi Ba and the others to read. So he had a lot of

The portrait of Zhou Enlai presented to Zhou Erliu by its painter, Wu Biduan, in 1978.

contact with Qi Ba and Qi Ma. He saw Qi Ba and his comrades work hard day and night for national affairs; hence, he had a deep understanding of their personalities and images. Because of my own childhood experiences, I felt touched when I learnt about Mr Wu's life experiences from Qi Ba and Qi Ma. I held him in high esteem.

Ms Wang Wuan used to work in the ILD, and my wife and I know her very well. She was Mr Wu's friend. She also understood that of all his relatives, Premier Zhou Enlai knew me and my wife very well and had confidence in us, so she suggested that we keep a copy of *Portrait of Zhou Enlai*. Mr Wu was very glad about this, feeling that it was significant to let Zhou Enlai's descendant keep a copy of his painting.

After I received the painting, I held it in my hands and examined it carefully. I was filled with admiration for the painter's extraordinary talent. The appearance of the deceased Qi Ba, especially his naturally dignified expression, made me feel as if Qi Ba was there in the flesh. I treasured this painting very much and kept it with me for decades. But a few years ago, when my house in Beijing needed to be pulled down and we were to be relocated, I was not in Beijing at the time and had to ask friends to take care of moving house for me. My treasured painting of Qi Ba went missing during the move, which made me feel incredibly sorry and remorseful.

In 2008, I went to Beijing for the commemoration of the 110th anniversary of Zhou Enlai's birth. I told my old friend Wu Zuqiang that I had lost Wu Biduan's painting. Surprisingly, Wu Zuqiang phoned Wu Biduan at once. What happened next was even more surprising, as well as touching. Wu Biduan was busy getting ready for a trip to the US, and I was to return to Shanghai after the commemoration activities ended. I left my address with Mr Wu, who said that he would send me a copy of the painting soon.

When I returned home to Shanghai, I received the painting very soon afterwards. Mr Wu said in his letter that all his sketches of *Portrait of Zhou Enlai* were in the collections of different museums, and this one was the only one he had left. Because his feelings for the premier were so special, he was happy to let me keep this one, which he had meant to keep for himself.

I understand that Mr Wu's journey to becoming a famous painter was inseparable from the care of Qi Ba, Qi Ma and the educator Tao Xingzhi. As for myself, if not for the care and love of Qi Ba and Qi Ma, I do not know what my life would be like. I appreciated Mr Wu's special feelings for Qi Ba, while having been presented with the painting twice is, to me, like a scene from a portrayal of history.

3.2. Shang Chengzuo

When my grandfather Zhou Henai was alive, he liked to collect classic books as well as cultural artefacts. His collection could fill 10 big camphor-wood trunks. When Qi Ba was young, he saw these collections, which aroused a profound interest in him. Qi Ba also talked about the research done by famous experts, such as Guo Moruo, Zheng Zhenduo and Shang Chengzuo, praising them for their special contributions to cultural research in China. He particularly praised Mr Shang for his learning and character, as well as his unique calligraphy, which he regarded as distinguished and representative for the south of the country.

Shang Chengzuo was born in 1902. He was a scholar of ancient scripts, an artist of bronze and stone seal cutting, and a calligrapher. His *Catalogue of Characters Found in the Yin Dynasty Ruins* (a more complete dictionary for the Shang oracle bone script), *Album for Seals*

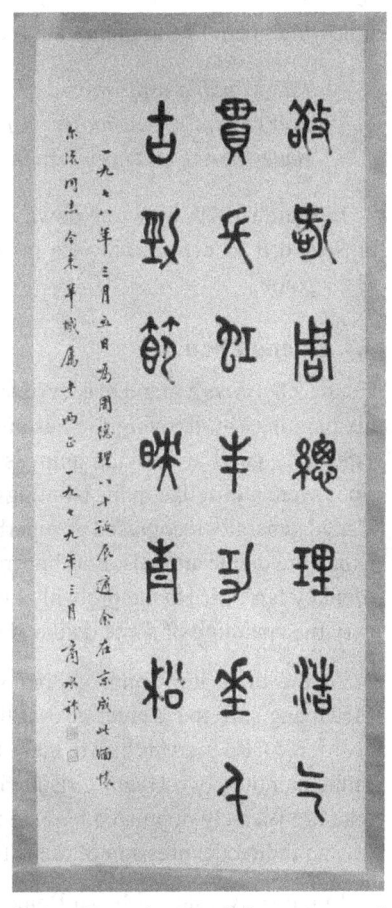

The calligraphy scroll in memory of Zhou Enlai by Shang Chengzuo. For the full translation, see below.

and *Official Scripts by Shang Chengzuo*, *Catalogue of Ji Jin Tu of 12 Schools* and others enjoyed a very high reputation internationally. When I was working in the UK, I helped the Chinese government send scholars to the UK to list and number the nearly 1,000 pieces of oracle bone scripts scattered round the country.

In March 1978, Mr Shang arrived in Beijing for the commemorative activities for the 80th anniversary of Premier Zhou's birth. He wrote the following poem to commemorate Premier Zhou:

> *Full of noble aspiration and daring is our beloved Premier Zhou. His tremendous achievements will be forever remembered, and his moral integrity mirrors the sturdy pine.*

In March 1979, he wrote down this poem in seal-style calligraphy and presented it to me when I was invited to visit Zhongshan University in Guangzhou.

3.3. Huang Zhou

Huang Zhou was a grand master of traditional Chinese painting. He created his paintings by drawing the customs of ethnic minority groups. He was especially good at drawing animals, such as camels, dogs and chickens. They were all lifelike in his paintings. The donkeys he drew were loved by all and generally recognised as superb. I have always been fond of donkeys, which are docile animals. For this, my wife used to mock me and call me a 'donkey fan'. Mr Huang probably knew about my hobby, so he made me a very nice painting of some donkeys.

At the time, the Gang of Four was running rampant, so people like Mr Huang suffered a great deal at their hands. Ignoring his own perilous position, Qi Ba tried his best to make the artists suffer less from persecution. In the painting, two Uygur girls are driving six donkeys. Both sides of the road are sparsely populated by bare trees. It was obvious that the painting was an indirect expression of the national situation at the time.

In the early 1980s, Mr Xu Beihong's wife, Ms Liao Jingwen, saw this painting. She said that both the figures and animals, which Mr Huang was excellent at drawing, were included in the painting. It was an excellent

The painting presented to Zhou Erliu by Huang Zhou.

piece of work, but its only flaw was that it bore no date. She insisted that Mr Huang add the date to the painting. At the time, Mr Huang was ill, and he could barely move about. Still, he quickly painted on the date and returned the painting to me. When I looked at the painting again, I noticed that, besides the date, he had added a few sparrows. The little birds were sitting on a tree branch and flying about in the air, twittering happily. He told me later that after the overthrow of the Gang of Four, he was happy, like people all over the country, and he was sure that the premier, who was in paradise, would be happy too. He thought that if I, the premier's descendant, collected the painting myself, which would have a distinctive significance, the premier's soul in paradise would be comforted.

3.4. Wu Zuoren

Wu Zuoren had been taught by Xu Beihong, who said that Wu Zuoren was an extraordinary and accomplished artist. Xu Beihong's wife, Ms Liao Jingwen, once said to me: "Wu Zuoren truly is a distinguished disciple of Xu Beihong. He has not only accomplished much in the arts, but is also upright in conduct."

In 1996, my wife and I went to see Mr Wu, who was very ill. Sitting in a wheelchair, he was almost blind and deaf. His wife, the famous flower painter Ms Xiao Shufang, bent towards him and said in his ear: "Zhou Erliu and his wife are here to see you." The face of Mr Wu was soon covered with tears and he said: "I'll never forget the care and help the premier has given me all my life." He couldn't speak for a long time; his wife was so surprised that she thought it was a miracle. At that moment, everyone in the room felt a shock, like lightning.

Before the liberation in 1949, Qi Ba sent Tian Han to sneak into Beiping (now Beijing) and advise Xu Beihong and Wu Zuoren to try and avoid being kidnapped by the KMT and stay in the city. Later, when he participated in the anti-rightist movement of 1957, Qi Ba defended Wu Zuoren and appointed him to be dean of the Central Academy of Fine Arts. During the Cultural Revolution, Qi Ba used the visit of President Nixon and the necessary decoration of the Great Hall of the People as an excuse, and called him back to Beijing. Mr Wu lived up to popular expectations and created a number of first-class works.

He painted me two pandas, as a gift. "I have painted you a pair of pandas as a present," he said to me with a smile, "for strengthening our friendship ties, and to show my gratitude to Premier Zhou." Then, meaningfully, he said: "I know you all like my camel sketches. All people know is that I intend to show that camels carry heavy loads, shoulder heavy responsibilities and have a staunch and unyielding determination. But I hope you two [my wife and I] will understand my underlying implication, which is that the camel represents my cherished memories of Premier Zhou, my admiration of his lofty character and his unyielding will to bear responsibility and blame, and his ability to turn a critical situation around and to serve the people with all his heart.

The painting presented to Zhou Erliu by Wu Zuoren.

3.5. Mu Lingfei

Mu Lingfei (1913-1997) was born in the village of Damujia, Longkou county, Shandong province. His real name was Qian, but he gave himself a style name, 'Lingfei', and another nickname: 'Old Tiger Man'. He had fallen ardently in love with painting at a young age. After he graduated from Shanghai Minzhi Middle School, he was introduced to two giants of Chinese traditional painting, the brothers Zhang Shanzi and Zhang Daqian, to study painting under their tutelage. He became an early disciple of the grand masters, as well as an early student of the Da Feng Tang art

Mu Lingfei's painting, presented to Zhou Erliu and Wang Zhangli.

studio. He was the well-accomplished student of two grand masters and he particularly adored Zhang Shanzi, who was famously called a 'tiger-mad' man. The tigers Zhang Shanzi painted were awe-inspiring. They glared at the Japanese invaders and the puppet armies, displaying the extraordinary fighting spirit of the Chinese army and people while strongly encouraging the Chinese people's resistance against Japanese aggression. Mr Mu absorbed the quintessence of Zhang Shanzi's techniques of drawing tigers while 'retaining his technique for drawing a landscape.

Mr Mu gave himself the style name *Ling Fei* ('rise high', 'fly'). The tigers he drew were full of life and soaring aspiration, which was enough evidence that he had inherited the true essence of his master Zhang Shanzi, and they were even more vivid than the tigers drawn by his master, which showed him to be the best in China. I was lucky enough to be presented with some calligraphy and several paintings by Mr Mu. I also learnt that like other famous artists, he was willing to contribute a painting to commemorate Zhou Enlai. The tiger he painted for me was full of vim and vigour: it reflected the heroic spirit of Premier Zhou Enlai in an imposing manner. With this painting, he tried to urge me to carry out Qi Ba's requests and never stop moving forward. I was so touched by him that I think it is necessary to introduce him to my readers.

Mr Mu made his home in Tianjin for many years. In 1982, through the Tianjin municipal cultural bureau, he invited me for a meal in an old restaurant in Beining park, well known for its elegance. During the meal, he told me about the time he studied painting with Zhang Shanzi. He stressed that an artist should not only have artistic accomplishments and creative enthusiasm, but he should also love the country, pay attention to how to conduct himself in society, and be a man of integrity. He talked about his visit to Mr Zhang Daqian in Shanghai in his early years, with whom he had sat down for a heart-to-heart. In a serious tone, he said to him: "Your teacher Zhang Shanzi once had a wish to draw 100 tigers in one painting. He is no longer alive, yet he was once your teacher and personally taught you how to draw tigers, so I hope you'll fulfil his wish."

He couldn't paint during the Cultural Revolution, which made him hate the Gang of Four very much. Premier Zhou's death grieved him, because the premier was a man he respected and loved. After the overthrow of the Gang of Four, he regained his enthusiasm for creation. He wanted to carry out his master's wish and paint the trend of the times, and this was the reason he called himself 'tiger-mad' in his old age. Now, his long monumental scroll, the traditional Chinese painting *The Hundred Tigers*, which he took great pains to complete, has been revealed to the public. It is a comfort to his tutor's soul in paradise.

Ms Fang Zhaolin was Mr Zhang Daqian's only female student. Though she made her home in England, she would continue to travel between China and the UK. Mr Mu and Ms Fang were students of the same tutor, but they were not meant to meet. Mr Mu entrusted me to be his liaison between him and her. After I had introduced them, they became acquainted and got on well. Mr Mu handed me a photograph of *The Hundred Tigers*, asking me to pass it on to Ms Fang to have it published in Hong Kong. Ms Fang then contacted a Hong Kong publisher, who was happy to publish it. However, because the painting was very long and the photograph Mr Mu had supplied was not clear enough for printing, the painting was never properly published, but during the process, it had caused a sensation both in China and abroad. The painting was praised as an exquisite work of art in the Chinese fine arts circle, a miracle in the history of Chinese painting. I have been told that the painting is now on show all year round in the hall of the People's Congress.

Mr Mu was a modest man. As a member of the CPPCC of Tianjin and a staff member of the Tianjin Research Institute of Culture and History, he cared for the country's united work front and the work that was being done in the culture and history sectors. He had set strict demands on himself and painted about 1,000 paintings, which adorned the rostrum in Tiananmen Square, the museums dedicated to Zhou Enlai and Deng Yingchao, and other museums in various places. He also donated his paintings to celebrate Hong Kong's return to China, and to disaster relief. His works have also been presented as gifts to presidents and government officials of foreign countries by both the central and local Chinese governments. The British Museum and some other overseas museums have collected Mu Lingfei's paintings.

Part Six

Corrections, Additions and Clarifications of the Historical Facts

Due to the tremendous role Qi Ba played in the Chinese revolution and the national construction, he attracted attention from researchers both at home and abroad. The fruits of the research were particularly substantial after his death. However, I noticed at the time that the data presented were usually insufficient or, in some cases, incorrect. During his lifetime, Qi Ba attached great importance to the accuracy of the historical facts — therefore, I think, besides taking a rigorous approach to their research, researchers also need to carry out their own investigations conscientiously. What they should not do is blindly copy the seemingly fashionable words or viewpoints of others.

Nowadays, information technology is becoming more and more popular. Intensive international communication enables the spreading of information at an astonishing pace and with various means. This is a double-edged sword. The unparalleled advantages of information technology are clear for us to see, but its negative effects are also very much evident. Books published overseas in which the truth has been bent are out in the open on university library shelves. Many foreign readers even feel as if they have found a treasure when they read these books. But the truth is that the publication of these books is a base act by certain individuals or organisations who have other plans.

As a descendant who has received the premier's teachings for 30 years, I sincerely feel that I must fulfil my duty to close up loopholes and clarify the historical facts according to my knowledge. I hope my action will be a comfort to the souls of Qi Ba and Qi Ma in paradise.

1. The Recipient of Zhou Enlai's Letter in 1921 Was His Second Uncle, Zhou Yikang

The letter Qi Ba sent from London in 1921 was addressed to Zhou Yikang, his second uncle — not his fifth uncle, Zhou Yiding, who has widely been reported to be the recipient of this letter for 30 years, since 1949. The reason for this misunderstanding is that Zhou Yikang was originally called Zhou Yiding — *ding* here means 'a tripod'. He changed his name to Yikang after he was adopted by his first uncle, Zhou Kanghou. He then gave permission to use the character *ding* from his original name to his cousin, in whose name *ding* means 'calm'. Later, Zhou Yikang became a *juren* and was then formally known as Zhou Henai (*nai* here means 'a big tripod'). The matter was finally clarified during the international conference in 2008, when we celebrated the 110th anniversary of Zhou Enlai's birth.

2. Zhou Enlai Did Not Go Directly to France to Study and Work

In 1921, Qi Ba was studying at Edinburgh University in the UK, rather than in France, as has been circulated among the common people. When my grandfather died, Qi Ba lost his source of income, while his sixth uncle refused to obtain a state grant for him as he regarded his nephew as a revolutionary. Therefore, Qi Ba went to Germany and France on a work-study programme, where he became a professional revolutionary. As he would say afterwards: "For me, joining the revolution either happened because of my own mature consideration, or because I was forced to revolt." In short, it was a choice driven by national calamity and family poverty, as well as his exploration of socialist theories.

3. The Young Zhou Enlai Did Indeed Visit Shaoxing

Qi Ba's ancestral home was in Shaoxing, Zhejiang province. In 1939, he took a special trip to the city and visited his relatives there. But people cannot seem to agree on whether or not he had been to Shaoxing in his childhood. As far as I can remember, Qi Ba's third younger brother, Zhou Enshou (style name 'Tongyu'), and his youngest cousin, Zhou Enzhu (my father), believed that young Zhou Enlai hadn't visited Shaoxing. But my

Corrections, Additions and Clarifications of the Historical Facts

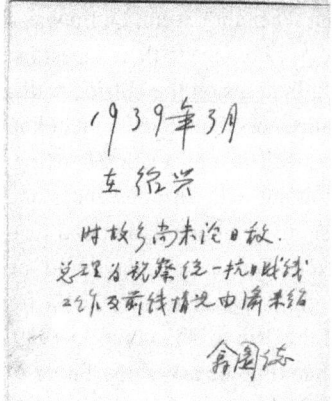

1939, Zhou Enlai in Shaoxing. After he returned to Chongqing from Shaoxing, he handed this photo to Zhou Enzhu to keep. "March 1939 in Shaoxing. At the time, our hometown had not yet fallen into the hands of the Japanese. The premier came to Shaoxing from Chongqing to inspect the anti-Japanese united front work. Xiyuan."

grandmother, Cheng Yizhen, and my grandfather, Zhou Yikang (Henai), as well as my great-uncle Zhou Yineng (Qi Ba's birth father) had taken young Qi Ba to Shaoxing. My grandma told me that when they went, Qi Ba was a child aged seven or eight with a bowl cut. To pay homage to their ancestors, they went to the graveyard, where they hung lanterns on the outside walls. They burnt incense and kowtowed to our ancestors. The locals, including those who looked after the graveyard, were full of praise for Shaoxing, saying that the place has a good *feng shui*; along with virtuous ancestors, Shaoxing produces talented people. Because my grandma had bound feet, she was carried to the top of the hill in a *sedan*. But uncle Tongyu told me that he had lived in the northeast and Tianjin, separated from Qi Ba for many years, so he had heard nothing about this trip to Shaoxing. In 1939, after Qi Ba returned to Chongqing from Shaoxing, he asked my father to organise the family tree and the photographs he had brought back. It seems that my father hadn't even been born when Qi Ba visited Shaoxing in his childhood, so he mistakenly thought the visit had not taken place. Moreover, the Zhou family tree circulating in China is the one organised by my father, who made some modifications based on the information Qi Ba brought back. As other family members made the reprints, it is inevitable that the family tree is inaccurate in places; still, its contents can be a reference for readers.

4. Zhou Enshou's Reasons For Dropping out of the Revolutionary Ranks

Zhou Tongyu is Qi Ba's third younger brother. After the failure of the Great Revolution in China (1924-1927), he stopped using his original name, Enshou, and instead began using his style name, Tongyu. After I learnt that the order of the seniority in the Engeneration did not conform to the standard, and that of the three generations, only the 'Yi' generation had a precise order of seniority, I followed Qi Ba's instructions and started addressing Zhou Enshou as 'uncle Tongyu'.

In 1954, I passed the entrance examinations for Nankai University. Uncle Tongyu was on a business trip and came to Shanghai by chance, where he reported my good news to Qi Ba. Qi Ba and Qi Ma were very happy

Corrections, Additions and Clarifications of the Historical Facts

Zhou Enshou.

and told him that they wanted to see me in Beijing, so uncle Tongyu took me with him to Beijing by train. From then until his death in 1985, I kept in close contact with him. In fact, I have a more comprehensive image of him than of my birth father. Since my birth, I had received the love of Qi Ba and Qi Ma when they took shelter in my family. Later, in 1946, they paid for my education, and from then on the custom was established that for anything related to my studies, health, work and marriage, Qi Ba would talk to me, while Qi Ma would mainly look after my daily needs. whenever I had a major issue involving work or studies, Qi Ba and Qi Ma often called uncle Tongyu and his wife to discuss it with them. After they had made their decision, they would then consult with me and I would carry out their advice. It was a strict, but also very democratic process. Of my generation, most of us were looked after by Qi Ma, because Qi Ba was very busy. I was the only exception: Qi Ba talked to me more. Hence, uncle Tongyu devised a rule that I must report to him whenever Qi Ba had had a conversation with me. I should also try my best to pass the contents of the discussion on to my sisters, brothers and cousins. I followed his request, and every time I told him what Qi Ba had said, he would take notes. I felt that it might be inappropriate for him to do so without Qi Ba's permission, but he was my senior and my contact with him was more extensive than the contact I had had with my birth father, so it was hard for me to say no.

In 1954, during my first winter holiday, Qi Ba received me at his residence. Though he was very busy, he spent almost the whole night talking to me, which surprised me. The main topic of our conversation was our family background. He emphatically pointed out that our old family had developed into a declining feudal family. He then listed 14 unhealthy social contacts among the family members. He felt that it was not good to just push them away into society, paying no attention to them or making no contact with them. He said that he should help them remould their characters and be progressive, not just shift the responsibility to society. But in view of their experiences and social foundation, he said, clearly affected: "It is not an easy thing to change them."

Qi Ba told me about uncle Tongyu's personal experiences in detail. When Qi Ba left Huaian, he was 12, while his brother, Tongyu, was six: the same age as Qi Ma. He attended the Nankai Middle School in Tianjin in 1921. At school, he joined the socialist Youth League in 1924, and that winter he became a party member. In October of 1925, he accompanied Qi Ma's mother, Yang Zhende, to go to Guangzhou, and in 1926 he registered at Huangpu Military Academy and became a fourth-term cadet. According to Qi Ba, Lin Biao was in the same class as Tongyu. In 1926, he took part in the Revolutionary Army's Northern Expedition, working as a propagandist in the general political department. During the campaign to attack Wuchang, he was wounded by enemy gunfire in his right foot. Guo Moruo, the leading cadre of the political department, assembled the manpower to take him off the front line. In the spring of 1927, he left his post without authorization due to a one-sided love affair with a woman, and went to Sichuan. Qi Ba told me that leaving one's post without authorisation in wartime was not an issue of private affections, but a serious breach of discipline. After the woman spurned him, he rejoined the troops. As secretary of the party organisation, Qi Ba severely rebuked his brother. Tongyu was placed on probation as an inner-party disciplinary measure. A disciplinary action like this, to lighten the punishment and see how the offender behaves, was appropriate and correct. It was to recover his losses and redeem his reputation, not, as the rumours spread by some people said, a dismissal from his post. In 1928, in spite of Qi Ba and Qi Ma's exhortations, he quit the party and withdrew from the revolutionary ranks. He went to Jilin to join his fourth uncle, and there he worked as a member of the checkpoint staff at the local railway station. In 1933, his fourth uncle died in Tianjin. After his own will, his birth father Zhou Yineng had him (Tongyu) adopted by his (deceased) fourth uncle. In July 1947, he was arrested by the inspection section of the Tianjin Garrison headquarters. According to Qi Ba, Tongyu was forced to write a confession. In 1979, the Organisation Department of the Central Committee reached a conclusion about him regarding this piece of history, and said: "Overall, comrade Zhou Tongyu did well during the time he was under arrest." Later, Uncle Tongyu explained that he had been authorised to leave the troops, but Qi Ba refused to listen to his statement.

When the CPC held its sixth congress in Moscow in June 1928, Qi Ba and Qi Ma went to the Soviet Union via northeast China. Aware that they were being followed by KMT secret agents, Qi Ba and Qi Ma disguised themselves and made contact with Zhou Enpu and Zhou Tongyu. They shielded them from the secret agents, and Qi Ba and Qi Ma safely arrived in the Soviet Union. Until 1949, as Zhou Binghua has said, except for the abovementioned episode, Zhou Enlai did not make contact with Zhou Tongyu on any other occasion during the 23-year interval. But my opinion is that Zhou Tongyu did well and contributed to Qi Ba's evacuation.

During the Cultural Revolution, uncle Tongyu was arrested and his children were scattered all over the country. Aunt Wang Shiqin was stressed out by the pressure, even though she was a woman of strong character. As I myself suffered from being politically persecuted, we felt sympathetic towards each other. She once said to me: "We, an aunt and a nephew, could be called 'friends in adversity'." In those days, she was in a difficult situation. I was worried that unexpected things might happen to her, so I would find time go to see her after I had been criticised at public meetings. Whenever I went on a business trip, I went to see my cousin Zhou Bingjun and his wife in Guangzhou, as well as my cousin Zhou Bingjian in Inner Mongolia and my cousin Zhou Binghe in Yan'an. We were on very intimate terms with each other, and Qi Ma praised me for this.

When uncle Tongyu became seriously ill, my wife and I went to Beijing hospital to see him. He demanded us to record our conversation. After a long illness, he died in 1985. Because his surviving children had all gone to the Babaoshan cemetery to prepare and receive the relatives who came to offer their condolences, I alone stayed with uncle Tongyu's remains in the mortuary. Being the sole relative on the spot and in accordance with the customs of the Beijingers, the make-up master, Ma Yanlong, requested that I hold my deceased uncle Tongyu's head and helped to lay his corpse inside the coffin. Dr Ma was very pleased with me. Breathing a sigh of relief, he said: "It's fortunate you are here, or I would not have known how to deal with the situation."

Afterwards, aunt Shiqin came to my house to thank me. In the past, I had given her two months' worth of my salary for her daily keep, and on that day, when she saw my empty house, she said, fervently: "You and your wife are honest people — you were when the premier was still alive, and even now, after his death, you and your wife are still strict with yourselves. It's not easy living like this for decades. Moreover, the facts clearly state that you highly value the sentiment. You and I are truly friends in need."

5. Cheng Yizhen Gave Cover to Zhou Enlai and Deng Yingchao

Cheng Yizhen was born in 1876 in Yangzhou and died at the advanced age of 90. When she married my grandfather in 1905, she met the seven-year-old Qi Ba. At the time, my grandfather Zhou Yikang (who was chief clerk to the civil and military governor) found Qi Ba's birth father, Zhou Yineng, a job in his office to look after the incoming and outgoing mail.

Zhou Enlai's second aunt and Zhou Erliu's grandmother, Cheng Yizhen.

Cheng Yizhen was very fond of Qi Ba and recognized his worth, regarding him as her own child. Later, in Beijing, Tianjin, Nanjing and Shanghai, she often took huge risks to give cover to Zhou Enlai and his birth father, Zhou Yineng, who was the liaison between his son and my family. She looked after them very well and treated them as close kin. I can still remember that whenever my father came home late, her face would be covered with tears. Inwardly, she was concerned for the safety of the family members, but she concealed Qi Ba and his father without the least hesitation and gave them accommodation. Qi Ba was deeply grateful for this and he remembered it with gratitude for over 60 years, never changing his attitude towards her. When she was 90 years old, Qi Ba informed the family that he would go to Shanghai to celebrate her birthday, but in the end he had to cancel the trip because he was too busy. To make up for his absence, he sent his chief guard, who would take some photos of her as mementos. But Qi Ma did go to Shanghai to see my grandmother.

In my early youth, Qi Ba reminded me to read Li Mi's *Chen Qing Biao* (*'Memorial to the Emperor Expressing My Feelings'*). I told him that I had read this prose work in primary school and could still remember the following, very touching sentences: "If it were not for my grandmother, I might not live today; but without me, it will be hard for her to get through her remaining years. So, grandmother and grandson depend on each other for survival." After I recited this, Qi Ba smiled. I have cherished the memory of this scene up to the present day.

In 1955, when Qi Ba learnt that someone from the family clan had called my grandma a concubine, he called me in to see him. He told me that when my grandfather married the Wang girl (they had similar family backgrounds), it seemed as though the Wang family had concealed the truth about her suffering from a congenital mental disorder. They only explained that she had caught the illness because she had offended the god of luck during the wedding ceremony. Therefore, the Zhou family had to arrange for her to live in the old house in Huaian until her death. My grandfather then married Cheng Yizhen, and they had one son, Zhou Enzhu.

Grandma Cheng came from a scholastic *xiucai* household that owned a couple of furniture factories. She herself was a fair maiden from Yangzhou, elegant and intelligent. Qi Ba also pointed out that my grandfather would inevitably have thought that, as tradition dictated, a man who had no children of his own would not be regarded as an object of filial piety, so it was possible that the Zhou family had concealed the truth from the Cheng family about his marriage with Wang for this reason. Nevertheless, the facts show that after their wedding, they were devoted to each other and treated each other with sincere respect.

Qi Ba said that it was probable that the Wang family had concealed Wang's illness from the Zhou family, while the Zhou family had concealed the marriage between Zhou Yikang and Wang from the Cheng family. But no matter what the truth was, the descendants of the Zhou family should never, ever, thoughtlessly call Cheng, whom he was so grateful to, a concubine. Qi Ma was indignant about the matter, too. She once said to me that such a form of address was extremely rude — an insult to the venerable old Cheng. Qi Ba and Qi Ma had once considered sending my grandma to Huaian to live out her final years, just as Zhou Angjun's concubine Wang and Zhou Yikang's ex-wife Wang had lived out their final years in the old house in Huaian. But they gave up this ide, because my grandma only had one son, and it was not a good idea to separate a mother and her son for long. So, they ordered me to go to see her in Shanghai during my holidays and paid for my travels. Qi Ma not only went to Shanghai herself to see my grandma, she also took out her own clothes, such as a padded silk jacket, for me to take to my grandma.

When my grandfather was still alive, my grandma would often follow him to the government compound. She also kept in touch with the wives of senior officials. Although she was not well educated, with her extraordinary appearance and her appropriate manners she slowly developed into a woman with the qualities as well as the manners of a girl from a wealthy and influential family. After my grandfather died, she continued to give cover and shelter to Qi Ba and his father. She brought up her son, who was only 13 when the father died, and managed to give him a higher education. Since my childhood, she had repeatedly said to me, in her thick Yangzhou dialect, that Zhou Enlai was a present-day *zai xiang* (prime minister) and an elite talent, whom my grandfather had paid great attention to nurture. Grandma also claimed that "although we gave Qi Ba financial help or cover when his life was in danger, this was not worth mentioning." So, after I grew up, I learnt not to have a 'dependent mentality' and go to Qi Ba to be repaid a debt of gratitude; on the contrary, as his junior, I learnt to maintain my respect, make my way in life by my own efforts, and not bother Qi Ba, because I understood that Qi Ba was a very busy man. Only by doing so have I become worthy of the teachings and expectations of the senior family members.

6. Zhou Enzhu As Deputy Manager of the Shanghai Xiangsheng Car Company

My father, Zhou Enzhu, whose style names were 'Runmin' and 'Xiyuan', was the 14th male member of his generation in the Zhou family. He was Zhou Enlai's junior by 10 years. He had received love from Qi Ba since the moment he was born. A graduate from the Shanghai law school, he became a lawyer. He was impaired in his left ear and suffered from a

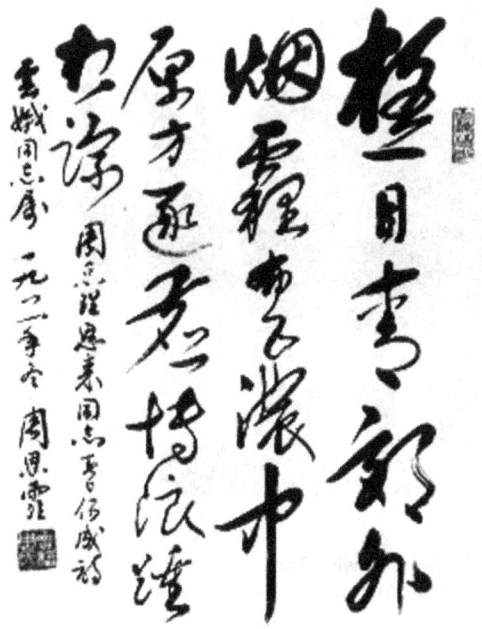

Zhou Enzhu's calligraphy rendering of Zhou Enlai's poem *A Random Verse on a Spring Day*. For the full translation, see Part One, chapter 5.1.

chronic lung disease, so he didn't do much actual work. Being a scholar, he was good at writing poems and prose, as well as calligraphy. He had intensively studied Beijing opera and Kunqu opera. Qi Ba used to urge him to keep in close contact with his Beijing opera tutor, the grand master Mei Lanfang. Starting in the 1930s, he worked hard to become a good amateur performer, meanwhile being responsible for passing Qi Ba's words on to Mr Mei, urging him to be progressive and to build up a relationship with the CPC. When I was a child, I often accompanied him to Mr Mei's mansion, where Mr Mei would tutor him in performing a play. In his old age, he became a consultant in the Shanghai municipal council, engaged in researching Beijing opera. He was also a member of the Shanghai calligraphers association, and his works were collected by Chinese and Japanese calligraphy fans.

Mei Lanfang's children with Zhou Enzhu at his home in Shanghai. From the right: Zhou Enzhu, Mei Baoyue and Mei Baojiu.

A student of his, Chen Chaohong, told me that in 1946, my father sorted out the material for the opera *Yu Zhou Feng*, which was in the Mei Lanfang style, and put it into a book. He also wrote an article about the play, which was published in July 1946 in the first issue of the periodical *You Yi Xun Kan*. He praised the fact that Mr Mei had stood up for what was right by refusing to perform for the enemy and the puppet regime during the anti-Japanese war. He then went on: "After the victory over Japan, Mr Mei returned to the stage and performed again. Today he will perform the Kunqu opera *Yu Zhou Feng*, to satisfy the audience's thirst for his performance. This play focuses on a *qingyi* [one of the main types of *dan*, or female roles, in traditional Chinese opera, traditionally dressed in black] in singing and action — one of Mr Mei's masterpieces. He has performed it many, many times, yet its magnificence never fades."

In 1946, when I met Qi Ba in Shanghai, he said to me: "I haven't heard from your father in a while. He may have died." In 1948, I learnt from my classmate Lu Guoxin that he had met my father when performing operas. Lu had asked Zhou Enzhu if he was the long-lost father of Zhou Erliu, but my father denied this for safety reasons. Afterwards, father and son met again, and we couldn't help laughing when talking about this anecdote.

In 1948, he secretly sneaked back to Shanghai from the liberated area in northern Jiangsu. Mr Gong Yuzhi once mentioned in his article that Zhou Enzhu might have had direct contact with Du Yuesheng, the Green Gang master. I discussed the matter with Jin Shan and Ms Luo Junyu, Luo Qinghua's wife, as they were both underground workers who had been in close contact with Du Yuesheng. According to them, Du had once offered my father the position of deputy manager of the Xiangsheng car company. Presumably, this position played a role in guarding against the dangerous KMT secret agents. They also told me that when Shanghai was liberated, the gangsters didn't inflict much damage on the city. The underground workers might have persuaded Du Yuesheng not to do so. Qi Ma also told me that my father had received permission from her and Qi Ba to sneak into Shanghai, which is contrary to the rumours saying that he acted without authorisation. Some of the family members even spread the rumour that he had sneaked back to Shanghai because he could no longer live the hard life in the liberated area. But, in fact, Wang Daohan (later the mayor of Shanghai) knew everything about my father's work in the liberated area. My father then called him 'Little Wang'.

7. Ma Shijie's True Experiences in His Old Age

My stepmother's father, Ma Shijie, was an important relation of Qi Ba's by marriage. As early as 1946, when Qi Ba met me in Shanghai, he asked me about Mr Ma's condition, who had been heedless of his own personal safety and stayed behind voluntarily in the liberated area in north Jiangsu after the civil war began. Qi Ba had also responded to Huang Yanpei's requests to pass my stepmother Ma Shunyi's letters on to Hui Yuyu, an official in the PLA's second military subarea in north Jiangsu, requesting the local government to follow the party's policy to care for Mr Ma and his family. (In the early years of the PRC, Ma Shijie and Huang Yanpei were colleagues. Ma was concurrently director of the department for internal affairs of Jiangsu province and its acting governor, while Huang was director of the education department. They knew each other very well.)

Qi Ba mentioned to me several times that Mr Ma was not just an old man from the last Qing dynasty, but one of the few enlightened gentry*. These gentry insisted on staying in the liberated area when the civil war broke out. All his life, Mr Ma pursued progress and sought moral integrity, expounding his ideas in writing and rendering his services to benefit the people and the world. Therefore, the historical facts relating to his achievements in life should not be forgotten. At the same time, Qi Ba pointed out that someone had fabricated a story and spread rumours about Mr Ma in a book overseas. This book was once in the Hoover Institute on War, Revolution and Peace at Stanford University in the US, and the author claimed that Mr Ma had died of persecution by Zhou Enlai and Zhou Enzhu. This utterly absurd claim was contrary to the historical facts, yet the misunderstanding and the negative impact on readers it has caused cannot be ignored. Qi Ba wished for me to pay attention to it and do something to clarify the related facts.

Ma Shijie, whose style name was 'Juanqing' and who was also known as

---

* The enlightened gentry is called *kai ming shen shi* in Chinese. They were individual landlords and rich peasants with democratic leanings who, influenced by the CPC's education and its policy of unity, favoured resistance against Japan, supported democracy and reduction of land rent and loan interests during the war of resistance against Japan, and, during the war of liberation between 1946 and 1949, opposed Chiang Kai-shek's rule and approved of the land reform.

Corrections, Additions and Clarifications of the Historical Facts

'Jiangshu', was born in October 1865 in Gaoyou county, Jiangsu province. His ancestral home was in Hexian county, Anhui province. He died of illness at home in August 1946, aged 81. During the Ming and Qing dynasties, the Ma clan was a prominent family in Hexian. There was a memorial archway in front of the family compound, with an inscription that told of the family's grandeur in those years: "*Fu zi ke di* ('fathers and sons take part in the imperial examinations'); *zu sun jin shi* ('grandparents and grandchildren are both successful candidates in the highest imperial examinations'); *liang chao jing jie* ('two dynasties honour their moral integrity'); *liu shi cheng en* ('six generations receive favours from the emperors')." During the Taiping Rebellion, around 1850, Mr Ma's grandfather, Ma Wanqing, moved the whole family to Gaoyou in Jiangsu. Mr Ma's father, Ma Weian, dealt with pawnshops and banking businesses who set up charitable institutions, such as orphanages. He also supervised the building of the local Wenmiao school. In the annals of Gaoyou, Ma Weian was referred to as follows: "He values friendship among people; he is eager to help those in need; and, although very wealthy, he is not mean when it comes to money."

During his childhood, Mr Ma obtained a *xiucai* position in the imperial examination. He went on to study hard and became a *juren* in Nanjing in 1894. In the following year, when he was ready to go to Beijing to take the highest-level exam, his mother died and he returned home to mourn her death. After he had fulfilled his term of mourning, he went to Beijing and worked as a compiler in the interior ministry. He then became a counsellor for the consultative assembly of the Qing government, and during his term he was sent to Japan to investigate politics in that country. Mr Ma was enlightened and had revolutionary leanings. After the 1911 revolution, he became director of the internal affairs department in the Jiangsu provincial commissioner's office, and then became head of civilian affairs in 1914. Later, he became director as well as inspector of a project to dredge the north Yangtze river, as well as a financial consultant for the Jiangsu canal engineering bureau. After 1920, Mr Ma withdrew from political life and went into business. Together with a few entrepreneurs — Zhang Jian from Nantong, Han Guojun from Haian and Huang Yanpei from Shanghai — he set up the Qinyuan Salt Company. They raised shares and recruited migrants to reclaim wasteland along the coastal areas in Dongtai, Nantong and Haian. They built dykes and produced salt from seawater, meanwhile improving the soil by dredging and burning plants to produce ash. They planted cash crops and introduced new varieties of cotton, maize, melon and fruit, as well as peppermint. Through all sorts of measures, they worked to promote local development by increasing employment and improving the environment. At the height of their business, they owned nearly 7,000 hectares of waste and cultivated land. Besides engaging in business, Mr Ma set up a primary school.

In 1924, Mr Ma cooperated with Huang Yanpei and Shi Liangcai (manager of the *Shen Bao* newspaper) to set up the Renwen Jiazi Association (*renwen* means 'humanity', *jiazi* means '60 years') and the Renwen Library, and to publish the magazine *Renwen Monthly*. The library focused on gathering information on politics, economics, culture, education and arts, and it also compiled a newspaper and magazine catalogue. In 1931, it received a grant of Rmb1m from Ye Hongying, so the organization changed its name to Hongyin Library, and was then renamed Baokan (*baokan* means 'newspapers and periodicals') after 1949. They also set up an education fund, concentrating on libraries and primary education in the country. When Huang Yanpei established the Chinese vocational school, Mr Ma was an active organizer.

When the September 18 or Mukden Incident took place in 1931, Mr Ma expressed his feelings in prose: "…alas! My hometown without flames of war is a thing of the past — the foreign power has invaded the northeast. Who will be there to worry about the fate of our country?" In that same year, floods caused a disaster in north Jiangsu, and he wrote: "…the merciless flood has seized our farmland; when will we have indestructible dams built?" His compassion for ordinary people as well as his patriotic feelings stand out from his writings.

Between 1931 and 1934, the Japanese were occupying northeast China while attempting to encroach on more of China's territory. The KMT authorities exercised a policy of surrendering to the foreign powers but suppressing the communists, and ignoring the ordinary Chinese living in an abyss of misery. Mr Ma and the manager of the *Shen Bao* newspaper, Shi Liangcai, shared common ideas. They became good friends despite their great age difference. When Shi was murdered in 1934 by KMT secret agents for his support of the anti-Japanese movement, the whole nation was aggrieved after hearing the terrible news. Mr Ma was indignant and resentful. With tears in his eyes, he wrote an elegiac couplet to mourn Shi's death, which showed the patriotic enthusiasm of this 70-year-old man: "Sad is the Creator; while our nation is confronting difficulties and dangers, another man has ceased to exist in Jiangsu. Curse evil society — your spirit will live on. Eternal life to you, sir."

Another thing he did also drew praise from the public. In the early years of the PRC, Mr Ma was acting governor of Jiangsu. One day, on his way home, he witnessed a sailboat sinking in the river; all the passengers on board lost their lives. He was so sad that he raised money and donated a steamer, *Puji*, to ferry people across the Yangtze river. Later, *Puji* changed her name to *Feiji*, but she went on working for many years under different management.

Mr Ma was one of the richest men in Gaoyou. 'Half-a-city Ma' was his nickname. He had a large residential compound, which was next to the Gaoyou government compound. There were 99 rooms and three entrances. The compound was divided into an eastern and a western part, with a porch and a back garden. Mr Ma had a wife and three concubines, and these combined gave birth to 22 children, of whom 14 grew up and lived in Gaoyou, Yangzhou and Shanghai. After the anti-Japanese war broke out, he moved to Shanghai and lived in Avenue Joffre (now Huaihai Road) and Route Tenant de la Tour (now Xiangyang Road South), thus becoming a neighbour of my family. When he was in Shanghai, he would often inspire the patriotic enthusiasm of our young children by telling us the long history of Chinese civilisation. Meanwhile, Liang Hongzhi and Yin Rugeng, the two traitors who were in collusion with the Japanese, tried to intimidate him and force him to work for the puppet government. Mr Ma rejected them, saying that he was in poor health and too old to work. Gaoyou was liberated at the end of 1945. Mr Ma kept a clear head about the situation. He had a high degree of confidence in the communists represented by Zhou Enlai, and thought that the communists would defeat the corrupted KMT and gain victory all over the country. For this reason, he ignored his family and friends, who had tried to persuade him to leave, but stayed behind in Gaoyou voluntarily. The KMT government disregarded the safety of the local people, wantonly and indiscriminately bombing the city of Gaoyou. Later, my uncle Ma Jiaji told me that because of the bombing, the back garden, where the temporary shelter for Mr Ma was built, had been levelled to the ground. Although he moved back into his living quarters, due to the shock and his old age, Mr Ma died shortly afterwards.

Qi Ba used to pay quite a lot of attention to the changes in Mr Ma's family, regarding them as a reflection of social development in modern China and thus as good material for historical research or literal and artistic creations, so he thought.

Mr Ma had confidence in the revolution and the CPC. This confidence, along with his own principle that 'my actions must benefit the people and benefit the world', had remained the same throughout his life. In early 1946, the land reform was launched in Gaoyou: this was a crucial policy of the CPC and, to some extent, the practical application and development of Sun Yat-sen's proposition, 'land to the tiller'. The implementation of this policy to enlightened, rich landlords was a comprehensive and precise example of the CPC's land reform policy, which also protected the landlords' interests. It not only roused their enthusiasm for the construction of liberated areas, but also encouraged the people in the areas controlled by the communists or the nationalists to learn about the CPC's policies, which would extend its influence.

Mr Ma actively cooperated with the local government, who arranged for a rickshaw to take him to the town hall to hand in his land deeds. As his grandson, I went with him. I saw that the government officials were very polite to him. When it was over, they dispatched a cadre to send us home. At the time, many local people had fled to Shanghai to avoid the bombings, including a small group who were sceptical about the CPC. The KMT then incited them to go to the UN Refugee Agency, trying to cause a disturbance in the city, which would make the Shanghai citizens who knew little about the communists sceptical about the CPC. At the time, Mr Ma's 12th son, Ma Jiashen, was working with the Refugee Agency. When Qi Ba heard about this from me, he thought that Ma Jiashen was from Gaoyou, so he hoped to clear up any misunderstandings by talking to these people in their own dialect. Qi Ba also hoped that Ma Jiashen would tell them that the war, provoked by the KMT, had been a direct reason for them to flee their home and had also destroyed the peace and construction works in the liberated area. Hence, Qi Ba went to see Ma Jiashen. But he arrived too late; he missed Ma Jiashen, but saw his sister instead, who received him. Qi Ba then explained to her: "I'm sorry I came too late. To avoid the secret agents, who may cause you trouble, my car had to be parked at the beginning of the lane. I walked to your house." This shows that Qi Ba was concerned about the refugees' problems, and was hoping to stop enemy agents from using the situation to fabricate lies and mislead the public. He paid great attention to the will of the people and was good at doing concrete work while still caring for his friends' safety. Besides visiting Ma Jiashen, he also wrote to the Central Committee, urging them to get rid of the ultra-leftists in the land reform movement. Getting rid of them could stop some bad people from stirring up trouble.

Throughout his life, Mr Ma told young people (including me) that under the leadership of the CPC and after the hardships, the Chinese revolution would succeed in the end. I firmly believed that the political foresight of these aged, enlightened gentry came to a certain extent from the revolutionaries, such as Zhou Enlai. These gentlemen understood that the nation's hopes rested on these revolutionaries. But my stepmother, Ma Shunyi, and her ilk deliberately fabricated lies overseas, absurdly blaming Zhou Enlai and Zhou Enzhu for her father's death. This is absolute nonsense. When Mr Ma died, Zhou Enlai was in Nanjing, while Zhou Enzhu was in Yancheng. They had no idea that Mr Ma had died of illness at home. Because most of the people involved with Mr Ma's death have died, I have recorded what I saw and heard about Mr Ma Shijie to stop the wrong person being accused and allow none of the correct historical facts to be neglected, thereby following Qi Ba's urges as well as my own wishes.

8. The Strict Pursuit of a Policy to Avoid Nepotism

Avoiding nepotism is one of the codes of conduct that Qi Ba strictly pursued all his life. He regarded petticoat influence as a chronic malady in Chinese society. Such social customs had been practiced for thousands of years, and the issue would relate to whether the party in power was able to maintain a good revolutionary tradition, or whether millions of people would be for or against the party. As premier, Qi Ba thought that he had to be strict with himself, setting an example for the cadres and the public. Hence, he had done everything in his power to stick to this principle.

After I was born, I was lucky to be loved and cared for by Qi Ba and Qi Ma. But in 1946, when I met them again in Shanghai, I had my first experience of their strict policy of avoiding nepotism. I remember that when Qi Ba suggested that I go with him to Yan'an, Qi Ma called him out of the room. After discussing the issue, they decided that I should carry on with my studies in Shanghai. As senior cadres of the party, their priority was to look after the children of the martyrs as well as the children of the other cadres, but not those of their own relatives. Then, it sowed the seed in my mind that I should learn from the lofty qualities of the veteran revolutionaries, to apply the same principle to myself and never to have a dependent mentality. In the years of hardship that followed, I was indeed able to overcome many unimaginable difficulties, and then joined the army. When we marched to the southwest of the country, after I found out that both my brother and I were assigned to do some confidential work at the Second Field Army's headquarters, I requested that I be sent to the frontline. After Chongqing was liberated, the members of the Chinese Youth League who were senior high school graduates had been given priority to work in large cities. To play an exemplary role, ignoring my poor health, I asked to be allowed to work at a basic level in small towns. Due to the rapid developments in the newly liberated areas, I had to change jobs and addresses constantly. Qi Ba and Qi Ma had once asked Zhu Hua to find out where I was because I never wrote to them, as I did not want other people to know I was a relative of Premier Zhou Enlai.

In 1954, I was admitted to Nankai University after passing the entrance examination. I worked part-time throughout my years of higher education. The president of the university, Liu Piyun, once jokingly 'criticised' me for not telling him that Qi Ba and Qi Ma had been looking after me for many years. I liked studying the English language when I was a child, so I came out on top in the university entrance examination. In my seven years at university, I studied both economics and English. I received full marks for all my courses and I was chosen to be a merit student in Tianjin. In 1960, when Chen Yi suggested that I start working in the foreign ministry, Qi Ba insisted that even though I met the requirements, because the foreign ministry had once been under his direct leadership, I find work in another department. Hence, I went to work with the Committee for Cultural Relations with Foreign Countries and the ILD. In those days, China had no pension system. The chances for promotion and salary increases were rare. Sometimes I had to give up the once-in-every-10-years chance in favour of other comrades under my leadership, resulting in my salary being too low in comparison to my title and post. In a meeting of the CCRFC's leading

Zhou Erliu with the Committee for Cultural Relations with Foreign Countries in Beijing in the 1960s.

party group, Director Huang Zhen used me as an example of cooperation with the premier, as well as of Zhou Enlai's strictness towards his relatives. Regarding my work arrangements, Qi Ma broached the subject with me after accompanying Qi Ba to Nankai University in 1956. She said: "You are always doing well in your studies. You depend mainly on scholarships, not on family influence. As for your relation to us, you have never mentioned it to the others. In my view, although we are strict with our relatives, due to social prejudice some people would not understand this, nor would they believe it. So, you should be mentally prepared, because you may not benefit but instead get hurt just by being related to us. As a relative and an elder, I feel that you have received some unfair treatment."

Later, during the Cultural Revolution, I worked as a manual labourer at a farm with the staff and students of the BSFLI. I was called back to Beijing after Lin Biao's downfall. Minister Geng Biao selected me to work for the ILD. Qi Ma congratulated me on my new job, thinking the role and

1966, Zhou Erliu and Wang Zhangli in Beijing.

its capacities would suit me. She was pleased that for all these years, the younger generation never requested them to exert any influence on our going to university or job transfers.

In 1980, my wife and I were assigned to work in the Chinese Embassy in the UK. She was a second secretary, while I was a cultural counsellor. My new post was in a lower position than my existing one, so the Organisation Department of the Central Committee was worried that it would affect my future promotion. I accepted this assignment despite the disadvantages. Meanwhile, my wife did very well at her job; when she was in a position to be promoted to first secretary, I pigeonholed the report for her promotion. This would obviously affect her remuneration and future job assignment.

After I returned to China at the end of 1984, the OD had originally arranged for me to take the position of vice president of the Chinese People's Association for Friendship with Foreign Countries. The then vice premiers, Ji Pengfei and Wu Xueqian, had given their approval. Considering Qi Ma was honorary president of the organisation, I didn't want to take the post. I preferred to be dean of the Shanghai Academy of Social Sciences, but the OD didn't agree with me. When Qi Ma learnt about this, she informed the OD that it would be better for me to take the other post because she was the honorary president of the CPAFFC. Finally, I took the post of vice president of Beijing University, as well as that of director of the Centre for Sociological Research and Development Studies of China.

In 1992, I was nearing retirement. The OD was considering to arrange for me to take charge of the centre for international studies under the State Council (later the China Institute of International Studies) or become vice president of the Chinese Tourism Association. But then, writer Han Suyin donated two million pounds to Nankai University to open the Centre for Zhou Enlai Studies. Representing the Tianjin municipal council, the party secretary and the president of Nankai University invited me to be the centre's director. Thinking that it would be ungracious for me to refuse, I agreed to go. However, I didn't want to replace Director Liu Yan, so I began working there as a consultant. Afterwards, when I went through the procedure for retirement, the director of the cadre department of the education ministry told me that I could enjoy the rights and privileges of a high-level official, but I told him that the rights and the privileges of the head of a bureau were quite enough for me. He was very moved, and my retirement procedure was completed that same day.

As far as I can remember, Qi Ba was also strict with his wife, Deng Yingchao, regarding the principle of avoiding nepotism. Although he was deeply in love with her and took care of her every need, he persistently refused to allow her to take the position of vice chairperson of the standing committee of the People's Congress. Besides, Qi Ma would never show herself whenever Qi Ba talked to me about my work. Even when they were on a tour of Nankai University, Qi Ma didn't show her face in public; as a result, the staff and students didn't know that she was also there. In 1973, when the All-China Women's Federation celebrated International Women's Day in the Great Hall of the People, Qi Ma (who was vice chairperson of the federation) chose to take part in some other celebrations while Qi Ba presented the meeting and gave a speech. In that same year I accompanied some foreigners on a visit to Yan'an. My cousin, Zhou Binghe, had gone to live and work in the countryside after graduating from middle school. The local government had given him preferential treatment, so he joined the army. Qi Ba didn't agree with this after he heard about it, so Zhou Binghe had to return to the countryside. When I was in Yan'an, I went to see the prefecture's party secretary. I thanked him for his care and concern for my cousin, but I also reminded him not to let my cousin get involved in fights between local factions. When I returned to Beijing, Qi Ma readily agreed with what I had done in Yan'an.

I am sure the abovementioned evidence will make my readers understand that I have always tried my best to do some practical things to give solace to my most respected Qi Ba and Qi Ma, who persistently pursued the policy of avoiding nepotism all their lives. They followed this path because they hoped their actions would slowly transform Chinese society and help to bring in a new system.

9. Treating Relatives Equally

During his lifetime, Qi Ba talked to family members about his principle of treating all relatives equally when dealing with family matters. In 2008, when we gathered in Huaian to celebrate the 110th anniversary of Zhou Enlai's birth, several members of the younger generation, such as Zhou Erjun, Zhou Erhui and Zhou Baozhang, talked to me about this principle of Qi Ba's. We agreed that some of us had forgotten about it and thus stopped putting it into practice. When I returned to Beijing, my nephew Zhou Guozhen expressed the same opinion to me.

In fact, after Qi Ba died, Qi Ma followed this principle when preparing for the funeral. The Zhou family is big, so she requested those living outside Beijing to stay in their own cities and not to come to Beijing; of those living in Beijing, only the eldest son of every household was allowed to go to the funeral. Yet some individual cases were granted permission by Qi Ma: I was the eldest son of the second household, so I attended the funeral, but my cousin Zhou Bingjian was an exceptional case. Because she had talked to Qi Ba on the phone when he was seriously ill, she received permission from Qi Ma to go, too.

When Qi Ma died, the funeral organiser followed the same rule. However, my cousin Zhou Bingde requested that my wife and I give up our places and let my brother Zhou Erjun and his wife go. I thought that if it was a necessary for them to go, they could just apply for it; there was no need to take our places. I travelled to Tianjin soon after Qi Ma died. Because she had always regarded Tianjin as her second hometown, while I had studied and worked at Nankai University in Tianjin, I went there to inform them about Qi Ma's death so that they would have time to send people to Beijing to attend the memorial service. When I returned to Beijing that same day, the vigil had already begun. Zhou Bingde said that I had travelled to Tianjin because I didn't want to attend the vigil, but the truth was that she had asked Zhou Ercui, who had just come to Beijing from Huaian, to give the relatives notice about the arrangements for the memorial service. Zhou Ercui had missed me, because she thought that I already knew about the arrangements. Only after I'd phoned Zhou Erjun did I find out about the arrangements, and was thus late for the vigil, resulting in a misunderstanding among some individuals in the family.

There is another case. I had been appointed vice president of the CPAFFC by the centre, and I was one of the candidates for the position of future president of the organisation. But Qi Ma was its honorary president; hence, to observe the principle of avoiding nepotism, I told the Organisation Department of the Central Committee that I would not go, and they created a new post for me as vice president of Beijing University. I have had some very enriching work experiences in my life. I have given no thought to personal gains or losses; on the contrary, I gave given up my own interests several times and let others take their chance. All this is on file. In fact, Qi Ma had eluded her relatives and staff to talk to me on how to deal with the persecution of the Gang of Four. It proved that she had confidence in me politically. On International Women's Day in 1973, when she was receiving the wives of foreign guests, she praised me and my wife in front of them. It is said that this was the only time in her life she praised a relative in public. I am proud of this and very grateful for it.

Various past events have brought about unnecessary misunderstandings and a negative impact, or, to some extent, damaged my reputation. I have been silent on the matter for over a decade, in the interest of family unity.

1992, Zhou Erliu and Wang Zhangli pay their last respects to the deceased Deng Yingchao, followed by Zhou Erliu's cousin Zhou Bingjun and his wife Liu Junying.

Corrections, Additions and Clarifications of the Historical Facts

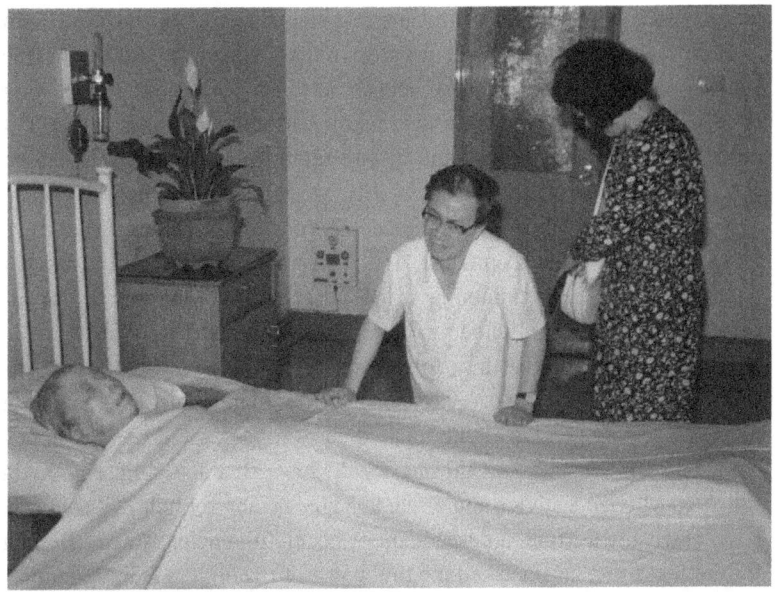

1992, Deng Yingchao on her deathbed. Zhou Erliu is grief-stricken. This photo was taken by a member of the Central Guard Regiment, without Zhou Erliu's knowledge. Wang Zhangli is standing to the side.

But I am old now, and thus I am using this opportunity to clear up some facts to comfort the souls of Qi Ba and the elder generation. I will try my best to live up to their trust.

Qi Ba had his own principles while dealing with family affairs. He discussed the matter with me many times, in 1946, between 1954 and 1955, and in 1964. He said that he was from a big and declining feudal family. Although I was young at the time, I interpreted what he said as follows: our family was large, and the good were mixed with the bad; for many of them, their minds and actions were guided by a feudal ideology; the result of the family's decline was that many of them had a low level of education, making it hard for them to fully bring their initiatives into play; and some of them were despondent and decadent, or careless when making political choices. Qi Ba told me that as the premier of a large country, he was very busy; therefore, he couldn't be in two places at once. But facing this big family, whose number was large yet whose individual circumstances were varied, he would still fulfil his responsibility to help most of them transform themselves, as their progress could lighten the burden on the state. It was necessary for every household to adopt the policy of treating all equally. There should be a distinction between right and wrong, but no distinction between close and distant relationships. Only by doing so could he win support from the majority. Qi Ma would sometimes cut in and say that they wanted to convince everyone and sincerely make them agree with each other's opinions, and to promote family unity. I thought Qi Ba's actions had something to do with his kindheartedness, broadmindedness and his childhood experiences. From his diary that he wrote in Japan we can see that in a foreign country, he had difficulty with his studies and daily life. It was Zhou Yikang (my grandfather) who gave him financial help. When his eighth uncle died of illness, there was no money for a funeral. Worried that no one would look after the children, Qi Ba followed Mr Gao's advice and wrote to Zhou Yikang for help. Thirty years later, when Zhou Ercui, a descendant of his eighth uncle, came to Beijing for the first time, Qi Ba asked me to travel from Tianjin to Beijing to meet him. He told me about the financial help my grandfather had given them, and hoped that we, the younger generation, could maintain the contact and affection between family members. This again embodied his principle of treating all household relatives equally, which means to lay importance on the principles and conduct of the individuals rather than their academic backgrounds, positions, family backgrounds, experiences, gender, or jobs.

10. 'Dislike, But Don't Avoid the Old Fogy' Zhou Yiliang

Qi B's sixth uncle was born on 17 July 1873. He was originally called Zhou Yiliang, but he changed it to Zhou Songyao, taking 'Xunzhi' as his style name. He was one of three *juren* in his generation of the Zhou family. Recommended by the governor of Jiangbei, Wang Shizhen, he held a post in the Qing government. In some modern-day reports, people have taken these words too literally and interpreted his post as the equivalent of today's secretary-general of the State Council, unaware that by doing so they overestimated his influence. The truth is that he was one of many secretaries to President Yuan Shikai. Later, in 1951, he was employed by the Central Research Institute of Culture and History. Qi Ba talked to me

Corrections, Additions and Clarifications of the Historical Facts

about this, saying that it was not him who had endorsed his uncle to take this job, and even clarified the issue in public. Zhou Yiliang had once written down information about each household, but some of it was incorrect. For example, he wrote that I had once joined the Fourth Field Army — but I had joined the Second, not the Fourth Field Army. In addition, my brother Zhou Erjun, who had also joined the army, was not included in the list of names. So, to stop the spread of falsehoods, we should check the information Zhou Yiliang has given about the later generations.

The American professor Chae-Jin Lee once wrote a book about Zhou Enlai as a teenager. According to Professor Lee, when Zhou Enlai passed the entrance exam for Nankai Middle School, Zhou Yiliang strongly opposed his nephew going to a 'foreign' school. In fact, the Nankai School was a modern private school. Its ideas about teaching and courses were more advanced than those at traditional family-run schools in China. After 1949, some party journals in Shaoxing published articles (without mentioning his name), saying that during the May Fourth Movement, Zhou Yiliang had developed a deep repugnance for the progressive students' anti-Yuan Shikai movement. He blamed Zhou Enlai and accused him of being an unworthy descendant who had strayed from the right path. He wrote to his fellow countrymen in Shaoxing, informing them of Zhou Enlai's 'inappropriate conduct'. When Qi Ba was preparing to go abroad to study, he asked for help from Zhou Yikang (my grandfather) and Zhou Yiliang. Both uncles were working in Nanjing. My grandfather immediately sent Qi Ba the money he had asked for, while Zhou Yiliang refused to help his nephew and accused him of being a 'swindler'. Qi Ba was very unhappy about this accusation. Later, Qi Ba wrote from England, requesting that Zhou Yiliang ask for some help from Governor Wang Shizhen and obtain a state grant for him. Zhou Yiliang ignored Qi Ba's request. However, despite disagreeing with Zhou Yiliang's behaviour, Qi Ba still showed respect to him and would celebrate the birthday of this longest-living member of the family.

Zhou Enshou, Zhou Yuyan, Zhou Enzhu and Qi Ba all talked to me about these circumstances, as well as their criticism of Zhou Yiliang. Qi Ba said: "This man of the older generation has kept his distance from the other households; they virtually never see each other. He has a bad reputation among the family members, who regard him as harsh and ungrateful, rich but cruel, and failing to educate his children in a proper way..." I also heard my grandmother and Qi Yeye (Qi Ba's birth father) talking about Zhou Yiliang. They said that he was not generous to other people. My grandfather and Zhou Yiliang were full brothers, and my grandfather cared about Zhou Yiliang and had often given him help. But after my grandfather died, Zhou Yiliang cared nothing for his brother's widow and son. He never went to see them. Zhou Yiliang's elder brother, Zhou Yiyu, was poor and sick. He died, dejected and at an old age, of illness in a temple. But Zhou Yiliang neither cared for nor thought about his brother, even though they were living in the same city. If my grandfather had still been alive, such a thing would never have happened. Qi Ba agreed with this opinion when he discussed the matter with me.

Qi Ba had once sought Zhou Yiliang out to gain information about governmental organisations and the salaries of officials at all levels in the late Qing dynasty, as well as in the early days of the PRC. When Qi Ba mentioned corruption in official circles, Zhou Yiliang said that he had been honest in performing his official duties. Qi Ba refuted this claim to his face, and earnestly pointed out that even if a section leader had been involved in corruption, it would be impossible for the secretary of a major warlord, like Yuan Shikai, to be clean. Qi Ba used his own birth father as an example, saying that the position of his father had only been equal to that of a section leader, and even he couldn't claim that he had been honest. When other people sent Zhou Yiliang antiques, calligraphies and paintings as presents, he accepted them, which could at least be regarded as economically unclean or a covert act of corruption. Zhou Yiliang accepted what Qi Ba had said, and told him that he felt ashamed. This conversation took place when Zhou Yiliang was 80 years old. To show that he cared for his uncle, Qi Ba, although very busy, held a feast to celebrate Zhou Yiliang's birthday.

Up until now, people have known little about Qi Ba's principles regarding the treatment of elderly family members. According to his principle, 'dislike, but don't avoid the old fogy', 'dislike' means to draw a clear ideological line for them, and 'don't avoid' means to try one's best to uphold affection within the family, giving these family members attention and proper care. So, I believe that during his days working with the Central Research Institute of Culture and History, Zhou Yiliang was aware of the well-intentioned arrangements made by the party and the government. He must have worked hard and accomplished something there. In short, it is not surprising that in the old days, this old fogy had had bad habits and been conservative in his thinking, and any exaggeration can lead to misunderstandings for those who know little about the truth. Besides, according to historian Jin Chongji, the tangled fighting between warlords in Jiangsu and Zhejiang provinces caused serious damage to people's lives and property. Qi Ba told me that after Li Chun, the military governor of Jiangsu, had died, Zhou Yiliang had sat at home doing nothing for a while, so he was incapable of putting a stop to the fighting among the warlords. These circumstances are not false rumours, but historical facts. Up until the present day, readers know little about Qi Ba's 'dislike, but don't avoid'-principle. I think publishers should pay more attention to it.

11. Shen Junru and Zhou Enlai Were Not Acquainted with Each Other during the Anti-Japanese War

Many authors of popular books mention that Shen Junru and Zhou Enlai were acquainted with each other in Chongqing during the anti-Japanese war. But this does not tally with the facts. My father was an early graduate of the Shanghai law school, where Shen Junru was dean of studies. Mr Shen was also master of ceremony at my parents' wedding. Between 1928 and 1931, he often came to visit my family in 44 Yong-an-li, North Sichuan Road in Shanghai, where he got to know Qi Ba. They trusted each other deeply. At the time, the KMT government had put a high price on Qi Ba's head, but Qi Ba and Mr Shen weren't afraid to meet in my family home. This is enough evidence to show that in the early years of his revolutionary career, Qi Ba was already skilled at getting along with non-party democrats and keeping up a long-term cooperative relationship with them.

Mr Shen's son was a doctor, and I was once his patient. He prescribed me some vitamin E supplements and asked me to take them for a long period of time. Mr Shen's daughter-in-law has associated with me and my wife for many years, and his granddaughter also keeps in contact with us. Mr Shen's grandson married my cousin Zhou Bingde. In this way, three generations of the Shen family have associated with the Zhou family.

12. How Dick Wilson Invented His Story

Dick Wilson was born in Epsom, Surrey, England in 1928. He was educated at Brasenose College, Oxford, and the University of California at Berkeley. He first travelled to Asia in 1952. He worked for the *Financial Times* before joining the *Far Eastern Economic Review* in Hong Kong as an editor from 1956 to 1964, and later worked as an editorial adviser in Singapore. From 1973 to 1981, he edited *The China Quarterly* at London University. His earlier books include *A Quarter of Mankind, Asia Awakes, When Tigers Fight, A Biography of Mao Zedong* and *A Biography of Zhou Enlai*. The latter has been translated into Chinese, and hence has had some influence on Chinese people both overseas and in mainland China.

In the early days of the 1980s, I was invited by John McLay, head of the International Culture Department of the British Foreign Office, to talk business. After I arrived, I saw that Dick Wilson was also there. It was the first time I met him, even though I knew that he had been working in Hong Kong and other parts of the Far East. Soon I found out our conversation had not been initiated by the British Foreign Office, but by Dick Wilson himself. He had requested them to be introduced to me. As we talked, I knew that he was writing *A Biography of Zhou Enlai*.

Afterwards, he invited me to his home, where I met his wife and his two adopted children from south Asia. After supper, he talked about the book he was writing. Firstly, he asked me if the material supplied by a certain person (Ma Shunyi), who had emigrated to the US from Taiwan, was true or reliable. I told him that this person had always been intentionally anti-communist. She used to slander Zhou Enlai and invent stories, saying that her father, Ma Shijie, had died being persecuted by Zhou Enlai's brothers. All this was sheer nonsense. Dick Wilson then took out Zhou Enlai's very fragmented family tree. I casually filled in a few names, such as Zhou Bingde, Zhou Bingjian, Zhou Erhui and Zhou Ercui. I didn't fill in my own name. I told him that this family tree was too uncomplicated and fragmented.

Corrections, Additions and Clarifications of the Historical Facts

I also told him that he should spend some time making a supplement and further revisions, but he failed to implement any corrections.

In 1960, Mr Wilson interviewed Qi Ba for 30 minutes in Nepal. He had no further contact with Qi Ba afterwards. Nevertheless, judging by the material he was gathering, he was serious about writing the book. However, in pages 65 to 67, he wrote that as a student in Europe, Zhou Enlai had been to Germany in 1923. In a place called Göttingen, he had met a young maid and slept with her, and duly became the father of a baby boy in 1924. After I read this, I told Mr Wilson that this was impossible, but he argued that it was not an invented story and that the information was from a reliable source, and refused to correct this error in his book. After my repeated complaints and appeals, he explained his thoughts on the matter to me. He insisted that Zhu De was the man who had fathered the baby. I further pushed him to clarify the facts until he couldn't deny them any longer, so he apologised for believing in rumours. He explained that he hadn't done it out of evil intentions or a conspiracy, but to satisfy the readers' curiosity about the leaders' romantic affairs, so that he could sell more copies of his book. I chided him right away: "A serious writer should never readily give credence to rumours and reprint other people's falsehoods at will. What you've done has shown that you are an irresponsible man." He finally agreed to add a footnote to acknowledge the whole story about the rumour spreading. The related article was published in *Stern* magazine in 1954. It said that Zhou Enlai had travelled frequently between Berlin and Paris in the summer of 1923, hence he had met a German woman in Göttingen. He had sexual relations with her and she gave birth to a boy. This story was written by Gerd Heidemann in 1954 and was widely carried in many international newspapers, which was why Dick Wilson had thought it a reliable and true story, and included it in his book. But in 1976, a German archivist found out that the romantic Chinese student in Göttingen was called Chu Ling Qin, born on 18 July 1898 in Shanxi province. Not only is his name completely different from Zhou Enlai's, but he is not even the same age. It's obvious that this man was neither Zhou Enlai nor Zhu De. In fact, when Qi Ba learnt about the story, he made a statement to the press that he had never been to Göttingen, concluding that the story was sheer fiction. Gerd Heidemann was forced to resign from *Stern* in 1983 when his purported 'Hitler Diaries' were subsequently proved to be forgeries. After the Europe-China Association had passed on all the information to Dick Wilson, he realised he had believed in rumours too easily and had made the mistake of carelessly spreading falsehoods. He thought it necessary to apologise to me and bring the truth of the matter to light. He wrote the following note:

With compliments,

Zhou Erliu,

Please see pages 67-68, and also the bottom of page 317, where I found proof that the Stern article was wrong!

With best wishes,

Dick Wilson

English writer Dick Wilson's apology.

This 'story' shows that Zhou Enlai was not only a distinguished and great man in China, but also, as his foreign friends pointed out, an esteemed historical figure who had incited change in the world. In the future, he may still have careless or deliberate rumours thrust upon his legacy, so we Chinese must take notice of such phenomena. The related department should attach great importance to it, watching out for these trends, studying the situation and taking appropriate measures to clear up rumours that don't tally with the facts, and thus defend the lofty image of Zhou Enlai. It is our responsibility and obligation to protect the interests of our nation as well as our national image. I hope that young readers who have little knowledge of the historical facts will pay more attention and conscientiously learn about the true history.

13. The True Story of Mrs Li Zhifan and Edgar Snow

Influenced by Qi Ba, Qi Ma [Deng Yingchao] also took a rigorous approach to historical research. She resolutely opposed any invented stories or exaggerations of an event.

In the 1970s, she approached me with two concerns, and these are her verbatim words: "Erliu, I am authorising you to solve two problems for me. The first is that in the drama *The First of August Storm*, a scene shows your Qi Ba busy with the fighting on the frontline in Wuhan, while I am pregnant in Guangzhou. Being apart, we frequently express our strong affection by writing sweet nothings to each other — very romantic. But the truth is that these battles were fierce, and we didn't hear from each other for some time. Nothing like that scene in the play ever happened. At the time, I was in hospital giving birth. It was only because of comrade Chen Tiejun's timely information that I managed to leave hospital and avoid persecution by the enemy. It was not a normal childbirth; the baby's head was too big, and it didn't survive the difficult delivery. Chen Tiejun didn't leave Guangzhou. She was executed later on, along with her fiancé Zhou Wenyong. The movie *The Wedding on the Execution Ground* tells the true story of their death. I hope you'll do your best to clarify this historical fact for me in China.

"The second problem is about the story regarding Edgar Snow and myself. After the Long March, your Qi Ba took on the important job of formulating a new plan (forming a united front) to resist Japanese aggression. Chairman Mao decided that I was to go with your Qi Ba. In March 1937, I arrived in Xi'an from Yan'an. After a discussion with your Qi Ba, I decided to go to Beiping [now Beijing] to get treatment for my lung disease so that I would have to spare no effort to do my work in the future. I changed my name to Yang Yi to hide my identity. I then used your Qi Ba's pseudonym in Hong Kong, Li Zhifan, and introduced myself to the others

In the summer of 1938, Zhou Enlai and Deng Yingchao met Edgar Snow, the progressive American journalist, writer and author of *Red Star over China*, in Wuhan.

as Mrs Li Zhifan. In May, I arrived in Beiping by train. Disguised as a son and a daughter-in-law from a wealthy family, the underground couple Xu Bing and Zhang Xiaomei received me. They arranged for me to recuperate in a sanatorium for ordinary people in Xishan (meaning 'Western Hills'). Another female student from Qinghua University was in the same ward. Her name was Hu Xingfen. Years later, after she learnt about my identity, she wrote an article entitled *Mrs Li Zhifan*, describing the days we were in the sanatorium together. This sanatorium was situated on Fushou hill, which was close to the rolling hills of the Yan mountains. At the bottom of the hill, there was a pine forest: quiet and safe, it was a good place to recuperate. But before long, the Marco Polo Bridge Incident occurred on 7 July. In the early hours of the 8th, the sound of artillery was heard near the sanatorium. I then received a letter from your Qi Ba: he had arranged for me to return to Xi'an by train through Suiyuan. On 30 July, after only three months in the sanatorium, Zhang Xiaomei and Nan Hanchen arranged for me to leave Beiping. We took a train to Tianjin. On that day, I dressed like a woman from a middle-upper-class family. Wearing sunglasses and a blue silk *cheongsam*, I tied my long hair with a matching ribbon. After my recuperation, I had a plump figure. When I got on the train, I found out that I was in the same coach as Edgar Snow, but we pretended we didn't know each other, and didn't speak. When the train arrived at Tianjin, the platform was full of Japanese military police. They arrested many suspects. For our safety, without saying a word, Snow and I quickly mixed with the crowd. This is what the situation was really like at the time. Snow was unable to give me any protection, except if he'd dressed me up as his maid servant. As a friendly Western journalist, he was in the habit of making up interesting stories at times, which Enlai and I never agreed with. I hope you can use your opportunity to work for foreign affairs to help me clarify the truth."

In the following years, I mentioned these two events to some friends working in the world of literature and art and in the Zhou Enlai research group of the Central Literature Research Office. It seems that these problems have been cleared up in the relevant dramas. But after Qi Ma died, many publications both in and outside China have continued to cite Snow's invented story. I am uneasy about this, feeling that I have let Qi Ma down. So, I hope my revelations about the truth in this book will draw the attention of the relevant departments and readers in China. Bringing the truth to light will not hinder the friendship between Qi Ma and Snow, but to allow these untrue stories to continue circulating is irresponsible and would have disappointed Qi Ma, who had personally urged me to clarify the facts.

Qi Ba also told me that some foreign writers liked to make up beautiful lies to please their readers. At most, these lies do not matter much, but we should not follow the example of these writers. It is rumoured that Mme Sun Yat-sen had similar views about Snow on the matter.

14. The Utterly Absurd Book, *A Heavy Load on Dad*

A Chinese peasant woman called Ai Bei from Anhui province wrote a book called *Jiao Fu Qin Tai Chen Zhong* (literally '*A Heavy Load on Dad*'). She was originally called Zhang Aipei. In her book, she claimed that she was the illegitimate daughter of the late world-famous Zhou Enlai, and that her birth mother was a beautiful woman from a capitalist family in Shanghai.

In her book, she said that the most important reason that Zhou Enlai was loved and esteemed by the Chinese and even by people around the world was because he was a person of high morals, including in his strict private life. His wife, Deng Yingchao, was a famous Chinese female leader, and to her, Zhou Enlai was a faithful husband. All these reasons made it very difficult to expose Zhou Enlai's privacy. As Zhou Enlai's own daughter, whether in public or in private, it was very hard for her to call him dad, because she would come under pressure from all quarters. These words of hers had won her some sympathy from readers. The book was sold all over the world in Chinese-language bookshops, and quite a large number of copies have been sold.

How could this book stir up the interest of those who knew little of the facts and took delight in reading it? There are profound social reasons for this. Firstly, Zhou Enlai was a world-famous, talented historical figure who was sincerely respected and loved by the Chinese, as well as by people around the world. Some people were curious about his so-called inside stories, and even took an interest in studying them. Therefore, writer Ai Bei capitalised on people's curiosity, and in order to sell the book, she stopped at nothing to get what she wanted.

To be honest, Zhou Enlai's moral image, as well as the images of other old comrades, not only helped to found new China and propel the country forward, but also won the understanding and support of people around the world. However, for some years, an unhealthy social conduct bred in and infested Chinese society, which caused many people to be disappointed and unhappy with the situation. Hence, some people who had ulterior motives thought that Zhou Enlai was the last, but also the hardest 'moral idol' to be destroyed, because, in the minds of the ordinary Chinese, Zhou Enlai was an example of a healthy and upright spiritual force. Such a force can unceasingly strengthen the cohesiveness of the Chinese people to advance the nation's fine traditions. Therefore, those who have evil motives will not hesitate to use dirty tricks to discredit Zhou Enlai and vainly hope to change the colour of China. That's to be expected when books like *A Heavy Load on Dad* are written and published. This phenomenon existed in the past, exists in the present, and I can state with certainty that it will exist in the future.

There is another reason why such a book can be published in Western countries. It is common and permissible for Western writers to make up interesting anecdotes about notable public figures. As far as I know, some Western writers and even some friendly personages have regarded this as a trivial thing that doesn't matter much. They think these anecdotes can entertain and attract more readers, and are no cause for criticism. Of course, there are people who think differently. For example, the former British prime minister Edward Heath once told me that because he was single, some small newspapers in England drew the conclusion that he was gay. He said that in England, people and social customs respect the privacy of the individuals. Generally, the ordinary people will not reveal, interfere with or comment on the private lives of others; however, politicians are under the scrutiny of the public. Any careless conduct will be exposed by the press, which can undermine their reputation as well as their political prospects. Hence, he made a statement to the public to clarify the issue. He thought that in the Far East, such as in China, the public usually pays more attention to famous public figures, setting much higher requirements for them (morally). This was not only demanded of them by traditional ethical standards, but by the group of politicians who were also party members. Because they were living in a new socialist country, people expected their leaders to lead by example; therefore, those ridiculous so-called 'incidents' that did not correspond to facts should be addressed by the affected individuals and the facts put straight, otherwise it could lead to misunderstandings between the people and their leaders.

As for Ai Bei, the relevant Chinese department investigated her and her family. Her birth mother was a peasant woman in Anhui province. At her home, without any knowledge of the investigation or any outside interference, she admitted that Ai Bei was her blood daughter. The truth has come out!

Besides, a reporter who was originally from Shanghai returned to China from overseas, having made direct contact with Ai Bei (in the US). The reporter noticed that Ai Bei's language and bearing showed that she had not grown up in Shanghai and Suzhou. Ai Bei could not speak the Shanghai dialect, nor could she relate any details of her mother as a young capitalist's daughter in Shanghai. Hence, this reporter despised Ai Bei's lies.

Also, the ridiculous accounts in the book are too many to list. For example, she wrote that Zhou Enlai's mother-in-law once took him to task, so to show his remorse, he stood in the rain the whole night holding an umbrella in his hand outside his mother-in-law's apartment. This is a laughable and base lie, because as premier of a large country, considering his complex environment, he was protected by his bodyguards round the clock. It was absolutely impossible for him to act alone. This case proves that this author acted against a writer's ethics and stopped at nothing to get what she wanted. Her ability to make up stories was dull and very poor.

Another incident comes to mind. Many years ago, an uneducated old woman from Huaian declared to the public that she had seen with her own eyes that Zhou Enlai and Deng Yingchao had secretly come to Zhou Enlai's birth place, Huaian, with Deng Yingchao's two illegitimate sons. To our surprise, this absurd, made-up story caught people's attention, and the relevant department sent people to investigate the matter. Naturally, the investigation came to nothing — a pure waste of people's time and money. The fact is that Deng Yingcaho had indeed given birth to a boy, but he died during the difficult delivery. Although Zhou Enlai missed his hometown, for all sorts of reasons he never returned after leaving the city when he was 12 years old. One of the main reasons is that the Chinese, especially the officials, not only have the mentality of wanting glory to reflect on their ancestors, but also the habit of returning home after obtaining wealth and power. As premier, if he returned to Huaian, he would inevitably burden the local people with organising a reception and it would also be hard for him to refuse any requests for special treatment by the local government. Therefore, as a party member, he made himself an example. He treated the idea of returning to Huaian with extreme prudence, and on this issue, he was indeed incorruptible and upright.

Some ill-intentioned people once openly declared in their articles: "Chinese society, including the party organisation and its members, becomes more and more corrupt every day. Only Zhou Enlai, that moral idol, remains untainted, though he could have been destroyed by the forces that sprang up from Ai Bei's book." Their evil intentions are self-evident. In the end, Ai Bei reaped what she had sown. She was spurned and despised by the Chinese. Many Chinese readers said to me that Ai Bei's book should change its title to *Jiao Fu Qin Tai Huang Tang* (literally 'Call Dad Utterly Absurd'). It would be best if one day we could witness all these ill-intentioned schemes falling apart and these people feeling ashamed and guilty.

Just like the other state leaders, Zhou Enlai had his daily movements recorded by his staff. Three of his security guards whom I knew, Cheng Yuangong, Zhang Shuying and Gao Zhenpu, issued a joint statement, declaring that what Ai Bei claimed was sheer fabrication and a pack of lies. This statement can also be a reference for readers.

Part Seven

Acting on the Teachings of the Deceased Qi Ba

Qi Ba and Qi Ma's Words Will Forever Warm Our Hearts

1. "You Are an Honest Child"

Geng Biao spoke to the cadres in the foreign affairs sector many times about the fact that Zhou Enlai himself was an honest man who liked people who were honest in word and in deed, but disliked people who boasted, flattered and toadied, held back unpleasant information, or catered to their superiors. As Zhou Enlai's nephew, in the almost 30 years of contact I've had with him, I did feel that this was the case.

As early as 1946, when he asked me about the real situation in north Jiangsu as well as about some family matters, I gave him both negative and positive answers and spoke frankly of right and wrong. He was very happy with my practical and realistic attitude, and said to me: "You are an honest child — this is very good."

One day in the 1950s, on my way to West Flower Hall, I saw a newspaper bulletin carrying the news that a Chinese delegation had given a speech at a UN conference. As I was in a hurry, I didn't read the news in detail, and Qi Ba unexpectedly asked my opinion on the matter. "It seems that it has been done just in time," I managed to reply. Staring at me, Qi Ba was clearly not happy with my reply. "Is your answer this simple?!" he asked me. Then I told him that I had only studied the matter in a hurry, so I didn't know any of the details. Smiling, Qi Ba said: "It's better to reply with honesty than boast or tell lies. I like honest people."

When Qi Ba invited Marshal Chen Yi to talk to me, he said to Chen Yi: "This child has a patriotic heart. He is an honest boy." When Zhang Yuan, Qi Ma's secretary, said to Qi Ba that I was the most honest of all my cousins, Qi Ba nodded his head, and replied that I was an honest and unsophisticated man.

During the Spring Festival of 1974, Qi Ba returned to his residence from hospital. This was the last time I spoke to him face to face. He inquired about the difficulties I had with my job, and asked if I had passed on his words to Qiao Guanhua and Li Qiang. I told him that I hadn't. He sighed gently, but said, satisfied: "You are still an honest man. That's fine. Leave the matter as it is." In those years, many guests from Australia and New Zealand chose to visit China during their summer holiday when the Chinese were celebrating the lunar new year. This usually meant that the foreign minister, Qiao Guanhua, and the foreign trade minister, Li Qiang, received the guests. The two ministers complained when I made the arrangements. When Qi Ba inquired about my work, I told him about the matter. He understood and trusted me. He agreed that I should urge the two ministers to find time for the reception in his name. I didn't, thinking it would be better for me to accept the complaints.

What still touches me today is that Qi Ba was concerned about the growth of young boys and girls. He had given me guidance on this issue. As a child, I was just what Qi Ba had called me: "an orphan but not an orphan". For my secondary education I went to a boarding school for boys. I had no experience with society and knew little about family life. Except for my grandma, I had few opportunities to make contact with women or girls. I knew nothing about their physiology or psychology. Qi Ba had a keen insight into such matters, and after I had been to university, he explained to me about certain physiological and psychological characteristics of the young female students. Recalling what he had said, I noticed that many of them conformed to scientific principles. He also pointed out that the bad social habit of treating women as inferior to men that had been left over from feudal society led to objectification. It was a problem that could not be overlooked, and the situation was worse in the country and in remote areas.

Looking back, Qi Ba's main reason for having long talks with me alone to give me guidance about growing up, education, jobs, and other things was that he knew that I was frank and reliable. I am grateful and have been proud of this all my life.

2. "Answer Them Based on Facts"

In 1963, my wife and I graduated from Nankai University and were assigned to work for the Committee for Cultural Relations with Foreign Countries. Qi Ba was very happy. He would talk to us and test our English during our conversations. What impressed me most was what he was thinking about the cultural construction of new China. The country needed to gain some experience, and he sincerely hoped that we would work hard and achieve something.

Once, he thoroughly analysed the four distinguishing features of Chinese cultural construction as follows:

1) Continuous and tenacious development is the main contribution China has made to the world. He said that the Chinese civilisation was one of four ancient civilisations that make up the heritage of humankind. Strictly speaking, it does not belong to one nation, nor is it the state's private property, so the disappearance of an ancient civilisation would be an irretrievable loss to the whole world. The enduring vitality of the ancient Chinese civilisation makes it a great subject to study. In modern times, we Chinese shouldn't resign ourselves to our backwardness, nor should we underestimate our own capabilities or be so conceited and arrogant as to have too high an opinion of ourselves. We should show respect for our old traditions, study them and make healthy advances while absorbing elements from excellent foreign cultures. Only by doing so will we live up to the world's expectations.

2) We must be realistic in the face of cultural competition. China's civilisation has won praise from the world as a representative of east Asia. But currently, some of our neighbours, such as North and South Korea and Japan, are trying to implement modernisation while trying to maintain their traditions. Some of their traditions originated in China and, based on these, they are exploring new

developments and trying to surpass us. Such competition is a self-evident reality. We must face it and take a grave view of the matter, meanwhile sharpening our own competitive edge to safeguard our cultural heritage and make further developments. We must learn about other countries' strong points to make up our weaknesses.

3) We must keep things in perspective while paying attention to day-by-day developments. China is a developing country with a large population. The country's development needs to be coordinated and carried out in different phases. Not everything can be done in one move; some problems need to be solved step by step. We must not take a laissez-faire attitude to uneven development or let it get out of control. Some problems, such as protecting the environment, require us to learn a lesson from advanced countries. We shouldn't pollute first and improve later, otherwise the losses will be irretrievable. Foreign countries have esteemed the philosophies of Confucius and Laozi and their application in daily life for centuries; we shouldn't sit still, doing nothing. We must intensify our studies of these ancient sages.

4) We must esteem creative exploration. As we are a young socialist country, there are lots of things to explore and learn about. We must act in accordance with the party's guiding principles for literature and art — that is, to let a hundred flowers blossom and a hundred schools of thought contend, and to discriminately absorb cultural elements from either our own or foreign countries. We must discard the dross and select the essence, to apply ourselves to making examinations and developments, and also to respect the creativity of writers and artists, keeping our own culture but making use of the excellent ones of others. I'll always remember what Qi Ba said in the early winter of 1964: "Building a culture cannot be done by launching movements. It is a huge task, so we shall not only rely on the theories of the experts, but also on the experiences of the people. By walking in the right direction and making improvements through the unceasing efforts of several generations, we will be able to build the Chinese civilization of the

future." He then added: "Your work is about cultural exchanges. It is certain that our foreign friends will ask you to name the distinguishing features of new China's cultural construction. Today, I have not had time enough to discuss it, so I'll only say a few words for reference. However, when you respond to that question, you should base your answers on facts."

In 1955, Qi Ba attended the Bandung conference in Indonesia. Since then, China has focused its diplomatic attention on Asia and Africa. In 1964, Qi Ba visited 14 Asian and African countries, which could be said to have been a continuation of the spirit of the Bandung conference, as well as an extensive and important foreign activity. Such a grand diplomatic event formed a background for the foreign cultural exchange work I was to be engaged in.

3. The First Lesson I Learnt during My Foreign Exchange Practice

Soon after I graduated from university, the CCRFC sent me on a trip abroad. In the autumn of 1964, I accompanied the Shenyang Acrobatic Troupe to Africa. In August, before we left, Qi Ba met me in his residence to prepare me for the Africa trip. He said to me that after my return I had to tell him not only what I had seen and heard, but also to sum up my journey for him.

Our initial plan was to visit Tanzania, Ethiopia, Burundi and Uganda, and several other countries. After changing flights in Paris, Kenya would be the first African country in which we landed. Because Kenya had become independent only the year before, we made no plans to perform, only to stay in the capital, Nairobi, for a short while and then travel on to other countries. In spite of this, Qi Ba requested us to include Kenya in our preparations. I knew little about any of the African countries, but after talking with Qi Ba, I knew that Kenya was an important and relatively rich country in the eastern African plateau. A major feature of the country's landscape were the grand canyons, and the climate was cooler than we Chinese had thought. Its population of 10 million made it one of the larger countries of the African continent. Qi Ba said that the Chinese foreign minister, Chen Yi, had visited the country once, and had told him that Nairobi was a charming city — its scenery had earned it the nickname of

Zhou Erliu in the capital of Kenya, Nairobi, 1964.

'little Paris'.

When I arrived in Nairobi, everything struck me as new. There were many plants and wild animals that were very different from those I had seen in Asia. The trees were very tall and straight, and looked as though they were towering into the sky. Some trees even had hotels built in them and had been turned into local tourist resources where many foreigners lived. The African elephants were large, much taller and heavier than Asian elephants. Their ears were nearly the same size as an Asian person. What I found most astonishing were the ant hills on both sides of the road, some of which were as tall as a man. At first glance, the African people all looked the same, but when one looked carefully, there were distinct differences in the colour of their skins, their stature, and particularly in their facial features. Having made contact with the local people, we understood that besides learning their nationality, we had to find out which tribe they were from, because every tribe had its own language, customs and ways of life and production. We must not get involved with those tribes who held historical grudges or were engaged in disputes.

After I returned to China, I reported to Qi Ba about my experiences in Africa. He took my observations seriously. He explained to me that although the historical records showed that a long time ago, Zheng He and his fleet had reached the country of Kenya on the eastern African coast, the Chinese were lacking in their understanding of Africa. Therefore, it was necessary to remind the Chinese in the relevant departments that they had to pay attention to learning about the national conditions of individual African countries. After thinking carefully, he then said: "It seems that African countries are not suited to the socialist system. The problems among the tribes have become big social issues, and if they are not handled carefully and skillfully, these issues can develop into political problems on a national scale."

Up to now, what remains fresh in my memory is that Qi Ba had urged me to learn more about the different countries and then to make a comparison between them. For instance, he said that he had heard that some of the former British colonies were richer and had a higher level of development than the former French colonies. This might be the result of the British emphasis on a market economy, which engenders inequality but creates the highest profits, while the French simply taxed the locals. Some Africans summed up this phenomenon as the British "feeding a hen to get the eggs" and the French "killing a hen to get the eggs". When Qi Ba came to this point, he indicated that if I were to go to Africa in the future, I should carry on with my investigations and do more comparative research. All these suggestions reminded me of one of the principles Qi Ba had been promoting since he was a teenager: 'We must immerse ourselves in research and experiments, otherwise we shall achieve no success.' I have benefited a great deal from Qi Ba's teachings. Twenty years later, when I was giving a speech at a conference held at United Nations University in Tokyo, Japan, I expressed the thought that China should intensify her studies of people's experiences in the world's most populous developing countries, such as India, Indonesia, Brazil, Mexico, Egypt, Nigeria and others, and to compare them with Chinese experiences since the economic reform in 1979. This speech of mine won the approval of the conference's participants from various countries.

4. Rare Open Praise from Qi Ba

It was common knowledge that Qi Ba was strict with himself in many respects and particularly in dealing with his relatives. Having set high demands for his relatives, he would criticise an individual, but it was rare for him to openly praise one. However, there were some exceptions. Between 1972 and 1975, I was lucky to be with Qi Ba when he was receiving foreign guests. For the reception, we always made very detailed preparations. But because Qi Ba would often ask the guests some unexpected questions, the preparation work was always more extensive, since any omissions would ruin the high-quality service during the reception. Once, Qi Ba asked a guest from New Zealand about the number of intermarriages between native Maoris and white Europeans. For such a question, the guests, even though they knew many facts about their country, were unprepared. Luckily, I had the information on hand, so I replied, which enlivened the atmosphere. "Your expert is very good. He can even answer a question like this, which makes us surprised and happy," the guests said to Qi Ba. He smiled and said: "Some of our cadres can do their jobs carefully and conscientiously. They have paid attention to learning facts. Well, to do a good job, more things are waiting for them to be learnt." Afterwards, some colleagues congratulated me for the rare praise I had received from Qi Ba in front of the others.

On another occasion, I accompanied Qi Ba to receive a foreign guest. It was a Sunday, and, without informing us in advance, Qi Ba recommended an article from *Le Monde* to the guest to read. He requested us to find a copy at once. The newspaper was in French, as well as some other foreign languages. It was inappropriate for me to ask Qi Ba which version he wanted. On Sundays, many newspaper agents usually only had one person on duty who might know a little about foreign-language newspapers, while the small agents would either not be open or not have the newspapers in certain languages. The premier would receive the guests in the evening, and the formal talks would begin after supper, when people had finished working and gone home. So, under the circumstances, I phoned the Xinhua news agency and the *China Daily*, telling the people on duty that the premier wanted *Le Monde* at once, hoping they could send some copies to the Fujian room in the Great Hall of the People for the premier and his guest to use. Because of the premier's high prestige, as expected, copies of the newspaper were sent shortly after I had made the phone calls. We picked up the French edition, which was just the one that Qi Ba wanted. The guest had been to China several times before, so he knew the country. He was amazed to see that the newspaper had been delivered so quickly. He congratulated the premier on the efficiency of Chinese workers. Qi Ba smiled: "Yes, they did well this time. But there is space for us to improve." Then he added: "Efficiency is the lifeblood of our work in foreign affairs, and in many other operations."

On International Women's Day in 1973, the Lin Biao Incident had been handled carefully. Seizing this opportunity, the premier went to the Great Hall of the People to announce the rehabilitation and apologise to the many foreign friends who were working in China but had been persecuted during the Cultural Revolution. His actions aroused a hugely favourable reaction in both China and the international community. Because she was practicing the policy of avoiding nepotism, Qi Ma went, unplanned, to a different location to celebrate Women's Day with the female family members of the foreign experts and some female foreign friends who were Chinese residents, rather than to the Great Hall for this important meeting. By chance, my wife was her interpreter, and Qi Ma was very glad to see her. She joked: "I thought, here comes a beautiful actress." Because my wife and I had been engaged in foreign affairs work for many years, we had seen Qi Ba and Qi Ma receiving foreign guests on various occasions. However, to avoid catching the attention of the others, we never went up to them voluntarily to say hello, keeping such a distance that few people knew we were related. Qi Ma was deeply touched by this. On that day, when the meeting had ended, she said to all who attended: "Zhangli did well during the Cultural Revolution. She also did well when dealing with her family and relatives." When she walked out, she turned round and said: "Erliu also did very well." Later, she told my other cousins about this situation. As it was very rare for Qi Ba and Qi Ma to praise their relatives in public, my wife and I felt extremely honoured and happy. The honour would spur us on to greater efforts, and we would work harder to let them feel satisfied and gratified.

5. Qi Ba Calls Me a "Little Jack-of-All-Trades"

To sum up my life, I have worked in industrial, agricultural, trade, educational and military circles, and in all branches of the party: government, military, civil and education. From 1949, when I joined the army, to 1954, when I passed the entrance examinations for university, I worked at the forefront in the southwest of China. After I graduated from university, I worked for the Committee for Cultural Relations with Foreign Countries and did what I could for new China's cultural exchanges with other countries. During the years before and after the Cultural Revolution, I often followed Chinese delegations to different countries, some of which Qi Ba would just have visited; as a result, Qi Ba jokingly remarked that I was imitating his movements and following in his footsteps.

During the Cultural Revolution, I worked with the workers in a pulp mill, a cotton mill, a porcelain workshop and a coal mine. I performed the same labours as the peasants in Henan and Shanxi provinces, and for two years I lived in a windowless room used for the storage of coffins. In the 1970s, China recovered its seat in the United Nations, and the relations between China and the US have improved ever since. I resumed my work on the foreign affairs front, and am lucky to have experienced and witnessed some of the major events and important diplomatic activities of those days. After the overthrow of the Gang of Four, I was a cultural counsellor in the Chinese Embassy in the UK for five years, the first cultural counsellor sent by the Foreign Cultural Exchange Centre (CCRFC, under the Ministry of Culture). My wife was also engaged in foreign cultural exchanges. She studied in England in 1973, becoming one of the first Chinese students abroad on a government scholarship. Later, she became a second secretary in the Chinese Embassy in the UK.

At the end of 1984, my term in the UK ended. When I returned to China, the OD assigned me to become either dean of the Shanghai Academy of Social Sciences (SASS) or president of the Bank of Communications, and concurrently a member of the Shanghai municipal communist party committee. I decided to take the post of dean of the SASS and went to Shanghai to report for duty. But after the procedure had been completed, I was called back to Beijing to take on the post of vice president of the CPAFFC, of which Qi Ma was honorary president. To steer clear of nepotism, I was also invited by Professor Fei Xiaotong to take up the post of vice president of Beijing University, for which I was accepted by the leaders of the country, Hu Yaobang, Zhao Ziyang and Li Peng, and concurrently became director of the Centre for Sociological Research and Development Studies of China at Beijing University. As such, the following sections are accounts of the positive results I achieved after my studies as well as of my creative applications of Zhou Enlai's ideology. Some relate the joint experiences of my wife and myself.

1. The Publication of the English Edition of *Speeches and Writings by Deng Xiaoping*

On 6 December 1984, the English edition of *Speeches and Writings by Deng Xiaoping*, one of a series of books about world leaders, was published in London by Pergamon Press. The first print run numbered 10,000 copies. The book evoked worldwide repercussions and was well received by readers, so the first reprint numbered 20,000 copies.

"As a member of the Chinese nation, I feel honoured to be a citizen of the international community. I am a son of the Chinese people. I deeply love my motherland and her people... Through our own labour, we will radically transform the backward aspects of our country so that, with an entirely new look, it will take its place in the front ranks of the nations of the world. Together with the people of other countries, we will advance the just cause of human progress." This fervent passage comes from the forward of *Speeches and Writings by Deng Xiaoping*.

The publication of the English version of the book provided the world with a window to learn about China and her economic reform. However, it took four years for it to be published in England. At that time I was a cultural counsellor in the Chinese Embassy in the UK, so I experienced the whole process of publication from up close.

The English version of *Speeches and Writings by Deng Xiaoping*, 1984.

Acting on the Teachings of the Deceased Qi Ba

1.1. A Party Committee Meets with Diverging Opinions

From 1980 to 1984, the CCRFC (later merged with the Ministry of Culture) assigned me to work in the Chinese Embassy in the UK. Huang Zhen was minister of organisation at the time. The CCRFC was at the same administrative level as the foreign ministry, and the ambassador and the administrative counsellor were dispatched by the foreign ministry. I was the first cultural counsellor dispatched by the CCRFC after China began its economic reform, and my job was mainly to deal with cultural exchange-related matters. I handled the visits to England paid by film director Xie Jin and actresses Qin Yi, Wang Danfeng and Liu Xiaoqing. I was also entrusted to persuade Zhou Caiqin, the daughter of Beijing opera grand master Zhou Xingfang, to return to China.

One day, the embassy party committee held a meeting to pass on a directive from China: to publish the English version of *Speeches and Writings by Deng Xiaoping*. The ambassador and the others thought that the publication would be of great significance. But it would be an arduous task — they were worried that they might not be able to get it done. Also, the majority of the embassy staff felt that there were no suitable publishers in England for the book, so, after some discussion, they decided to ask the Chinese side to try another method. But I thought differently. Although getting a book published was not my duty as a cultural counsellor, I thought it was an important matter. Because China's door had just opened to a crack, there was a necessity for the world to hear her voice. Deng Xiaoping was an important leader of the Chinese revolution and he was the chief architect of the Chinese economic reforms. Under his leadership, China began to open up, taking a step closer towards making contact with other countries. His speeches and writings would allow the world to understand more of China and her reforms. Besides, I felt a time-honoured affection for Deng Xiaoping. When I was a student at the Military and Political University of the Second Field Army, Deng Xiaoping was the political commissar, while Liu Bocheng was the commander. The Second Field Army's task was to liberate the southwest, and then the whole of China. Many of the new soldiers were young students from families of landlords. In view of this situation, Deng Xiaoping lectured us about the issue. He said that those who were joining the revolution must pass three tests: a military test, a land reform test and a socialist reform test. The lecture left a deep impression on me, and I could put it this way: it changed my life. After I graduated from the Military and Political University, I was offered the opportunity to be cipher officer for commanders Liu and Deng, but because I had listened to Deng Xiaoping's lecture, I asked to go to the front line instead. Later, Qi Ba inquired how Deng Xiaoping had told us to stand the test of being a socialist, and also said to me that Deng Xaioping was good at winning battles. Hence, from the bottom of my heart, I hoped the book would be published abroad.

1.2. I Am Mildly Rebuffed at My First Meeting with the Publisher

Before long, I returned to China. Firstly, I reported to Minister Huang Zhen about my work, then I went to the General Administration of Press and Publication of the PRC. I met with the section chief, Ms Zhou Shuiyu, my former colleague in the CCRFC. She was very happy to see me, and told me that she was worried about the publication of the English version of *Speeches and Writings by Deng Xiaoping*. It was very hard to deal with Robert Maxwell, the English publisher. She asked me to give her some ideas. Afterwards, she would be one of the key figures in handling the matter. If she hadn't told me about the difficulties they had met with, I would not have known about them.

Ms Zhou had likely told the director of Press and Publication, Song Muwen, about me, so Director Song received me. He told me about the importance of the publication of the English version, as well as the difficulties they were facing. He hoped that the Chinese Embassy in the UK would help them. Until then, I had not known that they had already contacted Maxwell, who had agreed to publish material about Deng Xiaoping and Zhou Enlai. Maxwell had come to China to discuss the matter, but the related department in Beijing did not want to disturb Qi Ma with the issue because she was old, so they only gave Maxwell material about Deng Xiaoping. After Maxwell had returned to England, nothing happened with the publication of the book, and Maxwell said that he had lost the material Beijing had given him, to some extent. Press and Publication was very unhappy about this, but London was too far away, and thus they wanted the embassy to do something to help.

Soon, I returned to the UK. I then made some inquiries and I learnt more about Pergamon Press and its owner, Robert Maxwell. Maxwell was born in 1923 into a Jewish family in Czechoslovakia. Both his parents failed to escape from the clutches of the Nazis. After the end of the second world war, he settled down in England. Although he had only been to school for three years, he was naturally bright and talented. Through his own efforts, he became a British newspaper tycoon with assets worth hundreds of millions, becoming a billionaire rich in stories. The *Daily Mirror and the London Daily News*, which Maxwell owned, were very influential. He was a successful entrepreneur, but he had an eccentric character and was hard to deal with. It was said that he kept up private connections with many of the world's political heavyweights. (He died in November 1991, having fallen overboard on his yacht. After his death, John Major, the British prime minister at the time, spoke highly of him.) I reported the information I had gathered about Maxwell to the ambassador, Ke Hua. He said that we ought to give it another try, so we went to Pergamon Press in London. Maxwell deliberately gave us the cold shoulder and let us wait. We knew he was in his office, but he simply did not come out. I thought it was not polite to treat us this a way, so, young and impetuous, I ignored diplomatic etiquette and forced my way into his office. He was very surprised when he saw me, and I said that we had been waiting for hours while his secretary had been overprotective of him.

1.3. Who Can Resolve This Difficult Problem?

After we explained to Maxwell that we hoped he would publish the English version of *Speeches and Writings by Deng Xiaoping*, he shrugged his shoulders and told us we should let him think about it. His perfunctory manner made ambassador Ke very angry. We walked out of Maxwell's office, and I told Ke that he should let me find another way. Though we had no other way, I had to find one. Meantime, Pergamon Press had put out advertisements about a publication featuring the paintings of Wu Zuoren, dean of the Central Academy of Fine Arts of China. Mr Wu and I were good friends, in spite of our great age difference. The publication date had been announced, and Mr Wu would personally be present at the ceremony. Mr Wu had been elected a deputy to the first, second, third, fourth, fifth and sixth National People's Congress — a deputy of the People's Congress was the equivalent of an MP in the UK, so the English respected Wu very much. Usually the English do not think highly of politicians, but artists, especially grand artists, enjoy the respect of everyone in society. Art has no national boundaries, so the English regarded Mr Wu as a guest of honour.

Wu was a man of my father's generation. He was another leading figure in the Chinese arts circle, like Xu Beihong. He had a deep affection for Premier Zhou, and after his death, he wrote poems of condolence and presented them to me. After the downfall of the Gang of Four he came to England on a state grant for cultural exchanges. But the money he received from the Chinese government was limited, so he was hard up and couldn't find a suitable place to live in London. After I learnt of his situation, as cultural counsellor, I felt I had a responsibility to help him, so I contacted Ms Fang Zhaolin, a well-known artist and the only female disciple of grand master Zhang Daqian. As she resided in London and Hong Kong, I arranged for Wu to live with Ms Fang for the time being. Wu was very grateful for my help, and, being an artist who enjoyed high prestige and commanded universal respect, he played an irreplaceable role in getting the English version of the book published. After I told him about the difficulties we were having, Wu said, straightaway: "If Pergamon Press doesn't want to publish Deng Xiaoping's book, I will not let them publish my paintings." His words put my mind at ease. Well, the English do things in a very planned way. The publication of Mr Wu's paintings was held as scheduled, and I attended with my wife. When Maxwell saw us, he said: "I'll publish Deng Xiaoping's book, and I'll try to get it done as soon as possible."

1.4. Maxwell's Wish

I knew that it would be much easier if Wu joined in our talks with Maxwell, so he went with me to his office. This time, Maxwell didn't make us wait, and he was very nice when he spoke to us. He told us that he was having several problems with the publication of the book. He had published many books about world leaders, and he had met with them all before the date of publication. However, he knew nothing about Mr Deng Xiaoping.

Acting on the Teachings of the Deceased Qi Ba

Given the situation, we knew that we could not force him to publish it. I had a discussion with Wu, feeling that Maxwell wanted to meet Deng Xiaoping but knowing that this was beyond our control to arrange. I then reported the issue to ambassador Ke, who also felt awkward. Although it seemed more difficult than we thought, we could not give up when we were halfway there. Hence, Wu and I went to see Maxwell again, hoping that he would change his mind. Before we went, Wu said to me: "You are a state cadre, a diplomat, and the nephew of Premier Zhou — let me speak to Maxwell." This time, Wu said to Maxwell: "We know that you are an influential publisher and that you have published books about many world leaders. Deng Xiaoping is the architect of the Chinese economic reforms. His thoughts on reforming and opening up embody the endurance of the spirit of Zhou Enlai. Deng Xiaoping's children have openly admitted that the line of Deng Xiaoping is the line of Zhou Enlai without Zhou Enlai. So, judging by experience as well as common practice, I believe Mr Deng Xiaoping will see you after you have published his book. We can help you fulfil your wish; although we can't promise anything for the time being, we will try our best to make it happen."

Maxwell was hesitant. We couldn't push him, so we gave him time to think. By chance, the general manager of the China Book Import and Export Corporation, Mr Cao, was in London. He had business contacts with English publishers, and he was also a friend of mine. I invited him to come to the embassy, where Wu and I talked to him about Maxwell. He agreed to help. Afterwards, I gathered that Maxwell had also learnt about me through Wu and Cao. After hearing that I was a scholar diplomat, he had apparently changed his attitude. Before long, he invited me and my wife to his house to attend an extravagant feast. His home was in Oxford, and the lawn outside his mansion stretched as far as eye could see. We saw police officers, there to maintain order. News of Maxwell's banquet appeared in the UK newspapers the next day. We could say that the banquet lost nothing in ostentation compared to royal banquets. Afterwards, he frequently invited me to his home and regarded me as his friend.

We then informed the Chinese side about the situation, and they soon sent people to contact Maxwell. Ms Zhou Shuiyu was one of them, and I heard they were progressing well. My term in the Chinese Embassy in the UK ended at the end of 1984. Just days after my return to Beijing, I was told that the press conference for the release of the English edition of *Speeches and Writings by Deng Xiaoping* had been held in London. It had caused a sensation in the West. The first print run was for 10,000 copies, and it sold so well that the publisher soon reprinted 20,000 copies. Before long, Deng Xiaoping received Maxwell at China's Beidaihe summer resort. After hearing the news I felt gratified, thinking my efforts had worked. Later, some colleagues from the Chinese Embassy told me that the administration counsellor had said that if it hadn't been for Zhou Erliu, the publication of Deng Xiaoping's book would have been very difficult; everyone involved had relied on him. Unfortunately, I didn't see the English edition of the book in Chinese bookstores, and when I went online, I saw not just one edition, but several. Today, the Chinese international influence is no longer what it once was. However, the days when I bustled around trying to get the book published in England are unforgettable.

2. Three Generations of India's Prime Ministers and the Five Principles of Peaceful Coexistence

In 1954, when the Indian prime minister Jawaharlal Nehru visited China, I was a student at Nankai University. Qi Ba asked me to come to his residence, where I saw the beautiful and colourful embroideries that filled the living room. Qi Ba said that they were gifts from Nehru; symbolising auspiciousness and blessings, these embroideries were an example of India's traditional cultural treasures. Before long, they were handed over to the foreign ministry, who then put them on show so that more people could view them. On that day, Qi Ba picked up a dozen cashew nuts from a plate on the tea table. He gave me the nuts to taste something new, saying that these were also gifts from Nehru. In those days, Qi Ba was in a very good frame of mind. The Five Principles of Peaceful Coexistence that Qi Ba had come up with were approved by prime ministers Nehru of India and U Nu of Burma, and then jointly promoted by all three. This had a great influence on the world. Never before had Asian and African countries been so united as after the Bandung conference in 1955. Thus, it was clear that the Five Principles had made a profound historical contribution in advancing world peace and developments, as well as human progress and unity. Interestingly, Qi Ba said that China and India were linked by common mountains and rivers, with both countries having a large population and ancient civilisations. Having been neighbours for several thousand years, it was a rare blessing in human history to live side by side in peace and maintain cultural exchanges. He even mentioned that the writer Zheng Zhenduo once thought that the image of Sun Wukong (the monkey king) in *Journey to the West* must have been influenced by legends of holy monkeys living near the Ganges in India. He also remarked that Indira Gandhi, the daughter of Nehru, was a young veteran revolutionary. In short, he hoped that I was not only interested in developed countries in the West, but would also pay attention to studying the relationship between China and India.

Three generations of Indian prime ministers.

In March 1982, during my time at the Chinese Embassy in the UK, I took part in a significant event that is still fresh in my memory. At the time, Indira Gandhi was prime minister of India. She was elected president of the India National Congress and had been prime minister since 1967. When her father, Jawaharlal Nehru, India's first prime minister, visited China, she also came and met Premier Zhou Enlai, and the Western media reported that Premier Zhou had made a good impression on her. In March 1982, when she visited England, I met her unexpectedly in London. At the time, Yehudi Menuhin, the grand master and tutor of music, was holding a violin concert for the Chinese child prodigy Jin Li in the newly built Barbican Centre. Menuhin was an American-born violinist who had been a child prodigy himself and attained great achievements in music during his lifetime. 'World citizen' was his nickname, as Great Britain, the US and Switzerland all claimed him as their own. He was made a Knight Commander of the Order of the British Empire and Right Honourable The Lord Menuhin OM KBE by the Queen of England. He had always been altruistic, performing for allied soldiers during the second world war and raising funds for charities. There is also a Yehudi Menuhin School in England, which trains musicians. He liked Chinese culture, and was very much influenced by the philosophy of his idol, Laozi. Of the many international politicians he knew, he held Premier Zhou in particular in high esteem. Furthermore, he believed that the sentiments held by the Chinese nation were valuable, making it easier for the Chinese to attain achievements in the audio and visual arts. His daughter was once married to Fu Cong, the famous Chinese pianist. They had a son and Menuhin requested me to help his grandson to go to China to study Chinese. Thus, I arranged for him to study at the Beijing Institute of Languages. Later, Menuhin told me that he had sent his grandson to Princeton University in the US to further his Chinese studies. He also asked me to translate his book, *Unfinished Journey*, into Chinese and get it published in China.

There is a reason I mention Menuhin when I am writing about the Indian prime ministers. For many years, the relationship between China and India had been locked in a stalemate, but the leaders of both countries, Deng Xiaoping and Indira Gandhi, believed that the two countries should put aside their historical issues and re-establish their good, neighbourly relationship for the sake of peaceful development in Asia and the world. Both were seeking a suitable breakthrough. Menuhin was willing to help; he was grateful to the Chinese for accepting the many Jewish people who fled to China during the second world war. As China had given these Jews a peaceful life, he would like to do something for China. Besides, he was a man of integrity who dared to speak up, and during the Arab-Israel conflict, he did not take sides, which was quite rare for a Jewish person.

Zhou Erliu with Yehudi Menuhin and Jin Li.

Menuhin invited Indira Gandhi to the violin concert for Jin Li. Usually, a leader of a large country such as India would not go to this sort of concert. But she accepted the invitation, which itself was a diplomatic gesture. During a break in the concert, Menuhin, Jin Li, my wife and I went to the VIP lounge to rest. Unexpectedly, Indira Gandhi was already there, waiting. She had some grey hairs and she looked thinner, but she was calm and steady and talked in a refined manner. She shook my hand very naturally and then said: "Jin Li can play at such a high level, it is indisputably due to Mr Menuhin's tutoring and guidance." Her praise of Jin Li did not only show her respect for the child, but also for China and even more for Mr Menuhin. Her appropriate remarks prompted me to talk about art, and then our conversation moved on to the communication between our two countries. Readily, she said that the relationship between China and India should be improved. Although more time was needed, the Five Principles of Peaceful Coexistence advocated by her father and Zhou Enlai were still the two countries' foundation for improving their relationship. She also recalled her trip to China with her father, saying that it had left a deep impression on her.

Zhou Erliu and his wife with Mr and Mrs Menuhin.

Since I had not received any instructions from China on the issue, I could only ask her: "What should we do?" She replied: "We can start with the economic and cultural exchanges, following the Five Principles jointly created by politicians of the elder generation to make progress step by step." I felt that despite the political changes that took place in those years, she still had faith and wanted to follow the Five Principles in dealing with the relationship between our two countries. Afterwards, I learnt that Deng Xiaoping had already expressed to Indira Gandhi that the relations between China and India should be normalised and that the two countries should seek common development. It seemed that when she was speaking to me she was repeating her response to Deng Xiaoping. She gave Menuhin the idea and she was well prepared when she went to the concert. Mr Menuhin was indeed the best candidate to take on the job.

In 1988, when I was vice president of Beijing University, I led a three-man delegation to New Delhi, the capital of India. Indira Gandhi had been assassinated, and her son, Rajiv Gandhi, had succeeded her as prime minister of India. Initially, Rajiv didn't want to enter politics, but his mother's sudden death pushed him onto the political stage. But this event happened to provide several chances for members of two generations of the Zhou family and members of three generations of the Nehru family to meet. Rajiv Gandhi was preparing for his China trip. He wanted to exchange some ideas with Chinese scholars, so he invited me to speak with him. He said that there were astonishing similarities between India and China, both historically and in the present day. Both were developing countries with a huge population; both had ancient civilisations that had made technological inventions; both had vast rural areas where conditions were comparatively backward but which were still populated by large numbers of people; both were seeking peace and development. However, the relationship between the two countries was difficult, and he didn't know what he could do to improve it. Therefore, he wanted to hear what my opinion was.

There had been a little episode before our meeting. As India was celebrating the centennial of Nehru's birth, many internationally noted

Zhou Erliu with the students of the Chinese language department, Nehru University, India.

figures went to India for the occasion. Personalities from all walks of life were saying that the Panchsheel (or the Five Principles of Peaceful Coexistence) had been invented by Nehru. Sternly but politely, I pointed out to Rajiv Gandhi that it was Premier Zhou Enlai who had first put forward the Five Principles, and that after winning support from prime ministers Nehru of India and U Nu of Burma, they jointly initiated the Five Principles, which was a genuine historical achievement. The Five Principles had been accepted as the general requirements for international exchanges. It is possible that young officers from the Indian foreign ministry did not know about this piece of history, and thus the publicity materials they produced could have misled the public. I hoped the Indian side would be able to do something to clarify the facts. At once, Rajiv Gandhi revealed his position on the issue, and soon a senior officer from the Indian foreign ministry apologised to me, saying that he was too young to know the historical details and that he was happy to withdraw the publicity materials. Because of this episode, whenever Rajiv received me later on, our talks generally went on pleasantly. I said: "It suits the two peoples' aspiration to develop Sino-Indian relations to keep following the Five Principles jointly initiated by China, India and Burma to deal with the problems we are facing today. All difficulties can be overcome." He readily agreed with what I said. In December of that same year, he visited China. Deng Xiaoping and Li Peng (the Chinese prime minister) had given a positive appraisal of Rajiv's visit to China.

Having gone through three prime ministers, three generations and different stages in development, we returned to the Five Principles in seeking solutions to the problems between China and India. This is proof that the Five Principles are just and full of vitality. They are also easily put into practice and are able to withstand the test of history.

During his visit to China, Rajiv Gandhi accepted my suggestions, and on all occasions he would openly express his wish that India would follow the Five Principles. In front of the Chinese people, he showed his good faith in the improvement of relations between India and China. Consequently, he was extensively well received in China and he ended his visit satisfactorily. Zhou Enlai's philosophy of 'seeking common ground while reserving differences', as well as its practical application, had once again been recognised and accepted internationally. The Five Principles, put forward under the guidance of the ideology, are not only a breakthrough in diplomatic theory, but an immortal contribution of Premier Zhou's to the peaceful development of human history. China and India have experienced twists and turns in their relationship, but in the end, India accepted and was ready to pursue the Five Principles of Peaceful Coexistence, which once again proved the significance of Premier Zhou's historical contribution. This contribution does not just belong to China and India, but to the whole world and all of humanity.

Although history moves forward unceasingly, the Five Principles will still remain standing. They were not only of guiding significance in the past, but are so in the present day and will be in the future. I remember Deng Xiaoping and some other Chinese leaders saying that after a trial of decades, the Five Principles seemed to have become universally applicable guiding principles. People will fully agree with this correct appraisal.

3. The Often-Told Tale of Joseph Needham and Lu Guizhen

3.1 How Did Joseph Needham 'Discover' China?

Joseph Needham was a British scientist. His masterpiece, *Science and Civilisation in China* — *SCC* for short — systematically introduced ancient Chinese achievements in science and technology to the world for the first time in history, emphasising the great contributions the Chinese nation had made to the whole world. Premier Zhou had highly praised Needham for his book, feeling that it had filled in the gaps in Chinese history. He also called the association between Needham and Ms Lu Guizhen a story that was on everyone's lips.

Needham greatly revered Laozi (Li Er, author of *Tao Te Ching*), so he chose Li as his Chinese surname and Yuese as his Chinese name. He was also known as Danyao and Shisu Daoren. He was very Chinese.

Needham was born in London on 9 December 1900, and he died in March 1995. His father was an anaesthetist. As he wanted to be a doctor, he studied physiology, anatomy and zoology at Cambridge University. After graduation, he accepted his tutor's suggestion to work in the laboratory of

Frederick Gowland Hopkins, who had won a Nobel Prize in Physiology or Medicine. He then won a scholarship to study biochemistry, specialising in embryology and morphogenesis, and discovered that the chemical process in a growing egg was like a "giant chemical plant". He received a doctorate degree and became a embryologist. At a young age, he was elected to receive a fellowship at Gonville and Caius College, Cambridge.

Needham married Dr Dorothy Moyle in 1924. His three-volume work *Chemical Embryology* was published in 1931 and established a new field of study. Dorothy was four years senior to Needham, and also a biochemist. In 1941, Needham was elected as a fellow of the Royal Society, the highest honour in English scientific circles, as was Dorothy, in 1948. They became the first husband and wife to be elected, and the couple enjoyed great prestige internationally.

In 1937, three young Chinese scientists (Ms Lu Guizhen among them) came to Cambridge for graduate school (one of them was under Needham's tutelage). They aroused Needham's interest in studying the Chinese language and culture. From 1942 to 1946, under the Royal Society's direction, Needham was director of the Sino-British Science Cooperation Office. He was also a scientific counsellor at the British embassy in Chongqing. During this period, he had a taste of the history of China and her achievements in all cultural aspects. Thus, an idea had formed in his mind that he would spend his lifetime writing a book about *science and civilisation in China*. When China was isolated, he was an indispensable link between Western and Chinese scientists in cooperation and exchanges. He also provided help to the areas controlled by the communists. In 1946, he was sent to France to be the first head of UNESCO's Natural Science Sector in Paris. He resigned two years later and returned to Gonville & Caius College, where he resumed his fellowship, and from 1966 to 1976 he was Head of College. From 1948, when he proposed to the Cambridge Press to write a book on science and civilisation in China, to his retirement in 1990, he devoted his energy to the history of Chinese scientific developments.

While writing this series, he studied 5,500 different Chinese and Japanese books, 4,000 in Western languages and 25,000 theses, pamphlets and photocopies. Though he had several assistants, he collected the data and compiled the index and bibliography himself. To obtain materials firsthand, he travelled all around China, investigating cultural relics and historical sites and visiting scientific and educational establishments, where he obtained much-needed supplies. The *Science and Civilisation in China* series has received widespread acclaim and has been translated in full into Chinese, Japanese, French, Italian and Spanish. Although he had achieved great success academically, due to his pro-China stance, the relevant English institutes conferred no academic title on him. But several decades later, in the 1980s, when he was 80 years old, he had become the scientist in possession of the most academic titles in the world. The related British institution awarded Needham the title of Doctor of Literature after Sino-Anglo relations had steadily begun to improve.

3.2. Lu Guizhen Gains Support from Zhou Enlai

In 1981, a grand ceremony was held in England to celebrate the 80th anniversary of Needham's birth. Many noted Chinese scholars attended, and so did my wife and I. There, I saw painters Wu Zuoren and Fang Zhaolin; Hong Qian, professor of philosophy at Beijing University; and Tian Rukang, professor of sociology at Fudan University. They had no interpreters with them, so our arrival made them very happy; thus, I became their simultaneous interpreter.

I also gave a speech at the ceremony, highly praising Joseph Needham's academic achievements. I used the words "uniquely qualified" to describe his research on the history of science and technology in China. I gave three reasons to support this designation: to undertake work of this scope over such a large span of space and time, one must have mastered all-round skills in science, technology and culture; one must have an intensive interest in the ancient Chinese civilisation; and one must be an extremely accomplished scholar of classical Chinese and English. Dr Needham was probably the only man who incorporated all three qualifications in a single person.

Everyone applauded after my speech. Needham and the representatives from the Chinese Academy of Sciences were happy with what I had said. For the first time, I discovered what an important role my limited English could play on such an occasion. An official from the British Foreign Ministry turned to his child, who he had brought with him, and said: "Zhou's speech was so good; could you do the same?"

1981, in front of the East Asian History of Science Library, Cambridge. From left to right: Joseph Needham, Fang Zhaolin, Lu Guizhen, Wu Zuoren and Zhou Erliu.

In the meantime, in China, it was being disputed whether the Chinese should employ Needham as an emeritus professor. Some were against the idea, but we followed the teachings of Premier Zhou and expressed our support for it. In 1983, with the cooperation of the Chinese Embassy in the UK, the China science and technology commission and the Chinese Academy of Sciences awarded Needham the first prize for natural science and made him emeritus professor of the Chinese Academy of Sciences' postgraduate department, as well as an honourable doctor of the Chinese Academy of Social Sciences. Needham was an honest man; he had once been a scholar and a diplomat, and he finally ended up being an eminently well-known man who owned the most academic titles in the world. For the last few decades, up until he was 80 years old, he would drive to his library to work every day. He did not only verify the advances in science and technology that had occurred in ancient China, but also commented on their contributions to world civilisation.

Ms Lu Guizhen had played a decisive role both by looking after Needham and collaborating with him on *Science and Civilisation in China*. In Needham's own words, she was the "inspiration and the driving force" behind this earth-shattering project. Lu was slight of stature, but her eyes were extremely bright. She was a scholar from Nanjing whose ancestors came from Hubei. She had been dean of a health research institute of the UN, and had been Needham's lifelong partner in writing *Science and Civilisation in China*. Needham's wife, Dorothy Moyle, was confined to a wheelchair due to illness, so Lu also helped Needham to look after Dorothy. The three of them formed a very special, fraternal, loving family. As Lu had a good income from her original job, she bought a house in Paris. The shares of a food company she had bought on the stock market had given her a stable income. But she was determined to sell her house in Paris and move to Cambridge to continue to support Needham and Dorothy financially. She looked after Dorothy while helping with Needham's research. Besides the money she had left after selling her house in Paris and her shares in the food company, she also accepted Premier Zhou's suggestion to assist Needham by going to Hong Kong to raise funds and get to know the people. Her efforts had allowed the research for the book to go on uninterrupted for several decades.

As an unmarried Chinese woman, Lu felt awkward in this situation. Though she had bought herself a house in Cambridge, others always regarded her and Needham as a couple. People forgot that Needham had a wife, Dorothy, who was frequently ill. Thus, Lu wanted to go back to China. She wrote to Premier Zhou, who eventually persuaded her to stay in England. Premier Zhou thought the cooperation between the three of them would make a brilliant and everlasting contribution that could be shared by all Chinese people, as well as people around the world. Just as the premier had said, their long-term fellowship and cooperation won Needham, Dorothy and Lu Guizhen acclaim, and theirs became an often-told tale in China and other parts of the world until they died, one after the other.

Lu Guizhen suffered from lung cancer, but she was a strong-willed woman, looking after two bigger-bodied people. In 1987, Dorothy, who had been bedridden for many years, died. On 15 September 1989, Needham and Lu married in the chapel of Gonville & Caisu College, Cambridge University. On that day, they had known each other for 52 years. At the wedding, Needham said: "Marrying a Chinese woman has proved my true love of Chinese culture." In November 1991, Lu Guizhen died of her illness in Cambridge. She was an outstanding English and Chinese female scholar who had become part of an unconventional family. With the care and support of premier Zhou, Needham and Lu broke away from common customs and pursued a special and everlasting international cooperation.

3.3. I'll Always Remember Them with Deep Affection

When I worked for the Chinese Embassy in the UK, I often went to see Needham, Dorothy and Lu because we were good friends. They lived in Cambridge and rarely came to London because of their age. In 1984, I finished my term at the embassy. They made an effort to come to London to attend my farewell dinner party, which moved me very much. In the

Zhou Erliu with Joseph Needham.

past, whenever I went to see them, they would tell me that they missed Premier Zhou very much and that they had been touched by his charming personality. Needham said that his spiritual strength for this project had been inseparable from the support of many Chinese friends, who Zhou Enlai represented. He said that if it hadn't been for the premier's support, this grand project would have been cut off halfway through. Every time Needham went to China to visit experts or to look up technical literature, he received support from Premier Zhou. When I was at his house, I saw Needham, in his eighties, studying the *Huo Long Jin* ('Fire Dragon Scriptures') of the Ming dynasty. He concluded that China had been the first country to invent the rocket. These were developed during the Song dynasty, but only for peaceful usage, such as the setting off of fireworks.

According to Needham, when the project was completed, the *Science and Civilisation in China* series would have seven volumes in 34 to 35 parts. Each part has a dedication, and the section entitled *Military Technology: The Gunpowder Epic* was dedicated to Zhou Enlai: "To the memory of Zhou Enlai, 1898-1976, leader of the Nanchang uprising in 1927, premier

Lu Guizhen, Wang Zhangli and Joseph Needham.

of the People's Republic of China, 1949-1976, the unswerving inspiration of the project, this volume is dedicated."

Originally, Needham thought that I was the relative of a high official and that I might not be able to undertake academic research. But after I had helped him to organise the material, he found out that I could do it both in Chinese and English. Also, I had a wide range of knowledge, so he hoped that I would become director of the East Asian History of Science Library in Cambridge. But in China, at the time, the government arranged people's jobs, and an individual could not select their own employment. So after I returned to China, I was unable to carry on with this project, which I regretted very much. Later, Needham asked painter Fang Zhaolin to find me in Beijing and to pass on his regards to me, which made me feel very touched. As part of the younger generation, I'll forever remember these special three people who formed one family and their precious friendship with Zhou Enlai. Until today, I have a collection of recordings of Needham singing folk songs in the Sichuan dialect. It is a reminder for me that the friendship between Needham and myself will last forever.

4. Dr Runcie, the Archbishop of Canterbury, Visits China for the First Time

The Archbishop of Canterbury is the most important leader of the Anglican Church of England. Being of the utmost importance among the numerous sects of the Christian religion, the Archbishop of Canterbury has an influence on both English and international communities.

Dr Runcie was Archbishop of Canterbury from the 1980s to the 1990s. Having studied history at Oxford University, he was also a scholar, acquainted with knowledge of the countries of the world and their histories. Runcie was born and spent his early life in the seaside city of Liverpool, where many Chinese men worked in the surrounding docks. He had witnessed the hard work as well as the hardships of these Chinese, who had left a good impression on him. He also became aware of the earth-shaking changes that took place after the founding of new China, as well as the rapid progress on all levels in the country. After comparing the present with the past, he felt that new China's achievements had not come about easily, so he understood and sympathised with China. He was willing to visit China to learn more about her and to make friends, as well as to improve the work in Christian churches in the country. However, in those days, his religious status made it hard for him to visit China.

The book presented to Zhou Erliu by the Archbishop of Canterbury, Dr Runcie.

Ding Guangxun, the Archbishop of China, then exchanged views with Dr Runcie. Ding expressed his wish for the two archbishops to visit each other's countries. But Dr Runcie was very worried. To avoid putting himself in a passive position, he didn't want his intention of going to China to be exposed ahead of time. For this reason, he secretly received me and my wife in Lambeth Palace, the Archbishop of Canterbury's seat in London. He told us about his thoughts and worries, and asked me to be the liaison, or a "[Henry] Kissinger", between him and the Chinese government. He wanted the Chinese side to arrange a secret visit to China for him. We told him that we were happy to help, but that organizing a visit, secret or not, was beyond our authority. He then talked about his status and viewpoints, which made us feel that he was open-minded and friendly towards China, taking a different attitude than he did to the Vatican.

But due to carelessness on the side of the British, his secret visit to China was quickly exposed to the public through the media. He summoned me for an urgent meeting, requesting me to help change it to an open visit in the hope that the Chinese government would support it, but still worried whether or not he would receive support from the British public.

I couldn't help thinking that in the 1970s, during President Richard Nixon's visit to China, when discussing the withdrawal of American troops

The Archbishop of Canterbury, Dr Runcie, with Zhou Erliu and Wang Zhangli.

from a certain area, the Americans repeatedly stressed that if they were to withdraw, other foreign forces would come in and replace them. Qi Ba convinced the Americans with reason. He used China as an example, saying that after the foreign powers had left China, the Chinese people filled in the gap, allowing no other foreign forces to enter. Another example was that after the Americans had driven away the British colonial powers and won their independence, it was the American people who moved in, making the US a no man's land for any other foreign forces to get involved. I was inspired by this idea of using one's own history to prove that problems could be solved, so I used English religious history, particularly the formation and development of the English state religion, as an example to show Dr Runcie that English Christian churches already exercised autonomy and self-support, and that the Church of England selected its own archbishops. All these practices were acknowledged both internationally and in English society. What China was practicing was the same policy as the English one.

After I had spoken, Dr Runcie almost struck the table in happiness. He said: "Excellent. We can only change people's minds by reasoning; so, let us use the historical facts to convince them." Soon Dr Runcie realised his long-cherished wish of visiting China, accompanied by Terry Whyte, his assistant in dealing with foreign affairs, who was almost 2m tall and who was very popular internationally. He was received by Archbishop Ding Guangxun and many Chinese state leaders. In his speech, his support for the Chinese religious policy (to remain independent from the Vatican, support itself and select her own archbishop) was warmly received by the Chinese public. His visit was a success, cleared away all obstacles and provided a successful example for future visits to China by his successors, as well as other senior religious persons. In view of this, I feel that besides learning from Qi Ba's noble spirit, which originated from his moral integrity, it is also valuable to put what we've learnt into practice. I believe that the formation of Qi Ba's charming character was also rooted in being the same on the outside and the inside, practicing what he preached, making an example of himself, and even in his intelligence and ability to convince people by reasoning, by using his sense of humour, or by speaking in a mild tone.

5. My Joint Research with Professor Fei Xiaotong

Fei Xiaotong was born on 2 November 1910 in the village of Jiangchun, Wujiang county, Jiangsu province. He died on 24 April 2005 in Beijing. Before his death, he had been vice chairman of the standing committee of the NPC, vice president of the CPPCC, vice chairman of the standing committee of the China Democratic League, and president of the China Sociology Association.

In 1957, he wrote an article entitled *Early Spring Weather for the Intellectuals*, in which he said: "Last January [1956], Premier Zhou's report about the intellectuals was like spring thunder, followed by the gentle breeze of contention of a hundred schools of thoughts, all the intellectuals' positive factors having been mobilised... The weather in early spring is rather changeable, and of course spring is always the most difficult season. When I took a closer look, the problems I saw were not few." Because of this article, he was called a rightist, a label he wasn't rid of until 1959, when Qi Ba and some other leaders defended him.

In 1981, Professor Fei was rewarded the Huxley Memorial Medal by the Royal Anthropological Institute of Great Britain and Ireland. My wife and I supervised his award ceremony, and we have been in close contact with each other ever since.

5.1. Mr Fei Invites Me to Work on the Seventh Five-Year Plan Research Project

I returned to China from the UK at the end of 1984. There were several job opportunities available for me: president of a Chinese delegation to a certain UN organisation in Europe. deputy mayor responsible for foreign affairs of a special (economic) zone in south China, or mayor of an important industrial city in north China. But because my parents, parents-in-law and children all lived in Shanghai, I requested to return to Shanghai to work. The deputy mayor of Shanghai, Ruan Chongwu, and the minister of the Shanghai organisation ministry, Zeng Qinghong, received me. They offered me both the position of president of the Bank of Communications and of dean of the SASS and concurrently vice chairperson of the Shanghai Association for Friendship for Foreign Countries. I chose the SASS.

In early 1985, the secretary general of the Shanghai municipal communist party committee (SMCPC) and the minister of the organisation department held a welcome meeting for me. About 20 people attended, the majority of whom were noted figures in the culture and education sectors. They included the director of the Shanghai foreign affairs office; the president of Fudan University, Su Buqing; the dean of the Shanghai Conservatory of Music, Ding Shande; the dean of the Shanghai Film Studio, Xu Sangchu, and others. Minister Zeng Qinghong had read my file and, knowing that I had not mentioned my relationship with Premier Zhou Enlai, realised that it was not easy for me. He was also surprised that so many famous people had come to welcome me. After the meeting ended, Director Ma of the culture bureau invited me and my wife to his home to have a chat. The minister of the municipal publicity department, Chen Yi, also went with his wife. They all knew Qi Ma very well, and also knew something about me. They hoped that I would stay in Shanghai permanently to work.

I wanted to work at the SASS very much. The dean, Zhang Zhongli,

Acting on the Teachings of the Deceased Qi Ba

and the party secretary, Hong Zhe, received me. Hong Zhe pushed me to report for duty as soon as possible by talking to a colleague of mine in the foreign ministry. Mr Zhang was also happy that I was to succeed him as dean of the SASS. He came to Beijing three times to invite me to go to Shanghai. Meanwhile, the SMCPC had allocated me an apartment. It seemed as if everything was ready for me to start working at the SASS, when I was suddenly asked to return to Beijing and take the position of vice chairperson of the CPAFFC. I was in shock, and refused to go. Because Qi Ma was the honourable chairperson of the CPAFFC, I was sure she would disagree with the arrangement. But the OD responded that it was an organisational decision that had been approved by the two vice premiers, Wu Xueqian and Ji Pengfei. The OD insisted that I withdraw my files from Shanghai and bring them back to Beijing. But as I expected, after I returned to Beijing, Qi Ma told me that I take any other job, but not that of the vice chairperson of the CPAFFC.

Prompted by these circumstances, Mr Fei came to me. He was a man of my father's generation and came from Wujiang county; I had done some

Fei Xiaotong and Zhou Erliu.

social research there, so we shared a common language. He told me that Hu Qiaomu (Mao Zedong's secretary) had talked to him about the fact that because Stalin regarded sociology as pseudoscience, the Soviet Union had stopped running their sociology courses. We in mainland China followed suit, and terminated our courses, too. Although Taiwan had stopped teaching the course for a while, they had sent students to the US to study the subject; hence, it was easy for Taiwan to reinstate the course.

Afterwards, Deng Xiaoping told Hu Qiaomu that we should re-establish sociology and anthropology in China. Hu then recommended Fei Xiaotong to take this job, which was made the key research project of the seventh five-year plan. Mr Fei was in charge of this project and concurrently worked as dean of the Research Institute of Sociology of Beijing University. Hu also hoped that Fei would actively take part in international academic activities, making foreign friends and helping foreign scholars to understand China, particularly post-economic reform. Fei was already 73 years old, and as his age did not allow him to take on part-time jobs, he was looking for a successor. He hadn't found a suitable one yet, so he came to me. He climbed

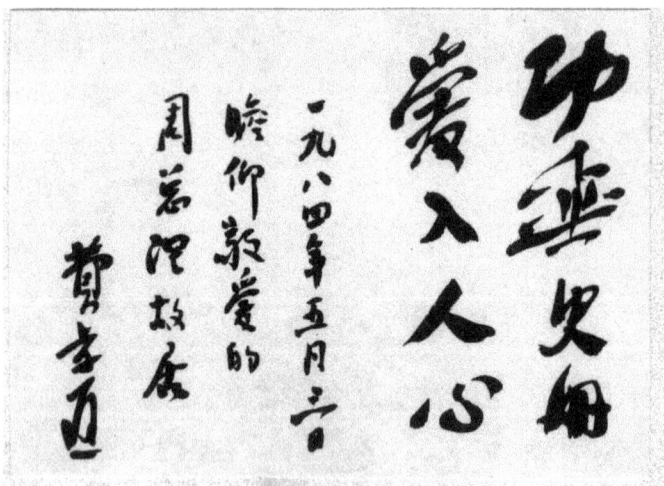

Fei Xiaotong's inscription in Huaian. "The whole world admires you; the broad mass of the people cherishes your memory and loves you. By Fei Xiaotong, when accompanying the former British prime minister James Callaghan to visit the old residence of Zhou Enlai in Huaian on 16 December 1986."

all the steps to my fourth-floor home, which touched me very much. As he was a very kind man and I respected him, I agreed to help him with his project. I was then appointed vice president of Beijing University, and concurrently dean of the Research Institute of Sociology. At the same time, Nankai University was trying to persuade me to become party secretary for the university, but I only accepted Mr Fei's invitation.

5.2. Hu Yaobang Writes "Boldly in Support" on My Report

After I had taken my post at Beijing University, Fei requested me to go to Tokyo to attend an international conference held by the rector of United Nations University. The UNU was not a university, but a UN institution that formed a bridge between the UN and international academic, policy-making and private communities. For the 1985 conference, delegates from 30 countries attended, and they discussed many issues, such as global warming and the rise in sea-levels. Many scientists thought they were indicators of global climate change. The rector of the UNU had followed the economic reforms in China with great interest. He discussed the successful experiences of the reforms with Fei and me, thinking they were of global significance as the majority of the countries in the world were developing countries. The result of our discussion was that with UN support, we set up a team to sum up the initial experiences gleaned from the Chinese economic reforms and do some comparative studies, comparing China to some other developing countries with large populations, such as India in Asia, Brazil in Latin America, South Africa in Africa, Egypt in the Middle East, etc.

When we had returned to China, Fei said to me that some of our research was neither purely anthropology nor sociology; if we carried on like this, we would not even know what we were doing. My view was that from a scientific standpoint, our research should be called 'development studies'. At the conference in Tokyo, I listened to the speeches of delegates from more than 30 countries, so I had come up with some ideas. I told him that though some universities in the West had started teaching the course, development studies was a multi-subject rather than a single-subject course. The aim of the course was to study developing countries. The Western countries had a sense of early warning: for example, the British had studied the Chinese textile industry, because it is a labour-intensive industry. Developing countries have labour forces, but are short of capital and technology. The textile industry can meet domestic demand and can also enter the international market. However, we didn't have a course like that in our universities, so I suggested that we first set up a centre for development studies.

Later, I wrote a report to the Central Committee in Fei's name, on which Hu Yaobang wrote: "Boldly in support." The two vice premiers also signed their names. The funding for the centre came directly from the finance ministry. The leaders of the State Council wanted the centre to be led by the government, but Fei wanted it under the leadership of the UFWD. However, the UFWD thought the centre's work was academic, which was beyond their management. As Fei had once been director of Beijing University's department of sociology, we decided the centre would be attached to Beijing University, externally calling it the Centre for Sociological Research and Development Studies of China. I was director of the centre for six years, while Fei worked as a consultant. I led the studies on coordinating development in China's urban and rural areas, a key research project of the state. Later, it was said that the successive leaders of Beijing University did not regard the centre as a necessity, nor could they find a director who was willing to take on the job. As such, the centre was closed down. More information about this will be provided later in this book.

5.3. Professor Fei Carries On with the Development Studies Programme throughout His Later Years

During the years I worked with Fei, he hoped that I would be able to concentrate on academic research. I respected his opinion. At the time, we had no title for our project, so I named it *Research on China's Coordinated Urban-Rural Development*. The CASS, who would examine and approve the project, also liked this title. In many of his articles, Fei used the phrase *mo shi* ('model'), but I disagreed with him on this. To me, 'model' meant people's habitual wording for 'accepted through common practice' — the implication, that we had set an example, could easily become rigid. I thought it should be *gou xing* ('configuration'), a word common in natural science education, which means objective existence and formation that can be measured. So, I proposed that the research should be interdisciplinary, and that by combining our knowledge of Chinese national conditions, we should be able to study how a developing country could become a middle-level developed country. This was my understanding of China's development at the time. Development as a learning endeavour emphasises coordination, so in this respect, I summarised the coordination between the following fields: politics, economics, society, culture and education, science and technology, and environment. The growth in these six fields must be coordinated while recognising the objective reality, the contradictory development of the subjective and objective, but also the fact that society is making progress despite contradictions. Later, a central party leader mentioned a similar view to mine in his speech.

A development of this kind should be divided into three phases. The first phase is starting up: beginning the reform in the countryside and developing the rural industries to create jobs for the surplus labour force, turning agriculture into industry through diversity. At this stage, the government is able to accumulate capital, train workers and open markets. I then propose the following policy: keeping in line with local conditions; retaining diversity; making adjustments according to changing circumstances; and seizing the opportune moment. In the early stages of economic reform, it was a certainty that the economic and cultural development would be uneven in different regions. Thus, we must attach importance to local realities and avoid striving to keep up with each other or copying indiscriminately, instead keeping pace with the times and making appropriate adjustments. The second phase would be for expansion, and finally, the reform would enter a relatively mature stage.

Internationally, a substantial number of people paid attention to my proposals. For example, various professors from the economics department of the University of California in the US approved of my policy and the three-phase theory. In 1991, George Washington University sent me a letter of appointment, inviting me over to do research on trends in Chinese economic development. After I finished, they would recommend me to the top 10 American universities. Despite Nankai University having agreed, I wanted to spend more time on my Zhou Enlai studies, so the George Washington University had to wait for two years.

I cooperated with Fei for six years and mainly focused on all-round studies of rural industrialisation in China. Studies about small towns, initiated by Fei, are well known both in China and abroad.

5.4. Mr Fei, Huan Xiang and I Discuss the Wenzhou model

Soon, Mr Fei, Huan Xiang and I went to Wenzhou via Hangzhou to do a survey. (Huan Xiang [1909-1989] was born in Zunyi, Guizhou province. He was once assistant to the Chinese foreign minister, party secretary, and vice president as well as a consultant of the Chinese Academy of Sciences.) The chief of staff of a publishing house, who was a member of the China Democratic League, also went.

When we arrived in Wenzhou, we saw that all the locals lived in Western-style buildings. The rooms upstairs were for people and goods, while all the ground floors were shops or workshops. They sold everything from electronic appliances to garments, and particularly buttons. Wenzhou was not far from Taiwan. Land was scarce in the region, but the population was large. The area was hilly, and several counties were impoverished and had to be subsidised by the state. However, the local people had a head for business. For example, they had begun selling Qingtian stone to France several hundred years ago. Before the economic reforms, the whole country wore dull garments with dull buttons; the people in Wenzhou spotted a commercial opportunity and raised funds to purchase small factories. By paying handsomely for technical staff, they slowly built up a sizeable button market in China and even abroad.

The economy in Wenzhou developed very fast, but many problems emerged in the early stages due to lack of a strong management team. Issues included the production of fake and shoddy goods, child labour, smuggling by sea, underground finance practices, and confiscation of the land for the building of graveyards (for this purpose, the lower land near the roads had all been taken). In one word: chaos. When we were in Wenzhou, we stayed in village hostels, and on our way to visit the local families we saw many scenes like these. Furthermore, it was said that the local people were of old imbued with capitalist thinking. Huan Xiang, a deputy to the NPC, thought that Wenzhou was a typical example of capitalism, and he was even thinking about reporting it to the centre after he returned to Beijing. Fei quite agreed with Huan's view, but felt that he must be cautious before making clear what his stand on the issue was, because he was not an ordinary scholar. So, he came to me to discuss the matter. He was very polite, saying that he had been engaged in rural studies for many years, but knew little about industry. Although he had promoted the development of small towns as well as rural industries, he could not make any real proposals. Although Huan's view had reflected the reality, drawing a conclusion was a grave responsibility, so he hoped that we would not make our judgement based on isolated incidents, and would let our experiences be used by future generations for reference. He also said that he had listened to the premier's teachings for many years while I had been to many places in China and abroad, so he wanted me to think of a proper formula.

I thought it over and decided to use the principle of 'small goods, big market', which formed the basis of the Wenzhou model. First, the economic reforms needed to solve three problems: the surplus labour, the people's demand for daily life in towns and in the country, and selling the product to international markets. Of course, many of the existing social problems should not be ignored, but under the correct guidance of the party and the government, with united wisdom and strength and by way of practice, the local people would be able to solve those problems.

After considering my proposal, Fei accepted, as did Huan. Huan also said that he originally thought that the children of the high officials could not do much practical work, so my case proved that he had been prejudiced about the matter. Later, he asked me to work at his centre for strategic studies.

There was an episode during our trip to Wenzhou. After we arrived in Hangzhou, I was in my hotel room writing an article; Fei and Huan were out. Suddenly, I heard some unusual noises. I ran out to have a look and saw that the director of the publishing house had collapsed after having a heart attack. I hurried to find somebody to help him and send him to hospital; he survived, but he couldn't go with us to Wenzhou. When we returned to Hangzhou from Wenzhou, he was out of hospital. One day, he asked me about our trip, and I told him what we had seen and thought. He began writing an article at once. The main gist was that the intrinsic structure of the Wenzhou model was based on small commodities, but a big market. After Fei read the article, he quickly came to see me because he thought it was me who had first put forward the formula of 'small commodities, big market', which received his approval and Huan's support. "I should not take credit for other people's ideas," he said, rather emotionally.

5.5. "We Do Well When We Work on Things in Tandem"

Mr Fei frequently travelled around to give speeches. The leaders of the local government often asked him for inscriptions, which he would write while on the train or in the sky. At times, somebody else would come and ask for one, and he always felt uneasy when seeing them waiting. Under such circumstances, he would come to me for help. Once, I wrote down: "*Bai gong zhi xiang, qian ping wan yang*" (literally 'home to hundreds of industries, thousands of assortments of goods'). He was very happy, saying that I had saved him. He said: "This is good. It mentions either the structure of the production or people's subjective initiatives, and it also verifies your consistent view that economics must integrate with sociology, to improve and perfect the practical work and to benefit the populace."

In Hangzhou, we reunited with the director of the publishing house and we all returned to Beijing. To express his gratitude for my hard work in Wenzhou, Fei wrote two poems for me:

> *The lakeside willows are light green,*
> *Hangzhou is no less beautiful than usual.*
> *Clouds cover the tomb of Su Xiaoxiao,*
> *Gone are the sweet voices of 20 years.*
> *Thousand miles away flew the seagulls,*
> *Mount Tiantai and Mount Yandang escorted my departure.*
> *Please show kindness to the ambitions of scholars,*
> *Kaffir lilies are in bloom at parting.*

In March 1986, I went to Wenzhou with comrade Erliu. We passed Hangzhou, where I composed two poems to Erliu as a souvenir. Fei Xiaotong.

Acting on the Teachings of the Deceased Qi Ba

Fei compared the three of us, representing two generations, to kaffir lilies, because he felt that we were all patriots.

From 8 to 23 June 1986, Fei accompanied Hu Yaobang while visiting England, France, Germany and Italy. He needed to give speeches in all these countries. Two manuscripts written in English had been prepared for him, but he liked neither of them. The one written in Hong Kong was too colloquial and the grammar was not correct, while the one written by Beijing University was too formal, unfit for a speech. Therefore, he came to me, asking me to write a speech for him. I got it done within a short time after some hard work. He was very happy with my English speech and he read it in three out of four countries, while the fourth country published it in print. When he returned to China, he was beaming with joy. "Very successful," he said to me. Fei's daughter came along on the trip, and she later told me that the reactions to her father's speeches had all been very good. Fei was very happy with my assistance, and he would say to me: "Let's answer the call of Premier Zhou and do what little we can to realise the four modernisations as soon as possible," or, "We are good friends despite of the great age difference between us." Later, he would often use the scripts I wrote for him for his speeches, or allow me to arrange plans for trips abroad or to design ceremonies for receiving foreign guests. Thus, he jokingly said to me: "We do well when we work on things in tandem!"

During these six years, I chaired seminars in Hunan, Shaanxi, Jiangsu and Zhejiang provinces. These seminars were not small in size, and attended by many representatives from these provinces. In 1994, the fruit of our project, *Research on Coordinated Urban-Rural Development*, was published. I truthfully presented my views, which I knew might not be the most practical, in this book. During our previous discussions, it turned out that Fei and even myself didn't agree with some of these views, so Fei mildly and indirectly pointed this out in the introduction. I was not happy with this book at all. Later, Oxford University Press published the second edition of the book, which I haven't seen with my own eyes. Anyway, I haven't seen many of the books published in my name, nor do I have the energy to safeguard my legal rights and interests.

I gratefully admired Mr Fei for his lifelong academic contributions as well as his devotion to doing research on the Chinese countryside. *Fifty Years of the Village*, which was compiled from the results of field research undertaken during the period of our cooperation, has had a great influence in both China and abroad. It opened another gate for Westerners to understand China. In his own style, Fei had written beautiful masterpieces, such as *Peasant Life in China*. Our cooperation is memorable, and I sincerely hope that my compatriots will pay attention to the studies on development that have been supported by Fei, and pursue them further.

Mr Fei cherished the memory of Premier Zhou. He had a great esteem for the premier and had even visited his birth place, Huaian, three times. In 1986, with the support of central leaders such as Hu Yaobang and my assistance, he invited the former British prime minister Mr Callaghan to come to Huaian. Fei, a most distinguished scholar and chairman of the China Democratic League, expressed his gratitude to Zhou Enlai for his efforts to rehabilitate the Chinese intellectuals in a particular way. In Huaian, Fei praised me in front of the researchers who were studying Zhou Enlai's thoughts, telling them that I ought to be consulted when it came to the history of the Zhou clan. He also told them that I was practical and dared to speak my mind, hence my taking part in the research would ensure that the historical facts were true and reliable. I knew that his praise of me, as well as his hope for and trust in me, came from his esteem for Premier Zhou Enlai. I was deeply grateful for being understood and treated well by him.

6. Former British Prime Minister James Callaghan Visits Huaian

6.1. Fei Xiaotong Meets Mr Callaghan by Chance

Professor Fei Xiaotong was a member of the delegation that accompanied the general secretary of the CPC, Hu Yaobang, on his visit to the UK, West Germany, France and Italy in 1986. Before he left China, he requested me to write his speech in English, the main gist of which was the development of the village of Jiangchun over the last 50 years. Fei was very happy when his speech was well received by audiences in all four countries.

The first stop on the trip was England. At Chatham House, London, Hu

Yaobang gave his speech, entitled *Understanding the Key of the Future Trends in China*, for an audience that included the former leader of the British Labour Party, as well as a former British prime minister, James Callaghan, who also chaired the seminar. Thus, Fei met Callaghan, and they got on well with each other. When Mrs Thatcher, the British prime minister and leader of the British Conservative Party, saw them sitting together, she said, jokingly: "It seems you two are sitting in the same long chair." Hu Yaobang laughed out loud after he heard her remarks.

James Callaghan served as prime minister of the UK from 1976 to 1979. He was born into an ordinary English family in 1912. His father died when Callaghan was nine years old. After he graduated from secondary school at the age of 16, he went to work as a clerk for the inland revenue department. He didn't receive any higher education, but, relying on his intelligence as well as his own efforts, he became the most powerful man in the UK. In addition, he was the only person who had served as prime minister, chancellor of the exchequer, secretary of state for foreign and commonwealth affairs as well as home secretary: a political idol who had started from nothing.

Fei had studied at the London School of Economics, so when he heard Mrs Thatcher's remarks, he assumed that she meant Callaghan and he had identical ideological views; also, he mistook Callaghan for an alumnus of the LSE. Hence, he hinted to Callaghan that he might invite him to visit China. In fact, they were engaged in animated conversation on certain topics, and Fei had given Callaghan the English translation of *Economics in Small Towns*. When he returned to China, Fei began the process of inviting 'alumnus' James Callaghan to visit China. The Chinese foreign ministry took the matter seriously, but after running several checks, they found that Callaghan had never been to university and had taken no senior post in the British government after being defeated by Margaret Thatcher in the general election; he had only served as non-executive director of a bank. Fei was caught in a dilemma, so he came to me for help. I understood relatively more about the British than he did, so, taking the actual conditions into account, I drafted a report that Fei then presented to the centre for approval. I also came up with an idea: I told Fei that he could communicate with Callaghan to see if he wanted to come to China and visit Huaian, the hometown of Zhou Enlai. After making contact with him, I learnt that Callaghan was happy to go to Huaian, so I felt sure of the matter. After discussing it with Fei, I wrote an invitation for him in English and invited Callaghan to visit China at his convenience; Huaian would be the second city he was to visit after Beijing. Initially, because Callaghan was no longer prime minister, the relevant department in China didn't hold out any hope for his being permitted to come to China. But unexpectedly for them, the British conservative government soon granted him permission and even equipped Callaghan with security guards for the trip. I believe Huaian may have played a key role in the success of inviting Callaghan to China. It helped that Zhou Enlai enjoyed some prestige and influence in the British Conservative Party, as well as with several senior civil servants, when they made the decision to grant Callaghan permission.

6.2. I Set Out to Huaian in Advance to Make Arrangements

After Callaghan's China trip had been given the green light, Fei invited me to join him in accompanying Callaghan. The main host was to be the National Political Consultative Conference. The director of the related NPCC department was to cooperate with Fei and myself. Fei once told the director: "For this reception, do what Zhou Erliu says." But I thought the NPCC was the host, not the foreign ministry, so I said to the director: "You make the arrangements; I am only assisting Fei with some practical things." In the following days, our cooperation went smoothly. The foreign ministry sent Chen Naiqing, a skilled female interpreter, to interpret for Callaghan. Ms Chen had been a young colleague of mine when I worked at the Chinese Embassy in the UK, and we were pleased to work together once more.

Fei asked me to go to Jiangsu in advance to report to the provincial leaders about Callaghan's upcoming visit to Huaian. After I had arrived in Nanjing, the party secretary, the governor and the minister of the UFWD of Jiangsu province received me, which showed that the province was taking Callaghan's visit very seriously. They arranged for a deputy governor, the party secretary and the mayor of Huaiyin to accompany him on his visit. The first party secretary of Jiangsu province said to me: "Huaian is only a county in north Jiangsu; it lacks the proper infrastructure for international exchanges. Callaghan used to be the British prime minister, so his visiting Huaian is unconventional. Such a high-grade visit has set a valuable precedent. Again, we experience the profound influence of Premier Zhou Enlai."

At the time, Huaian was a county under the administration of Huaiyin prefecture, lacking all sorts of assets. By car, it would take six to seven hours or more to get from Nanjing to Huaiyin if road conditions were bad. Then there were the further 15km from Huaiyin to Huaian. Although I was of a younger generation, even I felt tired after this journey. The Jiangsu government also decided that all members of the delegation would stay in the Huaian Hotel, the best in the town. The scenery was rural because it was surrounded by farmland, but the facilities only met the basic standards of an ordinary hostel; even a hot bath was hard to come by.

James Callaghan with Zhou Erliu.

Fei asked me to come up with a style for the reception. Remembering that Fei was noted for being a sociologist and anthropologist, I said to him: "You are a highly qualified intellectual who has entered politics, so the style should reflect the true colours of a scholar, wise and prescient."

He agreed with me. In this respect, he always had faith in me; on many occasions, he said to me: "We do well when we work on things in tandem." Thus, he trusted me to do it and set up no restrictions for me. I thought hard about this reception. In line with Fei's status and characteristics, his welcome speech would be lively, combining solemnity with wit and humour. So, during the welcome banquet, following my script, Fei said: "Chinese is one of the six working languages of the United Nations. As a former British prime minister, I hope you are brave enough to take on the challenge, and say a few Chinese words to us..." Everyone present laughed and at once the atmosphere became cheerful. Callaghan laughed heartily, and said, humorously: "To be able to do that, I need to go to back to school and study harder."

I knew that Fei liked to quote ancient poems, so at their farewell meeting I reminded him to express this interest of his. Thus, he quoted several lines from *For Wang Lun* by Li Bai, the Tang-dynasty poet: "The water of Taohua pond reaches a thousand feet in depth, but still it's not as deep as Wang Lun's feelings when seeing me off." He compared Callaghan to Li Bai and himself to Wang Lun, a comparison that both embodied the friendship between Fei and Callaghan and exhibited the essence of Chinese traditional culture. Originally, he was not sure whether the quote would be appropriate, but the result was unexpectedly good. After Li Bai's two lines had been translated and explained, Callaghan was very excited and greatly admired the exquisiteness and ingenuity of Chinese traditional culture. Callaghan was full of vigour for the duration of their farewell meeting. Afterwards, Fei said to me: "Quoting that poem worked very well."

6.3. Hu Yaobang Gives Callaghan a Courteous Reception

After Hu Yaobang learnt that Callaghan had come to China, he received him like an old friend. The others present were Fei, me, Hu Deping (Hu Yaobang's eldest son) and the interpreter. Hu Deping was the director of the secretariat of the UFWD, a low-key, kind and gentle man. He had made a good impression on me.

As soon as Callaghan saw Hu Yaobang, he said: "Zhou Enlai was the busiest man in the world. I know that you are very busy, too. I am very glad to have received such a warm welcome from you." He then went on: "Internationally, there are people who are sceptical about the Chinese economic reforms. Some are even taking a gloomy view; however, there are also people who think that these economic reforms will certainly succeed, and that the 21st century will belong to the Chinese. I'm a supporter of the latter view." We Chinese who were present were very much moved by his friendly and optimistic words. "Although in the UK, the two opposing parties hold different political views, regarding China, they share the same view on two things: trade with China and the appraisal of Zhou Enlai. Zhou Enlai was a man who understood Western culture. He was good at assimilating foreign cultures while retaining the fine elements of his own culture. Furthermore, he was nurtured by the Huai-Yang culture, which symbolised the strength of the genes of the extraordinary Chinese civilisation."

Callaghan's speech was wide-ranging and the atmosphere was relaxed. He also talked about environmental pollution caused by the improper behaviour of humans. He hoped that China would learn lessons from other countries and not follow the same old disastrous road in the development of her economy. Hu Yaobang showed his appreciation to Callaghan for raising such an important issue concerning humanity and its development. He said: "Solving this problem requires international joint efforts and cooperation. We are confronted with many difficulties. It is not easily done, which means we must take our time to solve this." Callaghan then asked Hu Yaobang: "How are you going to deal with nuclear waste?" "We can't throw it into space, can we?" Hu Yaobang said, jokingly.

Hu Yaobang held Zhou Enlai in great esteem. When he learnt that Callanghan was going to Huaian, he arranged for his son, Hu Deping, to come with us. Considering time restraints and security, Hu Yaobang asked for two helicopters to be sent to Nanjing, which then took the delegation straight to Huaian. Casually, Fei told Callaghan's bodyguard that one helicopter was Hu Yaobang's private helicopter, which made it an exceptional journey.

6.4. "China's Main Architect"

It was very cold in Huaian in December. The day of our flight was an ordinary one. Callaghan and Fei were in one helicopter, while Hu Deping,

Zhu Tonghua, myself and the rest were in the second one. The two helicopters landed safely on the sports ground of the Huaian middle school, which was being used as a temporary helicopter landing area. Huaian was a county-level city that did not have much contact with the outside world, so the citizens were astonished when they saw two helicopters landing. They ran to the sports ground from all directions. They certainly didn't expect a former British prime minister to step out of the helicopter. Indeed, Callaghan was the highest-level foreign visitor ever to come to Huaian, or even north Jiangsu, in the 1980s. The 76-year-old Englishman's visit to Huaian, which was thousands of miles away, excited the local government as well as the common people. On the school's sports ground, they welcomed Callaghan, which was quite moving to witness.

Besides security guards, Callaghan had brought with him a Bengali man and his wife. He was a banker, and it was said that he was the descendant of the founder of Bangladesh. Jokingly, Fei said that he was also the child of a high-level official. The banker had an assistant with him, who was in charge of the Beijing office of their bank. He was a Muslim from Pakistan.

Callaghan and his party were too high in spirit to be bothered by their fatigue. They went straight to visit Zhou Enlai's old home. Callaghan deeply respected and admired Premier Zhou. He spent many hours in the compound, looking at the buildings while asking questions. When he saw Hu Yaobang's inscription — 'an example to the whole party' — he asked me what it meant. I told him: "Although Premier Zhou has died, the whole party must follow his example and serve the people with all their hearts." "This allows me to see the relations between the former leaders and their successors. Secretary Hu has revealed the true voices of the Chinese people," Callaghan said.

The governor of Jiangsu, Ms Gu Xiulian, and the mayor of Huaiyin, Ms Xu Yan, were female leaders. Jokingly, Callaghan said: "It's not a lie that the Chinese women hold up half the sky. The CPC has attached great importance to the role women, which is wonderful. It is said that there are many distinguished women in China. Madame Deng Yingchao was Zhou Enlai's capable companion; they were a model husband and wife." Callaghan also left a comment in the visitors' book, which reads: "This is a great occasion to be present at the birth place of a man who was a major architect of modern China. His dedication to the work of building a nation based on the welfare of the people and of socialist principles has assisted China to face the 21st century. I express my deep admiration of his work and am happy that the people of Huaian county are proud of their famous son, and I hope for continued prosperity for all of its people. James Callaghan,16 December 1986."

James Callaghan in Huaian.

I have kept the photo of Callaghan's inscription with me until the present day. During his time in Huaian, several times and in public, Callaghan applauded Zhou Enlai as a great figure of the 20th century and an internationally acknowledged, important statesman. He gratefully admired Zhou Enlai's extraordinary talent and noble character. Time and again he told me that he sincerely felt happy and fortunate for the Chinese because new China had a world-renowned and famous leader: Zhou Enlai. He also said to me: "China's ability to develop quickly in the 21st century is inseparable from the hard work of the leaders, such as Zhou Enlai. The Chinese leaders of the older generation, through their efforts and hard work, have laid a solid foundation for China to walk into the new century and to realise the four modernisations. The main work in the future [for the Chinese government] lies in training and educating the younger generations…"

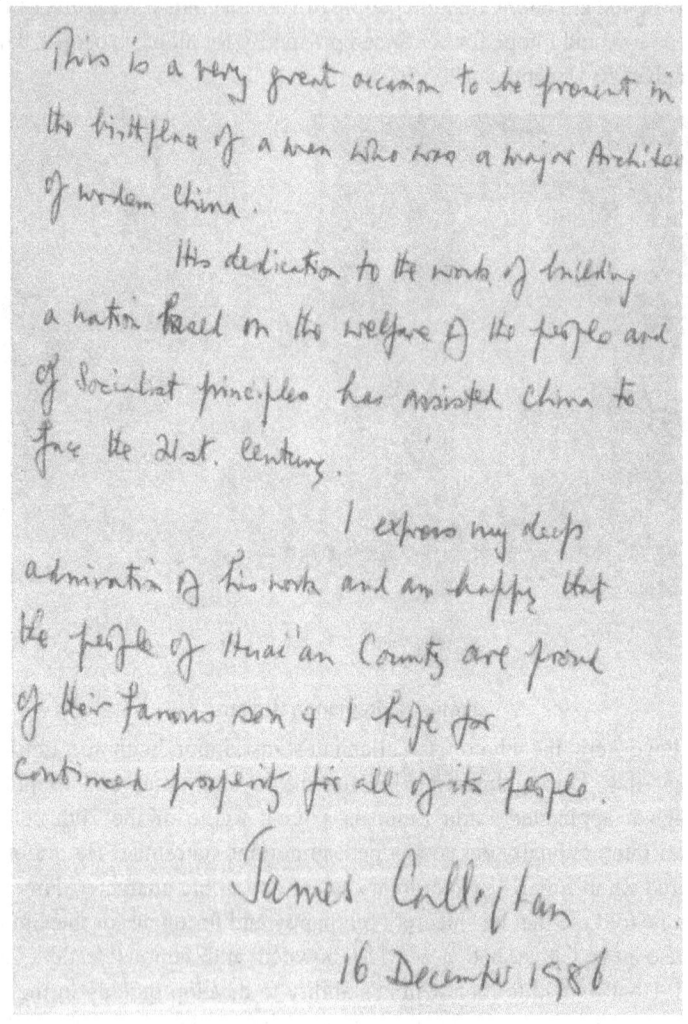

James Callaghan's comments in the visitors' book.

6.5. Callaghan's Practical Deeds for the Chinese People

During our short time in Huaian, we all stayed at the Huaian Hotel. I shared a room with Hu Deping. The hotel's facilities were not satisfactory, but Callaghan did not seem to care — on the contrary, he was thinking of doing something for Zhou Enlai's hometown. Earnestly, he said: "People all over the world think that Zhou Enlai and Deng Xiaoping sought truth and were pragmatic. I want to learn from Premier Zhou and do some practical things. I would like to donate $50,000 to Huaian." Hence, in Callaghan's name, his banker friend donated $50,000 to Huaian to start a small but efficient project to commemorate Zhou Enlai in a practical way.

This Bengalese banker also admired Premier Zhou. He also left a comment in the visitors' book, which read: "Zhou Enlai is the greatest and most influential world leader of the century. My wife and I are very lucky and excited to be able to visit his birth place. Zhou Enlai was not only a Chinese leader, but a world leader. The contributions he made during this century for the independence of many countries is unparalleled compared to those of any other world leaders. Written by friends of the Chinese people. 16 December 1986."

In Huaian, Callaghan and his party visited a power station, a chemical plant, and various other sites. I remember that they also watched a Beijing opera performance. On the journey back to Beijing, we passed Yangzhou. The secretary-general of the Yangzhou municipal party committee talked to me alone about some of his views. In general, they were: "We often and excessively pursue speed when it comes to practical work, which has resulted in us easily neglecting environmental protection and management, but environmental pollution will cause losses that will be hard to recover from." The secretary-general wanted me to pass his views to Fei, who could then report them to the centre. I told Fei about this, and during the remainder of our journey he talked to Callaghan about environmental pollution. "If Premier Zhou Enlai were still alive, how would he deal with a problem like this?" Callaghan asked Fei and myself. We then told him that Premier Zhou used to oppose the excessive enclosing of marshland for cultivation at Dianchi lake in Yunnan province. After we finished speaking, Callaghan agreed with us heartily.

Three of our guests were Muslims, so when we reached Yangzhou, I took them to a mosque to pay religious homage to the Islamic sages. Because Callaghan had no knowledge of my family background or social contacts, he did not know that I was a relative of Zhou Enlai. He only knew that I was a professor from Beijing University and that I had worked in the UK, so our conversations went on rather freely. During our tour of Slender West lake, he said to me: "Please keep an eye on where the money I donated has gone. More aid may be available in the future." It seemed that he was very concerned about how his donation was going to be spent. But due to changes in personnel, I had difficulty in keeping track of his donation, which has troubled me for the last few decades. However, I can say for certain that his money has been spent on the construction of Huaian.

In 2005, Callaghan and Fei both died, at the ages of 92 and 95, respectively. But the story of how they strengthed Sino-Anglo friendship ties, along with Callaghan's visit to Huaian, which boosted local economic reforms, will be recorded in the annals of the development of human history.

Concluding Remarks

The family members of Zhou Enlai's clan make up a large number, and each individual's situation or circumstances are varied. Generally, readers are willing to distinguish between family members by blood relationship, which is understandable. I support the idea that one who has close blood relationships and who is of exceptional ability and wisdom is doing well in his or her work to represent our whole family. However, Qi Ba emphasised 'treating all equally' — the principle he presented to later generations based on his tolerance, broad-mindedness and his respect for Chinese traditional culture.

All my life, I have been lucky enough to have received trust, training and teachings from Qi Ba personally. I am old now and my energy diminishes day by day; therefore, I oughtn't to trouble myself trying to avoid being suspected of having written this book only to gain fame and fortune. I couldn't help but express my reflections. I have done the best I can to leave behind, in words, some of the historical facts that are difficult for common people to learn about, as well as the love and teachings Qi Ba has given to me, hoping to add slightly to the intellectual wealth from which later generations will benefit all their lives, and to be on guard against omissions. In short, I did my best to recollect all this while writing down what was appropriate, expecting the reader to share these teachings with me.

All the parts in this book are independent from one another, and no limit has been imposed on their length, making them easy to read or circulate among the reading public. Trying to do this myself by taking the attitude of 'recognising the whole through observation of the parts', I have seriously and cautiously recorded and explored the historical truth.

Zhou Enlai's spirit and example will live on in the world forever. The saying 'the people's premier loves the people, and the people love the people's premier' is not false, but true. The lofty image he has left behind will forever be connected to China's future development. If it were not for Premier Zhou, who suffered injustice and, in his final days, made the biggest sacrifice, making multi-strategic adjustments and working hard to help to bring about their realisation, the consequences of the Cultural Revolution would have been much worse and more unpredictable. Every time history and reality have reached such a critical point, China and the world have been in need of such leaders. It was a mission brought about by circumstances. Anyone who had ulterior motives and who attempted to divide China was not only terrified by the sight of him, but also regarded him as an impassable obstacle; thus, some people attempted to get rid of him for good. Therefore, it is understandable that all sorts of efforts to blacken his name, distort the facts or even purely fabricate rumours have sprung up.

We of the later generations must be alerted by these phenomena and not slacken in our vigilance or follow the crowd blindly. It will be too late to repent if we inflict destruction on ourselves. If we can truly follow Zhou Enlai's example, continuing with the work left behind by the deceased premier and uniting as one, our dear motherland and her people will surely face an incomparably bright future.

While writing this book, I received help from the following people: Zhu Liang, Wu Biduan, Xu Dawei, Wu Zuqiang, Chen Ling, Chen Weiping, Chen Shiliang, He Pei, Zhang Yun, Zhang Xianrong, Jin Chongji, Ji Huamei, Nan Huaijin, Yao Jianping, Gao Qiufu, and Shu Yingyun. Here I want to express my heartfelt thanks to them. I also want to express my sincere thanks to the many other Chinese and foreign personnel who assisted me while writing, but their names will not be listed here. Due to my age and my physical condition, please forgive me for any oversights, omissions and mistakes.

Additional Comments:

The Work Engaged in By the Author in Recent Years to Pass on and Advance the Spirit of Zhou Enlai

* I have contributed parts of the collection of cultural relics on display at the 'Zhou Enlai in Shanghai' exhibition at the first conference of the CPC Museum.

* At the Zhou Enlai Museum in Huaian, an exhibition was held to display Zhou Erliu's collection of cultural relics, paintings and calligraphies.

* I have published multiple articles in memory of Zhou Enlai in *Century* magazine, the journals *Memories and Archives* and *Materials and Research on Shanghai's Revolutionary History*. These articles have been reprinted by other newspapers nationwide.

* I was interviewed three times by the Shanghai TV Studio channel *The Past*. The successive programmes *My Uncle Zhou Enlai*, *My and Zhou Enlai's Extraordinary Years*, and *The Last Contest* have been collected on the first part of the DVD *Dreams of Family and Country in Half a Century* (released by the China International Television Corporation). The programme *My Predestinated Relationship with the Indira Gandhi Family* was published in print under the title *Two Generations of India's Prime Ministers and the Five Principles of Peaceful Coexistence* in *Bai Nian Chao* magazine.

* I have given speeches about Zhou Enlai's life to students at Shanghai Jiaotong University, Fudan University, Donghua University, Beijing University, the Institute of Zhou Enlai School of Government at Nankai University, the Foreign Languages College of Tianjin Normal University, Huaiyin Engineering College, Nantong Agricultural Vocational Technical College, Shanghai Gezhi Middle School, Suzhou No. 1 Junior Middle School, and others.

* I have given a speech on Zhou Enlai's heads-of-government diplomacy at the second conference of the CPC Museum.
* I have given a speech about Zhou Enlai's life at the Sun Yat-sen Memorial Hall in Guangzhou.
* I have given a speech about Zhou Enlai's thoughts on economics at the Headquarters of China Everbright Group in Beijing.
* In 2008 and 2013, I attended international seminars organized by the department of Zhou Enlai studies at Nankai University, giving a speech and showing off several cultural relics.
* I have given a speech at an event for primary and middle school students to celebrate the 115th anniversary of Zhou Enlai's birth, which was jointly organised by the first conference of the CPC Museum, the Former Residence of Zhou Enlai in Shanghai, the Shanghai Municipal Education Commission and the Shanghai Education TV station.

Activities to commemorate the 110th anniversary of Zhou Enlai's birth. The backdrop reads: "Zhou Enlai in Shanghai: a photo exhibition to commemorate the 110th anniversary of the birth of Zhou Enlai."

Activities to commemorate the 115th anniversary of Zhou Enlai's birth. The backdrop reads: "Study for the rise of China: a theme activity of the primary and middle schools in Shanghai to commemorate the 115th anniversary of the birth of Zhou Enlai."

* I have introduced and identified Zhou Enlai's former address from the period of his early revolutionary activities in Shanghai. This is what I had recommended to be done many years ago and received support for during the first conference of the CPC Museum. During the third national survey of cultural relics, the Hongkou district government discovered that 44 Yong-an-li, Sichuan North Road had been Zhou Enlai's secret address during his early revolutionary activities in Shanghai. I confirmed and identified this discovery. The director of the local cultural bureau under the Shanghai cultural relics management committee, Tan Yufeng, said that Mr Zhou Erliu's introduction showed that between 1927 and 1931, Yong-an-li on Sichuan North Road had been a secret address for the party's revolutionary activities, and thus had a very high cultural and historical value. Of all the old revolutionary sites

that have been discovered in Shanghai, many were used secretly for revolutionary activities only for a short period: some were not used for more than several days, and the longest time that one was used was only a few months. At present, none have been discovered that were used for several years, other than Yong-an-li. The *Liberation* newspaper and some others carried this news and gave it a high appraisal.

Appendix 1:
List of the Zhou clan descendants of Xuanyuan, the Yellow Emperor of Xishan (page 7)

In the *Records of the Grand Historian*, (Sima Qian) clearly recorded the bloodline of our clan from Xuanyuan, the Yellow Emperor, to Emperor Ping of the Eastern Zhou dynasty. The descendants of Prince Lie, the youngest son of Emperor Ping, were then listed after their ancestry was verified with the Zhou clan's family trees, such as the family tree in the *New Book of Tang*, volume 74 (book 2), the *Grand Family Tree of the Zhou Clan of Xishan*, the *Family Tree of the Zhou Clan of Lianxi,* the *Family Tree of the Zhou Clan of Luling*, the *Family Tree of the Zhou Clan of Yuecheng* and the *Family Tree of the Zhou Clan of Shantang* in Xiangtan of Hunan. The following list is for reference within our clan.

The list starts from the Yellow Emperor, but there is a dispute surrounding generations 50 to 59. Some people say that our clan members are the descendants of Zhou Bo, while others say that we are the descendants of Zhou Ren. Although both Zhou Bo and Zhou Ren were descendants of Prince Lie, which branch the future generations of the clan descended from is still to be put to textual research.

1: Huangdi; the Yellow Emperor, surname: Ji, given name: Xuanyuan.

2: Xianxiao

3: Jiaoji

4: Emperor Ku@

5: Houji^

6: Buzhu

7: Ji Ju

8: Duke Liu

9: Qingjie

10: Huangpu

11: Chaifu

12: Huiyu

13: Duke Fei

14: Gaoyu

15: Yayu

16: Duke Uncle Zulei

17: King Tai of Zhou^

18: Jili^

19: Ji Chang^

20: Ji Fa; Emperor Wu of Zhou established the Zhou dynasty.

21: Ji Song@

22: Ji Zhao@

23: Ji Xia@

24: Ji Man

25: Ji Yihu

26: Ji Jian

27: Ji Xie

28: Ji Hu; 841 BC - 828 BC Gonghe regency.

29: Ji Jing

30: Gongsheng

31: Yijiu; Emperor Ping moved the capital to Luoyang in 770 BC.

32: Ji Lie; Prince Lie, the youngest son of Emperor Ping, was named Marquis of Rufen, and he is regarded as the first ancestor of the Zhou clan.

33: Zhou Mao^

34: Zhou Wen^

35: Zhou Sheng^

36: Zhou Xing^

37: Zhou Yan^

38: Zhou An^

39: Zhou Hong^

40: Zhou Ming^

41: Zhou Yin^

42: Zhou Shou^

43: Zhou Rong^

44: Zhou Xiu^

45: Zhou Xiong^

46: Zhou Hui^

47: Zhou Kuan^

48: Zhou Yuan^

49: Zhou Cheng^

50: Zhou Yong^; the ancestral name Ji was formally changed to Zhou.

51: Zhou Yuandao

52: Zhou Bo; named Marquis of Jiang by Emperor Gaozu of Han.

53: Zhou Yafu; served as prime minister for Emperor Wen of Han.

54: Zhou Mi

55: Zhou Ze; received the highest degree in the imperial examination between 149 BC and 143 BC.

56: Zhou Miu

57: Zhou Yishan; received the highest degree in the imperial examination between 80 BC and 74 BC.

58: Zhou Kan; received the highest degree in the imperial examination during 73 BC and 49 BC.

59: Zhou Shouli

60: Zhou Dang; received the highest degree in the imperial examination between 25 AD and 56 AD.

61: Zhou Yu; received the highest degree in the imperial examination between 58 AD and 76 AD.

62: Zhou Rong; served as administrator of Shanyang between 76 AD and 89 AD.

63: Zhou Xing; served as shangshulang [literally 'gentleman of the masters of writing'] in the imperial court between 120 AD and 121 AD.

64: Zhou Jing; served as grand commandant in the imperial court between 168 AD and 172 AD.

65: Zhou Yi; served as mayor of Luoyang in the Eastern Han dynasty.

66: Zhou Yu; b. 175 AD, d. 210 AD. Served as grand commandant for the kingdom of Wu.

67: Zhou Yin; Marquis of Douxiang in the kingdom of Wu.

68: Zhou Zuan; general for the kingdom of Wu.

69: Zhou Min; served as Leftside Zhonglang General in the Western Jin dynasty.

70: Zhou Fang; Marquis of Xunyang and general during the Western Jin dynasty.

71: Zhou Fu; served as a general in the imperial court during the Eastern Jin dynasty.

72: Zhou Chu; served as a general in the Eastern Jin dynasty.

73: Zhou Qiong; served as a general in the imperial court during the Eastern Jin dynasty.

74: Zhou Xiao; served as a general in the imperial court during the South and North dynasty.

75: Zhou Xing; served as governor of Yizhou during the South and North dynasty.

76: Zhou Qiang; served as a provincial administrator during the South and North dynasty.

77: Zhou Lingchao; provincial administrator, Marquis of Baocheng during the South and North dynasty.

78: Zhou Biao; Marquis of Pengling during the South and North dynasty.

79: Zhou Caiqing; Marquis of Yongcheng, served as governor of Dezhou during the Sui dynasty.

80: Zhou Guiren; received the highest degree in the imperial examination in 617AD.

81: Zhou Guizhu; received the highest degree in the imperial examination between 627 AD and 650 AD.

82: Zhou Wenying; received the highest degree in the imperial examination between 650 AD and 656 AD.

83: Zhou Anshi; received the highest degree in the imperial examination between 668 AD and 670 AD.

84: Zhou Ruxi; received the highest degree in the imperial examination between 685 AD and 689 AD.

85: Zhou Hongqian; received the highest degree in the imperial examination between 742 AD and 756 AD.

86: Zhou Congchang; received the highest degree in the imperial examination in 765 AD and served as the administrator of Lianzhou and Baizhou; the first ancestor who moved to Daozhou.

87: Zhou Yu; received the highest degree in the imperial examination in 805 AD.

88: Zhou Weijian; received the highest degree in the imperial examination between 821 AD and 825 AD.

89: Zhou Rang; received the highest degree in the imperial examination between 841 AD and 847 AD.

90: Zhou Yanpu; received the highest degree in the imperial examination between 847 AD and 859 AD.

91. Zhou Yubin; received the highest degree in the imperial examination between 901 AD and 904 AD.

92. Zhou Congyuan; received the highest degree in the imperial examination between 960 AD and 963 AD.

93. Zhou Zhiqiang; scholar, but did not serve as an official during the Song dynasty.

94: Zhou Fucheng; received the highest degree in the imperial examination between 1008 AD and 1017 AD.

95: Zhou Dunyi; architect of Neo-Confucianism.

96: Zhou Tao; received the highest degree in the imperial examination between 1086 AD and 1094 AD.

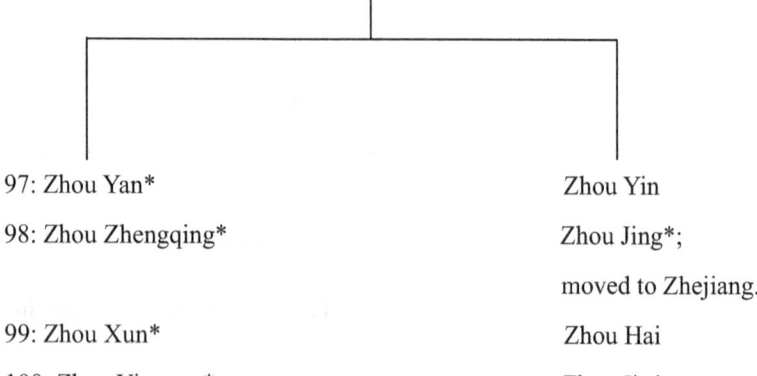

97: Zhou Yan*   Zhou Yin

98: Zhou Zhengqing*   Zhou Jing*; moved to Zhejiang.

99: Zhou Xun*   Zhou Hai

100: Zhou Yinggao*; style name Xiyuan, moved to Wuxi.   Zhou Jin*

101: Zhou Hui*	Zhou Ke	
102: Zhou Sheng*	Zhou Wenyu	
103: Zhou Bangzheng*	Zhou Maolin	
104: Zhou Zhicai	Zhou Ao; ancestor who moved to Shaoxing.	
105: Zhou Tianyou	Zhou Wanyi; settled in Shaoxing.	Zhou De; settled in Wujiang.
106: Zhou Weixin	Zhou Wenhui; ancestor of Zhou Enlai.	Zhou Xixian; ancestor of Lu Xun.
107: Zhou Huazu*	Zhou Mao*; ancestor who moved to the Houma village of Shaoxing.	
108: Zhou Liangwu*	Zhou Wan*	Zhou Qin
109: Zhou Boyu*	Zhou Shou*	Zhou Xuan
110: Zhou Chi	Zhou Qing*; Ming crown prince's guardian and grand academician at Dongge	Zhou Ang; settled in Baoyouqiao in Shaoxing
111: Zhou Shou*	Zhou Shuzhuang*	Zhou Yong*
112: Zhou Sichen*	Zhou Zong*	
113: Zhou Daosheng *	Zhou Fu*	Zhou Yizhai
114: Zhou Zhesun	Zhou Shun	Zhou Nanzhou
115: Zhou Lunyuan	Zhou Qi*	Zhou Zhiyan
116: Zhou Ao	Zhou Qianxiao	Zhou Huai
117: Zhou Zizhe	Zhou Maozhang*	Zhou Shengzu

118: Zhou Zhifeng	Zhou Ruxiang	Zhou Huang
119: Zhou Jinchen	Zhou Xizuo	Zhou Shaopeng
120: Zhou Wenhuan	Zhou Buchao	Zhou Xiongzhan
121: Zhou Buchan	Zhou Yinglin	Zhou Peilan
122: Zhou Yu	Zhou Wenhao	Zhou Ruizhang
123: Zhou Xuezhu	Zhou Yuantang*	Zhou Lingnian
124: Zhou Xianglian	Zhou Guangxun*	Zhou Fuqing*
125: Zhou Wenxun	Zhou Panlong*	Zhou Boyi
126: Zhou Fupei	Zhou Yineng	Zhou Shuren
127: Zhou Lizao	Zhou Enlai	Zhou Haiying
128: Zhou Boquan		
129: Zhou Tianshi		

Notes:

@ was emperor

^ inherited the title of Marquis of Rufen

* became an official after receiving the highest degree in the imperial examination

Autumn 1998

Appendix 2:
The archive copy of Zhou Henai being announced as a successful candidate for the imperial examination on the provincial level (page 30).

Zhou Henai, style names Tiaozhi and Yangchu, b. 11 December 1867 (the second child), passed the imperial examination at the provincial level in 1894. Rank: *fugongsheng* (additional tribute student) for Kuaiji County, Shaoxing, Zhejiang province. Occupation: lecturer.

20th-generation great-grandfather, Mao, style name Yuanbo, received the highest degree in the imperial examination during the Yuan dynasty and served as Left Prime Minister in the imperial court. He was named Duke of Yiguo. His wives Sima and Shi were named Ladies of the First Rank.

19th-generation great-grandfather, Wan, served as the magistrate of Huaian Prefecture, an official of the 6th rank. His wife was named Yiren.

18th-generation great-grandfather, Shou, received the highest degree in the imperial examination.

16th-generation great-uncles, Yuan and Jin, successively held the posts of Investigation Censor of Shanxi province and the Administrative Commissioner at Shandong and Fujian provinces.

15th-generation great-uncles, Rong, Ji, Su, Xian and Xian held the post of Medical Officer at county level.

14th-generation great-uncles were Jing, Xian, Ning, Xian, Fu, Quan, Ying, Rang, Gong, Sheng, Qi, Wei and Yi.

13th-generation great-uncles were Zhao, Hua, Gui, Fan, Wenying, Zhang, Fu, Lu, Wencai, Wensheng, Wenkui, Wenxiang, Wenyuan, Wenxian, Shan, Hu, Wenlin, Wenli, Wenyu, Wenrui and Wenpei.

Appendix 3:
Zhou Enlai's letter to Zhou Enzhu (page 96)

The envelope:

Please hand over this letter to Mr Cui Di, Yongheng Bank, 266 Ningbo Road, Shanghai, who will then pass it on to Mr Zhou Runmin. Fabi50000 in cash is enclosed. Deng, Chongqing.

The letter [page 1]:

Dear brother Run,

I have heard nothing from you since we parted from each other six or seven years ago, and I am so relieved after receiving your letters one after another. Only it seems to me that your wife is not kind and gentle, and you are in an awkward predicament that increases my worries about you. As I was very busy with the work for the political consultative conference, I did not reply to you at once. But I am sure you will forgive me for my late reply. I am sending you 50,000 fabi in cash at the convenience of a friend, for your extremely urgent needs. You should stay in Shanghai for the time being, not to come to Chongqing.

Appendix 4:

Zhou Bingjian's letter to Zhou Erliu (page 115)

Night, 5 December 1973

Dear brother Erliu,

You might have received the letter I wrote you last time. With this letter, I am sending you the group photo that was taken when you came to visit us.

How is your work and health? How is the family in Beijing? I have not heard from Erjun and his wife Zaijun in five years. Please pass my regards to them when you see them. Don't forget that I miss them very much. When I am in Beijing, I will definitely go along with my brothers and sisters to visit you, Erjun and Zaijun.

I have received the books you sent me and I am very grateful for your help. I will make the best use of my time to learn more things, allow myself to meet the demands of the new international situation and accomplish the task assigned to us by the party and society.

Do you see Qi Ba and Qi Ma often? Please give my best regards to them when you see them. (I will of course write to them myself.)

Everything is fine with me, so please don't worry about me. Finally, I hope everything goes well with your work and wish you the best of health.

Bingjian

Appendix 5:

Deng Yingchao's letter to Zhou Erliu on 28 November 1956 (page 186)

The envelope:

Mailbox 191, Nankai University, Tianjin
To: Comrade Zhou Erliu
From: All-China Women's Federation, PRC, Deng

The letter:

All China Democratic Women's Federation

28 November 1956

Dear Erliu,

I have received your letter. After the party's eighth National Congress, I was ill due to the workload. Now I am taking a remedial rest, so I cannot say much in my letter. We don't have a spare one of the item you are asking for, so I am sending you Rmb40 with this letter so you can buy it for yourself in a nearby shop. That will be much better than if I buy it in Beijing and send it to you by post.

Hope to receive more of your letters.

Best wishes,

Qi Ma

Appendix 6:

Jin Shan's letter to Zhou Erliu (page 304)

Comrade Erliu,

I haven't seen you in a long time, and I hereby I present my regards to you and Zhangli.

I am sorry to bother you. Ms Zhou Caiqin is the daughter of the deceased noted Beijing opera performer Zhou Xinfang. She went to England to study drama in 1950s, and thus she has made some achievements in drama. (I have enclosed her resume.) She is willing to come to our drama institute and give some short-term lectures. We want to know more of her actual circumstances so that we can decide whether or not to invite her. Can you please help us to find out more about her and write to us as soon as possible?

Currently (China) is organising the National Congress and the Chinese People's Political Consultative Conference and the situation is very good.

With best wishes,

Jin Shan

About the Author

Zhou Erliu was born in Shanghai at the end of 1929 and was educated at Nankai University, Tianjin. He was director of the Centre for Sociological Research and Development Studies of China, vice president of Beijing University, cultural counsellor at the Chinese Embassy in the UK and an adviser as well as a researcher at the Zhou Enlai Study Centre, Nankai University. He has also held posts at director level in the International Liaison Department of the Central Committee of the Communist Party of China, the cultural ministry and the Committee for Cultural Relations with Foreign Countries. After China's reform and opening–up to the outside world, he published several books on social science and some other articles. In 1980s, he was chief editor of *A Study on Urban-Rural Coordinated Development*, which was a key research topic for China's philosophical and social science studies during the Seventh Five-Year Plan.